Party Animals

A
HOLLYWOOD
TALE
of
SEX, DRUGS,
and
ROCK 'N' ROLL
STARRING
the
FABULOUS
ALLAN CARR

Party Animals

ROBERT
HOFLER

DA CAPO PRESS
A Member of the Perseus Books Group

Designed by Timm Bryson
Set in 9.5 point New Caledonia by the Perseus Books Group

Cataloging-in-Publication data for this book is available from the Library of Congress.

First Da Capo Press edition 2010
ISBN: 978-0-306-81655-0

Published by Da Capo Press
A Member of the Perseus Books Group
www.dacapopress.com

Da Capo Press books are available at special discounts for bulk purchases in the U.S. by corporations, institutions, and other organizations. For more information, please contact the Special Markets Department at the Perseus Books Group, 2300 Chestnut Street, Suite 200, Philadelphia, PA 19103, or call (800) 810-4145, ext. 5000, or e-mail special.markets@perseusbooks.com.

10 9 8 7 6 5 4 3 2 1

CONTENTS

INTRODUCTION

And the Phone Rang

July 5, 1999. The phone call came early that Sunday morning.

"Can you see the house today?" the real estate agent asked. "It's the Ingrid Bergman house. She used to live there. I think it's exactly what you've been looking for. It goes on the market tomorrow, Monday. But I can show it to you today *exclusively.*"

Brett Ratner assured his realtor, Kurt Rappaport, that he would be right over. He wrote down the address: 1220 Benedict Canyon Drive. The house was available, suddenly, because someone had died, suddenly. Someone named Allan Carr, said Rappaport.

Ratner wondered: Could it be *that* Allan Carr? The very same Allan Carr who produced the top-grossing movie musical of all time, *Grease,* as well as the most absurd movie musical of all time, *Can't Stop the Music* starring the Village People in their first and last big-screen appearance? Was this the party-central house that Ratner read about as a kid—this virtual pleasure arcade of 1970s hedonism that rivaled Hugh Hefner's Playboy mansion—that is, until 1980s reality hit hard and Allan Carr produced what Hollywood vets were still calling the worst, most embarrassing Oscars telecast ever? Was he about to enter the Beverly Hills home of Allan "you'll-never-throw-another-party-in-this-town-again" Carr? *That* Allan Carr?

In addition to its illustrious, and sometimes infamous, film-world pedigree, the house at 1220 Benedict Canyon Drive carried an evocative, cypress-scented name. Hilhaven Lodge rested on the side of a steep hill a mere mile from where Ratner had recently taken up residence, at the legendary Beverly Hills Hotel on Sunset Boulevard and Crescent. He could walk there in half an hour, but since this was Beverly Hills, the custom dictated that he drive. And besides, he could get there faster if he took his Bentley.

In Billy Wilder's last film, a 1978 box-office disaster called *Fedora,* William Holden plays Wilder's stand-in: an old-time movie producer, who, because he can't finance his latest opus, is forced to complain, "The kids with beards have taken over! Just give them a hand-held camera with a zoom lens!"

Wilder, of course, was referring to such hirsute, relatively young upstarts at the time as Francis Ford Coppola and Steven Spielberg and Martin Scorsese and George Lucas, who had revolutionized the entertainment industry. But twenty years later, it was the boyish and brash Brett Ratner who sported the big beard and the even bigger box-office success, *Rush Hour,* starring Chris Tucker, a stand-up comic with few Hollywood credits, and Jackie Chan, a martial-arts star from Hong Kong with absolutely no Hollywood credits. That cop comedy made back its $33-million budget in its first weekend and went on to gross five times that much. Sometime around that film's second month of release, when *Rush Hour* hit the almighty $100-million mark, Ratner moved into the Beverly Hills Hotel and promptly began to think about realizing his dream of living in an old Hollywood house. And not just any old Hollywood house. He didn't want, for instance, Norma Desmond's mansion on Sunset Boulevard, to bring this story back to Billy Wilder. That manse, which actually stood across town in Hancock Park before it was unceremoniously plowed under to make way for a much-needed filling station on Wilshire Boulevard, looked too monstrously Gothic by half. Ratner didn't want Nathaniel West's idea of Hollywood grandeur gone bad. Ratner wanted a place like Woodland, Bob Evans's estate, where Greta Garbo once slept and, momentarily, achieved her ultimate dream "to be alone." The *Rush Hour* director recently attended a party at the *Chinatown* producer's sixteen-room house, and had fallen in love with its understated French Regency style.

With fewer than half as many rooms, Hilhaven Lodge was far less grand than Evans's Woodland but more storied in movie history, because Ingrid Bergman (and Kim Novak, too) didn't just sleep there. She owned the joint. Ratner could only hope that Bergman's extraordinary talent for acting extended to picking houses. As he was soon to learn, *Gone with the Wind* producer David O. Selznick bought the Benedict Canyon house for Bergman when he feared that his moody Scandinavian star might return with her husband, Dr. Petter Lindstrom, to Sweden. As his gift of enticement to make Bergman stay put in Hollywood, Hilhaven Lodge made good business sense for Selznick, despite the reported $40,000 price tag. With Ingrid happily living there, he could continue to loan his star to other studio chiefs for four times the amount he was paying her in 1944.

Although the address reads 1220 Benedict Canyon Drive, Hilhaven Lodge anchors itself not on that serpentine road but rather at the top of a cul-de-sac that runs off the east side of the drive and up a narrow evergreen corridor to the house. Racing along Benedict Canyon Drive, Ratner nearly missed the turnoff on the right that leads to this cozy enclave of three addresses, one of which is the Ingrid Bergman house. That's what Rappaport called it, "the Ingrid Bergman house," although its present owner was a man named Allan Carr, who, at this point in his life, was as dead as the Swedish movie star had been for the past sixteen years.

It was a legendary house, because legendary things had happened there to legendary people.

Beyond the gate, the driveway makes a steep upgrade to the house on the hill and its adjacent cottage. It was here on the driveway that Ingrid Bergman, in typical Hollywood style that was so atypical for this otherwise introspective Swede, rolled out a thirty-foot red carpet to welcome her future paramour, director Roberto Rossellini, to the West Coast in 1946. She admired his films *Open City* and *Paisan,* destined to be classics of Italian neorealism, and when that latter title won the New York Film Critics award for best foreign film, he cabled her in mangled English I JUST ARRIVE FRIENDLY, to which she cabled back WAITING FOR YOU IN THE WILD WEST. They would make five beautiful movies together and nearly as many beautiful babies.

By the time Ratner first saw Hilhaven Lodge, the red carpet had long been rolled up and a yellow Mercedes-Benz now occupied the driveway. It carried a curious designer license plate: CAFTANS. Ratner walked up the flight of flagstone steps to the front door. Built of chiseled fieldstone and redwood, the house came topped with a wood-shingle roof and looked like a hunting lodge out of *Rebecca* or some other Daphne du Maurier novel set in Cornwall-on-the-Pacific. To Ratner's immediate right on the grounds, the rectangular pool came courtesy of Dr. Lindstrom, but the small stone cottage nestled beside it was very much part of the lot's original 1927 design. If Rossellini had been impressed, or more likely dumbfounded, by the red carpet, it was the cottage by the pool that won his heart: It was here that his affair with Mrs. Lindstrom began shortly after the Italian director's benefactor, producer Ily Lopert, stopped paying his bills at the Beverly Hills Hotel and Dr. Petter Lindstrom invited Rossellini to live free of charge on the grounds near the big house, which Ingrid affectionately called "the barn."

Rappaport greeted Ratner at the barn's front door, and after the potential buyer took one step inside the foyer, he succumbed to a severe case of décor whiplash. The charming hunting-lodge façade gave way immediately to frou-frou white lattice, gold mirrors, a grotto-like stone fountain, and an altar of sorts that featured a silver-framed portrait of Ingrid Bergman, circa *Notorious*. Ratner stepped closer to read the inscription:

> To Allan,
> I'm glad to see the Swedes are still paying for this house.
> Love, Ingrid

Allan Carr and Ingrid Bergman. Never had one Hollywood residence linked two more disparate personalities. How ever had the ebullient Jew from Illinois gotten the cool Swede from Stockholm to inscribe her own photo? Less of a mystery were "the Swedes" who paid for the house. In addition to Bergman, there was Ann-Margret, the erstwhile kitten with a whip whom Allan Carr had groomed from Las Vegas stardom to Oscar-nominated film glory, if, in fact, rolling around in a small mountain of baked beans and screaming "Tommy" was anyone's idea of glory.

With Rappaport pointing out the architectural details, Ratner's aesthetic disorientation continued to spin his bearded head around and around. As he would later observe, "The bones of the house were solid, but Allan Carr kept peeking out."

As in life, and now in death, nobody could miss him.

At Hilhaven, the low-ceilinged foyer leads to an explosion of space in the living room. No wonder Ingrid had nicknamed it "the barn." A vast beamed and vaulted room, its peak rises to an awesome thirty feet, and straight ahead, the granite fireplace with its old scroll inscription HILHAVEN LODGE could have been lifted from *Citizen Kane*'s Xanadu. To the right, a sweeping bay window with an equally extensive window seat offers a panoramic view of the pool and cottage. No doubt about it, thought Ratner: This is classic, elegant Hollywood architecture. But what about the chandelier that dripped crystal over a Lucite grand piano, and high above it, as if ready to swing through the oak rafters, a life-size portrait in painted plywood, by Gary Lajeski, of the recently departed master of Hilhaven Lodge—Allan Carr himself!—his avoirdupois badly disguised in a signature caftan as the breeze wafts through shaggy blond-streaked hair, his plump left hand placed in proud ownership over a violet-filled urn? Allan must have posed for the portrait at the pool outside, as if he were the reincarnation of Hadrian on a summer retreat to Capri—or was it Mykonos?—with the guys. In case anyone didn't know the once proud owner of Hilhaven, there was another Allan Carr portrait, this one in oil on canvas, placed in honor over the bay window. It showed a somewhat younger and slimmer man, this one decked out in white suit and Jew-fro.

The living room contained only a few pieces of nondescript furniture. It was, after all, a party house to be filled with famous people, not intimate conversations, and expensive tchotchkes. But if the now-deceased owner of Hilhaven Lodge had skimped on sofas and chairs, he made up for it with a stunning display of Lalique and Baccarat crystal that sent the room swirling with light that reflected off dozens of photos under silver frames, most of which featured Allan with the stars he'd managed over the years—entertainers like Peter Sellers, Mama Cass Elliot, Rosalind Russell, Sonny Bono, Dyan Cannon, Tony Curtis, Petula Clark, Herb Alpert, Marvin Hamlisch, Joan Rivers, Marlo Thomas, and Melina Mercouri, as well as a wide range of personalities who made sense only as a Dadaist collage: Sophia Loren, Che Guevara, John Travolta, Mae West, Placido Domingo, Jayne Mansfield, Ronald and Nancy Reagan, the Village People, and Roy Cohn. "There were more photos of Roy Cohn than you can believe," Ratner would later note. Or, as Allan Carr himself used to put it, "Walk around the house and you'll see my life on the shelves."

If the bones of the living room were solid and untouched, the steps leading up to the bedrooms had run afoul of a 1970s disease known as Mylar strips. At the top of those stairs, one bedroom sported a small bronze placard on the door. It read: THE OLIVIA NEWTON-JOHN ROOM, and sure enough, it looked very much like a movie set. In fact, decked out in pink and beige, the room replicated the movie set where its designee, together with Stockard Channing and Didi Conn, dreamed about high school boys in the musical film *Grease*. Long ago, it had been Bergman daughter Pia Lindstrom's bedroom. Fifty years later, only one thing spoiled the delicate tableau of lace and chintz. A shiny dialysis machine kept company next to the frilly double bed.

The three upstairs bedrooms were beautifully proportioned and cozy, and once he removed the wall-to-wall carpeting and animal-skin throw rugs, would really be rather lovely, in Ratner's opinion. They were nice guest rooms, but the prospective owner required something a little more spacious for himself.

Rappaport pointed his client back downstairs to the "master suite."

The careful architectural play of the grand and the intimate at Hilhaven Lodge impressed Ratner. After the tremendous space—both lateral and horizontal—of the living room, the adjoining dining room and country kitchen, with its copper bar-grill, offered a less imposing, friendlier place in which to relax. Even the familiar, old-world charm of the kitchen, however, surprised with an eccentric touch, in this case, a neon sign that beamed MAKE AND DO, MAKE AND DO. On his way back through the living room, Ratner noticed something he missed on his first pass through: There on the back wall, framed and under glass as though the shroud of Turin, rested a fancifully embroidered white caftan.

Finally, Rappaport welcomed Ratner to the master bedroom. He emphasized the word "master."

If the Lucite grand piano, the rough-hewn portrait in plywood, the opera chandelier, and the veritable forest of Lalique and Baccarat objets were mere fingerprints of camp humor, the master bedroom fairly suffocated the visitor in an aesthetic that could only be described as disco by way of Louis XIV. Bathed in colors of royal red and papal purple, a heavily fuzzy and mirror-striped Mylar wallpaper literally enveloped the room. Even the floor oozed an intensely layered feel of faux animal skins stacked on top of blue shag carpeting, the color of which crawled up the stone fireplace. The room's centerpiece, logically, was a bed, but not just any bed. Here was a super-king-size four-poster that belched forth enough matching red and purple velvet pillows to keep all of old Europe's monarchs in robes for centuries. As Ratner immediately described it, "My God, it's a gay version of Bob Evans's house!"

The laughter, however, never left his throat. At the foot of the four-poster waited two red velvet slippers that would never make another early morning call of nature to the bathroom. It wasn't much of an exaggeration when Ratner remarked, "They're still warm."

Amidst the room's deep, oxygen-deprived plushness, only one element of the décor seemed as jarringly out of place as the dialysis machine in the upstairs bedroom: A modern stainless refrigerator stood like a military guard next to the king's bed, its chrome handle padlocked shut.

If life isn't fair, then it's downright berserk in Hollywood, where a couple of ill-placed fiascos can not only negate one's successes but define one's life. It's what happened to the man who owned Hilhaven Lodge. Brett Ratner, a Miami Beach schoolboy, had yet to crack his first box of Trojans when Allan enjoyed his twin hits, *Grease* and *La Cage aux folles*, which seesawed perilously amidst the titanic blunders of *Can't Stop the Music* and the 1989 Academy Awards tele-cast, which featured a tone-deaf Rob Lowe serenading an unknown actress in Snow White drag, among other widely alleged affronts to the film community's sense of its own dignity and self-importance.

A bookcase next to the four-poster contained the brutal evidence: a loose-leaf of typewritten sheets titled "Production Notes, the 1989 Academy Awards, Producer Allan Carr" and, beside it, photos of Allan posed next to the cowboy, the construction worker, the cop, et al., from *Can't Stop the Music.*

But those distant remnants delivered less than half the man. Other photos and memorabilia spoke to his greater legacy: Allan Carr was Hollywood's pre-miere party giver during the town's most indulgent era, and it made no differ-ence that he was often obese and always gay and considered himself very ugly for as long as he could remember. His party invitations shone like gold in the most beauty-obsessed, homophobic city in America. Just as he gave each of his homes a name—Hilhaven in Beverly Hills, Viewhaven in Manhattan, Surfhaven in Hawaii, and Seahaven in Malibu—Allan titled his gala fetes as if each were a full-blown production worthy of an Academy Award: the Rolodex Party, the Rudolf Nureyev Mattress Party, the Truman Capote Jail House Party, the Elton John Horse Party, the Night on the Nile Party, the Cycle Sluts Party, the AC/DC Disco Party, as well as the opening-night party for *La Cage aux folles,* the most expensive in Broadway history, and the opening-night party for *Can't Stop the Music,* which required the north plaza at Lincoln Center to fulfill Allan's fantasy.

The bedroom's bookcase also told the story of a man at war with his own body. Like a movie that alternately fast-forwards and flips into reverse, the pho-tographs captured a man who could look boyish well into his middle age and then, only a month or two later, turn grotesquely fat, his flesh obliterating not only his large brown eyes but the features of what was a delicately chiseled face.

Rappaport motioned to Ratner. He wanted to show him something special.

As the realtor explained it, there used to be his and her bathrooms in the Lindstroms' day, but that was before Allan Carr converted one of those lavato-ries into a mammoth closet, which (in addition to housing a Barney's supply of men's clothes) was the fabled residence of over a hundred designer caftans. They ran the gamut from understated beige linen to Mexicali-mirrored-medal-lions-with-fringe muumuus to the wedding-white ensembles that Allan, after nine or ten costume changes, often slipped into for a party's final hour as if to announce, "The bride has arrived so it's time to say goodnight."

Rappaport also showed off a bit of modern gadgetry. At the flick of a switch, the two closet doors slammed shut, activating an alarm system that not only signaled the Beverly Hills police but jump-started the closet's individual ventilation system. With the doors automatically locked, the closet functioned as a vault with its own air supply and no visible phone lines. Allan had hired the very best, Gavin de Becker, who designed the security systems used to screen threats to the senior officials of the CIA, as well as the Supreme Court justices and members of Congress.

As Ratner later described it, "You press the panic button and 911 comes. I'd never seen so many cameras. This man was paranoid."

Hilhaven Lodge impressed, but it wasn't until Ratner visited the basement that he experienced architectural love at first sight.

It was a fairly nondescript low-ceilinged basement by Beverly Hills standards: One room contained a high-tech chrome gym, the other a pool table with a cheap imitation Tiffany lamp overhead. But that was before Rappaport turned a switch and a yellow-and-red neon sign lit up to announce his entrance to the ALLAN CARR DISCO. The sign led to a narrow room with an even narrower bar, the requisite glass shelves behind it stocked with liquor bottles, sphinx-embossed drinking glasses, and intriguingly, yet another neon sign, which spelled a bit of exotica in ice blue lights: BELLA DARVI BAR. And beyond that, through yet another doorway to his right, Ratner beheld Studio 54.

Or Studio 54 as imagined by an ancient Egyptian midget. Ratner estimated the room to be not more than eighteen by eighteen feet, and although small, it crammed in a pharaoh's tomb's worth of ersatz antiquities that ranged from two life-size gold-dipped Egyptian spear carriers, who guarded the front entrance, to a lapis lazuli table retrieved from some sarcophagus of the deeply drugged imagination. Wall murals reflected the overall pyramid-disco motif in its presentation of veritable armies of chariot riders and bizarrely winged hieroglyphic characters, completely unashamed to put their sizable erections on display. One life-size mummy sported an anachronism: A coal miner's light beamed from his forehead. As for the dance palace itself, the requisite disco ball dropped amidst golden palms and a sky of tiny blue Christmas tree lights that reflected off the copper-floor earth below. Maybe Allan Carr couldn't make up his mind what to call his mini-pleasure-dome. After the two neon signs in the antechamber, Ratner spotted yet a third on the room's back wall, this one in understated white. It read simply CLUB OSCAR. Framing the DJ's booth, two raised gold leather banquettes floated above the mirror of a copper floor. Even the banquettes sported names—REGINE, MALCOLM FORBES, STEVE RUBELL—names that recalled an era redolent with platform shoes, coke spoons, and popper headaches. Multicolored pillows were strewn about to polish the copper floor, and Ratner almost tripped over them, accidentally brushing his leg against one of the booth's small black tables, which caused it to spin, spin, spin. This time he did laugh out loud. Here was the perfect temple for snorting a line of coke and, with half a revolution of the table, giving your friends a toot, too. He looked up. Overhead, a black "eye" in the ceiling spied down at each table. These mini-cameras, in turn, fed back to a TV set in the master bedroom. With a flip of the channels, Allan and his inner circle of close friends and one-night boyfriends could watch, from the comfort of his four-poster, Hollywood's most famous noses stuff themselves with blow. How many infidelities had he witnessed? How many tales of indiscretion had he launched just for the fun of it?

For Ratner, it was as if the $3.6-million asking price were an afterthought.

"I'll take it!" he said, standing in the middle of Allan Carr's basement disco. "I'll buy Hilhaven Lodge."

one

Ingrid, Kim, Allan

In late April, Allan sent out invitations for his party on May 26, 1973. This was Beverly Hills, and Allan wanted to make sure that his famous friends—and they included famous people he wanted to make his friends—would have time to adjust their schedules for his fete on Memorial Day weekend.

That spring, the Hollywood community looked upon Allan Carr with bemused curiosity, especially after gossip columnist Rona Barrett revealed that all 200-plus pounds of him had "streaked" through Chasen's restaurant one night in March. Allan protested Barrett's report with a nondenial. "It was a private party and I gave them a little bare shoulder with a slip of my mink coat," he told people.

Allan could have sued the gossip columnist, but her timing was so impeccable that he invited Rona to his party instead. The event melded two momentous occasions: his purchase of Hilhaven Lodge and his thirty-third birthday, which was actually his thirty-sixth. If either milestone left anyone unimpressed, Allan designed an inducement that made Hilhaven Lodge, not its new owner, the ticket. He needed only to showcase its legendary status—first, with his fairy-tale sketch of the house, and second, by borrowing some storybook copy. Allan believed wholeheartedly in first impressions. "If your invitation isn't fabulous, then your event isn't going to be fabulous," he decreed. Printed on an elegant cream-color rag-cloth paper, the party invitation for his housewarming showcased Allan's newly purchased four-level manse together with a smiley-face sun gleaming in the sky above and an equally smiley-face duck floating in Dr. Lindstrom's

pool below. It took Allan hours to find just the right script, which could best be
described as King Arthur font, and even more hours to tweak the prose that
would establish him forever in the Hilhaven firmament:

> In the fabled hills of Beverly, there was an enchanted castle (see illus-
> tration) nestled neatly in a sunlit canyon of the kingdom. And this castle
> had been built in a bygone age, when there had lived in it a famous and
> exceptionally photogenic princess. Many years later, a man passed by.
> He was a man who managed well, and his name was Allan, and he said,
> "Hoohah, such a castle," and he moved in. Upon settling in, he pro-
> ceeded to invite the worthies of the kingdom to aid him in the warming
> of his house.

The invitation went on to describe the castle as "Hilhaven Lodge" and the
"Occupants of the Castle" as "Ingrid Bergman, Richard Quine, Kim Novak,
James Caan, Allan Carr."

The more vital information was relegated to a few words:

> And that is how you happened to be invited to Allan Carr's Birthday-
> housewarming open house. Sat., May 26, eight p.m. 1220 Benedict
> Canyon. Cocktails and buffet RSVP 274 8518.

Allan's business manager, Daniel Gottlieb, had found the house, and though
its $200,000 price tag in 1973 dollars proved daunting, Allan felt he couldn't af-
ford not to buy it. "Ingrid Bergman lived here!" he exclaimed, as if his owning
it sealed his destiny in ways that only money could buy. Allan knew better than
anyone: Nothing announces a person's ascendancy in Hollywood like a historic
Hollywood house.

Before he actually owned Hilhaven Lodge, Allan first needed to see Hilhaven Lodge, and for one of his initial tours he enlisted a new friend to accompany him there. Richard Hach was a *TV Guide* columnist, who, in time, would
position himself to even better advantage for Allan's filmland ascendancy when
he migrated across town to the *Hollywood Reporter*. "James Caan was renting
the house at the time," Hach recalls. Caan had just scored his greatest triumph
by playing the testosterone-drenched Sonny in *The Godfather*, but he spent
none of his newfound lucre on furniture. "There was a mattress on the floor in
the living room, and a basketball hoop nailed to the wall there," adds Hach.

Allan described the Caan aesthetic with less charity. "It was pig city," he said. "Caan turned Ingrid Bergman's house into a Jewish gymnasium." The basketball hoop was the first thing to go. If Caan didn't take the mattress with him, Allan kept it to indulge his favorite sport: watching young men wrestle.

Allan also approved the master bedroom's four-poster bed with overhead mirror, the legacy of Kim Novak's brief occupancy of Hilhaven in the 1950s. (The actress lived there with her *Bell, Book and Candle* director Richard Quine, who owned the house and sold it to Allan.) Otherwise, the joint needed major renovations, which only added to Gottlieb's concerns. "Allan couldn't afford it, but he wanted it because it was a statement of his arrival in Hollywood," says Hach.

The house was also perfect for the weight-impaired Allan Carr. In his redo, he forged a new entrance to the master bedroom from the living room, replacing a few steps with a gentle ramp that gave him easy access between the two rooms. "Allan rarely visited the second-floor bedrooms," Hach says.

Allan was a big man, despite his five-foot six-inch frame, and at his peak, which he scaled often, Allan weighed 310 pounds. The legendary publicist Warren Cowan remembered his first meeting with Allan in the mid-1960s, when he brought Ann-Margret to the Beverly Hills offices of Rogers & Cowan. Allan wanted Cowan to handle her publicity chores—that is, if Allan could make his way through the PR firm's front door. "He had to walk sideways, and it wasn't a small door," said Cowan.

Allan once complained to comedy writer Bruce Vilanch about having to wear a cast on his foot. Vilanch asked what happened. "I stepped off the curb," Allan replied. His 300-plus pounds so overwhelmed Allan's small-boned body that his ankle cracked under the pressure.

On the evening of May 26, 1973, Allan weighed something less than a baby whale. Unlike his age, he didn't lie to party guests about the poundage. Fat is one thing, encroaching middle age quite another. Hilhaven figured large in his master plan to gain social entrée to the Hollywood elite. The other part—besides an illustrious client list that he managed—involved a gastric bypass operation that literally stapled off eighteen feet of his intestines. "It was so life-threatening. It was a very rare procedure then," says Ann-Margret. "Finally, Allan had to go to Louisville to have it done."

Prior to his bypass, Allan produced two movies with Ann-Margret's husband, Roger Smith: *The First Time,* starring Jacqueline Bisset, and *C.C. and Company,* noted for featuring a nude love scene between Ann-Margret and Joe Namath in his sophomore film effort. During the *C.C. and Company* shoot, Allan posed for pictures with Joe Namath, and he held the playboy football-star-turned-incompetent-actor personally responsible for his body overhaul. Allan took one look at the photos. "I was shocked," he said. "I got the pictures back and you could not see the bike. Just me—the blob—and the motorcycle outfit and the Gucci shoes!"

C.C. and Company died at the box office, as did *The First Time,* and those two flops momentarily put Allan's producer ambitions on hold. Acquiring Hilhaven and losing a hundred pounds, Allan believed, could make him a Hollywood player again. "He was just not pleasant to look at," says Roger Smith.

While Allan never fessed up to having an eye job, he reveled in discussing every detail of disposing of half his digestive tract. The one operation was routine, the other dramatic. And Allan never missed the opportunity to eschew the former and embrace the latter. On the night of his birthday/housewarming at Hilhaven, Allan made his grand entrance with the words, "Body by Dr. Rex Kennamer!" In case anyone arrived late and missed that salutation, he spent the remainder of the night bragging about the bypass. To the press.

"I use the old trick—dress in blue around the middle," he offered. "But that operation really worked."

"What operation?" a reporter asked.

"The bypass."

"When was that?"

"Oh, let me see. Around the time *Sleuth* opened."

The master of verbal inversion, Allan turned bombshells into yesterday's news and made a front-page story out of absolute drivel. Regarding Dr. Kennamer's handiwork, he couldn't stop talking. "Well, I mean, my stomach looks like Joe Namath's knees, the doctors have done so much to it. It's not a pretty picture, let's face it," he blabbered.

Someone of Allan's fervid imagination could even put a provocative spin on the folds of loose skin that draped his newly deflated body. Always ready with the choice moniker, Allan ruefully dubbed it "my elephant skin." He wanted the skin tightened, but no doctor would oblige him there. "They tell me my skin has lost its elasticity, and if I regain the weight, I'll burst!" he bragged.

Other topics discussed at Allan's first Hilhaven party included the recent unspooling of Bernardo Bertolucci's *Last Tango in Paris* at the Cannes Film Festival (an outraged Earl Wilson called it "pornography") to the ongoing Watergate scandal (Jimmy the Greek gave odds of 100 to 1 that Nixon would be impeached and 1000 to 1 that he would resign). But those were minor distractions as Allan's guests eagerly explored the legendary Hilhaven, and stood in line to take tours of the cottage where Bergman and Rossellini trysted so many years ago. There were even more radical dieting tips to be learned—like the one Allan picked up from Ann-Margret after her near fatal twenty-two-foot fall at a theater in Stateline, Nevada, in 1972.

"I had to have my jaw wired shut, and I could only drink through a straw," she recalls. "Allan was so impressed with how much weight I lost that he had his own jaws wired shut too." (When Steven Spielberg's shark epic hit the screens in 1975, wags immediately applied its title, *Jaws,* to Allan.)

Here were two survivors who needed each other. She had endured a fall of twenty-two feet; he had endured the removal of eighteen feet of his innards. He was her manager; she was his fantasy. "Allan was a true confidante to Ann-Margret," says his client Marvin Hamlisch. "Was Ann-Margret his alter ego? Probably. If Allan could have been in show business as a performer, he would have wanted it. He was made for it. The only life he knew how to lead was a showbizzy life."

Allan singlehandedly reinvented the B-movie star Ann-Margret for Las Vegas. That makeover included Hamlisch's music services, as well as the full glitz treatment of dancers on motorcycles and Broadway-like technical pyrotechnics that the gambling audiences had never seen before. Ann-Margret was talented, but not so gifted that she didn't need Allan to fill in some blanks. "She's not a great singer or dancer," Allan opined. "But she's malleable, and she wants to succeed." He told her what to sing, how to do her hair, what gels belonged in the spotlights. Most managers take their 10 percent and think that the answer is to go from job to job. "Allan saw that it wasn't about getting work," says Hamlisch. "He saw the big picture. It wasn't a two-year plan. His was a twenty-year plan."

Roger Smith put it more simply: "Ann-Margret owes a lot of her career to Allan Carr."

Other performers who relied on Allan's concert/nightclub expertise were Cass Elliot, after the Mamas and the Papas, and Dyan Cannon, after *Bob & Carol & Ted & Alice.* "He did every step," says Cannon, "from the costumes to the back-up singers to the cities on the tour. He demanded the final say, which is why we parted ways."

Allan disagreed with her on the latter part, and forgetting that it was she who hired him, he insisted, "I fired Dyan Cannon. She didn't do what I wanted her to do." When it came to being a diva, Allan showed them how. "I don't do hand-holding," he maintained. "If they need that, then they get someone else. Their dishwasher breaks, they gotta call someone else."

Allan and Cass Elliot parted ways more amicably, if unexpectedly, when, after two acclaimed sold-out performances at London's Palladium, the thirty-three-year-old singer died of a heart attack brought on by her extreme obesity. Coincidence or not, she and Allan bounced around in the same 200-to-300-pound weight range. Allan commiserated, "She always seemed to be on a diet of some kind or other, always losing and gaining weight." He could have been talking about himself, and knew it.

Allan hired Bruce Vilanch to write jokes and patter for a number of his clients, including Mama Cass. "Cass Elliot and Allan Carr were two Jewish fat kids who wanted to be something other than what they were," says Vilanch, "and they saw the other as helping to make that possible."

Mama Cass had fourteen months left to live when she made her way up the Hilhaven Lodge driveway for the first time, to celebrate her manager's thirty-third (or thirty-sixth) birthday and new ownership of the house. It was not an easy journey regardless of one's physical condition. In what was to become a party ritual, Allan hired a phalanx of burly security guards to check each guest before any of them made the trip from Benedict Canyon Drive up the long cul-de-sac to his house. The guards communicated with other security men at the top of the hill via walkie-talkies, then sent the guests up the hill in escorted vans. Torches on long poles illuminated the driveway where Ingrid's red carpet once welcomed Roberto. Hundreds of white gardenias punctuated the night air as the torch flames lent the towering ficus a romantically ominous flair, as if the Great Gatsby had been transported five decades into the future across 3,000 miles from East Egg to the West Coast.

John Kander, composer of *Cabaret* and *Chicago*, wasn't much of a party person. "But I would drive by Allan's house when I was staying in Beverly Hills, and it always looked like the most exciting parties—the torches, the limousines, the valet, the music," he said.

And security. Always lots of security. The Charles Manson murders of Sharon Tate and others in 1969 took place only a mile up Benedict Canyon Drive. Like many in the film community, Allan remained ultracautious (his newly installed "panic room" a testament to such fears), but not so wary that he wanted to remain stuck in the hippy-macramé-LSD years.

"I want to bring glamour back to Hollywood," he often said. "Everybody, let's dress up!"

To show them what he meant, Allan demanded that his security men wear tuxedos in an age when young men no longer knew how to work a bow tie. The well-fashioned guards pointed the way up the zigzagging stone stairs to Hilhaven Lodge, where its oversize host and his absurd Lucite grand awaited them. "One of the six in the world!" Allan said of his piano. Black and white silk draped the rafters of the living room, and outside, black moiré covered the chairs on the terrace. "Do you think Allan is as rich as he seems to be?" asked his friend Joan Hackett.

Lee Remick wondered, "Why the black-and-white theme?"

"Ever heard of Cecil Beaton?" Allan shot back.

Sidney Poitier, Peter Sellers, Ann-Margret, Dyan Cannon, Gregory Peck, Gene Kelly, Michael Crichton, and Kirk Douglas also visited Hilhaven Lodge during Allan's first year there. "It was like going to the movies only in 3-D," says Joanne Cimbalo, a friend who had known Allan since their grammar-school days in Highland Park, Illinois. She was the sibling he never had, and they remained in close, constant contact throughout his life. Each autumn, Cimbalo mailed Allan big packages of leaves—"at the height of their color," she says—so that he could spread them across his Beverly Hills lawn and feel at home.

Allan liked to mix it up at his parties, and that included famous friends and friends like Cimbalo, as well as strangers who were young, pretty, and willing. "Everything happens at parties!" Allan crowed, and in addition to the fun and sex and drugs, he meant business as his clients brushed shoulders with the film world's top agents, studio execs, and producers, as well as the old guard of Billy and Audrey Wilder, Janet and Fred de Cordova, Irving and Mary Lazar, Virginia and Henry Mancini, and Monica and Jennings Lang, the once-famous agent-producer who, Allan used to tell the youngsters at his parties, "got shot in the balls by Walter Wanger." He also invited select members of the press, because, if it wasn't written up in *Variety* or the *Los Angeles Times,* the party didn't happen, in Allan's opinion.

One reporter wanted to know why no one was dancing on the oak floor that Allan erected over his pool.

"Because they're all doing business first," said Andy Warhol superstar Pat Ast, who was yet another Jewish fat kid whom Allan befriended. "Then they'll eat, then they'll dance."

Clients who missed an Allan Carr party didn't remain an Allan Carr client for long. Such an affront warranted the inevitable next-day phone call, which invariably began, "Hello. It's Allan. I hope you were really sick last night."

When Allan said he wanted to bring back glamour, he didn't mean something that reeked of leftover absinthe or molting feather boas. While he adored Hollywood's old guard, he defiantly broke their rule never to mix with the rock 'n' roll set, and through Hilhaven Lodge, he provided the meeting ground where movie stars and rockers could party together. If Elton John, Bernie Taupin, Alice Cooper, Harry Nilsson, Rod Stewart, Ringo Starr, and Bianca and Mick Jagger weren't there on the evening of May 26, they certainly attended one or more of the dozen other get-togethers that followed during Allan's first season on Benedict Canyon Drive.

In the early days of Allan's party-giving, before he had turned the cottage into his office, he relied on Richard Hach to send out the invitations. At one party, United Artists executive David Picker, responsible for inking the James Bond franchise, turned to new-boy-in-town Howard Rosenman, fresh off an affair with Leonard Bernstein back in New York City and already in production with a few TV movies, to say, "Allan must have invited his Rolodex."

Actually, it was two Rolodexes: his and Hach's.

"We cross-pollinated lists," Hach confirms.

As long as Allan plied them with food, liquor, drugs, and sex, the guests didn't seem to mind when their host said clunky things like "I'm instant Elsa Maxwell!" Whoever the hell she was. The food was good, the drugs and sex even better.

That first summer at Hilhaven, the parties merged deliriously into each other. So many people spent so many nights at Allan's house that many who attended don't remember being there the night of May 26, and many who think they were weren't. His housewarming was followed in quick succession with fetes honoring a lazy Susan array of celebrities that ranged from Elton John and Martha Raye to Rudolf Nureyev and Mick Jagger, who didn't make it to the party in his honor. "But that didn't matter," says Hach. "Bianca Jagger showed up, and besides, Mick Jagger was at half a dozen Allan Carr parties that he hadn't been invited to."

"It was just before the Robert Stigwood disco period," says Alice Cooper, "and Allan was the social butterfly who had a million different parties because he was always promoting something." Cooper called it a "family thing" since the parties usually included fellow rockers Elton, Rod, Mick, Ringo. "For a while there, we were out almost every night," he recalls, and Allan was the catalyst that brought them together with the movie and TV people. "I became friends with Groucho Marx. We'd go to Allan's and it would not be surprising to find Mae West sitting next to Rod Stewart or Salvador Dali or Jack Benny. Those people did hang out there," says Cooper.

"Allan was the bridge between new and old Hollywood," says *Flashdance* producer Peter Guber. "When I first came to Hollywood, he gave parties on a scale of what you read about in Harold Robbins."

Allan's parties weren't the only starry gatherings in town. Agent Sue Mengers's dinner parties were strictly A-list, as were the weekend salons over at Joan Didion and John Gregory Dunne's house. "What made Allan's parties unique is that you just didn't know who would walk in the door," says agent Ron Bernstein.

Batman Forever director Joel Schumacher agrees. "It was like Noah's ark. His parties were two of everything."

"Allan's parties were loud, vulgar extravaganzas to which he invited half the town," says critic and *Gong Show* regular Rex Reed.

Who knew? The next person through the door could be Rita Hayworth or L.A. Philharmonic conductor Zubin Mehta, Diana Ross or rock mogul David Geffen, Sidney Poitier or porn star Harry Reems or a neighbor's good-looking pool boy. It was Allan's introduction of the rockers to the movie mix, however, that really shook up Hollywood. "He was a force that drove that kind of thinking in the 1970s," Guber adds.

Time magazine put the epicenter of the rock star/movie star confluence at two points on the Los Angeles map. A club called On the Rox occupied the second floor above the Roxy on the Sunset Strip. Unofficially, people called it Lou Adler's Living Room, since it boasted an exclusive list of only forty members. Most of them were rockers but a few made movies, including Jack Nicholson, Warren Beatty, Ryan O'Neal, and his pubescent daughter Tatum in the flush of her *Paper Moon* Oscar-win days.

As *Time* put it, there are "only two places where L.A. music and film personalities can meet informally." On the Rox was one. "The other location is Allan Carr's house in Benedict Canyon," *Time* continued. "If a rock, film or TV performer wants to cross over, his journey must begin here." The newsweekly went on to call Allan Carr "the king of the A list."

Although few among the rock set became his clients, the Rod Stewarts and the Keith Moons of the world found an equally protective "career doctor," as Allan advertised himself, at Hilhaven Lodge. "The rock people don't come from affluent backgrounds," he observed. "They're not used to socializing in chic and elegant style." Whether Mylar staircases and Lucite pianos are hallmarks of true elegance, Allan countered with Cristal Champagne, Petrossian caviar, and stone crabs flown in from Florida. More important, Allan and his rock friends bonded over an interior decorator named Phyllis Morris, who reveled in the moniker that *Time* magazine gave her, "la dame du flash." She specialized in zebra rugs, Borsalino mirrors, St. Regis candelabras, and Corsican coffee tables—an aesthetic best described as loud and lacquered.

"Rock people are just like the movie stars of the 1940s," Morris proclaimed. "It's exciting to watch them spend money. They're looking for something that says they've arrived. They're creative, emotional, uninhibited. And in their homes you'll find an atmosphere of uncontrolled funk."

She could have been speaking of Allan Carr, and as it turned out, her pièce de résistance was to be his AC/DC Disco, installed for $100,000. That basement retreat rivaled Hugh Hefner's mansion and grotto only a few blocks away. "There was a whole rash of new stars then. It was movie stars and rock stars. It was party central between Allan's house and the Playboy mansion," Alice Cooper recalls. Hefner, whom Allan had talent-scouted for in the early 1960s, provided the girls. In a less explicit way, Allan provided the boys, bringing a bisexual frisson to an era that was still militantly hetero but increasingly curious about the sexually outré. If they didn't experiment, the people on Allan's guest list had read about homosexuality in *The Joy of Sex* and *Everything You Wanted to Know About Sex*, and they'd seen it in new movies like *The Boys in the Band*, *Midnight Cowboy*, *Fellini Satyricon*, and *Sunday, Bloody Sunday*.

"Nobody in those days ever said 'gay,'" notes Alice Cooper, who predated the sexual ambivalence of David Bowie's Ziggy Stardust persona by a few years. In 1973, the oddly named male rock star Alice Cooper reigned atop the pop music field, having broken U.S. box office records set by the Rolling Stones. Teenagers came to his concerts not just to hear his brand of heavy metal but to watch the "shock rocker" decapitate baby dolls, throw live chickens into the audience, and fiddle around with a guillotine. Sexual ambivalence, if swathed in enough blood, fake or otherwise, was one thing. Confirmed homosexuality registered somewhat lower on the social totem pole. Even in Hollywood, its name remained unspoken despite the Stonewall Riots only four years earlier. Alice Cooper explains, "It was a much more heterosexual period, a hedonistic era of excess. Hollywood was Sodom and Gomorrah, and Allan Carr's house would have been that clubhouse."

Straight stars liked it. Closeted gay stars liked it even better. As Allan used to tell them, "You can't go out and be yourself. So if you're going to be naughty, come to Casa Allan and carry on!"

Over the years, some of the biggest celebrities, regardless of their sexual orientation, showed up at Allan's parties on a regular basis, "whether they would admit they were there," says Allan's friend Gary Pudney, a longtime ABC vice-president. "He got beautiful people to let their hair down at his house, to get down and dirty. Allan was able to bring out the worst in everyone and have a wonderful time of it."

It was Allan's unspoken goal to bring gay into the Hollywood mainstream. "Only at Allan's parties would you find Louis B. Mayer's daughter Edie Goetz chatting up some young hustler that Allan had picked up the night before," says Howard Rosenman, producer of *The Celluloid Closet*.

"There would be these big Hollywood stars, and then you would see these beach kids. You'd think, What are they doing there?" says *Hairspray* producer Craig Zadan.

Allan referred to these kids either affectionately or dismissively, depending on his mood, as "the twinkies." For the gay half of Allan's guest list, they were a major attraction. When Brett Ratner became the proud owner of Hilhaven Lodge, he heard the stories repeatedly. "So many gay guys tell me they fell in love in this house," he says. Not that the fun was restricted to same-sex attractions. As a famous TV actress once joked to Ratner, "If you ever find a broad's panties in that house . . . "

Whether his guests were hetero or homo, the gayest thing at an Allan Carr party was unquestionably Allan Carr. "He was really out there," says Gregg Kilday, who profiled Allan many times for the *Los Angeles Times* and the *Herald-Examiner*. "But of course, the press would never write about anybody being gay in the 1970s for fear of libel. They used the code word 'flamboyant.'"

Or "epicene," as *Time* did in its profile of Allan.

To the press, Allan's mantra told Hollywood to "get back to glamour!" Privately, "He was making it up as he went along," says Richard Hach. "He was pretending. He was living his fantasy the way he thought it should be." If he wasn't yet the great Hollywood producer that he had longed to be since his childhood in Highland Park, Illinois, Allan Carr would instead be the great Hollywood party giver—until the rest of his fantasy fell into shape.

Not that Chasen's catered every Hilhaven party. Since Allan would often invite 200 people and 300 showed up, the quality of the food, the décor, and the entertainment varied radically. Business manager Daniel Gottlieb was right. Allan couldn't afford his house, nor could he afford to entertain extravagantly several times a month. In hindsight, publicist-turned-producer Laurence Mark (*As Good As It Gets, Dreamgirls*) jokes that Allan gave the first "product-placement parties." Chicago Pizza Works catered a few events, and Allan made sure to sprinkle his parties with members of the press—the *Hollywood Reporter*'s George Christy, *Variety*'s Army Archerd, the *Los Angeles Herald-Examiner*'s Wanda McDaniel, the *Los Angeles Times*'s Jody Jacobs, and Liz Smith's legman Jack Martin—who, in turn, were encouraged to write up the events. It was an era before journalists and Hollywood celebs had declared war on each other. "Allan would get the caterers to do a lot of it for free in exchange for being able to advertise that they had done the party. Allan saved money and they got free publicity. It was marketing," says Hach.

Some parties didn't make the papers, and whether the Fourth Estate was present or not, the code remained in effect: If it's gay, it doesn't see the light of day.

In early April 1974, Allan further expanded his social circle of celebrities to include the artistes of the classical ballet world when Rudolf Nureyev came to town with the National Ballet of Canada. Allan had first met the Russian-émigré dancer through his close friend the screenwriter Bronte Woodard, who was variously described as "a good old gay southern boy," "a comical version of Truman Capote but without the poetry," and "a sweet guy who did lots of drugs." Even before the party honoring the National Ballet of Canada, Allan and Nureyev enjoyed a high-profile friendship of low expectations.

"Allan could never understand him because of his thick Russian accent," says Hach. Over dinner at the Bistro Garden in Beverly Hills, "Everybody would pretend they were having a conversation, but they didn't know what Nureyev was saying."

It didn't matter. Nureyev gave Allan the perfect excuse to throw a party on April 9, 1974, and *tout* L.A.—Bianca Jagger, Paul Morrissey, Jack Nicholson, Anjelica Huston, Diana Ross, Roman Polanski, Charles Bronson, Zubin Mehta, Michelle Phillips, Aaron Spelling—showed up at Hilhaven to honor the Russian émigré, as well as celebrate Marvin Hamlisch's recent triple Academy Award wins (*The Sting, The Way We Were*) and Mrs. Harold Robbins's birthday. To honor the award winner, Allan unveiled a seven-foot replica of the Oscar known as "The Marvin" ("I feel like Secretariat," gushed the composer), and for the

Mrs., he rolled out a cake fashioned in the shape of the Robbins's yacht, the pleasures of which Allan had recently enjoyed with his good friend Dominick Dunne.

Three guests of honor didn't prevent Allan from inviting an unofficial fourth: The previous month, Robert Opel entered the Oscar history books when he "streaked" the telecast by running across the stage naked. During the day, Opel toiled as an ad man, but at night he dreamed of being a stand-up comic. Until that gig arrived, Allan made use of Opel's brief fame to *épater le Hollywood bourgeoisie*, and the streaker obliged by wearing a floor-length cape, silver cod-piece, stiff white collar, and formal black tie to the ballet party. He then announced poolside, "Everyone should take their clothes off and be counted!" at which Opel obeyed his own commandment by discarding everything but his collar and tie.

For his part, Nureyev spent the evening licking sartorial wounds. Decked out in satin Cossack pants, knee-high cobra-skin boots, and matching tunic, he should have been a singular sensation. Then Rudy got an eyeful of Peggy Lee's bodyguard only to discover that the hunk was wearing the very same knee-high cobra-skin boots. "No! No! I didn't know [Nureyev] would be wearing them, really!" the bodyguard protested.

The real highlights of this party, however, weren't the celebs but rather the young and nameless men, like Peggy Lee's bodyguard, who were fast becoming an Allan Carr trademark. *L.A. Times* gossip Joyce Haber remarked on them obliquely in her coverage of the party honouring the National Ballet of Canada.

"If [Easter] Bunnies were lacking, muscle-bound young men were not. Mae West would have had as much of a ball as Nureyev," wrote Haber. Those two sentences were a promise that both Allan and Rudy delivered on at a following party, which featured a much more exclusive, if less famous, guest list.

"Nureyev was sexually insatiable," noted writer Dominick Dunne, a frequent visitor to Hilhaven. "For one party in his honor, Allan hired a hustler for every room in his house so Nureyev could be serviced on the spot, if he so chose."

This is what came to be known, unofficially, as the Nureyev Mattress Party, which might have been pay-back for all the women Rudy had to dance with on that previous evening.

"It was a midnight party," recalls publicist David Steinberg, who performed press chores for Allan's client Peter Sellers. The invitation—an obvious joke of sorts—required that all guests bring a mattress to gain admittance. Steinberg lent one member of the press some old bedding. "I was always looking to buy a story," Steinberg explains. "I did it as a favor to the journalist. What did Allan do with the mattresses? I assume they were for reclining."

The Mattress Party was one of Allan's strictly men-only affairs, which didn't necessarily mean there were no reporters present. "If it was mixed, I would have been invited," says Steinberg.

Producer Howard Rosenman attended, and as he recalls, Allan welcomed his Russian guest of honor with an abundance of Beluga caviar and Stolichnaya vodka and Hollywood rent boys. Curiously, it was the latter dishes that Nureyev never got around to sampling, although reports circulated that other guests made quick use of them. At one point in the evening, Rosenman wondered when he was going to see, much less meet, the world's greatest dancer. Then he heard someone cry out into the jasmine-filled night air, "Nureyev's getting fucked in the lanai!"

Actually, it was the cottage—the same one where Bergman and Rossellini kicked off their illicit affair. Some revelers could only wonder if Allan had told his guest of honor of the cottage's illustrious history and Rudy had taken it upon himself to embellish the legend. Rosenman estimated the line outside the tiny stone house, now being used as Allan's office, at twenty-five men. He peaked inside the door. Yes, Nureyev was on his back, his heels banging away on a Smith-Corona.

"But that wasn't so unusual," says Rosenman. A few weeks earlier a similar orgy, with Nureyev as the object of too much affection, took place on Saturday afternoon at Bronte Woodard's house on Mulholland Drive. Once again, the dancer showed immense decorum by using a guest cottage, not the main house, as the scene of his multiple quick-fire assignations.

Since the cottage's carpet was good enough for him, Nureyev had no use for the many mattresses that Allan, jokingly, had requested in return for admittance to Hilhaven that evening. The bed offerings, instead, ended up on the floor of Ingrid Bergman's "barn," the few pieces of furniture there having been pushed aside to turn the room into a venue for a veritable sports marathon. "There were all these young, hairless boys wrestling," says Rosenman. "That's how Allan had sex. He watched these guys wrestle."

Rosenman and others had a name for Allan's young men. They called them the "fetuses."

It was, however, Nureyev's far more famous physique that Allan chose to immortalize in his "Marvin" statue. No sooner did *People* magazine report the Russian's modeling assignment than the Academy itself threatened Allan with copyright infringement, and within the week, assistants had no choice but to wield sledge hammers and reduce The Marvin to so much rubble for the Dumpster.

A similar fate befell a much-beloved Christmas tree that Allan couldn't bare to throw out. When he renamed it his "Easter bush," that new moniker graced newspaper reports of a spring party at Hilhaven, and quicker than Rona Barrett could say "Passover seder," the Beverly Hills Fire Department showed up to remove the dead-tree hazard from their fine city.

Notable novelties appeared at other parties as well. At a birthday party for Elton John, Allan made a present of a pony that he'd rented for the evening. "There was something about 'being hung like a horse,'" Alice Cooper recalls. The horse gag played well at the party, and everyone had a good laugh when Allan paraded the pony around the pool, which had been outfitted with several mermen. The full extent of the joke, however, eluded the birthday boy, and the following day, Elton John sent an assistant to Allan's house to collect the gift, only to learn that the horse had already been returned to its stable in Beachwood Canyon.

"Elton John was probably expecting Secretariat," says Alice Cooper. "Elton John was the kind of guy who once gave Rod Stewart a Rembrandt for a birthday present."

Where the rocker's generosity knew no bounds, Allan's did, because he was far from being a multimillionaire. While he spent lavishly on gifts, Allan expected gifts in return, and more than one birthday party degenerated into a tantrum when a much-anticipated present failed to arrive at Hilhaven Lodge. It wasn't always easy being his friend.

"There was the good Allan and the bad Allan," says one of those friends, David Geffen. "He could be warm, loving, generous, larger than life. Or angry, unhappy, miserable, fucked up. You never knew which Allan you were getting until you got there."

In 1974, Allan wasn't even a millionaire, despite all appearances to the contrary. It baffled some friends how Allan, in addition to his Hilhaven lifestyle, could afford a bigger hotel suite in Vegas than his client Ann-Margret. "But that's the way he lived," says ABC's Gary Pudney. Or as his erstwhile client Joan Rivers put it, "He lived a big Hollywood life."

In time, Allan would figure out how to pay for that life.

two

Deaf, Dumb, and Blind Ambition

Chicago Pizza Works and other product placements aside, Allan needed vast infusions of cash to keep himself, Hilhaven Lodge, and his perpetual parties going at hyper speed. Ten percent of what his stable of stars made was hardly enough, especially when his number-one client, Ann-Margret, suffered from that near-fatal twenty-two-foot fall onstage in 1972. It put her career on hold, and while she had scored two years earlier in Mike Nichols's *Carnal Knowledge*, playing the suicidal sex object Bobbie, her film work since then languished. In fact, the debit side of Allan's ledger had grown so awash with red ink that it forced him to recall some party gifts to a few young friends.

"One afternoon, there were all these fiesta-colored Honda Civics in the driveway at Hilhaven," recalls Bruce Vilanch. One of Allan's accountants sent the dire warning to Hilhaven that too many car payments were due, and it would be best for the many Hondas to be returned to the dealership. "And these surfers types could be seen marching angrily down Benedict Canyon Drive," adds Vilanch.

Returning a lot of used Japanese compacts put a tourniquet on the financial hemorrhaging, but Allan knew he needed more than a manager's cut of his clients' income. He needed a big piece of the producer's pie. Due to his close ties to the world of rock 'n' roll, Allan was one person working in Hollywood who knew all about the Who's *Tommy* and how Aussie producer Robert Stigwood wanted to turn the rock opera into a movie courtesy of Columbia Pictures.

It was Allan's challenge to sell Stigwood on the all-American (by way of Sweden) Ann-Margret to play the mother of a blind, deaf, and dumb pinball wizard British boy, Tommy, to be played by the Who's Roger Daltrey, who was exactly three years younger than Ann-Margret. She, in turn, would be Allan's entrée to the financially rewarding job of promoting *Tommy* to the world. As Allan sold himself to Stigwood, "Columbia doesn't have a clue how to advertise this movie."

By the time Columbia Pictures green-lit *Tommy,* the studio's stock had hit a historic low of $1.50 per share, the result, in part, of producer Ross Hunter's ill-fated attempt to turn *Lost Horizon* into a movie musical starring the non-singing actors Liv Ullmann, Peter Finch, and Sir John Gielgud, who played an Asian guru named Chang. In the wake of such a major misfire, Chemical Bank and Bank of America put a low-ball cap on how much Columbia could spend on any one motion picture: a paltry $3 million bucks.

Stigwood's right-hand man, Freddie Gershon, exhausted his goodwill whenever he tried to pitch *Tommy* by telling middle-aged movie VPs that the title character was a deaf, dumb, and blind boy who played pinball. Nor did it help when he switched the subject to the Who.

"The What?" they asked.

And even with *Goodbye Yellow Brick Road* topping the pop charts, the words "Elton John" left a void in most movie-exec eyes.

Columbia's new heads Leo Jaffe and David Begelman were equally skeptical of *Tommy,* but a Young Turk named Peter Guber, also freshly hired at the studio, championed the project.

"Making *Tommy* was a nightmare from the time of its conception to the acquisition of rights to the casting to the financing," says Gershon. A somewhat easier sell was Ann-Margret. Fiftyish moguls like Begelman and Jaffe had at least heard of her. It helped, too, that Stigwood found her manager intriguing. "Robert was convinced that Allan was indeed imaginative, creative, bombastic, passionate, and slightly demented," says Gershon. Besides, "He needed someone to drive the studio and Peter Guber needed an ally."

While Allan promised Stigwood the immediate delivery of Ann-Margret, he hadn't exactly informed his client of that decision. Like so many otherwise knowledgeable movie types, the actress claimed some ignorance of the Who's platinum double-album *Tommy,* oft referred to as the first rock opera. "I'd only heard a couple of songs from the Who's album and I wasn't aware that the band had staged it as a play," says Ann-Margret.

The actress seemed a little oblivious of the project even when Allan broke the news that she'd won the coveted role to play a thirty-year-old rocker's mother.

"You just got the part of Nora!" Allan told her. "In *Tommy*!"

"What?" she asked.

"It's the rock opera. By the Who. It's the hottest script in town."

She wasn't so sure. In addition to the music, Ann-Margret drew a blank on the movie's director. "She had never heard of Ken Russell," says her publicist, Bobby Zarem. The feeling, or lack thereof, was mutual. When Stigwood screened *Carnal Knowledge* for Russell, the director nodded his approval and then asked, "But can she sing?"

By taking good care of Ann-Margret, Allan took even better care of himself. His 10 percent of her fee was insignificant compared to the six figures he would get from Stigwood to promote *Tommy*. "I'm going to make it an event!" said Allan. He and Guber joined forces to present a variety of marketing plans, and that included the winning "See me. Feel me. Touch me. Heal me" campaign that ultimately became the film's big catch line. Allan also convinced the studio to feature Jack Nicholson, despite his playing only a cameo in the film, in all the electronic media. "Allan showed Columbia the route to market the film. It would be an emotional, theatrical experience. There would be a story, not just a record cut," says Peter Guber.

It impressed the powers at Columbia Pictures that Allan secured no fewer than five consecutive segments on the Mike Douglas TV show to feature Elton John, Ann-Margret, and Tina Turner in quick rotation. "It was unprecedented to get such TV coverage in those days," said Warren Cowan, who handled publicity chores on the film. Mike Douglas would sell tickets to the masses, but he wouldn't fulfill Allan's greater goal: to make Allan Carr a legend. To take his "instant Elsa Maxwell" persona national, all he needed was a *Tommy* party venue to equal the size of his ambition.

The film's central imagery of a pinball arcade led Allan to visit F.A.O. Schwarz, the most magnificent toy emporium in the world. "But it was too obvious a choice for the opening-night party," he conceded after one quick tour of the Fifth Avenue store. He dreamed of someplace *special*. For sheer size, he could never top Mike Todd's opening-night party for *Around the World in 80 Days*, staged at Madison Square Garden on October 17, 1956. And for sheer class, Truman Capote's Black and White Ball set the standard for Manhattan elegance by cramming so many celebs into the Plaza Hotel's ballroom that no one could remember the guest of honor (the *Washington Post*'s Katharine Graham). What Allan needed to promote himself, and *Tommy*, was a New York landmark that didn't define the word "party" so much as defy it. Such a place would make his choice irresistible and, therefore, newsworthy. If Allan came up with the idea all by himself, others stood ready to take full credit.

"Allan's *Tommy* party in the subway was lifted from my *What a Way to Go* press party on the subway," said Warren Cowan. In 1964, Cowan invited reporters to join the film's cast—Shirley MacLaine and Gene Kelly included—to ride the subway to the World's Fair in Queens, New York. The publicist claimed that he and Allan had discussed the logistics of that event when planning the *Tommy* party.

Not everyone agrees. "Allan came up with the subway concept himself," says Kathy Berlin, a Rogers & Cowan publicist. "We'd sit around and throw out ideas." If Allan heard an idea he liked, he'd screamed, "Aaaaaaaaah! Get in the car. We're going there."

That's two versions of what happened. The third is more complicated.

Since Allan held the reins on the entire *Tommy* promotion, he brought on a press agent to help him stage the monumental party. Enter Bobby Zarem, who had recently bolted Rogers & Cowan to start his own firm. While Allan earned upwards of $150,000 to create the drum roll for *Tommy*, he bestowed upon Zarem a rather slim slice of that sum—$5,000, to be exact—to help with more press-specific duties. Having repped Ann-Margret for five years, first at Rogers & Cowan and now at Zarem Inc., Bobby Zarem was well acquainted with the ways of Allan Carr.

"When Allan hired me [in 1970] to do publicity for Ann-Margret, he made it a condition that I spend 50 percent of my time on him. Of course, Ann-Margret was paying 100 percent of the fee," says Zarem.

For the all-important *Tommy* party, Allan wanted to replicate the film's anarchic mix of rock and opera. Opera is refined, rock is gritty. Opera is high culture, rock is low. The *Tommy* party must reflect these contradictions, Allan believed. "This was the days before the Internet and *Entertainment Tonight*," says Freddie Gershon. One party could make a difference, if it were grand and special and outrageous enough to receive the media saturation of the day, which translated into articles in *Time, Newsweek,* the *New York Times,* and the AP.

According to Zarem, Allan left it to him to find the appropriate party place after F.A.O. Schwarz proved too ordinary. "There's a scene in *Tommy* which is all white and glass and metal, so I went around town looking for a site that was white and glass and metal," says Zarem, who discovered just such a place in the new subway station at Sixth Avenue and 57th Street.

After long negotiations, New York City's Metropolitan Transportation Authority signed off on the unusual project, a first in its history. In effect, Allan rented the new (and as yet, unused) mezzanine level of the subway entrance for his *Tommy* party. The affair would be catered with tables set up for 600 guests to dine and dance only one floor below the street and one floor above the active subway tracks. Allan dreamed of ornate candelabras and vast floral arrangements to give the cavernous space an intimate, romantic glow as hundreds of candle flames reflected off the glass and metal. "But the MTA stopped us there due to smoke inhalation," says Zarem.

There were other hitches, too. Angry at Zarem for having recently departed their company, Warren Cowan and his partner, Henry Rogers, bad-mouthed the renegade publicist by labeling the party-in-a-subway concept as "dangerous." But to no effect. "Stigwood was already sold on the idea," says Zarem, and wasn't about to cancel what he knew would be a publicity-grabbing event.

Stigwood made a huge donation to the Police Athletic League to help grease another New York City department, and from the time the premiere screening of *Tommy* ended at 8:30 p.m. until 9 p.m., the city's finest made sure that all lanes of traffic on the Avenue of the Americas (aka Sixth Avenue) between 54th Street and 57th came to a halt as hundreds of invited guests traipsed from the Ziegfeld Theater to the subway, a red carpet protecting their high heels and patent-leather shoes from the street grime. One hundred cops on horseback also ensured their safety so that the hoi polloi wouldn't disturb the first-nighters on their pilgrimage northward. Allan prayed for mild weather and got it on the night of March 18, 1975. Any cold wafts coming off Central Park failed to disturb the phalanx of formally attired partygoers, and even the occasional horse turd steaming in the gutter only added to the overall sense of displaced, antic fun.

"Everybody thought it was the greatest goof of all time," says Gershon. "This was a crowd that ranged from the carriage trade society and the press mixing with rock stars and movie folk. But many of them had been to see the Cockettes and had gone to Andy Warhol's Factory. Anything avant-garde was very de rigueur for them. And Allan tapped into all of that."

Most relieved among the first-nighters was Peter Guber, whose head had been stewing in the *Tommy* pressure cooker for months. The dailies on the film confounded Begelman and Jaffe, who complained that Ken Russell's bizarre visuals didn't add up to a conventional narrative. "I was having sphincter arrest for weeks before *Tommy* was released," says Guber. Then he heard the opening-night ovation at the Ziegfeld. "I was so relieved, like I'd taken a giant Percodan."

It was a happy audience that left the theater to make a three-block journey up Sixth Avenue and down one flight of newly cemented, not-yet-filth-encrusted steps into the subway mezzanine, where an eight-foot long *Tommy* sign fashioned from 3,000 cherry tomatoes, radishes, cauliflowers, and broccoli greeted them. When someone asked Allan why all the vegetables, he shot back, "Didn't you see the movie?"

Guests expecting the usual garbage-urine odor inhaled instead the fresh construction smell mixed with the perfume of thousands of fresh-cut flowers. "Forty thousand dollars worth of flowers!" Allan announced.

The *Tommy* invitation requested "black tie or glitter funk," and in the definitive words of *Women's Wear Daily,* the subway that evening showcased every look from "terrific to terrible."

Allan made sure that no one ate the vegetable signage by offering a buffet comprising 50 pounds of octopus flown in from the Bahamas, 600 oysters from Virginia, five 30-pound lobsters from Nova Scotia, a 20-pound king crab from Alaska, 100-pound rounds of roast beef from Omaha, and pastry fantasies ripped from Ken Russell's own imagination as seen on the screen only minutes before. This was one of Allan's more spectacular Hilhaven spreads. "But bigger!" he told New Yorkers.

Trains rumbled below, only occasionally drowning out the piped-in *Tommy* score, as those 700 guests fought over the 600 seats. It was a scene of such unbridled frenzy that Elton John, lightly dusted with black sequins, remarked, "I've never been so frightened in my life!"

Allan reveled in bringing the press together with the movie stars, the rockers, and Manhattan's Old Guard. New to his mix were the drag queens. If Allan didn't discover them at the *Tommy* party, he certainly learned to promote them there. "The party was almost a costume ball," says *Tommy* publicist Kathy Berlin. "But leather weird." Having just seen *The Rocky Horror Show* on Broadway, Allan proclaimed transvestites an absolute must for any opening other than a Gristedes. Some people disagreed. The odd amalgam of cross-dressers and society matrons unnerved no less a notable than Pete Townshend, who complained, "I just hope none of them turn up at any Who concerts."

Tina Turner was no less indelicate. "We have a little bit of everybody here, and not everybody has soul," she remarked only moments before taking her seat in a roped-off section of the subway near a bugle-beaded Ann-Margret. Even though it wasn't his movie—he merely promoted it—Allan broke protocol and lavished the film's stars with gifts, and those trinkets included silver-plated hypodermics (similar to what Tina Turner wields in the movie), which the singer promptly displayed to good photo-op use with her new friend Ann-Margret.

In this crowd, only Andy Warhol sank to the level of being totally, unashamedly star-struck. "I just wanted to see Ann-Margret," he gushed.

Allan gambled that the paparazzi would go wild, shooting Prince Egon von Furstenberg, bauble maker Elsa Peretti, senator's wife Marion Javits, and Revlon's Henry Kuryla as they danced the night away in front of a bank of token booths. Where else in the world could photographers land a shot of Anjelica Huston and her date, Halston, passing through a turnstile to get to the champagne bar? On what other planet could photographer Ara Gallant scout the subway tracks for errant rats with supermodels Appolonia and Maxime de La Falaise looking on? And was it true that fashionistas Jackie Rogers and Stephen Burrows actually threw their emptied clams on the half shell onto those same tracks?

Around midnight, Allan personally thanked the cops by inviting them off the street and into the subway for a little food and drink. Over a hundred of them had been stationed above ground to keep the crowd of club kids, bums, and late-night dog walkers in their place. As the men in blue descended, people who had never been in a subway before felt the urge to ascend. Returning to street level, many of them had a whole new attitude about life down under. "I love this idea of music in the subways," said Maxime de La Falaise. "I just talked to a policeman for about a half hour and I told him he should suggest to his bosses that there be music piped into the subway system. All those people would be too busy dancing and listening to the music to even think about mugging anyone."

At around two in the morning, Allan's biggest party to date wound up, and he enjoyed a good laugh as the police force walked off with the centerpieces, a souvenir for their respective wives and kids in the Bronx.

The stars and socialites had left long ago, and as was their custom, the glitter gays and the drag queens were the last to fold up tent that night in the subway. One young partygoer lamented, "It's not easy being gay. Not today, the way everyone is trying to get in on the act. Just look at this crowd. They're so thrilled by all their pretended decadence."

Actually, those words were spoken 3,000 miles to the west seventy-two hours later when Allan moved his *Tommy* party to West Hollywood's gay disco Studio One, where reporter Gregg Kilday from the *Los Angeles Times* uncovered "a tribe of bearded men dressed as leather-studded motorcycle women, another man in a cellophane jumpsuit, a female impersonator sashaying around in the character of Mae West," not to mention Paul and Linda McCartney and David Frost, whom Allan had booked to host an In Concert special on the movie.

Although the scene was Studio One, the young gay's comment could have been uttered in the New York subway as well. At night, Manhattan's 10 percent dined in the homosexual demimonde of George Paul Rozell's ubiquitous *Satyricon* parties only to traipse off the following Monday to nearby office buildings, where most of them pretended to be straight. During the week that *Tommy* opened, *Newsweek* published a story on New York's disco world in which it revealed that "cross-sexual cavortings do not play to limited audiences these days. At Le Jardin, the likes of Bianca Jagger, Truman Capote, Lee Radziwill and Andy Warhol regularly turn up to turn on by joining in." What *Newsweek* dared not reveal to its booboisie readership is that such out-there personalities as Capote and Warhol were gay. Only the year before did the American Psychiatric Association remove homosexuality from its list of mental disorders. Gay bars and discos flourished at night, but the next morning's newspaper, including the liberal *New York Times,* continued to run editorials advocating a don't ask/don't tell policy for homosexuals teaching in the public school system. It was a city where the annual Gay Pride parade, instead of being given a primo berth on Fifth Avenue, took up a mere two lanes of traffic on lowly Seventh Avenue.

Although hardly an activist—"Allan was totally apolitical," says Roger Smith—he also never blew with the inhospitable 1970-80s winds that saw David Geffen dating Cher and Elton John marrying Renate Blauel. "Allan never had the 'fiancée,'" says Joan Rivers. "He was always openly gay."

"If Allan was seen with a woman, they were just hanging out," says reporter Gregg Kilday. "He never presented the woman as his 'date.'"

If journalists weren't going to report on his sexual orientation, Allan saw no reason not to push the envelope, and he did that with the "glitter funk" (read: ambisexual attire) of his bicoastal *Tommy* parties.

What he could not have choreographed that March was the mixed company that *Tommy* kept. The movie opened within days of such passé turkeys as Peter Bogdanovich's *At Long Last Love,* an homage to Cole Porter, which put a lid on Cybill Shepherd's film career for at least a year, and Barbra Streisand's lackluster follow-up to *Funny Girl,* the not so *Funny Lady.* In comparison, despite the film's mixed reviews, *Tommy* emerged as the edgy new kid on the movie-musical block.

All endings must have a beginning, and in a way, Allan's successful promotion of *Tommy* both established his working relationship with Stigwood and, just as effectively, signaled the beginning of its slow unraveling.

Lila Burkeman, a U.K.-based promoter, had known Allan since the mid-1960s, when he arrived in London with Ann-Margret to see Laurence Olivier in *Othello*. Allan was so humongous at the time that he had to wedge himself into the theater seat in order to sit sideways. Burkeman also knew Stigwood and planned the *Tommy* party—on a gaggle of yachts—for its launch at the Cannes Film Festival, two months after the Gotham premiere.

"Allan Carr was a perfection creation of that whole 1970s hedonistic era," she recalls. "And Stigwood had a marvelous ability to pick the right people to do things for him." The two men could use each other because, in a way, they were near opposites. "Robert is a bit of a recluse, even though he entertained lavishly. He would fall asleep at some of his own dinners. Allan always took the spotlight."

When the two men met, supersuccess was but a flicker in Allan's eye, whereas Stigwood had already managed the Bee Gees and Cream and produced *Jesus Christ Superstar* onstage. Such an enormous difference in their status did not deter Allan, and somehow, despite Stigwood being its producer, *Tommy* quickly transmogrified into Allan's movie in the eyes of the press and, hence, the world.

"Stigwood didn't talk. It was easy for Allan to upstage him," says Kathy Berlin.

And even more important, "Allan was synchronistic with the film," says Peter Guber. Flamboyant, loud, visual, hysterical. The result was that Allan's name appeared thirteen times in the *Los Angeles Times*'s coverage of the film's premiere. Poor Stiggie. In the same article, the man who actually produced *Tommy* got to read the name Robert Stigwood only once.

three

Three-Piece-Suit Negotiations

After the subway *Tommy* party, all New York knew what L.A. had long known: Allan Carr was America's premiere party giver, someone who glittered like gold and measured less than an inch in depth. But amidst his many sparkling, giddy events, Allan possessed a savvy business head that heretofore had gone unheralded. The perception of him as nothing more than Hollywood's gayest gadfly was about to change.

His client Marvin Hamlisch had been working on a stage musical with choreographer Michael Bennett. Bennett had not yet solo-directed a show, although Broadway impresario Harold Prince did give him a codirector credit on the Stephen Sondheim musical *Follies*, in 1971. Like most geniuses, Bennett was a driven, determined talent who knew what he wanted. On *Follies* and the previous Sondheim musical, *Company,* which he choreographed, he never played the indebted novice, and he often clashed with the theater veterans around him—and won. At the time that Hamlisch entered his professional life, the thirty-one-year-old Bennett had already spent months at the Public Theater in downtown Manhattan, talking to Broadway dancers about their offstage lives and how they managed to keep their careers going before hanging up their leotards at age thirty or younger. Using those interviews as his guide book, Bennett looked to conceive a new theater piece that would meld song and dance to salute the unsung heroes of the stage musical: those so-called gypsies who travel from show to show on the Great White Way.

Despite his great success in Hollywood and Las Vegas, Hamlisch wanted nothing more than to write for the theater, and he'd already written three songs for Bennett's show when its creator made a request that Hamlisch was not supposed to refuse.

"Michael wanted me to write another dance song," Hamlisch recalls, "and I protested that we were getting away from the show, which was about the dancers, not dancing."

That's when Bennett did the unthinkable and fired Hamlisch. Bennett, his sizable ego switching into fifth gear, thought he didn't have to kowtow to anyone, and that included a multi-Oscar-winner like Hamlisch. Dancers dance, and this musical was all about dancers. Besides, Bennett held an ace in the show's lyricist, Ed Kleban, who was also a composer. Apparently, Bennett knew Kleban much better than Hamlisch did.

"I was sure Ed would hold firm, that he would tell Michael that without me he was leaving," says Hamlisch. But he should have known, "That only happens in the movies. In real life, it goes this way: Since he also wrote music, Ed said he was ready to finish the score by himself."

Unceremoniously canned, Hamlisch recovered his ego by making a quick phone call to his manager, who had only recently installed his seven-foot "The Marvin" statue in the foyer of Hilhaven Lodge. Allan adored Hamlisch and he adored him even more after he accomplished his 1974 Academy Award trifecta. With men like Hamlisch and Joe Namath, Allan enjoyed tweaking their hetero male vanity by making gifts of full-length mink coats or sending them enough flowers to fill a diva's office. With Bennett, a fellow control-freak and homosexual, Allan took a completely different tack: He booked the next flight to New York City, and, within twenty-four hours, had set up a meeting to help negotiate a rapprochement between his client and Bennett. Hamlisch desperately wanted to finish the musical. But he told Allan, "I don't want Michael to think I'm his rubber stamp." That assessment left Allan little room to negotiate. One doesn't win three Oscars in a two-hour span and not grow a healthy ego in the process.

Allan's first words to Bennett: "Michael, you are the most important person. . . ." And from there he continued to flatter and stroke and kiss ass until Hamlisch found himself happily welcomed back into the musical-theater fold. "That's the kind of savvy you can't take away from Allan Carr. He was two people in one," says Hamlisch. "There was the wild guy for public consumption and then there was this very smart guy who listened to people and listened to ideas and knew when to act on them and knew how to get things done."

Bennett's lawyer, John Breglio, agrees. "They were having a lot of difficulties on the show. Allan, however, was always the kind of guy who avoided those kinds of confrontations," says Breglio, who, at the time, was only a few years out of Harvard Law School. "He did everything to patch things back up. So many people thought of him as this flamboyant overweight guy who would gossip and regale you with stories. But he was a very astute man who was dead serious and cared deeply about his client's career. He could concentrate on fixing things up and making it all work."

Allan could also play protector when his client needed a cushion to sustain the blows. Shortly after Hamlisch's triple-Oscar win, ABC came calling. A producer at the network, David Kennedy, wanted to put together a TV special with the composer, but after long negotiations, the deal continued to languish and ABC got nervous. Allan couldn't put off the inevitable any longer. "Marvin is really involved with this musical about dancers," he told Kennedy.

"What is it? A Broadway show?"

"No, right now it's just a workshop."

"A workshop?!"

"That he's doing Off-Broadway."

"He's turning down a fucking TV special so he can do a fucking workshop Off-Broadway?" Kennedy asked in disbelief.

It's a conversation that Allan never repeated to Hamlisch. He knew when not to put business before passion, and Hamlisch returned the favor when he asked Allan if he would take his mother, Lily, to the opening of *A Chorus Line* at the Public Theater on May 21. But Allan's work didn't end there. It deeply annoyed him that some of the New York critics didn't fully appreciate Hamlisch's work on the musical. Or as the composer recalls, "People forget that in some of the original reviews for *A Chorus Line* the music got killed to smithereens." Allan made sure that those offending critics received a recording of the score, and as a result, they rereviewed it much more favorably a few weeks later when Hamlisch's "fucking workshop" moved uptown to the Shubert Theater to become one of the longest-running shows in Broadway history.

four

Sluts' Night Out

After the Nureyev Mattress Party, Hilhaven Lodge rightfully took its place as *the* gay party house in Los Angeles. Except for the occasional all-out orgy, Allan made sure to keep his house hospitable to straights who wanted to see what everyone was talking about in this new post *Roe v. Wade* era of sexual liberation when *Last Tango in Paris* entertained the masses and *The Devil in Miss Jones* landed a review from Vincent Canby in the *New York Times*. While office decorum dictated that homosexuals remain in the closet, nighttime integration allowed gays to be seen as the engine fueling the social circuit on both coasts. It was a coy one-foot-in-both-worlds approach that had already been used to sell movies as widely divergent as *Women in Love* and *Cabaret,* and would be exploited to the max by publisher Clay Felker with his "bisexual chic" cover lines for *New York* and *New West* magazines.

More than any other Hollywood power broker, Allan brought the ambisexual aesthetic to Los Angeles and pushed it into the open, if not the daylight. The wrestling matches and the orgies starring Nureyev were one thing. What made Allan unique was his ability to bridge Hollywood's gay and straight worlds—much as he had the Old and New Guard and the movie-star and rock-star worlds—by making Hilhaven *everybody's* playground.

He did it by titillating, if not shocking, movieland's elite.

Enter the Cycle Sluts.

On the evening of July 4, 1975, David Geffen, Cher, Liza Minnelli, Lorna Luft, James Caan, Mario Puzo, David Janssen, Buck Henry, Tony Richardson,

Hugh Hefner, Rex Reed, Sidney and Joanna Poitier, and Altovise and Sammy Davis Jr., along with 300 other people, came to Hilhaven to see the new pop group that Allan touted as clients. The Sluts were ten very bearded men who wore female S&M leather gear—studded bras, corsets, chaps, high-heel boots—as they cranked out a rather diluted brand of heavy-metal rock. The group's emcee, Michael Bates (aka Cycle Slut Mother Goddam), saw a message in their outrageous makeup, if not their music. "We don't pretend to be singers or dancers," he said. "We take away stereotypes and labels by holding them up to be ridiculous. There's no social redemption involved." Whenever the Sluts took a break from their drums and guitars and vocals, they continued to entertain by brandishing whips to flick at flying insects navigating the Beverly Hills night air. Apparently this was not enough to entertain Allan's guests, because as host he also devised a circus theme for the party, and once again made Mick Jagger his guest of honor. And once again Mick Jagger didn't show since he preferred to attend only those parties to which he had not been invited.

The party's circus theme took form with clowns and palm readers and a Puerto Rican band (accompanied on the bongos by George Schlatter and George Hamilton) and a mermaid floating in the pool—this was fast becoming an Allan Carr trademark—and no fewer than three banquet spreads: one by Westwood's Chicago Pizza Works (again); another table serving Mexican or "Montezuma's Revenge," said Allan; and the third offering Chinese cuisine. Allan, who had a name for everything, called it "Charlie Chan's Fantasy."

At the food bar, Rex Reed complained that "a bunch of hustlers from Hollywood Boulevard" had cut in line, and worse, they advertised "amyl nitrite" on their T-shirts. Wearing a leopard print bathrobe, Allan laughed and called the drug wear "cute," but even he knew that some damage control was needed when his security team warned that a drag queen had OD'd on his front lawn and the police were on their way.

"I don't have a front lawn," Allan cried in defense. "What happened was a crasher collapsed on my neighbor's lawn."

It was one overdose Allan didn't have to disown. As Bruce Vilanch describes the general Hilhaven vibe, "People were so chemically altered then. You could have people like Gregory Peck's wife, Veronique, or Louis B. Mayer's daughter Edie Goetz or Billy Wilder's wife, Audrey, talking to Allan's latest boy toys."

More damage control: When word circulated that all the bedrooms were locked, many gay guests took it the wrong way and wondered in delight if perhaps Nureyev was back in action. Allan tried to dispel the locked-doors rumor.

Only two bedrooms had been barricaded, he told the roving journalists. "One where the servants change and one where the Cycle Sluts are getting dressed. Liza, Lorna, and Altovise Davis are helping them get made up," he insisted.

It would be reported in the *Los Angeles Times* that Hugh Hefner looked "aghast" when he caught sight of the Sluts. With their muscled gender-obliterating mien, they compelled few people to listen as they performed. "Out came the Cycle Sluts, these guys in leather chaps with their bums hanging out," Lorna Luft recalls. "People were shocked—people like the Irving Lazars and the Henry Mancinis. People thought Allan had gone loopy, but then everybody had a really great time."

Allan believed in the Cycle Sluts and thought the party would give them the needed exposure to land a recording contract. "This is the future of show business!" he announced to Poitier, Geffen, and Wilder.

Allan reveled in the bizarre, yet idolized old Hollywood. "That took him back to his childhood of sitting in a movie theater, that was his solace," says Luft. "We talked a lot about his seeing my mother in movies." Watching the daughter of Judy Garland watching Gene Kelly watching the Cycle Sluts crack their whips, Allan knew his party plucked the right nerve.

After the show, when old Hollywood, and much of the new, thought they'd seen enough bearded men in dominatrix gear and left Hilhaven, a few of the boys at the party went skinny-dipping and the girls—Lorna Luft, Liza Minnelli, Altovise Davis, and Lucie Arnaz—retired to the backyard to play volleyball with the Sluts. In his *Variety* column, Army Archerd made his usual long list of notables present, then went on to comment about those "nameless Hollywood residents who made the sweet smell of summer even sweeter . . . their perfumes mingled with the smell of pizza, pretzels, enchiladas and chow mein. Coke and Champagne tastes also mingled."

What Archerd's purple prose left unsaid is what Allan's friends knew. He liked to watch boys wrestle and sometimes, throwing off his caftan, he would get down with them in his skivvies. "It was a horrifying sight," says Howard Rosenman. The lord of Hilhaven Lodge always encouraged his guests to indulge themselves in any way possible, and he helped them in those endeavors by providing the drugs as well as the sexual contacts of easy conquests. Allan's own carnal knowledge, however, knew its bounds.

Even as a boy, Allan knew he was gay. "It is just something you know," he told Dyan Cannon. "All my friends were interested in girls. I wasn't." When

Cannon asked if he ever felt traumatized by his sexual orientation, Allan said no. "But sometimes people answer too quickly," Cannon offers.

Joel Schumacher found Allan to be "a survival story of a lot of pain. Being gay has been a plus in my life. Then there are those people who have made it a plus but went through hell to get there," says Schumacher, who put Allan squarely in the latter category.

David Geffen had known Allan when the Dreamworks founder was still an agent at William Morris in the 1960s. "Before Allan decided not to be very fat, he was a happier guy," says Geffen. "He hadn't really discovered sex at that point. Which led to all kinds of complications."

Another longtime friend agrees. "I think Allan was a virgin until quite late in his life," says Gary Pudney. According to the ABC executive, Allan didn't find love, or some facsimile thereof, until September 1975. Pudney had rented a house in Puerto Vallarta and invited Allan to come down to relax and party for a few days. Unfortunately, Allan's luggage didn't make the same airplane, and Pudney had to take him into town to buy clothes. There in the ladies' section of one boutique, Allan alarmed the shopkeeper with his ululant cry of happy discovery when he found one especially outrageous caftan: It was bright red and very Mexican with lots of fringe, jewels, and medallions that sparkled and made noise like a wedding getaway car. Allan couldn't wait to put it on, and wearing it out of the store, he proceeded to down several margaritas, get smashed, and fall in love with a beautiful young blond. "I think it was the first time he went to bed with a man," says Pudney. "He had not slept with women."

The next morning, Allan told his TV exec friend, "This guy has changed my life." Allan was in love at last, he said, and so happy that he couldn't stop talking about his affair. Love is forever until it's over, and for Allan, eternity could be counted on two hands. "Over the years, Allan had half a dozen relationships," says Pudney, "He had a mental picture of a fantasy man, and he would try to find that figure."

These men were inevitably young, beautiful, tall, well built, perfect—everything Allan felt, and knew, he was not.

five

Capote's Retreat

Diana Ross, Peter Sellers, Lucille Ball, Dominick Dunne, and a few hundred other Hollywood notables were stunned by the summons delivered to their doorstep that crisp November day. Most subpoenas are delivered by a plainclothesman. This one was handed to them by a uniformed officer of the law. "It was quite a shock to receive it," observed Dunne. "When you open the front door and someone is serving you a subpoena, your heart stops!"

The joke was pure Allan Carr. In his mind, the party scheduled for December 14, 1975, began three weeks earlier when those three hundred "summons," i.e. invitations, went out by way of a few dozen unemployed actors dressed up in cop costumes. The law-enforcement theme carried right through to the December 14 party itself, held in the Lincoln Heights Jail in northeast Los Angeles. The prison, which once housed 2,800 convicts, shut its doors shortly after the Watts riots in 1965, and in recent years sat deserted except for its occasional use by film companies in need of an ugly, dank jail.

On that mid-December night, most of Allan's guests rode in limousines that took them past downtown L.A. and the gaudy lights of Chinatown, where banks are disguised as ersatz pagodas, and through an anonymous neighborhood that few of them had ever seen, and never much cared to visit again. Lincoln Heights is the dumping ground of the city's vast transportation departments, its asphalt-paved lots filled with menacing-looking bulldozers and trucks. The hills of Elysian Fields park rise to the northwest, only to be blotted out, momentarily, by the Lincoln Heights Jail. Limo drivers followed the instructions of Allan's invitation/summons, which directed them to cruise up North Avenue 19 and past the prison's stern, multilevel edifice, its meager front lawn strewn with weeds and litter. There, guests were greeted by police officers, who motioned with their flashlights to drive up the ramp to the parking lot. Two more cops then approached the car, and were just as quickly replaced with two other guys in striped prison uniforms. "That looks like a good one. Take that car. It's our getaway car," said one of the inmates.

"Yes, we'll go to Mexico," said the second convict, who, along with his partner in crime, repeated this exchange a couple hundred times in the next two hours.

More actor-cops appeared with a list of names that read PRISONERS at the top of the page. "Move them on to booking," an officer ordered as he motioned to the elevator that took all guests to the jail's second floor. There, they were fingerprinted, frisked, and had their mug shots taken.

Once they were checked through the security gates, guests could then wander about the cells, which had been deodorized and gussied up for the night. Instead of the expected sweat and urine, the aroma that hit them was of high-end fish food that Allan had flown in from the Gulf Coast and northern California. Lobster, salmon, and Chilean sea bass overflowed from several New Orleans carts parked among dozens of small cocktail tables, each of which had been appointed with votive candles, crystal and silver, and brown linen tablecloths.

At the last minute, amidst the early arrival of a few unfashionable guests, Allan took a final survey of the place, and freaked. "There are no ashtrays!" he screeched. "They'll mutiny!" Allan followed his initial mortification with four-letter tirades that sent several gofers scurrying to rectify the egregious omission. Allan's verbal abuse sometimes shocked his childhood friend Joanne Cimbalo. "If he talked to me the way he talked to his assistants, I would have collapsed on the spot," she says. Whenever Cimbalo repeated her criticism to Allan, he invariably shot back, "I'm the only one who should be collapsing!"

On the occasion of his jailhouse party, Allan turned his impromptu tantrum on all the cops, inmates, and lady wardens who milled about, courtesy of a costume-catering company called the Doo Dah Gang. "Do something!" he yelled.

Nothing about this event had been easy. Allan continued to bask in the accolades for his *Tommy* subway party, but for that event, he relied heavily on the resources of Columbia Pictures. Now he was party giving on his own largesse and muscle.

"I have a headache from all the red tape," Allan cried, referring to what the city's Economic Development Office put him through to rent the jail for the night. "Actually, the week," he added. "It took a few days to turn this place into something other than a pig sty, which it was."

Dominick Dunne praised the clean-up crew. "The bathrooms were fit," he recalled. "That's where everyone was piling in for the coke."

When they weren't imbibing, Allan's guests made more practical use of the toilets. Since many of the prison johns were in the open, Allan splurged on some strategically hung burlap curtains, and it tickled him when he found Charles Bronson standing guard for Jill Ireland. "He didn't want anyone peeking at his wife!" Allan said with a giggle.

Marvin Hamlisch knew and appreciated Allan's split personality. "If you needed a deal, bring in Allan No. 1. If you wanted a wild party with lots of co-caine, bring in Allan No. 2." Tonight belonged to Allan No. 2, but Allan No. 1 never disappeared completely since he knew when it was important to introduce his clients to someone more important, especially if that VIP had snorted too much coke.

The jailhouse theme came courtesy of the evening's guest of honor and his most famous book, *In Cold Blood*. Truman Capote had recently escaped New York City to accept his first acting gig, in the Neil Simon movie *Murder by Death* at Columbia Pictures. Back on the East Coast, Capote enjoyed leper sta-tus after spilling a bunch of society beans in *Esquire* magazine about Babe Paley and other members of the Park Avenue world. An early look at one of the chap-ters, "La Cote Basque 1965," from his long-awaited but never-delivered novel, *Answered Prayers,* had won him no praise among the literary set and lost him entrée to the Beautiful People, as they were known. One of them, Mrs. William Woodward Jr., found herself so unraveled by "La Cote Basque" that she com-mitted suicide on October 10, seven days before the offending *Esquire* issue hit the stands. In a rare gesture of discretion, Capote resorted to using a pseu-donym, Ann Hopkins, for Woodward, whom the 13,000-word short story ac-cused of tricking Mr. Woodward into marriage and then murdering him "after he got the goods on her and threatened divorce," as gossip doyenne Liz Smith revealed in her syndicated column. Other society types who were maligned without the benefit of pseudonyms included the Duchess of Windsor, Princess Margaret, Gloria Vanderbilt, Babe Paley, Mrs. Joshua Logan, and the late Joe Kennedy.

Capote may have been considered infamously outré on his home turf, but on the night of December 14 in the old Lincoln Heights Jail, he remained a lit-erary genius with people who read Liz Smith but not *Esquire* or *In Cold Blood*.

It didn't matter. Allan knew that the L.A. crowd had seen the movie version of his best seller, and besides, who among them were starring in a Neil Simon movie?

"This isn't one of those 'come to a party' parties," Allan claimed. Translation: Allan demanded that his guests dress up, play a role, act like *somebody*. To goose things along, Allan occasionally called out to let the "prisoners" know who had just arrived to have his or her photograph taken. "Peter Sellers is being mugged with the dog Won Ton Ton! Go and watch!" he brayed.

For those who had already watched Lucille Ball and Charles Bronson and David Niven and Christopher Isherwood and Princess Toumanoff and Diana Ross and Francesco Scavullo and Margaux Hemingway being mug-shot, the Doo Dah Gang's boys and girls conducted tours of the nearby gas chamber as the Linc, a five-piece chamber music group, played old favorites like "Jailhouse Rock" and "Killing Me Softly with His Song."

"I always knew I'd end up in jail," said *Midnight Cowboy* director John Schlesinger.

"I bet I'm the only one who's been here legitimately—500 times," cracked *The Onion Field* author Joseph Wambaugh, a former cop.

At last, Truman Capote himself stepped out of the prison elevator wearing overly tinted specs and a gangster-ish mix of big-brimmed black Borsalino, double-breasted tuxedo, and what he called "my Brazilian dancing shoes," which sported red leather and rubber soles. Allan's *Hollywood Reporter* friend Richard Hach played chauffeur for the night, and picked up Capote at his Malibu rental (the writer had recently bolted Mrs. Johnny Carson's place in Beverly Hills) to bring him across town to the jail. "I was an old friend of Truman's and Allan wanted to know Truman," says Hach, identifying the raison d'être for many Allan Carr get-togethers.

Capote tried to downplay his expulsion from New York City. "Oh, I just thought it would be fun to do something different," he said of starring in *Murder by Death*. Like Allan's jailhouse party, the movie played off Capote's sleuth status, care of *In Cold Blood*, and cast him as an eccentric millionaire who invites five detectives to his house to solve a murder. "I probably won't act again. It was just for a change from working on the book, and I knew I didn't have time to take a vacation."

If anyone asked about his "La Cote Basque 1965" contretemps, he told them not to worry. "Carole Matthau and Gloria Vanderbilt absolutely loved it," he said without apologies. It was but a warm-up for what he would soon tell Liz Smith:

"Why, if anybody was ever at the center of that world, it was me, so who is rejecting whom in this? I mean I can create any kind of social world I want, anywhere I want." Anywhere, that is, but Los Angeles. As Capote told Allan's guests, Los Angeles was "the no place of everywhere" and he could never live there. "In New York City," he said, "I can get a bowl of onion soup at 4 a.m. I can get my tux cleaned at 4 a.m. and I can enjoy the sexual favors of a policeman at 4 a.m."

At 10 p.m. in L.A., Capote could do better than onion soup, but when he looked at all the raw seafood in a nearby cart, he nearly passed out. "I'm ordering rice and beans. I'm having jailhouse food," he said, and instead ate nothing. The hurly-burly of Allan's party left its guest of honor strangely unnerved, and he soon retreated to one of the cramped eight-by-ten-foot cells with sink and exposed toilet. Capote left it to the 500 other guests to dance and eat and smoke dope in the common area. Dominick Dunne wandered into another cell and for a moment his gaze met Capote's. "There was such sadness in Truman's eyes," Dunne recalled. "He never recovered from that snub of Mrs. Paley's. This was not his new milieu—Hollywood, and it wasn't up to what he was used to in New York."

Worse, the new and older Capote wasn't anything like the old and younger Capote. "It could have been fun if Truman had been Truman, but he was subdued that night. He wasn't fun," says Joseph Wambaugh, who'd been a friend ever since Capote slipped Mrs. Wambaugh a mickey one night so that "Truman could be alone with my cute cop husband," as she put it. In addition to Capote being in a funk, it also put a crimp in Wambaugh's evening when one movie actress got smashingly drunk and, turning bitchy, kept berating the Doo Dah Gang's attempts to impersonate cops, inmates, and guards.

As with any party, the guest of honor is merely an excuse for the revels, especially those that involve heaps of drugs and the incongruous sight of famous people in evening dress in a decaying jailhouse. It didn't really matter if Truman was the life of the party or stuck away in a cell or asleep in Malibu in his rented bed. He was, in the end, just another celebrity. "Allan had two kinds of friends at his parties," says publicist David Steinberg. "He had famous people and he had more famous people." But this being Los Angeles, Allan couldn't invite the kind of society people who truly impressed Capote. Betsy Bloomingdale? Dorothy Chandler? Capote wouldn't know them if he stumbled over them.

The *Los Angeles Times*'s society writer Jody Jacobs called it "the party of the year" and likened it to Capote's own Black and White Ball from 1966 in New York.

But not everyone was so impressed. Christopher Isherwood's longtime partner, painter Don Bachardy, complained, "It was one of those occasions that was thought to be very wry, but when it came down to the actual night, it was very tedious. The jail cast a pall over everything." But not all was lost for Isherwood's lover. "I met Diana Ross that night. She looked like a real star, very glamorous," Bachardy notes.

"The joke of the jailhouse party was who had been there before," says Bruce Vilanch, who, in the end, took a position somewhere between Jacobs's rave and Bachardy's pan: "It was campy and silly and theatrical and what people liked in that period of time."

Even Allan had to admit that his Jail House Party wasn't as "spectacular" as Capote's Black and White Ball. "But it was probably more inventive, since we had to take an abandoned jail . . . and refurbish it," he said. Whatever anyone else thought, the event got Allan precisely want he wanted—lots of press—and something that he needed even more. Quite by accident, the party turned him back into a movie producer. And a successful one at that. He would soon be a multimillionaire at long last—and just in time.

six

Survival Techniques

Having invited John Schlesinger to his Truman Capote Jail House Party, Allan scored with that gesture by promptly receiving a dinner invitation from the British director. As usual at such Hollywood affairs, the conversation quickly devolved into the subject of everyone's ongoing projects, real or imagined, and when Allan asked the Oscar-winning helmer of *Midnight Cowboy* about his next film, Schlesinger casually mentioned that he wanted to bring the best-selling book *Alive!* to the screen.

Allan wanted to know: Was this the story about the rugby players whose plane crashed in the Andes and they ended up eating each other to stay alive?

Schlesinger nodded. "Yes, that story. But you know, there's a Mexico cheapo version that is already out in theaters there."

That simple exchange was Allan's good fortune and Schlesinger's big mistake.

In the coming months, Allan planned to visit Mexico City to open *Tommy* there and take a much-needed vacation. After a successful launch in Western Europe, Robert Stigwood had set his sights on Mexico and South America, and needed his ace marketer to handle the new round of promotions. With Schlesinger's *Alive!* rattling in the back of his head, Allan arrived in Mexico City to find the cheapo version playing at a theater near his hotel. He glanced at the marquee: *Supervivientes de los Andes*. Curiosity drew him closer. People stood in line praying; some clutched rosaries; a few were on their knees. The movie's Spanish-language poster contained only one word that Allan knew, but it was the right word—"canibal"—and together with the visuals of goggled young men caught in a blizzard, Allan felt a mild jolt in his gut. "Does anyone speak English?" he asked the sidewalk crowd. "What does . . . *supervivientes* mean?"

A woman on her knees looked up, her fingers braided with holy beads. "Survivors," she said. "Survivors de los Andes." Rather than drop to the sidewalk, Allan bought a ticket to see the movie, which left him both appalled and exhilarated. Later that night, he could hardly sleep as his mind raced to find a way to sell his idea to Stigwood. The next day he placed a phone call to his friend at the Robert Stigwood Organization, Freddie Gershon, who had recently been promoted to president of the company.

"Freddie, you're not going to believe this," Allan began. "I just saw a movie called *Supervivientes de los Andes!*"

"*Supervive* what?" asked Gershon.

"You know that John Schlesinger movie *Alive!* about these rugby players who resorted to cannibalism when their airplane crashed over the Andes in 1972?"

Gershon knew of the project, vaguely.

Allan informed his friend that Schlesinger was working on that same story, after he finished the Dustin Hoffman picture *The Marathon Man,* but that *Alive!* would never get made because they—Allan and Gershon—would beat him to it by acquiring this Mexican movie. Best of all, they could pick it up cheap. As Allan explained, Roman Catholics south of the border loved the story because, even though it was ghoulish, it was blessedly not immoral. The pope himself had declared the real-life rugby players not guilty of mortal sin since they restricted themselves to eating only dead meat. Allan believed that American moviegoers would eat it up too.

The subject matter of *Survive!*—cannibalism—bothered Gershon, but as Allan insisted, audiences love to be disgusted. And besides, "they eat the dead ones to stay alive, they don't kill anybody," he kept saying.

The quality of the film also concerned Gershon. A hit in Mexico did not automatically translate into a hit north of the border, especially a Spanish-language film that would have to be dubbed, not subtitled, in English to score at the U.S. box office. Allan had to level with his RSO friend there: "It is so badly made it looks hideous. But I think it will work."

Despite Allan's assurances, Gershon continued to worry about the dubbing.

"It will work because the actors have scarves around their faces," Allan said. "It's cold in the Andes, so we don't have to worry much about synching. That's a good part of the movie."

Allan tinkered with the economics of transforming *Supervivientes de los Andes* into *Survive!* It would work if they could acquire the film for under half a million, with another $350,000 to be spent on editing and the licensing of stock footage of avalanches and snowstorms. If they could bring it in for under a million, Allan believed, how could they not clear at least a million in profits?

To sell the idea to Stigwood, Gershon knew Allan had to present his full economic plan, as well as his ideas on how to market the movie, because it was there—as a marketing person—that Stigwood considered Allan an unqualified genius. And if anyone knew how to sell cannibalism to the American masses, it was Allan Carr. His pitch to Stigwood went like this. "The audience for *Survive!* is the boys who want to have the girls grab them because they're so revolted by it all. The girls have to look away and scream, and so they grab their boyfriend's arm. It's a makeout movie!" he insisted. "It's not a horror movie. It's a makeout movie!"

Allan also detailed his marketing campaign: "You know how they've been talking about this ratings systems and how mothers have been complaining about the need for there to be a ratings system not just for sex but violence? We'll have our own rating for violence, and it will be a giant box on the poster and it says . . . 'Caution: the scenes of cannibalism in this film may be too strong for some audience members.'"

For Allan, *Survive!* meant no more mortgage on Hilhaven Lodge, no more parties catered by Chicago Pizza Works, no more returned Civic Hondas, and it gave him his dream to be a real Hollywood player with a place in Malibu, one in Hawaii, and maybe even another in Manhattan.

To Gershon's mild surprise, Stigwood liked the idea of picking up a grade-C Mexican movie about rugby cannibals stranded in the Andes during a blizzard. "If we can pick it up for half a million," Stigwood cautioned. He would put up all the money but be 50-50 partners with Allan since Allan found the film and would be responsible for re-creating and marketing it.

With that low price tag as his compass, John Breglio, the same young lawyer who repped Michael Bennett's *A Chorus Line,* flew to Los Angeles. "It was the first thing I did for Stigwood," says Breglio, "who was then the most successful independent mogul in the entertainment business." Allan's idea of picking up *Supervivientes* made economic sense to Breglio, because the John Schlesinger–optioned book *Alive!* had been hugely popular. "It was a great way of telling the story without having to buy the best seller."

Breglio met with Rene Cardona Jr, who not only produced *Supervivientes* but directed it and adapted the script from the book *Survive!* which, unlike the book *Alive!* was something less than a best seller. The lawyer offered Cordona $100,000 up front plus a piece of the action. "It was a real deal. If the picture made money, they stood to make a million or three or four million," Breglio says.

Although their meeting lasted three days, no deal materialized since the Mexican filmmaker and his lawyer had no interest in being taken to the cleaners by a bunch of Hollywood gringos. Unable to make them budge, Breglio phoned Allan and Stigwood with an alternate plan. "Just give me half a million dollars. Let's just buy them out. Let's forget the back end," he advised.

Cardona liked his money up front, and for a half million dollars, Breglio acquired worldwide rights, excluding several Spanish-language countries, and paid for the rights to the Mexican negative on a twenty-year lease paid over a period of five months. Stigwood and Allan had their movie.

"But don't look at it just yet," Allan warned. "Let me fiddle with it first."

As he worked on *Survive!* Allan needed a quick cash infusion to keep his party lifestyle on track. For a brief interlude, he switched back to wearing his promoter hat and put together a movie campaign for producer David Picker, who paid him a quarter million dollars for his marketing services. "Allan had done a brilliant job on *Tommy*," says Picker, who wanted him to do the same for his new movie, *Won Ton Ton: The Dog That Saved Hollywood*.

Again, it was the unexpected outrageousness of the party on April 26, 1976, that distinguished Allan's campaign for *Won Ton Ton*, set in 1920s Hollywood and featuring star cameos of Joan Blondell, Phil Silvers, Milton Berle, and Edgar Bergen, among other movie legends.

As part of his manufactured hoopla, Allan "signed" the film's star, a tan-and-black German shepherd named Augustus Von Schulmacher (aka Won Ton Ton), as a client and conceived a party that required everyone to bring a pet cur to the Paramount lot. Actually, "We hired thirty dogs," says the studio's then-VP of marketing, Laurence Mark, "and most of the celebs were handed the dog on their way into the party."

Which may have been the reason why actress Marisa Berenson held Paramount responsible for her rented dog's pissing on her in the limousine and sent the studio a dry-cleaning bill.

Allan got his friend Merv Griffin to cover the premiere on his TV talk show, but the coup de théâtre was the appearance of Paramount founder Adolf Zukor, age 102, together with 1930s Paramount queen Mae West, age 83, who claimed that her back-to-back hits, *She Done Him Wrong* and *I'm No Angel,* saved the studio from bankruptcy in 1933. For Mae West, it was as if those movies had un-spooled yesterday. Zukor, for his part, reserved his remarks for Won Ton Ton when he demanded, "I want your chair!" The 102-year-old man got what he wanted, but not before the canine star left a puddle of pee where Zukor was about to sit.

Adolf Zukor and Mae West. "Only Allan Carr would have thought of that duo!" quips Mark. "The whole thing was utter bliss."

More problematic was Won Ton Ton, who found himself aroused every time he posed for photographs. After careful inspection, Allan pinpointed the camera lights as the erotic stimulant, and not Mae West, who paid inordinate interest in the dog's inflated appendage, and he recommended that a rubber band be strate-gically placed around the dog's genitals to prevent him from getting an erection.

"It was an amazing event, devised by Allan," says Picker. "Unfortunately, no one went to see the movie." Like *Tommy*, the *Won Ton Ton* party generated lots of press. Unlike *Tommy*, the *Won Ton Ton* movie generated no heat at the box office.

Pocketing his quarter of a million for marketing *Won Ton Ton*, Allan returned to work on *Survive!* which he knew would bring him the big money. He bought footage of avalanches from Disney. He rephotographed portions of the film through various gradations of netting to disguise the snow as something other than painted cornflakes. Most important, he whacked a few reels out of the film to bring its playing time down to an easily digestible ninety minutes. And he dubbed it into English—all for under $300,000. True to his word, he didn't stray from the budget.

Only then did Allan let Stigwood, Gershon, and Breglio look at the movie, which had now cost about $850,000. Stigwood told Allan, "It's terrible, but it's everything you promised." Stigwood especially liked that it ran an hour and a half, which made it possible to cram in more screenings in its first weekend be-fore the bad word got out. Also, Allan was right. *Survive!* was a young person's movie. Anyone under thirty would definitely be revolted—but in a good way.

Screening rooms in Los Angeles were booked for Allan to sell his surefire hit movie to the town's studios. He started with the big guns: Warners, Fox, Co-lumbia, Universal.

The reaction was uniform:

"Whoa! What kind of crap is this?"

At least, that's what various studio chiefs told Freddie Gershon.

"We were vilified," he recalls. Allan and Stigwood received not one offer for *Survive!* until, far down on their list of studios, Sam Arkoff of American-International saw it and came up with a deal. Arkoff, known as king of the B movies, had founded A-I with director Roger Corman, and often bragged that he personally created two movie genres of little repute: beach-party and outlaw-biker pictures.

"I'll give you a $1-million advance against 50 percent of the profits," said Arkoff.

Or, as Gershon explains it, "'Against fifty percent of the profits' is like saying 'You'll never see another dime.'"

Stigwood wanted to take Arkoff's offer. At least his RSO would clear $150,000 and not lose the entire $850,000 investment.

Allan balked. "This movie can make us millions!" he believed. "We're throwing it away!" He insisted on at least one more screening, in this case, for Paramount Pictures. One of the glorious, legendary studios, Paramount had experienced serious economic fallout by the time RSO set up a *Survive!* screening for Barry Diller and Allan's new *Won Ton Ton* chum David Picker. Having recently relinquished his VP slot at ABC, where he'd pioneered the movie-of-the-week genre, Diller came to Paramount just as the studio receded from its *Godfather I* and *II* glory days. By early 1976, the new chairman and CEO of Paramount was no longer so new, having been unable to deliver a box-office winner. Worse, "Paramount had nothing for the summer" of that year, says Picker, whom Diller had recently made president of production.

The two Paramount chiefs took one look at *Survive!* and Diller said he hated it.

Picker thought it was a piece of crap too. But he disagreed with Diller on the movie's box-office potential. "We can make money from this," Picker said. "And besides, we don't have *anything* else for the summer." As Picker explained his strategy, "If we strike only 400 prints, we can move it from theater to theater on word of mouth." Diller shrugged and said OK. "We don't have anything else," Picker repeated.

Allan pushed for the Paramount deal. "Let's go for broke," he told Stigwood.

Unlike Arkoff, the guys at Paramount weren't giving Allan and RSO a dime. Instead, Picker promised to match, in prints and media, the $850,000 that had already been spent on *Survive!* They would be 60-40 partners, with the studio getting the larger percentage of the gross until the movie broke the $4-million mark at the box office, at which point the split would be 40-60, with RSO and Allan now getting the larger percentage.

"Between that and the 400 prints," Allan said, "I'll get a house in Malibu out of this movie!" He had never been more confident of anything in his life.

Allan's cannibalism film opened well on August 4, bringing in a quarter million dollars on only twenty-six screens—good enough to deliver the astoundingly ominous No. 13 slot on *Variety*'s box office chart. Then it exploded. For the next three weeks, by adding only a few more screens, *Survive!* grossed well over $1 million in each of those sessions, bringing it to the No. 2 position, right after Mel Brooks's *Silent Movie* and right ahead of the big-budget thriller *The Omen*, starring Gregory Peck.

On the strength of those numbers, Allan purchased his Malibu house, one that sat high on a bluff over Trancas Beach. He bought it for $1 million when he was thin, because otherwise he could never travel the forty steps that separated it from the Pacific Ocean. He dubbed it Seahaven. "I'm the Elizabeth Taylor of houses. I marry every house I go to," he said.

Allan knew *Survive!* would continue to live up to its title in the coming weeks when he read reviews like Frank Rich's diatribe in the *New York Post,* which labeled the movie "a patently false snuff film that simulated the disembowelment of a woman for an audience's erotic pleasure" and "the experience of sitting through it is so degrading it makes you want to rush home and take a shower." Halfway through the pan, Allan ordered his assistant to send Rich a bouquet of roses.

He enjoyed the fact that people were calling *Survive!* "that Mexican delicatessen movie," and knew precisely how to work those bad reviews to his advantage. "The only thing most people know about Mexican movies is Buñuel and Tijuana porno," Allan told *Variety.* "This is something in between. Buñuel it is not, but it is a very entertaining picture that the public really likes." Allan knew how to work a quote, and took special pleasure in the "Tijuana porno" comment, which he repeated ad nauseam. He gave it a sanitized spin when speaking to reporters at family newspapers like the *Los Angeles Times.* "The eating sequences are brilliantly done," he noted.

When occasionally reporters pressed him too hard, Allan claimed marginal responsibility. "Hey, I didn't ask the plane to crash and I didn't ask them to eat their friends!" he said.

Not everyone in Hollywood found pleasure in the lucrative bad reviews for *Survive!* Pissed as hell were the makers of the competing Andes cannibalism film, *Alive!*

"We're not terribly happy about [their] jumping up and down saying they broke ground for us," said Mike Medavoy, West Coast production chief at United Artists. Two years earlier, UA had bought the rights to *Alive!* written by two survivors of the airplane crash.

Allan never missed an opportunity to retort to a retort. "There was no other project," since UA had not yet announced a start date, he told reporters.

Medavoy shot back. "Ours will be a class-A movie with a class-A director and a class-A budget. I don't think they've taken the steam out of our film. It will stand on its own."

As Allan predicted, UA soon pulled the life support on *Alive!* and John Schlesinger never invited Allan to have dinner at his house again. Then again, Allan could take solace in the deed to his new Malibu house.

No sooner did he own Seahaven, however, than Allan feared he might have to put it back on the market. That unlikely premonition came in the form of *Variety*'s Labor Day 1976 report on weekend grosses. Allan alerted Gershon. Suddenly *Survive!* was no longer in the top ten. It was sinking and sinking fast at the box office. Everybody on the RSO side of the project wanted to know what had happened.

As the powers at Paramount explained it, once *Survive!* hit the $4-million mark, it no longer made sense for the company to make media buys now that they were getting only forty cents on the dollar.

"Are you crazy?" Gershon told Picker. "Go ahead and reverse it, we'll go back to 60-40 in your favor." Telegrams were exchanged, and "that was the whole agreement," says Gershon. The next week *Survive!* was once again the No. 1 movie in America, taking in $1.4 million—and it stayed in the top ten for several weeks. Allan called it one of those "strange deals," in which he made as much money as the studio. "And that just never happens. It's a textbook case of just how you sometimes get lucky in Hollywood."

Allan was happy. RSO was happy. Paramount was happy. "We all had a bonding relationship over this demented movie," says Gershon, "and Allan got us that relationship. Without it, Stigwood would probably not have brought them *Saturday Night Fever*. It was Allan Carr who started that chain of events."

Tacky as it was twisted, *Survive!* brought Allan his first million dollars—plus a few more. "It's a fabulous day," he said of the accomplishment. "I do all this because it is creative fun."

Only later, when he was really rich did he develop a modicum of discreet bravado. "After $10 million, you shouldn't talk about how much money you have. It's major bad taste," he believed. "You'd just be astounded at how different people treat you when they know you have more than $10 million."

Regarding his new enemies at United Artists, Allan blew them off with a one-line joke. Since he'd just bought the screen rights to the Broadway musical *Grease*, he offered the wounded party a novel revenge, suggesting, "Maybe they will make a film called *Vaseline*."

seven

B'way's Bastard Child

Marvin Hamlisch, luxuriating in his hypersuccess with *A Chorus Line,* couldn't stop talking up this new Broadway musical he'd just seen. "If ever you're going to make a motion picture, *Grease* is it," he told his manager-friend. Allan eventually agreed to see the show, despite its "unpleasant" title, because Hamlisch made it a threesome, inviting his *Chorus Line* collaborator, Michael Bennett; that Allan couldn't resist. *Grease* had already been running for over two years even though its story of a bunch of horny 1950s high school students had been eschewed by the Tony Awards and the usual geriatric Broadway crowd. *Grease* attracted, instead, theatergoing neophytes who were dismissed as "the bridge-and-tunnel crowd" from New Jersey and Long Island. Cutting-edge musical theater it was not, and such an illustrious legit combo as Hamlisch and Bennett looked more than a little out of place among the Jersey youngsters as they all walked through the lobby of the Royale Theater to take their seats. Allan was the third wheel that evening, and while his expectations were low, he respected Hamlisch's opinion. Perhaps, too, a paparazzo would catch him with the *Chorus Line* duo and he'd get his photo in the *New York Post.*

Sometime between "Greased Lightning" and "Look at Me, I'm Sandra Dee," Allan forgot about camera angles and instead experienced a *Grease* epiphany. This musical was his high school story, or, at least, his high school story as he would like to rewrite it. The plot about hip leather greasers versus the plaid-covered nerds reverberated for him, especially the love angle that had the

47

square girl Sandy (i.e., Allan) turning into a floozy to get the sexy guy Danny. "God, it's even set in Chicago in the 1950s!" Allan gushed.

After the show, he took Hamlisch and Bennett to a late dinner at Joe Allen restaurant, a theater hangout best known not for food but its exposed brick walls, which showcase posters from flop tuners—*Dude, Via Galactica,* among them—that are legendary for all the wrong reasons. Over his chicken pot pie, Allan let his two companions know his plan: "I have to make this into a movie."

Let others go broke with sophisticated, avant-garde theater. Allan had the proud taste of a wealthy adolescent; and the very next day, he inquired into the stage rights. Unfortunately, the option to bring *Grease* to the movies was held by Ralph Bakshi, a filmmaker who had recently scored with some edgy, almost X-rated, animated films. As he'd done with *Heavy Traffic* and *Fritz the Cat,* Bakshi planned to turn *Grease* into a long-format cartoon.

"Which is all wrong," Allan said when he got the bad news. Then he forgot about *Grease,* only to remember it at precisely the right moment.

Lunching at Sardi's restaurant one day, Allan spotted Kenneth Waissman and Maxine Fox across the crowded dining room. He winked at the two *Grease* producers, and on his way out of the famed theater eatery, he decided to make nice. "So when's your movie coming out?" he asked.

"It's not," said Waissman. "The rights came back to us."

"Really?" said Allan. "I'm doing a picture deal with Paramount and I'd really be interested in producing the movie version of *Grease.*"

"Call me after lunch," said Waissman, who never expected to hear another word from Allan Carr, since "Allan was waving and talking to everybody else in Sardi's that day." After his own *Grease*/Bakshi turnabout, the Broadway producer tended to discount these Hollywood types.

Forty-five minutes later, Allan made good on his promise to phone. "I *really* am interested in producing the movie version of *Grease,*" he began. More than ready to sell their musical, Waissman and Fox sold the option for $200,000, which Allan considered quite a bargain for such a long-running show. At that time, Allan didn't have $200,000 in quick change, so he "bought it on the installment plan," as he described it, giving the Broadway producers a few thousand dollars every month.

It was the era of tuner sophisticates like Stephen Sondheim and Bob Fosse, and many on Shubert Alley considered *Grease,* with its easy pop-rock melodies and bare-bones staging, "the bastard child of Broadway," as Allan dubbed it.

The theater may have been his first love, but even on this turf, he considered himself the outsider. Allan could relate to *Grease*'s interloper status, especially when he learned that young people ("under thirty" in theater parlance) were going to see *Grease* again and again. Repeat business, as Allan knew, is what turns a hit movie into a blockbuster movie.

Grease began as a community theater production in Chicago, scheduled to run only four performances over two weekends in February 1971. But the show, written by two local guys—Jim Jacobs and Warren Casey—caught on with the Windy City audiences, and one year later, it opened on Broadway at a bargain-basement cost of only $100,000, compared to the then-record $750,000 spent on the Stephen Sondheim extravaganza *Follies* a few months earlier.

When Allan began his rights negotiations, both *Follies* and the 1972 Tony winner for best musical, *Two Gentlemen of Verona*, had shuttered, while Tony loser *Grease* continued to pack them in, albeit at discounted prices for its young audiences. In negotiations, he and Waissman enjoyed a good working relationship before reality fouled everything by week's end. Allan wanted the earliest possible movie release date for his investment while Waissman, fearing that the movie would cut into his stage-show ticket sales, wanted that date postponed. These talks caused a major freeze between the two parties, and when they bumped into each other at industry events, Allan indulged in this habit of looking through Waissman to say clever things like, "Who are you?"

Their deal went to arbitration with the Dramatists Guild, which settled in Waissman's favor with a 1978 release date. "It seemed like a long time into the future," says Waissman. Allan knew how to hold a grudge. Since he didn't win that battle, he thought he could waive the option money. "It forced him to bring in Stigwood," says Waissman, who also thought it would be a good deal if his percentage was based on gross after break-even rather than a back-end deal. "My feeling was at that point $500,000 or $250,000—what is the difference?"

In its wisdom, Paramount Pictures jumped at the savings, because "while Michael Eisner thought the movie could be a success, Barry Diller didn't have great faith," says Waissman. In Allan's opinion, everyone at Paramount was "nervous," and that included Eisner, who had been brought on by Diller to revitalize the studio. (And Eisner did with *Saturday Night Fever, Happy Days, Cheers,* the *Star Trek* franchise, and, of course, *Grease*.)

Allan's wrangling and perseverance paid off. He also secured one major caveat from the stage producers, and that was the rarely won interpolation clause. In essence, Waissman agreed "that if some of the music from the stage musical wasn't quite right for the movie, [Carr and Stigwood] had the right to add additional songs to the picture."

Both Stigwood and Allan wanted there to be a *Grease* title song, something the stage show lacked. To add new songs by new songwriters—it was a major, if not outrageous, concession. "Something that composers for the legitimate theater never agree to," said Allan, who knew full well that Casey and Jacobs were not Lerner and Loewe. In this case, Allan asked for Camelot, and he got Camelot.

However, before he and Stigwood could commission composers Barry Gibb, John Farrar, and Louis St. Louis to write new songs, before John Travolta and Olivia Newton-John were cast as high school sweethearts Danny Zuko and Sandy Olsson (née Dumbrowski), Allan needed to get Stigwood's attention. It was Stigwood, after all, who was looking for properties to fulfill his three-picture deal with Paramount.

The Aussie producer wasn't averse to putting his money into a movie musical, but as he continually pointed out to Allan, movie musicals weren't making money. In fact, there had been few box-office winners since Barbra Streisand made her film debut in 1968's *Funny Girl*. Then again, Stigwood was banking on his *Sgt. Pepper's Lonely Hearts Club Band* to make him a ton of money at the box office. But unlike *Grease*, "*Sgt. Pepper* has the Beatles. It can't lose," said Stigwood.

Allan didn't quite know how to convince Stigwood of *Grease*'s commercial validity until he contacted a mild-mannered cinematographer named Bill Butler, who was extraordinarily busy with two back-to-back projects: *Jaws*, directed by a young director named Steven Spielberg, and *One Flew over the Cuckoo's Nest*, directed by a new Czech director named Milos Forman.

Butler and Allan made an unlikely partnership, but like so many family men, the avuncular cinematographer, who rarely raised his voice above a whisper, took an immediate liking to Hollywood's loudest, most "flamboyant" producer-manager, and vice versa. Back in the 1970s, when Hollywood was enjoying the golden age of *The Godfather* and *Taxi Driver* and *American Graffiti*, many producers considered their next picture a work of art beyond reproach. "Allan's attitude was different," says Butler. "He was 'Hey, let's have fun making a movie.'" That playful approach to the job even carried over to his personal life. "Allan was gay as could be, and that's part of what I liked about him. He wasn't trying to hide anything," adds Butler, who remembers one meeting at Seahaven in Malibu. Allan had just gotten back from Hawaii. "And there was this young boyfriend Allan had picked up there. There was a surfboard in the back of his convertible. I loved him for that."

Since the cinematographer had never seen *Grease,* Allan flew Butler to New York City to see it onstage. Later, the two men met at an Italian restaurant in Philadelphia to work out how they could "make it not a Broadway thing but a movie." Stigwood was coming to town, and had set aside a small window of time for their *Grease* sales pitch. With the help of some colored crayons and a paper tablecloth, Butler laid out his vision of *Grease:* Because young audiences preferred realism to musical fantasy, *Grease* would be a realistic musical. "Let's put it in a real high school and make it as real as possible," Butler told Allan. He started with the show's song "Greased Lightning," in which the Kenickie character fantasizes about his dream car. Butler scribbled a few frames of celluloid on the paper tablecloth, then explained, "We'll have the character slide under a real car and then 'transition' to a musical dream sequence in which he sings." It was Allan's job to sell that concept to Stigwood.

Rather than meet his potential *Grease* collaborators in a restaurant or hotel room, Stigwood chose a more convenient location for the confab. "We met in Stigwood's limousine," Butler recalls. "Allan was the greatest salesman you could ever imagine. Stigwood was cold and distant, he didn't want to deal with me. I was just a cameraman." Allan presented his "realistic musical" to Stigwood, who bought the concept in about ten minutes.

Allan needed to reinvent *Grease* for the screen, but not too much. One of his first hires was choreographer Patricia Birch, who had been with the stage show since it opened in New York. Birch was five feet tall. She sported a pixie haircut. But she was no pushover. Also, she knew the property better than anyone and, therefore, was not an easy convert to radically rethinking the material. "But I got used to the idea that 'Greased Lightning' was going to be a fantasy in the movie," she says. At the time she thought, "Well, we've gone glitzier here than I would have liked. It had been set in Chicago. We lost some of the toughness with the palm trees in California. But you gain some, you lose some. Allan recognized what made the show successful, and what we preserved in the movie were the students' relationships."

Allan's play for power, once he had Stigwood's money, continued to expand. He even gave himself the task of writing the *Grease* screenplay. What did it matter that he could not write and was so bad at spelling that his first attempt at a designer license plate came out JAMANI when he meant it to read GEMINI, his astrological sign? He took care of that minor deficiency by bringing aboard his close friend Bronte Woodard, "who can handle the punctuation," said Allan.

Grease was set in Chicago. Allan was from Chicago. As he saw it, *Grease* was *his* high school story—after he and Bronte made a few changes.

eight

High School Confidential

If it's true that the greatest celebrities are those who completely reinvent themselves, then Allan started earlier than most.

"I made it closer to my own high school memories," Allan said of bringing the *Grease* stage show to the screen. In the original musical, most of the high school characters are greasers. At Allan's Highland Park High School outside Chicago, none of them were—except when the students play-acted at being tough for the school yearbook and hand-held the sign "hood" in case their leather jackets, unlit cigarettes, and carefully pressed blue jeans failed to complete the picture. These teenagers were the progeny of doctors, lawyers, and big businessmen, not the offspring of car mechanics, beauticians, and waitresses. "Money was not the social dividing line," says Allan's childhood friend Joanne Cimbalo. "All our families had money."

Highland Park was only twenty-five minutes by commuter train from those hard Chicago streets that spawned the delinquent leather-clad teens who first inspired songwriters Jim Jacobs and Warren Casey to write *Grease*. But in terms of income, social status, and expensive landscaping, Highland Park may as well have been on the other side of the continental divide. The L.A. palm trees that Patricia Birch objected to in the movie would be the least of Allan's changes. Or as Jim Jacobs later complained, "The whole nitty-gritty of these tough kids was gone."

Moviegoers today know Highland Park as the town of expansive blue-grass lawns and quiet oak-lined streets and tastefully oversized colonial and Tudor houses that are home to the Goodsens, the Jarretts, and the Buellers in, respectively, *Risky Business, Ordinary People,* and *Ferris Bueller's Day Off,* all of which were filmed in Highland Park. The small town is just one of a select group of wealthy communities that line the North Shore of Chicago.

Allan's house looked something like those movie houses, except that his home had all of Lake Michigan for its backyard. "Allan's house was a couple of steps up from the rest of ours," says his high school friend Robert Le Clercq, who attended several parties there. High on a bluff overlooking the second biggest lake in America, the split-level house was known as party central for the students of Highland Park High School and, later, nearby Lake Forest College where Allan almost, but not quite, got his B.A. degree. With the waterfront as their dramatic background, the parties at the end of the short cul-de-sac known as Lake View Terrace afforded its young guests catered food, torch lights on tall sticks, polished oak dance floors erected over the lawn, and the music of George Stewart's band. Even when Allan was sixteen years old, hamburgers and 45 RPMs played on an old Motorola were not his style.

Back then, Allan Carr was known as Alan Solomon, the only child of Ann and Albert Solomon, who were divorced by the time their only son entered junior high school. Both parents were successful Chicago merchants. Albert owned a large furniture store; Ann sold the finest shoes and handbags at her fur and leather-goods boutique. They made plenty of money, and neither stinted at lavishing it on their son, who invariably got his way—if money could buy whatever it was he wanted.

The young Alan, as it turned out, wanted a lot. When Ann and Albert first took him to Florida on spring break, a ten-year-old Alan insisted that they get off the train in Atlanta to spend the night so he could visit the theater where *Gone with the Wind* held its 1939 premiere. Or the time he flew to Detroit, at age twelve, to see Bette Davis in *Two's Company* and didn't notify his parents until right before the matinee, when he long-distanced them to say, "Don't worry. The show is over at 4:45 and I'll be home around 7 tonight." Or when he needed money to be a Broadway investor, at age fifteen, and got his parents to put $1,500 into a Tallulah Bankhead vehicle called *The Ziegfield Follies,* which promptly folded on the road.

While Alan lived most of his teen years with his father, it was the nearly biweekly trips to New York City to see Broadway shows with his mother that made her his arts patron, if not his clear favorite as parent. It didn't matter that she had to pay scalper prices to land primo seats to the original productions of *South*

Pacific and *Wonderful Town*. Best of all were the ducats she brought to *Around the World in 80 Days* premiere at Madison Square Garden on October 17, 1956. Producer Mike Todd played ringmaster, complete with whip and red jacket, while his princess-attired bride-to-be, Elizabeth Taylor, stood at his side. It was there that Ann's son met his role model for life: "That's when I knew what I wanted!" Whether the world needed it or not, Alan Solomon vowed to be the next Mike Todd.

His parents paid all the bills and Alan threw all the parties; otherwise, he didn't talk much about Ann and Albert except to say that his father found him to be "an embarrassment." With cultivated adolescent insouciance, Alan said it didn't matter much what his parents thought of him, as long as they gave him the money to invest in Broadway shows and escape to New York City and Fort Lauderdale.

A letter from Camp Indianola, however, gives a more complicated interpretation of that father-son relationship. Written in 1950 when Alan was thirteen, the handwritten missive expresses his "hope" that the August heat is not unbearable in his father's Chicago store. "It is very hot and the flies are terrible here," Alan wrote from Lake Mendota, Wisconsin. "Only 3 weks from today and I'll be home. I can hardly wait. . . . Lots of parents here this wk-end and lots of dads staying over nite. Will you be up next Sunday for a few hrs. I hope? Say hello to everybody at the store. It won't be long now! I love you very much."

It is signed "Your best pal, friend, boy, son, Alan."

An overweight child who was saddled with thick glasses from an early age, Alan had no choice but to avoid those sports that essentially defined boyhood in the Midwest, and gravitated instead to more sensitive pursuits like dressing up in drag to play the titular role in *Charley's Aunt* and posing for yearbook photos with the theater department's Garrick Players girls. His appearance as a teenager is what could best be described as "fubsy," an antiquated word meaning chubby and squat. "Fubsy" also conjures up the clown role that Alan played throughout his school years.

"At home I was secure," he said, "but at school I felt I was not physically attractive and this exaggerated my desire for approval, to be amusing, to be liked. That's why I came on so strong."

Five days a week at Highland Park High, Allan stepped over the foyer's floor plaque that told him to "Dream. Believe. Achieve." He dreamed and he believed but he did not achieve very much gradewise. Neither was he known as a particularly good student at Lake Forest College, where his studies invariably took a backseat to the parties, the clubs, the school plays, and the endless campus pranks that sprang from the school's busy social network of fraternities and sororities. Here was an institution of higher learning better known for its bucolic, picture-perfect campus than its academic standards. As more than one 1950s grad described it, "Lake Forest is the place you went if your parents had money and you couldn't get into any other college."

Being Jewish was pretty much the norm in Highland Park, but that was not the case in the neighboring town of Lake Forest and its college. Here the citizens were solidly Gentile, and Alan's ethnicity automatically denied him admittance to four of the five fraternities on campus. Only one, Tau Kappa Epsilon, allowed Jews and other minorities as members. "The other fraternities were the jock ones, but the TKEs were the artsy ones," says David Umbach, a fellow theater devotee whom Alan first befriended in high school.

In college, Alan preferred to hang out with the Gentile jocks rather than the artistic ethnics. Or, as Groucho Marx once explained it, "I don't want to belong to any club that will accept me as a member."

Alan kept his eye on one of the exclusive jock frat houses, Phi Delta Theta, that excluded all minorities. "Our national chapter wouldn't permit us to pledge Jewish people," says James Kenney, another Lake Forest classmate. Such an obstacle only made Allan more determined to belong, and eventually his persistence paid off when the fraternity accepted him as a "social *affiliate*," explains Kenney.

Alan was delighted, because, as he often told people, he wasn't Jewish. Technically speaking. "My mother is Roman Catholic," he said. He also told people that his aunt was a nun. Perhaps it was the truth. "I don't ever remember anything about temple or a bar mitzvah," says Joanne Cimbalo.

Being Jewish, or not, was only one roadblock he confronted in finding acceptance among the Greeks. "Alan loved the Gamma Phi Betas," recalls another coed, Margaret Neely. "They were rich girls and very attractive, and Alan loved hanging out with them." In this case, Jewish was the least of it. They were girls, he was a boy, but Alan knew better than any of them how to dress, do their hair, and walk in high heels. It didn't really matter that his entry into the Gamma Phis involved a mock ceremony. He *belonged*. "Alan wanted to be in a sorority, and so he went through a pinning ceremony," says Neely.

In 1956, such behavior didn't read as gay, surprisingly. For a more retiring type, it might have spelled disgrace. But Alan was defiant in his demands to flaunt the rules and yet be accepted within the social box of the conservative

Eisenhower era. If his fellow students dared laugh, Alan was there to laugh first. They said, "Isn't he interesting?" Or, at worst, "Isn't he bizarre?" Homosexuality wasn't discussed, not even in the theater department, and that taboo extended to the year 1957, when Lake Forest College boldly put on the gay-themed play *Tea and Sympathy*. "It was a very restricted time. Gay or straight, no one was having sex much, certainly not openly," says David Umbach. "You didn't talk about sex, particularly gay sex." Even in college, Umbach and Alan never acknowledged to each other their sexual orientation. But Alan knew. "The other boys were interested in girls. I was not," he would admit many years later.

In high school, Umbach and Alan bonded, and their both being homosexual probably had something to do with that friendship. It certainly had a lot to do with their both being "theater nuts," as Umbach recalls. "I was green, from the corn country, and Alan was so sophisticated. He showed me the theater world of Chicago."

Highland Park boasted its own major cultural institution in the summer Ravinia Festival, its grounds a short three-block walk from the Solomon home. When Allan wasn't entertaining his friend David with tales of his latest trip to New York City, he took him to see concerts at the festival and in Chicago. Umbach says, "We went to places I never would have thought to go, like to see Mae West at the Blue Note. It was very raunchy for the 1950s." They also saw the bawdy, and openly bisexual, nightclub performer Frances Faye, and it shocked them when the singer took to the stage of the Blue Note and introduced herself with "I'm Frances Faye and I'm gay, gay, gay!" Alan and Umbach thought it meant she took drugs.

One evening, Alan invited his high school friend to see Carol Channing in a road production of *Wonderful Town*, and bragged that he had already met the Broadway star at a party in New York City. Umbach didn't believe his friend, and to prove himself, Allan wangled his way backstage to knock on Channing's dressing-room door. When she dutifully appeared, her bright orange outfit caused Umbach to gasp. "And she definitely remembered Alan and invited us in and we had a wonderful, long conversation with her," says Umbach. "Even as a teenager, Alan was a very recognizable, unforgettable person. He pushed his way into places."

On another theater outing, the two teenagers took in a performance of the musical *Pajama Game*, which featured the memorable "Hernando's Hideaway" number. At one point in the show stopper, the stage goes dark and a character cries out to her boyfriend, "Poopsie! Poopsie!"

Umbach turned to his friend. "You are Poopsie!" he said.

Alan threw his head back to squeal with delight. He fell in love with the moniker and immediately adopted it for the slug "Poopsie's Column" that appeared above his theater reviews in the Lake Forest College newspaper, *The Stentor*. He even created a brand of awards, the Poopsies, not to be confused with the Tonys or the Oscars or the Emmys, to bestow upon local theater talent. They honored "true excellence in the theater." To everyone else, including many Lake Forest students, Alan wrote brutally negative reviews. Margaret Neely, who edited *The Stentor*, used to complain, "Alan, could you go a little easier on the school productions and not be quite so abusive?"

Her lack of ethics shocked Alan. "Margaret, you're the editor and I'm the artist, and I've got to say what I want to say. This is freedom of the press!" he insisted.

If Alan had no problem attaching his own name to the theater reviews, he knew the limits of freedom when it came to penning the anonymous "Through the Keyhole," *The Stentor's* must-read gossip column. It was an act of sheer stealth for Alan to breathlessly report on the romantic goings-on of the coeds and jocks each week of the semester. "No one knew he wrote it," says Neely. Every week Alan slid his typewritten news under the dorm-room door of Neely's boyfriend (and future husband), Roger Wilhelm, Lake Forest's star basketball center. Often confused with baseball great Hoyt Wilhelm, the six-foot-six college athlete acted as conduit between his editor-girlfriend Neely and Alan, which made the gossip column as much an act of tabloid journalism as it was one of personal infatuation. "Alan was always attracted to Roger and several other men who were athletes, and I'm sure that was an operating factor," Neely says of Alan's commitment to "Through the Keyhole."

As their college tenure progressed, Alan and his gay friend David Umbach saw less of each other. Alan preferred the company of the tony Gamma Phi Beta girls and the manly Phi Delta Theta jocks, who saw him as a novelty. He was their klutzy younger brother, but also the smart aleck who could level any physically strong but mentally dense adversary with the well-delivered, lethal quip. It helped, too, that he had been blessed with a confidence man's voice—unwavering and in control even when he didn't know what he was talking about. His Greek friends might have called him a "mascot," but Alan rejected such second-class status. He was equal but separate and therefore special, maybe even singular. It was a respectful, loving social dichotomy he was to nurture with dozens of straight family men and women throughout his life.

On the making of the movie *Grease*, Allan Carr often said that he was an expert on the subject of young outsiders because, "Like many kids, I was not too popular."

With the exception of *Charley's Aunt*, he didn't star in many school plays, but he did write all the theater reviews. He wasn't voted prom king, but he did throw the best parties. He didn't find love, but he called himself "the matchmaker" in the college newspaper. He wasn't the senior class president, but in many ways, he was the most high-profile student on campus.

"He advertised himself," says Franz Schulze, a Lake Forest College professor. "Students recognized him as Poopsie. He was very, very stout and made no bones about that. And in a way he took advantage of his uniqueness." Even his many Poopsie columns and reviews carried a pen-and-ink caricature that humorously captured Alan's already jowly, nearly shapeless face.

But high-profile is not the same as popular, nor can it be confused with handsome. If he lusted after the school's top athletes, he kept it to himself. "Alan wasn't a beauty," says Umbach. "His sexual inclination would have been to be shy and not bring it up until later in life when he could control it."

Regarding the opposite sex or his own sex, he didn't indulge—except when it came to that de rigueur date for the junior prom, and even then Alan took a pretty but less-than-available girl, Margie Tegtmeyer, who had momentarily split from her boyfriend (and future husband). "Alan knew Bob [Cohen] was taking someone else," Tegtmeyer recalls. Back in 1957, Margie qualified as a safe bet, in Alan's estimation, one who wouldn't be interested in a goodnight kiss or follow-up date. The Lake Forest junior prom qualified as the big date night, and college students there didn't decorate the gym for the event. They rented the expensive *Milwaukee Clipper* to cruise Lake Michigan. Margie and Alan had a "very nice time," as she remembers, but her prom date wasn't anything like Bob Cohen. "Alan was very concerned about what I'd wear and he brought flowers to go with what I wore. He was thoughtful about those things," she notes, even if he was inordinately nitpicking about the décor, the place settings, the music, and anything else having to do with proper entertaining. "This shouldn't be there," he said of one flower arrangement. "It should be *there*."

Whether it was his weight, his homosexuality, his ethnicity, or his troubled family life, "Alan didn't feel he ever fit in, both in high school and college," says Joanne Cimbalo. "He found excitement, he loved to entertain, and he was always going going going. But in his reflective moments, he never found peace. Never."

By his senior year in college, Alan's weight had already ballooned his five-foot-six frame to well over 200 pounds, and he had even begun to wear caftans or muumuus on campus to disguise his burgeoning obesity. If he had simply retreated to a corner of the campus, Alan might have been ridiculed or, at best, ignored. But he possessed too strong a personality to be dismissed, and despite the fact that he was now dressing, in essence, like a woman, and an extravagant woman at that, Cimbalo never heard him referred to as a sissy, a queer, or a fairy. "His clothes, like his weight and his interest in Broadway, were just one more thing that made him unique," she says. What most students didn't know was that the high-profile Alan Solomon never graduated from college. Semester after semester, he put off fulfilling the school's science requirement and waited until the second semester of his senior year to take biology. He failed the course.

While that ignominy only solidified his outsider status, at least to himself, he took out career insurance by quickly setting up a postcollege job prior to his nongraduation.

"We reopened the Civic Theater in Chicago," says Jack Tourville, a Lake Forest College alum who also came up short on graduation credits. The reason for their double failure was easy to pinpoint: Instead of studying biology that final semester, Alan enlisted Tourville to emcee the annual Lake Forest *Garrick Gaieties*. The show was a success, their studies were not. They wisely decided to pursue success.

"We'll become theater producers!" Alan told his friend.

Before he got down to the nitty-gritty of raising money, acquiring stage properties, and securing a theater, Alan set forth his top priority as an impresario. "I'm getting a new name!" he said. "There are too many Solomons in Chicago."

He even hired a lawyer to change his name to Alan Carr. (The "Allan" came a few years later when a numerologist suggested the change.) When the judge asked him why he needed a new name, the newly monickered young man replied, "I'm divorcing my parents!" Always the performer, Allan knew it would get a reaction in court. But secretly, in the back of his mind, "I was really thinking about that marquee. I was thinking of billing and how a name looked in a newspaper ad."

If the new Mr. Carr divorced his parents that day in court, he failed to notify Ann and Albert Solomon of that split when he asked them to bankroll the new Chicago Civic Theater. It was their money that bought an impressive 1958 season: Eva Le Gallienne in *Mary Stuart*, a repertory offering of Shakespeare's *Measure for Measure* and *The Tempest*, plus Bette Davis and Gary Merrill in

The World of Carl Sandburg. Alan had seen the Merrills perform the Sandburg offering in Oshkosh, Wisconsin, and promptly barged his way into their dressing room. "I don't want to be rude," he began the conversation, "but why are you playing in this auditorium?"

"Good question," said Davis, who liked the boy's spunk.

Alan let her know, "I think you should come to Chicago. Carl Sandburg is from Chicago."

He had more than just his parents' money to start a first-class theater company. Alan laid the groundwork for the Civic Theater by assiduously courting the favor of the *Chicago Tribune*'s entertainment columnist Herb Lyon and its chief theater critic, Claudia Cassidy, who, in turn, lavished much ink on the project. It was Cassidy who suggested the venue, which heretofore had been used as a rehearsal space for the Lyric Opera of Chicago.

Cassidy also cooperated when it came to the reviews, but there was nothing that she could do about the box office. Undeterred, Alan and his friend Jack Tourville set out to put together a spring 1959 season. Alan had recently seen Lorraine Hansberry's *A Raisin in the Sun* on Broadway and wanted to bring it to Chicago, where the play is set. The tyro impresarios sat down with the play's producer, Philip Rose, and Alan threw out a box-office guarantee number. "It was too much money," says Tourville. But his partner told him not to worry. Alan Solomon was now Alan Carr, and he knew that showmen from Flo Ziegfeld to Mike Todd often had to lie to get what they wanted. The trick, he believed, was to lie so extravagantly that he instilled confidence. Tourville saw finances in a different light. "It was scary for us," he recalls.

Alan wanted to round out his spring 1959 season with *Eugenia*. It had been a flop on Broadway, but it was a flop starring Tallulah Bankhead. Bankhead was now touring in it, and Alan and Tourville drove to Detroit in hopes they could convince the tempestuous, and cocaine-addicted, actress to bring the show to Chicago.

"We sent her roses and we visited her backstage," Tourville recalls. "It was a terrible show. She admitted as much. It needed work."

After one desultory performance, Bankhead sat in her dressing room and listened as two postteenage producers made their pitch. She didn't bother to change out of her robe, but had already consumed half a bottle of scotch. "Alan and I shared some thoughts with her and preconceived notions of what we wanted to do. That kind of stuff. And then we gracefully got out of there," says Tourville.

Bankhead never made it to Chicago that theater season. *A Raisin in the Sun* did arrive, but under the auspices of another producing entity, and Jack Tourville joined the army. He told Alan that he couldn't keep taking Albert Solomon's money, since their first season with the Civic Theater failed to break even and it was unlikely that their second season would be any different. "It was an exciting time," says Tourville. "But my dad was concerned and Alan's relationship with his father was not good. It was through his mother that Alan got the money. His father had crumbled and moaned and finally just said OK."

But without Tourville's business acumen and emotional support, Alan also called it quits. It helped that he got a job offer from an unlikely source.

"I was starting this new TV show and hired Alan Carr to be my talent director," says Hugh Hefner. The show: *Playboy's Penthouse*. It lasted only a couple of seasons, but it spawned the magazine's vast network of Playboy clubs, and introduced Allan to the world of booking talent—talent that included Ella Fitzgerald, Lenny Bruce, Joan Baez, Judy Collins, and Bob Newhart, and even some performers, like Marlo Thomas, Mama Cass Elliot, Joan Rivers, Phyllis Diller, and Ann-Margret, who never made it on the show but ended up being managed by Alan Carr as soon as he migrated from Chicago to Los Angeles.

It's often said that famous people never look back. Allan Carr was different. He looked back often, which is why he could never stop running.

nine

It's Pepsi-Cola Time

Broadway is hardly a bastion of street reality and grit, but in the hands of Allan and his friend Bronte Woodard, *Grease* lost whatever real dirt it once possessed. Choreographer Patricia Birch, the only major creative talent to work on both projects, may have worried about the substitution of California succulents for Chicago asphalt, but in the end, she felt that Allan and Woodard's screenplay kept the show's adolescent soul. "Those high school kids were popular in any school. They are archetypal. If you look at any high school class, you find the outsiders getting left out, people vying for position," she says.

John Travolta spoke for Allan when he analyzed the movie's success: "The 1950s didn't have a lot of great causes. Everything was more dull, bland, and complacent. And in a lot of ways, that's the way things are today in the 1970s. I think audiences can relate to that."

It's not as if Allan were messing with a hard-hitting teen classic, like *Rebel Without a Cause,* when he rewrote *Grease. Grease* is, and always was, a light-hearted musical. Allan never apologized for sanitizing his greasers. The movie would be his story. It was never to be *their* story. "I based my changes on my high school in the Chicago suburbs, where the kids were not all greasers, like in the stage musical," he said. "They were tough but good kids, and by moving the setting to the suburbs, I made it closer to my own high school memories and, much more important, more resonant for a wider audience. To that end, I also cleaned up some of the raunchy language."

If cinematographer Bill Butler channeled Busby Berkeley for *Grease*, Allan kept to an equally 1930s aesthetic—one that had much to do with "Mickey and Judy put on a show." Regardless of the approach, the powers at Paramount Pictures never really cared for *Grease*. Box office prognosticators were much more excited about Robert Stigwood's other upcoming movie musical that summer, *Sgt. Pepper's Lonely Hearts Club Band*. And so was Stigwood, who viewed *Grease* "as Allan's movie," says the *Sgt. Pepper* screenwriter Henry Edwards.

Paramount wanted its TV star Henry Winkler, of *Happy Days*, to headline *Grease*. "The Fonz," tired of playing greasers, passed—much to Paramount's disappointment and much to Allan and Stigwood's delight. Stigwood had his eye on John Travolta ever since the teenager auditioned for the Broadway production of *Jesus Christ Superstar* in 1971. "That kid's going to be a star!" Stigwood said at the time. From his opposing catbird seat, Allan also claimed credit for the young actor's subsequent stardom, and often told the story that a headshot of Travolta, sent to him by publicist Ronni Chasen, led to Travolta's being cast in *Grease*. Regardless, it was Stigwood who first signed the young actor, not only to *Grease* but to the producer's three-picture contract with Paramount, which began with *Saturday Night Fever* (and ended with a big thud called *Moment by Moment*).

Travolta made only two requests before agreeing to star in *Grease*. He told Allan, "I want blue black hair like Elvis Presley and Rock Hudson in the movies. It's surreal and it's very 1950s." And since the Danny Zuko character doesn't sing very much in the stage version, Travolta wanted his Zuko to get another song in the movie. Allan immediately promised him the Kenickie number "Greased Lightning."

From the beginning, the bigger casting quandary had to do with the female lead character, good-girl Sandy Dumbrowski. Very few names got tossed into the actress blender. "Carrie Fisher couldn't sing and Marie Osmond wasn't that interested," says the film's casting director, Joel Thurm. When those two options didn't materialize, Allan mentioned Olivia Newton-John. He'd met the pop singer at a dinner party given by fellow Aussie Helen Reddy of "I Am Woman" fame. It was a setup of sorts, arranged in part by Reddy's husband, Jeff Wald, who knew that Allan wanted Olivia for the role.

"One day, Allan Carr was there at Helen Reddy's house. We had never met," Olivia Newton-John recalls. She sat next to him at the dinner table, and Allan made exceedingly little chitchat before broaching the subject of *Grease*. She'd seen the musical in London with Richard Gere in the lead. When Allan first suggested that she play the all-American Sandy, Olivia jumped *away* from the offer.

"But I'm Australian," she said.

"We'll make Sandy Australian," Allan replied.

"I'm twenty-eight years old. I'm too old."

"Everybody in the movie will be too old. It's a comedy."

"I don't know if I have chemistry with John Travolta."

"You'll meet John. He's fabulous!"

"I'm not sure about the music."

"We'll write new songs for you."

Thanks to Allan, "No one else was really seriously considered for the role," says Thurm. "Allan was smart. He needed someone who was a star, could sing, *and* could play an ingenue. It was not an easy role to cast."

The Paramount execs remained leery about almost every aspect of *Grease*, and that included the casting of Olivia Newton-John. "But Allan was adamant. It was his idea to cast Olivia, and he kept pushing," says director Randal Kleiser.

Much as he reinvented Ann-Margret, taking her from kitten with a whip to a serious Oscar-nominated actress, Allan wanted to take pop music's girl-next-door and turn her into a vixen. Just as in college, if Allan couldn't be one of the Lake Forest sorority girls, then he would tell them what to wear to get the boys. He knew exactly how to package Olivia Newton-John for male mass consumption.

"She is goody-goody two-shoes. And in front of your eyes, you're going to see her become hot stuff!" is how Allan put it to the Paramount brass. Leave subtext to losers. When he was on a marketing roll, Allan spoke only in exclamation points as if titling a Broadway musical: "Put her in spikes! Put her in Spandex! Put her in peddle pushers! Put her in lots of makeup! Tease her hair out to here! I'll make a hot tamale out of her!"

Finally, Paramount agreed and Olivia Newton-John agreed, but on one condition.

"I have to have a screen test," she insisted.

Stars always refuse to audition, but this one was different. Olivia Newton-John had already made *Toomorrow,* a sci-fi musical in which aliens kidnap a pop music group, and she didn't want to mar her singing career with a second movie disaster. "I worry about making another mistake," she kept telling Allan.

To help woo her, Allan sent Travolta to Newton-John's house for a meeting. Whatever happened there, she reported back to Allan, "Yes, we have great chemistry!"

Then came the screen test. "Olivia worried about looking too old, so we used very soft lighting," says Joel Thurm. And to show that her off-screen chemistry with Travolta was no fluke, the casting director chose the drive-in-movie scene where Sandy slams the car door on Danny's crotch.

"But it didn't pop," says Thurm. He took another look at Jim Jacobs and Warren Casey's book and decided the problem wasn't his actors but rather Allan Carr and Bronte Woodard's new screenplay. Kleiser agreed. "Let's use the original script," said the director, and they went back to having Sandy throw Danny's ring at him. She slams the door, and screams, "Do you think I'm going to stay with you in this sin wagon? You can take this piece of tin!" Grabbing his loins, he replies in pain, "Sandy, you can't just walk out of a drive-in!" With those words reinstated, the scene clicked. It would be the first of many on-set rewrites. While "the screenplay effectively opens up the stage play," says Kleiser, it also added a lot of campy humor that was pure Allan. In one scene, the school principal, played by Eve Arden, tells the student body, "If you can't be an athlete, be an athletic supporter."

"That was Allan's!" says Kleiser.

With his two leads secured, Allan proceeded to cast the supporting players. Forget the palm trees or the excising of a few dirty words. It's here that Allan's showbiz aesthetic replaced the original urban grime of *Grease* with pure Hollywood cotton candy. He fought and won to cast stars from his school days— Eve Arden, Frankie Avalon, Joan Blondell, Edd "Kookie" Byrnes—as featured players. They were hardly anything like the pedestrian teachers who populated Highland Park High, but they were, Allan believed, his real teachers—the ones who taught him at countless Saturday matinees the world according to MGM and 20th Century Fox.

Sometimes Allan's novel approach to casting *Grease* got too creative for the Paramount powers—like when he made a controversial choice to fill the role of Coach Calhoun.

Herbert Streicher, better known as Harry Reems, had appeared in over a hundred porn movies, including the instant classics *Deep Throat* and *The Devil in Miss Jones*. If those films didn't make him rich (he received $100 for his day's work on the Linda Lovelace opus), they made him infamous, as well as one of the nation's better-known felons. In 1976, the U.S. government convicted Reems on federal charges of conspiracy to distribute obscenity across state lines. In the following days, Allan met Reems at one of Hugh Hefner's many "First Amendment" fund-raisers, held to help defray the legal costs of attorney Alan

Dershowitz, who, in a few years' time, would achieve even greater courtroom fame by getting Claus von Bülow acquitted of murder charges. As Allan readied *Grease,* he and Reems became good acquaintances, if not close friends, over evenings spent watching old movies at the Playboy mansion in Beverly Hills. After a screening of *Casablanca,* Hef's favorite movie, Allan popped the newly acquitted Reems an unusual proposition.

"I'm making the movie version of *Grease,* and I'm going to get this part for you," he said. "You'll be the coach in my new movie."

"When do I audition?" asked Reems.

"We don't need an audition," said Allan, repeating what would soon become one of his favorite, and most abused, lines.

Reems nearly fell backward into the lobster dip. "Finally, a breakthrough!" he thought to himself. While Hefner and others had been generous in footing his legal bills, Reems remained broke and unemployed. Despite his acquittal, porn companies continued to reel in the aftermath of the Reems conviction, and respectable movie producers were not about to take up the slack in the actor's employment. They included the Paramount brass, who eschewed putting ex-porn stars on their payroll, especially for family fare like *Grease.*

"They bounced me out of the cast," says Reems. "They thought they might lose some play dates in the South. Allan felt terrible about it."

Allan, in fact, felt so terrible that he wrote Reems a personal check for $5,000.

The X-rated star wasn't the only casting casualty. Lucie Arnaz considered herself Allan's personal favorite to play *Grease*'s "knocked-up" bad girl Betty Rizzo. Then came the audition, even though there wasn't supposed to be an audition.

Michael Eisner, the new president of Paramount Pictures, took keen interest even in the minor detail of who would play a supporting role in a $6-million film that he'd inherited and didn't really think would make money.

"You're in it," Allan assured Arnaz. "Mike Eisner just wants to see all our choices. He doesn't have a veto."

She went through the pro forma motions, and that included reading for Allan, Eisner, and Kleiser. As Eisner sat chin in hand, Allan beamed encouragingly at Arnaz as she performed with Jeff Conaway, who'd already been cast as Kenickie, the character who "impregnates" Rizzo in what turns out to be a false alarm. Afterward, Arnaz believed that she'd "cinched the reading."

Paramount's new president saw it from another perspective. He took one deep breath as he shook his head in amazement. "Wow! The entire time you were reading I was thinking that your father, Desi Arnaz, used to own this studio—and now I run it," said Eisner.

Outside in the parking lot, Allan's response was equally doubt-provoking. "We'll know in a couple of days," he told Arnaz. She waited four weeks and, hearing no word from Allan, the actress pulled herself out of contention and signed to perform in a touring production of *Bye Bye Birdie*. Arnaz gave him the news on a Wednesday. The next day, talking on the phone with one of his clients, Allan let out a triumphant war cry when Stockard Channing casually mentioned how much she enjoyed playing a car thief in a little movie called *Sweet Revenge*. "You can play Rizzo!" he exclaimed. The thirty-three-year-old actress screen-tested on Friday, and arrived on the *Grease* set the following Monday to play teen-slut Betty Rizzo. "It all happened in twenty-four hours," says Channing.

To show his gratitude to Lucie Arnaz, Allan concocted a rather bizarre rumor. "I had picked Lucie Arnaz to play Rizzo, she was perfect," Allan told friends. "Paramount wanted Lucie to test with John and Olivia, just to see how the three of them looked together, but her mother, Lucille Ball, wouldn't let her do a test." According to Allan, Lucy said, "I used to own that studio, my daughter doesn't have to test." Allan added, "No test, no part."

Arnaz calls Allan's story "ridiculous. My mother really never got involved like that in my career," she insists. (Also, both Allan and Eisner were wrong about Arnaz's parents' running Paramount. Their Desilu production company purchased the RKO facilities, which later became part of Paramount.)

Grease began filming on June 23, 1977, at the Venice High School in Venice, California. Two days earlier, Allan threw a party at Hilhaven, but at the last minute, he had to be a no-show for his own fete, having been felled by a kidney infection and rushed to Cedars-Sinai. The entire cast showed up at Allan's party, including the last-minute invites of Stockard Channing and Lorenzo Lamas, his hair bleached so as not to compete with Travolta's new blue black do. Lamas would be playing Tom Chisum, meant to rhyme with "jissum" since the character rivals Danny for the affection of Sandy. Allan wanted Stephen Ford to play the role, but only a few days earlier, the son of President Gerald Ford quit the project despite his being a guest at a few Hilhaven Lodge parties. "Ford knew we would exploit him," says Joel Thurm. Allan took the rejection well. "He was just as happy that he had the son of Fernando Lamas and Arlene Dahl as that of President Ford," says Thurm.

The *Grease* kickoff party was notable for a number of reasons. In addition to "everybody getting smashed," says Stockard Channing, the highlights included Olivia Newton-John's sliding under a table when Kenneth Waissman introduced her to Patricia Birch, who coaxed the fledgling movie star from her hiding place with words of encouragement. Another tender, if less spontaneous, moment developed when the actress held John Travolta's hand a minute or two. Allan may have been recuperating a few blocks away in Cedars-Sinai, but word of Olivia's loving gesture was enough for him to alert gossip columnist Rona Barrett, who dutifully reported:

> Good news for die-hard movie-buff romantics who remember the good old Hollywood days when the actors and actresses met on a movie set and fell in love as the whole world looked on. My sources say it's happening again on the set of *Grease,* where stars John Travolta and Olivia Newton-John came together first as costars, but are now discovering each other personally and liking what they see.

In time, matching John Travolta with a mate of the opposite sex turned into a cottage industry, and Allan together with a number of the actor's handlers paired the bachelor star with Kate Edwards, Marilu Henner, Priscilla Presley, Cher, Brooke Shields, and Allan's client Marisa Berenson.

At Allan's *Grease* party, the occasional question arose, "Where are Jim and Warren?" as in Jacobs and Casey, the original writers of *Grease.* Casey was out of town. "But I was here in Los Angeles," Jacobs recalls. If his noninvite to Allan's party was a clue, the songwriter knew his lowly status for certain when filming began on the Paramount lot. Jacobs recognized the famed Paramount gate from the movie *Sunset Boulevard,* in which the silent-movie star Norma Desmond, played by Gloria Swanson, is almost turned away before a veteran guard allows her to enter the hallowed studio walls. Jacobs wasn't quite so lucky when he pulled up to that black iron gate.

"Sorry, your name isn't on any list," the guard told Jacobs.

Neither Jacobs nor Casey ever got to visit the set. "That's Hollywood, man!" Jacobs surmises. "They're like, 'Even though you wrote this, we know we can make it better than you can.'"

Bit by bit, some of Jacobs's original dialogue for *Grease* eased its way back into the movie. As Travolta himself told the scribe during filming, "Don't worry.

We're getting your script in there." Having performed *Grease* hundreds of times on the road, Travolta knew the Jacobs/Casey book by heart, and when he didn't think something worked in front of the cameras, he often asked Randal Kleiser, "Let me try doing something like this," and he would quote the original stage show. Kleiser would listen, and then say, "Oh yeah, that's better."

The film's new songs weren't so easily massaged. On Olivia Newton-John's suggestion, her LP producer John Farrar wrote "Hopelessly Devoted to You" and "You're the One That I Want." Which caused a minor pique of jealousy in Travolta, who also wanted a new song to sing. Since "Greased Lightning," sung on stage by the Kenickie character, wasn't enough to assuage the star's ego, Allan went to Louis St. Louis, who had handled dance and vocal arrangements for the original Broadway show.

"You know, girls' names songs were big in the early 1960s," St. Louis informed Allan. He mentioned a few—"Cherie Baby," "Paula," "Renee"—and suggested that Travolta get a new song called "Sandy."

Allan clapped his hands in excitement. "You should go back to the hotel and write it!" he announced.

The assignment marked a major rapprochement between the two men. Years earlier, St. Louis put together an act for Alexis Smith, which opened at the Fairmont Hotel in San Francisco. Allan had seen the show and hated it, and later taunted the composer-arranger in that hotel's lobby by telling friends in a very loud whisper, "There's the guy that ruined, absolutely destroyed Alexis Smith!"

St. Louis preferred not to think about that previous encounter as he drove back to the Sunset Marquis hotel to write "Sandy." It took him twenty minutes to write the song and get his friend Scott Simon to flesh out his one verse, "Stranded at the drive-in," into full lyrics. The next morning, he rushed to Hilhaven to try his luck on the Lucite grand piano, playing the song for Allan at 10 a.m. and again at 1 p.m. for Stigwood's executive producer Bill Oakes and yet again at 3 p.m. for Travolta and Stigwood himself. "At 4 p.m. it was my song, and I had a deal," St. Louis recalls. His gift to himself: a new navy blue Honda Prelude.

In the end, Olivia Newton-John got to sing the most new songs, but it was movie star John Travolta who benefited more from headlining with this recording star. On *Grease*, "They each had a most-favored-nations contract, which means that he got what she got and vice versa," says Thurm. "People made more from the record *Grease* than the movie *Grease*."

If Allan missed his own *Grease* kickoff party, he skipped few days of production despite his recurring health problems. In a way, *Grease* was an extension of the parties he gave at his father's house in Highland Park. At least once a week, Allan brought a celebrity to the set, whether it be Rudolf Nureyev, George Cukor, Jane Fonda, Kirk Douglas, or psychic spoon-bender Yuri Geller. They'd stay for about an hour, and then, as it often happens on movie sets, their interest invariably began to wane in the wake of too much downtime. Sometimes Allan would announce a visit with much fanfare, then cancel. "He had infections from the stomach staples," says Thurm, and they would necessitate a return to Cedars-Sinai for massive injections of antibiotics. And if it wasn't the stomach staples, it was problems with his kidney stones or his hips, which had begun to bother him as a result of the bypass, which had leached his bones of needed calcium. Appearance meant everything to a man of Allan's delicate condition, and if he couldn't measure up to his own impossible standards of physical perfection, he made sure that his stars did.

Just as he advised the girls of Gamma Phi Beta how to dress, he spent an inordinate amount of time on what his *Grease* actresses wore onscreen.

"Stars do not wear poodle skirts!" he informed Olivia Newton-John, and promptly put her in Spandex.

Allan also obsessed over Stockard Channing's red-and-black polka-dot dress in the movie's dance-contest scene, and insisted that the camera pan from her shoes up to her face. He called the camera movement "very Ava Gardner!" In another scene, he pushed aside the makeup artist, grabbed an eyebrow pencil, and personally applied freckles to the actress's face. "Allan was kind of a nasty mother figure," Channing recalls. "He never liked your hair, what you were wearing."

With the guys, he showed equal impatience, as well as attention to detail. When John Travolta thought his ill-fitting jeans didn't allow him enough room to bump and grind sufficiently, Allan retired his star to a waiting limousine for an impromptu sartorial consultation. Twenty minutes later, Travolta emerged a new man but wearing the same old Levi's.

Even when Allan lay flat on his back in Cedars-Sinai, his spirit never left the set. "Allan had all kinds of deals for contests and these prizewinners," says Randal Kleiser. One group of would-be actors came in the shape of out-of-town journalists. "They'll go back home and write their articles, saying how great the movie is," Allan told his director. "Find a place for them in the movie." Kleiser rolled with the punches of Allan's movie-as-circus. He took one look at his randomly assembled crew of small-town reporters—often referred to as "those press-junket whores"—and decided, "Well, they're old enough. They could be teachers," and cast them as faculty chaperones in the dance-contest scene.

During another hospital sojourn, Allan phoned Kleiser to give him more casting news: "I've got thirty contest winners who must be in the movie. I'm flying them in next week and they must be in the movie."

"Where am I going to put them?" asked Kleiser.

"You'll figure something out," said Allan. End of conversation.

Kleiser sandwiched this latest bunch of nonprofessionals into a scene where students flee the school at semester's end. "They were winners of various department store contests, like 'Win a Spot in *Grease*,'" says Laurence Mark. "Allan turned *Grease* into a complete and utter romp." Allan may have been the first and only producer in Hollywood history ever to be "thrilled" to chat up the studio apparatchiks in charge of department store tie-ins. "There were many people who thought that was low-rent," says Mark. "Nothing was too low-rent for Allan," who believed in creating buzz any way he could.

He worshipped at the shrine of product placement. For Olivia Newton-John's big song, "Hopelessly Devoted to You," a Pepsi-Cola sign looms brazenly on the character's back porch. Pepsi signs were also supposed to populate a hamburger hangout called Frosty Palace. Instead, the set designer used posters from another slightly more iconic soda-pop company.

"Who did this?!" Allan screamed when he visited the set, only to discover that the Frosty Palace moment had already been committed to celluloid. "Who let those fucking Coke signs in my movie? I've got a deal with Pepsi. It has to be Pepsi-Cola!"

Later, in the film's postproduction phase, some poor flunky had to hand-paint out the Coke signs behind Olivia Newton-John's head. "You can see it's blurry in the final film," says Kleiser.

ten

Only Half the Phone Book

"Producing *Grease* made me feel like I was the president of my class," Allan said.

Early in the filming, Allan asked some of his actors to pose with him for "a class picture," as he put it. Didi Conn, who played the destined-for-a-beauty-school character Frenchy, recalls that momentous afternoon. "There were all these cool greasers around him, and Allan was this honorary greaser, and that was something he never was in high school," she says. "He was happy finally to be the hot guy on campus. He liked that role."

Tellingly, Allan decided to be different from all the other guys in that photo, and opted not to wear a leather jacket and jeans. Instead, he wore Bermuda shorts. *Plaid* Bermuda shorts.

"He just beamed when he came on the set," says Stockard Channing. "Allan had been very sick and he loved all of these boys and girls hugging and kissing him and being affectionate. He really believed in that glossy high school world, which is probably why he tapped into the gestalt of what so many people feel about high school."

While he was riding high with the production of a new movie musical, Allan decided to capitalize on his newfound producer status with an überparty. Unlike the *Tommy* Subway Party or the Truman Capote Jail House Party, this one would not have the gimmick of a funky locale. It would be a real class act—and he'd stage it at his new Malibu beach house, Seahaven. "I'm going to hold a party that runs over two nights," he announced. He called it his Rolodex Party.

"People with last names A–L will be invited on Friday night. Those with names M–Z on Saturday night."

Producer David Picker had joked that Allan invited his entire Rolodex to the Hilhaven Lodge housewarming party back in 1973. Five years later, Allan took that gentle jab and turned it into a party theme to publicize *Grease* and show off Seahaven. According to *Variety*'s Army Archerd, it was the house "that *Survive!* bought and *A Chorus Line* furnished."

"Everyone in Hollywood was trying to get an invitation to *that* party," says producer Howard Rosenman.

Allan knew it would be his best party to date. "It felt like the opening night of a Broadway show," he said. And to back up that claim, he rolled out a yards-long red carpet on Old Malibu Road and even set up a few klieg lights in case any of his guests couldn't find their way. And that was just Friday! The following evening he did it all over again, in total inviting over 750 of his best friends to a two-night party.

Allan was proud of his multilevel beach house, which resembled his Highland Park home in that it sat high on a bluff overlooking the water. Allan took almost a year to decorate Seahaven, and he was eager to show off the fake palm trees and real ostrich feathers and peacock-and-pheasant-feathered dining table—"Every one of them molted. I couldn't hear of anything being killed," said Allan—and enough mirrors to stock a fun house. Allan wanted Seahaven to be a veritable jungle of kitsch, and he enjoyed pointing out the entryway's big round fish tank, which, he told guests, featured "very, very expensive" tropical fish. (A caretaker, who filled the tank, revealed that no fish ever cost more than $35.) Never one for understatement, Allan glued Valentino fabric to the walls and used it to also sheathe his "conversation pit," that 1970s architectural oddity otherwise known as a sunken living room. He considered the Valentino fabric a classy touch, because it restricted the décor to the colors gray, white, and silver. And so it hurt when, on the second night of the Rolodex Parties, his Malibu neighbor Merle Oberon—looking preternaturally young at sixty-six years next to her even younger husband, Rob Wolders, of indeterminate age—advised Allan on how to treat mold in an oceanside house. "Get rid of the wall fabric!" Oberon ordered as soon as she stepped inside Seahaven.

Other Malibu residents dealt with their own soap operas that weekend. Dani and David Janssen, who lived next door and were estranged, made amends at the Rolodex Party. Britt Ekland, having just broken up with Rod Stewart, told her sob story to George Hamilton, who had just broken up with his date for the night, his soon-to-be-ex-wife Alana Hamilton, who a year later would marry Rod Stewart. Hamilton, in turn, offered Ekland his Malibu couch for the night, while the *Hollywood Reporter*'s George Christy wondered aloud why "George and Alana are seeing each other more now that they are separated."

Where the invitation for his Cycle Sluts Party had read "glitterfunk," Allan asked everyone to wear "beach chic" to his Rolodex Party. Keith Carradine came in a jogging suit. Gossip columnist Rona Barrett wore a terry beach robe and diamonds. Struggling photographer (and ex-wife of the Canadian prime minister) Margaret Trudeau arrived in a simple suit. Sophia Loren's husband, producer Carlo Ponti, showed up in a checked jacket and open-neck shirt.

Allan insisted that his client Stockard Channing attend both nights, so she could meet important people. No sooner did she walk into Seahaven than he rolled his eyes. "It's all wrong," he said of her Halston knockoff, then whispered, "Never leave the house unless you look like an eight-by-ten glossy." He suggested a more appropriate outfit for Saturday night, and picking some lint off her dress, he turned to kiss a drag queen made up to look like Bette Midler.

That first night, Allan changed his outfit three times, donning first a scarf caftan by La Vetta, followed by a Japanese obi jacket with harem pants, and finally an Egyptian fisherman's tunic and pants. After so many trips to Cedars-Sinai, he looked svelte that weekend, and proud of it. One more jaw wiring and he'd get himself down to under 200 pounds, he promised. He'd recently gone to the hospital to have the bypass removed, hoping somehow that it would relieve his chronic problem with kidney stones. He told guests, "I am confident that I can now maintain my weight. There is no doubt I want to stay happy about the way I look more than I want to eat."

If he was on a diet, Allan didn't think it fair to make his guests stick to veggie sticks and brown rice during the two nights of the Rolodex affair. Now that he could afford better, he eschewed the pro bono food of Chicago Pizza Works in favor of the Studio Grill's chef, Tom Rolla, who prepared a buffet menu that included his newest invention, a fresh crab and lobster mousse. Also served was a "wall of seafood," as Allan described the hors d'oeuvres.

Partygoers John Travolta, Olivia Newton-John, Michael Eisner (but not Barry Diller, with whom Allan was already feuding), ABC's Gary Pudney, William Morris's Stan Kamen, Roger Vadim, Lee Grant, Michele Lee, Johnny Carson and his producer Fred De Cordova, and Steven Spielberg obeyed Allan's weekend dictate, with the A through L's arriving on Friday night and the M through Z's waiting until Saturday.

A notable exception was Anjelica Huston, who broke the alphabet rule by attending the second night and regretting her decision the minute Roman Polanski, her major courtroom nemesis, stepped through the front door of Seahaven. The big news at both parties was (1) Roman Polanski's rape trial and (2) Cher's breakup and reconciliation with Gregg Allman after nine days of marriage. Allan had invited the Polish émigré, as well as the rock-pop couple. At that moment in time in Hollywood, they could make any party by their mere appearance. If Allan didn't land Cher and Gregg Allman for his party, he got the other 50 percent, and in his opinion it was the better half: Polanski.

On Saturday night, Allan noticed a sudden change in the room's temperature, and looking around, he saw the *Rosemary's Baby* director—all sixty-five inches of him—in the doorway. Even though he was already standing, Allan motioned for everyone else to rise, and he led an ovation for the much-maligned Polanski, who'd been accused of the statutory rape of Samantha Geimer, a thirteen-year-old from Woodland Hills, on March 10. Everyone in America, much less Malibu, had been following the trial and knew that the film director had taken nude photos of the girl after plying her with champagne and Quaaludes at Jack Nicholson's house up on Mulholland Drive. Sometime during the impromptu photo session, Nicholson's ex-girlfriend, Anjelica Huston, returned to the house to pick up some belongings, and no sooner had she expressed outrage at Polanski's underage company than the police arrived. Polanski accused Samantha's mother of the tip-off. The police booked Polanski. In a surprise twist, they also booked Huston after finding cocaine in her purse, and in exchange for immunity on all charges of drug possession, the actress gave evidence for the prosecution.

"The DA's case would be weak without some supporting testimony from Anjelica Huston, who could place me in the house and the room where [the thirteen-year-old] and I had made love," Polanski wrote years later in his autobiography. Huston's testimony had been nasty. She called Polanski a "freak" and ridiculed his story that the photographs were for *Vogue*. The night of the Rolodex Party, Polanski told Allan's guests that he couldn't really blame Anjelica for accepting the deal, "though it left me feeling slightly bitter," he said.

Polanski was now free on his own recognizance, having paid a $2,500 bail, and he tried to keep a low profile—until the Rolodex Party—and the photographers at Seahaven went wild. With the trial going on, Polanski's appearance on the second night of Allan's party propelled it from a must-attend event to one for the record books, giving the Malibu event the softest brush of scandal. With his standing ovation for Polanski, Allan let Hollywood's most recently in-

dicted rapist know that he was a welcome guest, and the gesture moved Polanski
to tears, even though not everyone approved. "Only in Hollywood," complained
Alana Hamilton.

For two evenings, Allan had it all. *Survive!* and *A Chorus Line* made him a
multimillionaire, and with *Grease* now before the cameras, he was clutching
the producer's brass ring. No longer was he somebody who got lucky recycling
a Mexican flick. Allan was a Hollywood power broker, and he liked having that
power. Friends noticed that it brought out a new side to his personality. As his
school friend David Umbach had observed, Allan "wasn't a beauty. His sexual
inclination would have been to be shy and not bring it up until later in life when
he could control it."

A true Hollywood player at long last, Allan could now "control it" with a
vengeance, and when he wasn't flinging out his arms to say, "I'm Allan Carr and
it rhymes with star," he approached young men with a newfound confidence.
He no longer tried to seduce or be seduced or even roll out a mattress on the
pretext of a late-night wrestling match. He instead took a shortcut to the object
of his desire, and asked point blank, "Cash or career? What will it be?"

eleven

Grease on Track

"He saw me as a worker bee on *Grease*," says Randal Kleiser.

Allan had a way of treating fellow homosexuals like mere employees and straight male friends like the brothers he never had. Despite Kleiser and Joel Thurm's exemplary work on *Grease,* it was the film's cinematographer, Bill Butler, whom Allan sought to adopt as an honorary brother of sorts, and he rewarded Butler in ways that went far beyond the dollars of his contract.

One weekend, as he drove his *Grease* cinematographer to Malibu, Allan let go with a surprise.

"Your salary on this picture is not enough," Allan said.

"It's a very good salary," Butler replied.

Allan shook his head. "I want you to have a piece of this picture." And out of his own percentage of the gross, he handed Butler one point of the gross profits from *Grease*. "I'll have our lawyers write it up tomorrow," Allan said. And he did.

As filming on *Grease* continued into its final days, Stigwood and Allan began to turn their attention to the film's title sequence, which had been animated at great expense by John D. Wilson. Stigwood wasn't happy with the music and got the Bee Gees' Barry Gibb to slap together an alternate tune. Allan thought it was great, but Kleiser disagreed. "The beat of Gibb's song is out of sync with the editing," said the director. "The lyrics don't reflect the movie. They're too serious."

Gibb wasn't smiling when he suggested, "So why don't you shoot a serious scene for the movie?"

Ill fitting or not, the title song "Grease" helped sell 13 million albums in the soundtrack's first year of release, and Gibb received a full 1 percent of the net profits on the movie for his songwriting effort.

Early in the producing process, Allan and Stigwood divided their respective fiefdoms. Stigwood handled the music, Allan masterminded the film's production and promotion, and they basically stayed out of each other's way. "Robert was quiet, he made his presence felt, but his style was much more laid back," says Laurence Mark. "Allan was much more out there in every way. They complemented each other that way nicely."

Until they didn't.

The showier of the two men, Allan sometimes got credit—or took credit—where none was due. It began with *Tommy,* and now Stigwood watched as his producing partner leveraged a similar publicity grab on *Grease.* Reporters often mentioned Allan as the producer of *Grease,* with no ink spilled Stigwood's way. It's difficult to say whether it was a *Variety* or a *Los Angeles Times* profile of the fabulous Allan Carr, "the producer of *Grease,*" that pushed Stigwood out of the backseat.

"It made Stigwood nutty," Kevin McCormick says of the hoopla surrounding Allan. It was McCormick who brought Nik Cohn's *New York Magazine* article "Tribal Rites of the New Saturday Night" to Stigwood's attention and, in turn, became executive producer of *Saturday Night Fever.* McCormick recalls a phone call that Stigwood placed to Allan: "He started making fun of Allan's clothes, how ridiculous he was. It was hurtful."

For much of the filming and postproduction, the two men didn't speak and instead used go-betweens like McCormick and Freddie Gershon to relay messages. It wasn't until the Hollywood premiere of *Grease* that they met again, face to face. "They pretended it didn't happen," McCormick says of their long-distance blowout. "But they both knew it had."

On June 2, 1978, *Grease* premiered in Hollywood at the Chinese Theater. Allan came with Elton John, and they double-dated with Stockard Channing and her husband, David Debin. In the limousine, the rocker told the actress, "I really like your singing in the movie," and on the strength of that high praise, she paid little attention to anything else that happened on the way to the theater. Stigwood brought Lily Tomlin, who was starring in his upcoming *Moment by*

Moment with John Travolta, who arrived with Olivia Newton-John. John wore black leather, Olivia a vintage prom dress. "There was total panic in the streets outside the theater," says Randal Kleiser. Channing was dumbfounded by the crowds, which "recalled the golden age of Hollywood!" Allan exclaimed. Since the buzz on the film had been so subdued, the actress never expected multitudes of people on the street. "Everybody in the business was puzzled by it. *Grease* was dismissed," she says.

Except by the public. *Saturday Night Fever,* which had opened late the previous year, had certified John Travolta as the No. 1 heartthrob in the country, and the girls of Los Angeles showed up in force on June 2 to make sure that no one mistook him for a one-hit fluke. Paramount, meanwhile, continued to downplay *Grease.* The big movie musical that spring/summer was Stigwood's other extravaganza, *Sgt. Pepper's Lonely Hearts Club Band.* "At its premiere party they had caviar and shrimp," Kleiser recalls. "For *Grease,* they served hot dogs and hamburgers."

Allan turned the McDonald's food into a plus, calling it "teen cuisine" in honor of his high school movie. Ignoring the studio's indifference to *Grease*— "Paramount hated it beyond belief," says Freddie Gershon—Allan secured a big TV special, which went out to 126 markets. According to the *Hollywood Reporter,* Paramount flacks gave the credit to studio toppers Michael Eisner and Barry Diller, but that scenario is unlikely since the special is titled "Allan Carr's Magic Night." It began taping on premiere night outside the Chinese Theater and continued to the after-party on the Paramount lot, where Allan gave himself the emcee honors by interviewing both John Travolta and Olivia Newton-John (who had changed into something less comfortable, a skin-tight flaming pink jumpsuit), much to Stigwood's chagrin. The studio did splurge some capital to re-create the film's big dance-contest scene, set in a high school gymnasium, and the exorbitant cost pissed off at least one cast member.

"We sweated all last summer at Venice High School making the movie," said the film's Kenickie, Jeff Conaway. "And now Paramount's built an air-conditioned set just for the party that we could have filmed the movie in without sweat!"

Four days later, Allan moved the party to New York City and Studio 54, which had been open only a year but already defined the disco era with its shirtless bartenders, its amalgam of celebs and street people, and its cocaine-sniffing half-moon signage that dropped over the dance floor at midnight. The *Grease* festivities began earlier that evening at Elaine's restaurant, where Patricia Birch toasted Allan before a hundred friends, including Woody Allen, Ann Miller, Rita Hayworth, Francesco Scavullo, George Plimpton, and Stephen Sondheim. Then Allan bused them all across town to Steve Rubell's disco, where he revealed that he'd been approached to do a Blackgama "What Becomes a Legend Most" ad. "I'll wear a mink caftan, what else?" he told Rita Hayworth, who was wearing her own summer fur that night.

For their Studio 54 entrance, John and Olivia repeated their leather and Spandex routine, and no one seemed to notice, once again, that the budget allowed for only hot dogs and burgers to feed the hungry premiere freeloaders.

Despite the restricted budget, Allan managed to hire society florist Renny Reynolds to dress the place up with some vintage cars. Their owner insisted they be emptied of gasoline on the city streets. It was a safety no-no that promptly brought out the police, as well as the fire department, which required the vehicles to seek relief in a nearby gasoline station. The cars then had to be hand-pushed back to Studio 54. Most of them went unscathed.

"There was a 1950 Chevy convertible that got a bit trashed because people climbed in and [cigarette] burned the seats," says Reynolds. "So we ended up having to pay for new seats. But the party was wild. Fabulous!"

Allan couldn't have cared less about the auto fracas. He wrapped himself instead in the glory of his three big party coups: Grace Jones, Elizabeth Taylor, and Liza Minnelli, who had recently pocketed a Tony for her turn in *The Act*. His three lady stars so distracted Allan that he failed to notice a major altercation at the front door when the writers of the original *Grease* stage show couldn't get past the notoriously arrogant doormen at Studio 54. Broadway producer Kenneth Waissman spotted Jim Jacobs and Warren Casey in the crowd. "These are the authors of the show," he said. "They don't need tickets!"

In a way, the real parties for *Grease* weren't held at either Paramount or Studio 54 but in Allan's basement at Hilhaven Lodge. As he readied *Grease* to open that June, Allan announced his other major production that season, one that would come to define, more than even the Rolodex Party, his stature as Hollywood's premiere party-giver. On June 4, 1978, two days after the *Grease* fete at Paramount, Allan Carr unveiled what he claimed to be the first basement disco in all of moviedom. Let others have their antiquated ballrooms and tennis courts. He brought the lights, sounds, half-naked boys, and drug culture of Studio 54 to Beverly Hills. That night, he called it, simply, the Allan Carr Disco. "Or if you prefer, the AC/DC Disco," he offered, abbreviating the title with his own personal bisexual letter play.

As the guests made their way to Hilhaven Lodge's refurbished basement—
the same basement space where Mama Cass, Petula Clark, and Ann-Margret
once rehearsed for their manager—Allan and his valet, John, stood over them
in his immense closet/vault and proceeded to encase the lord of Hilhaven Lodge
in a *Ten Commandments*–style caftan and cape, complete with Day-Glo geo-
metric hieroglyphics and Victor Mature shoulder pads. The occasion was so immense in his own imagination that Allan set up a video camera to record it for
posterity.

"This was made for me for the opening of the disco," he said of his glittering
outfit. Allan gazed at himself in multiple floor-length mirrors that recalled the
final scene in *All About Eve*, where the image of a young girl, Phoebe, also encased in a beaded cape, is fractured into endless replications of itself. John the
valet flattered Allan on his "Mary Tyler Moore" smile, and Allan returned the
compliment. "Did you model caftans in *GQ* before you became a movie star?"
he asked John.

Intoxicated with his own impending success, Allan let his valet know, "These
are the good old days. We're doing it now. I don't feel I've missed anything. Yes,
I would have liked to have been around for Ingrid Bergman and Clark Gable,
but I don't feel I've missed anything." And with that, he spun around and
around in front of the mirror, his broad-shouldered cape swirling about him
like a latter-day Phoebe, ready to take his place in the movie pantheon next to
Margo Channing and Eve Harrington.

Downstairs in the disco, Allan didn't stint, hiring star DJ Don Blanton, who
had recently performed at Studio 54 and Odyssey. The song "I Feel Love"
blared as guests first confronted the Allan Carr Disco sign, which led to the
Bella Darvi Bar and the Edmund Purdom Lounge (the restroom) and beyond
it the copper-encased pleasure dome itself, complete with a disco ball and a
life-size mummy with a light beam stuck in its head. "It's someone who used to
work for me. I had him mummified," Allan told John Travolta.

He then broke away to share a private moment with Olivia Newton-John,
who honored Allan by having her hairdresser go through much trouble to put
tiny braids in her otherwise flowing blond hair. "This is our new play place.
There's a back entrance. I'll make a key for you," Allan said, referring to a secret
exit through the laundry room.

A handsome blond man snuggled passed him. "Didn't I see you in *Holocaust*?" Allan asked.

"No." And the man walked on.

"Well, it looked like *Holocaust!*" cracked Allan, miffed at his anonymous guest's lack of attention.

The disco's architect, Phyllis Moore, congratulated Allan on the fabulousness of her creation. "It cost me $100,000!" Allan bragged to everyone. Then he turned to Moore to threaten, "If you copy this all over town for $18,000, I'll kill you!"

Despite the din from the DJ, a loud explosion made every semisober person in the room jump. "We had a champagne injury already!" Allan exclaimed. He turned to complain to Dominick Dunne, "You stepped on my caftan!"

Since his good friend Jacqueline Bisset couldn't make the party, Allan felt free to tell her *Greek Tycoon* costar Camilla Sparv, "You're a major actor-performer. You were the only one in the movie I sympathized with."

Throughout the evening, Allan took up the slack whenever the other one hundred people crammed into a space built for ten ran out of compliments. "It's a soul train for rich kids," he said of his disco. "Just when you think I've run out of ideas. . . . This is *Playboy*'s penthouse." He pointed to the copper nameplates nailed into the two leather banquettes that flanked the room. "Regine, Malcolm Forbes, Steve Rubell. I can't wait for them to see it," he said.

Not everyone loved being immortalized in Allan's basement. When he told Joan Collins that he wanted to showcase her Egyptian heritage—she played Princess Nellifer in 1955's *The Land of the Pharaohs*—the English actress took one look at the Bella Darvi Bar, not to mention the Edmund Purdom Lounge, and notified her impresario friend that she was having none of it: "Listen, I am living, working. And don't you dare name a room after me as though I were dead!"

The disco was but a prelude. That very June weekend, *Grease* took in over $9.3 million and barely missed beating the No. 1 film, *Jaws 2,* which made only half a million more at the box office. The one-two punch of this movie duo shook Hollywood and prompted a big page-one story from *Variety,* which boasted, "The unprecedented has happened in the film industry: never before have there been two day and date opening smash pictures reaching the stratospheric weekend box office heights of Universal's *Jaws 2* and Paramount's *Grease.*"

Everybody in the movie business read that page-one story in *Variety,* and one of the first to congratulate Allan in person was Ron Bernstein. That summer, the literary agent was repping Larry Kramer's scabrous novel *Faggots,* a no-holds-barred exposé of the gay vacation town Fire Island Pines, New York. "I really wracked my brain on who would have the chutzpah to make this movie," says Bernstein, and he admits that "nothing could have been more incongruous" than selling it to Allan Carr in his post-*Grease* glory days. Nonetheless, he made the pilgrimage to Hilhaven Lodge, and Allan greeted him poolside in his white tent. "Like I was seeing a potentate in Saudi Arabia," the agent recalls. "There were hundreds of pillows stacked everywhere and at least a dozen copies of *Variety* laid at Allan's feet."

"Did you see the *Grease* grosses in St. Louis?" Allan wanted to know. "Did you see the *Grease* grosses in Chicago? I understand Middle America."

Congrats and other business niceties aside, Bernstein finally got around to mentioning *Faggots,* at which Allan gave him a look that slid rapidly from incredulous to dismissive. "I don't think that's what America wants now," he said. Then putting aside his Illinois-boy hat, Allan asked under his breath, "So how juicy is it?"

Bernstein could not lie. Kramer's *Faggots* fairly oozed semen on every page, but Allan might be interested in at least taking a look. As the agent described it, the novel contained "this terrible send-up of Barry Diller."

Allan couldn't contain himself. "Oh, let me read it!" he exclaimed.

That was Monday morning. The following week, *Jaws 2* stumbled at the box office and *Grease* replaced it as the No. 1 film, a position it held for an astounding five straight weeks. And for five straight weeks—plus several months—Allan enjoyed every moment of his newfound fame. "Something happens where you get recognized," he sermonized. "But I've been doing the same thing for five years now. Suddenly, you're the hot new kid in town," he said, recalling what happened to "Spielberg after *Jaws* and Travolta after *Saturday Night Fever*. It's like Dolly Levi at Ma Maison. I'm at a table between Jack Nicholson and Jack Lemmon, and it is shallow but I've arrived."

Allan was right on both counts. He had arrived. And it was shallow. But most important, his *Grease* success meant that whenever anyone tried to rub his nose in his gayness or his fatness, he could now fling the abuse right back. A few days after *Grease* became the No. 1 movie in America, Allan decided to celebrate by lunching at Le Dome and wallowing in everybody else's envy. Allan, his royal blue silk caftan flowing, walked by one table and heard a fellow producer remark, "Look, she's wearing one of her dresses again!" Allan seized the moment to strike as the restaurant fell silent. "Keep a civil tongue in my ass!" he replied.

As David Geffen described the change in his friend, "*Grease* was the best thing that happened to Allan, and it was the worst thing."

And his parties grew more lavish. When Allan received the Producer of the Year award from the Cairo Film Festival, he returned from Africa to throw himself a Night on the Nile Party. As if the disco in his basement wasn't flashy enough, he extended its Egyptian décor to every room in Hilhaven Lodge, and even rented scenery from the movie *Cleopatra* to help immortalize his overseas prize.

And his parties grew more intimate, too. In addition to spinning records for the 300-plus affairs, Don Blanton worked the turntables at what Allan called his "private parties."

"I'd get a call at 3 or 4 a.m. to play at Allan's disco," Blanton recalls. When the twenty-one-year-old DJ would arrive for these early-morning affairs, he invariably got frisked by security man Gavin de Becker, who made sure that Blanton wasn't carrying a camera or recording device. He always cautioned the young man, "What you see here you don't repeat."

As Blanton recalls, "Those clandestine parties had a lot of powerful people at them, a lot of top politicians who people wouldn't think were gay, and Allan arranged these meetings for them to be with boys late at night and I'd be the DJ." They were small gatherings of half a dozen guests, and included men like Merv Griffin, Roy Cohn, and fedora-wearing attorney Harry Weiss, a West Hollywood legend who had fashioned a lucrative business out of representing homosexuals who'd run afoul of the law. Despite his $200 fee to play music for a couple of hours, Blanton came to resent Allan's early-morning private parties. He was a star disc jockey at the height of disco mania. "And these young guys, these little brats would come up and request songs, a favorite song, and I was reduced to playing these punks' requests," Blanton says of having to spin "Rock the Boat" ad nauseam.

There was never a paucity of young men delusional enough to think that their movie careers depended on being guests at an Allan Carr party, whether it be intimate or one of his blowout affairs. If that well of eager supplicants ever ran dry, Allan's assistants could always make a quick trip to the Odyssey disco, which was Blanton's real "night job." The DJ booth there offered a panoramic view of the dance floor below, and it was not unusual for celebrities to send their assistants to Odyssey to check out beautiful young men and women who, in turn, could be whisked off in limousines to someone's bedroom in the Hollywood hills. "The Odyssey was a juice bar. It didn't serve alcohol," says Blanton. "So there was no eighteen-year-old age limit."

Whether the party at Allan's was big or small, press-worthy or private, what very few of the guests, famous or anonymous, knew was that the disco ceiling in the basement held video cameras. "Allan used them to monitor what was going on while he was in his bedroom so he knew who did what to whom," says Blanton.

One Hollywood notable who escaped being immortalized on Allan's home video system was the one person Allan most wanted to capture there. It rankled Allan that Barry Diller never partook of the Hilhaven festivities. Or that he didn't show any delight at *Grease*'s box-office lucre. But then, *Grease* wasn't really Diller's movie, and it upset the CEO that the success of such a little film could eclipse his pet project, the prestigious *Heaven Can Wait*, directed by and starring Warren Beatty. Because Allan's piddling teen movie musical got in its way, *Heaven Can Wait* failed to reach the exalted top slot on *Variety*'s box-office chart.

There were other reasons, too, for Diller to be repelled by the *Grease* producer. "Barry is very elegant, plays it very close to the vest," says Howard Rosenman. "Allan was the exact opposite: outspoken and tacky."

Allan gave a more detailed analysis of why Diller didn't want him to succeed. Despite the fact that *Grease* was well on its way to becoming the highest-grossing movie musical in the world, and eventually grossed over $341 million, Diller dismissed Allan's hard-won accomplishment. First *Survive!* and now *Grease*. Allan did much for Paramount's bottom line, and it hurt him that Diller never genuflected at the altar of his twin hits. As Allan explained the situation, "Barry can't believe that a queen who wears caftans and is so out and visible could make as much money as I did. Because of *Grease*, I made him sign the biggest check he has ever signed, and he will never forgive me."

twelve

Oscar's First Consultant

While Allan and Paramount people not named Barry Diller continued to sink their well-manicured toenails into the plush box-office numbers for *Grease,* trouble loomed across the Hollywood Hills at Universal Pictures. Studio chiefs Lew Wasserman, Sid Sheinberg, and Thom Mount had flown to Detroit for a preview screening of *The Deer Hunter.* Not one for the JuJu Beans crowd, Michael Cimino's drama offers a somber portrait of Vietnam War vets. The screening did not go well.

"The worst preview I'd ever seen," says Mount, then president of Universal. "*The Deer Hunter* died."

The film's producer, Barry Spikings, held a postmortem with Universal's top brass, and together they made the difficult decision to shorten the film's considerable three-hour running time. Ultimately, "We realized we'd cut the heart out of it," says Spikings. "We put it back together. But Universal was nervous how to market it."

Spikings can't recall why Allan was indebted to him back in 1978, but Allan did owe him for *something.* One afternoon, Spikings, desperate after his Universal showdown, decided to collect on Allan's debt to him. "He was in his cabana at the far end of his pool, dressed in a very relaxed fashion, drinking champagne," says Spikings, an English gentleman who prefers business suits and ties to the normal Hollywood attire.

Allan was gracious as he remained seated in his plush throne of pillows. He extended a hand.

"I've come to call in a favor," Spikings began.

"That's fine. What is it?" Allan asked.

Spikings proceeded to tell him about his hard-hitting film, directed by Michael Cimino and starring Robert De Niro as a Vietnam War vet who returns home to despair and the suicide of a fellow soldier, played by newcomer Christopher Walken. Called *The Deer Hunter*, the film previewed in Detroit. "But it didn't go well," Spikings said. "We need someone to market the film, someone like you, Allan."

Allan listened. He liked having his ego stroked as he drank champagne. "You want me to sell a long movie about poor people who go to war and get killed? No thank you," he said, and promptly finished off the Cristal.

"I've got a car waiting," said Spikings.

With a heavy shrug, Allan slowly lifted himself up out of the pillows, slipped into flip-flops, and let himself be sped away to the Universal Pictures lot in the San Fernando Valley, where Spikings had taken the liberty of reserving a screening room.

The next day, Allan sat in Sid Sheinberg's office, telling the CEO, "This is an important movie, and I want to run the marketing campaign. I know exactly how to sell this movie. It is an incredible movie." Allan Carr may well have been the only person to have seen *The Deer Hunter* who actually believed it could be a hit. After the previous day's private screening, Allan had embraced Spikings and wept. He even shed tears when he spoke to Sheinberg. Much to Spikings's surprise, Sheinberg called in Universal's marketing and distribution department, and introduced them to Allan on the spot. He told them, "This is the man who is going to market *The Deer Hunter*."

It was well known at Universal that the legendary Lew Wasserman viewed cable TV as the death of the movie business. Both Sheinberg and Mount repeated that edict, but Allan dismissed Wasserman's assessment of cable as if it were so much gnat dung. "The way to get this film the Academy Award attention it deserves is to play it on the Z Channel. I don't care what Lew thinks," he said. The blasphemy of his statement nearly leveled the walls of Wasserman's palace.

Allan's concept was not only revolutionary. In 1978, it was considered box office suicide to release a movie on cable *before* its initial theatrical release. Allan, however, didn't care about the negligible cut in ticket sales that the tiny Z Channel viewership would take from the film's overall receipts. He considered it "nothing!" Allan wanted to give the film a heavy, media-doused patina of prestige. Only three years old, the Z Channel in Los Angeles showed an eclectic lineup of foreign-language and independent films, and often showcased them with letter-box and rare director cuts long before those terms were known to the general moviegoing audience.

"We will cultivate the right audience," said Allan. He had his gaze fixed not on the box office. "*The Deer Hunter* is an Oscar winner!"

It baffled him why Universal would preview a quality film like *The Deer Hunter* in Detroit. In his opinion, a more agreeable environment would have been the Little Carnegie Cinema in New York City, where the audiences, as Allan described them, "were edgy and sophisticated." He also insisted that the film must open in only two theaters—one in New York, the other in Los Angeles—for a mere two weeks at the end of the year. Then rerelease it wider after the Oscar nominations were announced. "It's definitely a gamble," Allan cautioned.

"I'd never seen that before," says Mount. "It's a common pattern today. But it was unheard of in 1978."

According to Mount, "Allan's campaign for *The Deer Hunter* was the beginning of Oscar consultants. Now everybody does it."

If Mount and Spikings gave Allan full credit for their turnaround success, they weren't the only ones. "I saved *The Deer Hunter*," Allan believed. "Universal would have buried it in Iowa last fall if I hadn't seen it and hollered that this is a masterpiece and then fought for it."

Cimino's Vietnam War picture went on to be nominated for nine Academy Awards and won five, including best picture. On Oscar night at Spago, Christopher Walken, who won for his featured performance, dedicated his statuette to Allan, saying, "I want you to keep this six months out of the year because if it weren't for you, I wouldn't have it."

Spikings also wanted to give Allan something special, and thought a trip to the Rolls-Royce dealership in Beverly Hills would be an appropriate way to show his gratitude in the days following the Academy Awards. There in the showroom on Olympic and Robertson, the stylish *Deer Hunter* producer pointed to a black Bentley. Allan smiled in appreciation, but his eyes kept darting to an older Rolls in the window—a white convertible with royal blue upholstery.

Spikings spoke glowingly of the black Bentley when his wife, Dot, took him aside to whisper, "Allan doesn't want the black one, dear. That's your taste. He wants the blue-and-white convertible."

The Deer Hunter's Oscar campaign so impressed Universal's Thom Mount that he wanted to make Allan head of marketing at the studio. But flush from

Grease, Allan declined. He was determined to make more movies, movies as good as Cimino's Vietnam War picture.

Allan's *Deer Hunter* miracle turned him into a marketing legend in Hollywood. It was, however, not a hat he cared to wear again for just any old film. A movie executive once made the mistake of approaching him at Le Dome to ask a favor: "Would you market this new film *Ishtar?*"

Allan had already been to an early screening of the Elaine May–directed comedy starring Dustin Hoffman and Warren Beatty as a couple of third-rate lounge singers, and he wanted nothing to do with the film. He didn't whisper back his reply. He shouted his nay vote so that everyone in the restaurant could hear: "*Ishtar* is 'rat shit' spelled backwards!"

The Deer Hunter remained Allan's last foray into movie marketing. "Allan always dreamed of producing a movie that would be recognized around the world as quality," says Mount. "He had commercial success. He lived nicely and made money. But the desire to do something that was culturally transcendent was a big issue for him."

Of all his *Deer Hunter* cohorts, Allan remained closest to Mount. They bonded over Cimino's movie, as well as an article in *New West* magazine that coined a fresh term for Hollywood's newest breed of movers and shakers. The Maureen Orth piece, "The Baby Moguls," listed a group of successful and preternaturally young Hollywood players (Mount, Paula Wagner, John Landis, and Don Simpson, among them), who eschewed the old status symbols—Beverly Hills mansions, Le Dome dinners, Jaguars and Porsches—in favor of a round-the-clock work ethic that left little time for hanging out with Bob Evans and Sue Mengers. At age twenty-nine, Mount had already occupied the president's slot at Universal for a couple of years, and he took much pride in having developed the studio's Youth Unit, which put out movies like *Fast Times at Ridgemont High* and the defining Brat Pack film, *The Breakfast Club. Grease* fit into that youth mold, but in 1978, Allan had already passed the forty mark, even if he judiciously shaved off a few years. Orth's article profiled people who were at least ten years younger than Allan and who saw his houses, cars, and jewelry as antistatus symbols.

Allan didn't care. He clung to his youth hit *Grease* as admittance to the club. "I'm a baby mogul!" he said. "The baby moguls will be important. We will take over this town!" Allan knew a great press ploy when he saw one, and indeed, profiles of the baby moguls were suddenly everywhere: *Time, Newsweek,* the

Los Angeles Times. Whether he rightfully belonged in that company, he glommed on to Orth's rubric, if not the credo of her article.

"I hit California at just the right time," Allan said. "Right after *The Graduate* changed everybody's life. Before that movie, they thought everybody old was brilliant. Afterward, anyone who was young was smart. I rode in on the youth movement."

Allan believed that his friendship with Mount, plus *Grease,* made him a baby mogul, and as a result, he and the young Universal president shared conversations that Allan could never enjoy with men of an older generation. "Allan obviously had a healthy attitude about being gay at a time when that healthy attitude got you a lot of raised eyebrows," says Mount. Many in Hollywood were shocked by Allan's openness, but those people of a younger, more liberal bent found Allan to be "immense fun," says Mount.

Allan turned his homosexuality into a calling card and, for those who wanted to play along, a game of one-upmanship. First, there were the caftans. Then the gender-bending parties. And if Allan really liked someone, he launched into a no-holds-barred brand of gossip.

"OK, did you sleep with so and so?" Allan asked Mount.

"Allan, leave me alone!"

"I'll tell you who I slept with!" And so Allan did. In graphic detail.

On other occasions, he could be extremely cautious about giving offense, and it was not unusual for him to ask permission to indulge himself if he were traveling on a friend's yacht or private jet. "Do you mind if I make out with my boyfriend?" Allan would ask his straight hosts.

He idolized straight men like Mount, Marvin Hamlisch, and his *Grease* cinematographer, Bill Butler, and afforded them a respect that he didn't always extend to people who shared his sexual orientation. For many heterosexuals, Allan played a quasi-paternal role that didn't stop with the 1 percent of *Grease* grosses that he bestowed upon Butler. "There was a long list of people Allan liked in Hollywood who were down on their luck," says Mount. "I'd seen him write out $20,000- to $50,000-checks and send them in the mail."

thirteen

His Second Biggest Mistake

While Allan's motives for bringing *Survive!* to America were purely cash-driven, *Grease* emerged as the more personal project, playing as it did off his outsider status in school and his overweening need to belong. But now that he was "rich, rich, rich," as he let people know, he wanted to bring the sexual derring-do of his parties to the big screen. Although Roger Smith would claim that his friend was "completely apolitical," Allan's desire to push the erotic envelope played off the sexual politics of the late 1970s and led him to make Hollywood's first, and only, big-budget gay musical. He was, in his own festive way, an accidental activist, and the idea to make a big-budget gay musical got its start, says Bruce Vilanch, "with everyone being heavily soused."

The alcohol started flowing at a dinner party given in the Beverly Hills home of actress Jacqueline Bisset and her current boyfriend, a garment-businessman-turned-realtor named Victor Drai. It was Allan who personally took credit for making the thirty-four-year-old actress an international sensation by convincing the producers of her latest film, *The Deep*, to use a poster that featured her in a sopping wet T-shirt. He didn't care that Bisset herself surmised that the poster reduced her breasts to "something like two fried eggs on a platter." (Or that the producer of *The Deep*, Peter Guber, denies categorically—"1000 percent no"— that he took Allan's advice.) With or without Allan's help, *The Deep* became one of the top-grossing films of 1977.

After too much booze and food, Allan convinced everyone at Bisset's dinner party to accompany him to the Palladium in Hollywood to check out a taping of the weekly syndicated TV show *Don Kirshner's Rock Concert*. The Village People were to perform, and Allan's keen interest in the group had grown in tandem with their record sales, which were a few million more than those of his own gay group, the Cycle Sluts. Also, it was a happy coincidence that, shortly before the Bisset/Drai dinner, he'd met Jacques Morali, who conceived and literally "cast" the cop, the American Indian chief, the construction worker, the cowboy, the biker, and the soldier who were the Village People. Since Morali and his business partner, Henri Belolo, were traveling from Paris to Los Angeles to attend the Kirshner show, Allan looked forward to a follow-up meeting. Morali was also primed. Shortly before the Palladium engagement, he told Belolo, "I met this guy who did *Grease*. He's in love with what we're doing. He wants to meet us." It was everything two starstruck boys from France needed to know. "Allan Carr wants to make a movie with us!"

Allan and Morali had much in common: They were gay, they made no bones about being gay, they liked things gay, and if they really loved something gay, their enthusiasm knew no bounds. There at the Palladium on Sunset Boulevard, Allan didn't just love the Village People. "He wanted to represent the Village People," says his *Hollywood Reporter* friend Richard Hach, who was part of the entourage that night, along with Bruce Vilanch and Bounty-paper-towels spokesperson Nancy Walker, whom Allan repped as a client. The overall camp sleaze of the Village People concert so moved Allan that he found himself dancing in the aisle with *The Deep*'s poster girl to the songs "Y.M.C.A.," "San Francisco," and "In the Navy." Then Allan got hit in the head with one of his epiphanies. "Instantly, I see a film. I want to do a movie musical with the Village People!" he told his friends.

These revelations came often to Allan. "It was typical of the thing he did," says Hach. "He would see something and turn it into a production whether that be a live stage show, a TV show, or a movie."

The Village People, Allan decided, were a movie. They were big. Disco was big. He had to look no further than a recent *Hollywood Reporter* headline to put it all in perspective: "No Cooling of Disco Fever as Operators Eye $5 Billion Year." Allan believed, "A Village People movie could be bigger than *Grease*." The dollar signs danced somewhere between his big brown eyes and his even bigger aviator glasses.

The world of Moroccan showbiz is not a vast one, and as it turned out, Belolo, who hailed from Paris by way of Casablanca, knew Drai, and over the next few weeks there were more dinner parties at Bisset's house. Allan listened to

Belolo and Morali, who told their story of how they literally assembled the Village People. Morali, whom Belolo referred to as being "very openly gay and a crazy cruiser," frequented an S&M bar in the meatpacking district of Manhattan called the Anvil, which featured a young dancer, Felipe Rose, who worked as a go-go boy for fifty dollars a week.

Rose's gimmick was to dress up as an Indian (to call his act "Native American" might do grave offense to those proud people) in a costume of bright feathers and flapping loin cloth right out of Central Costume. It was quite an act, but then again, it had to be exceptional to keep the customers liquored at the bar instead of spending all night in the Dungeon (i.e., the basement), where everything from blow jobs to fist fucking was de rigueur. Popping up from the Dungeon one night, Morali spotted Felipe and the idea struck him: American icons of masculinity. "We'll make a group of macho American men!" he told Belolo.

In fact, Morali, who wrote the music, and Belolo, who wrote the lyrics in French and then had them translated into English, hired Victor Willis and a few anonymous studio singers to record their first album, *Village People,* in spring 1977. They didn't get around to "casting" the cop, the construction worker, the soldier, et al., until the following autumn, at which time the Village People had already sold 100,000 copies of "their" first LP. Then six months later, almost as an afterthought, the release of "Macho Man" made the airwaves and the album went on to sell 2 million copies.

Belolo's heterosexuality didn't deter him from helping to mastermind a gay group, and he harbored few qualms when it came to following Morali's lead in researching the homosexual lifestyle in Greenwich Village and Fire Island Pines. He chalked it up to his openness as a Frenchman, or at least, his not being American. Plus, he adored his baby-faced business partner. "Morali was openly gay and he had no shyness about it," says Belolo. "His dream was to bring some of the gay life to the mainstream," with the operative word being "some."

The same could be said of Allan, who bought the Frenchmen's spiel and found the Village People's gayness a singular plus for movie audiences. "The girls want to take the members of the group home and their boyfriends aren't resentful, and that's what makes movie stars," he reasoned.

When Morali and Belolo told their story of inventing the Village People, right down to the leather chaps and red back-pocket kerchiefs, Allan exclaimed, "That could be a fantastic movie! I want to make this movie!" Some of the group's gayer aspects would have to be adjusted or disguised or obliterated. But those were minor details, he let them know.

The topic of how gay was open for debate—for a few days, anyway. Allan did talk about it with his faithful *Grease* cinematographer. "There were many discussions on how gay the movie would be, whether the Village People would be gay or like they were on their tour," says Bill Butler. "Onstage in their tour, they were just kind of there and you made up your own mind." Which is the way their creators preferred it. "Belolo and Morali were more interested in their possession of their enterprise than anything else." Indeed, even the Village People took it upon themselves to warn journalists not to bring up the subject of the group's gay genesis when they interviewed Morali.

In the beginning, Morali and Belolo liked the way Allan "adapted" their gay-rags to a semi-straight-riches story. Says Belolo, "Morali became an American guy named Morell, and my role was divided into three: the head of a record company, a lawyer, and a supermodel."

Jacqueline Bisset would play the supermodel. "That's how Hollywood works," says Belolo.

Only she didn't. When Bisset bailed, much to Allan's disappointment, he offered the role to Olivia Newton-John.

"Allan liked the combination of Olivia with the Village People," says Bruce Vilanch. "He thought it was milk toast and sleaze."

"Maybe if Allan had said that to me it would have worked," Olivia Newton-John jokes.

But he didn't. And in the end, she didn't. "I just didn't like the script," she says. And there was the other matter: the music: The pop singer wanted John Farrar, her "Hopelessly Devoted to You" composer, to rework his magic and write her songs for the Village People project. Morali and Belolo, who had no interest in sharing a piece of their recording profits, nixed that idea, which led Allan to launch into one of his more spectacular hissy fits. Not against Morali or Belolo—after *Grease*, he understood profit points better than anyone—but Olivia Newton-John. Since he had fought the Paramount executives to cast her as Sandy, he took personal credit for making the singer an international movie star. For Chrissakes, he'd even named a bedroom in his house after her! And *this* is how she repaid him?! It especially hurt that the project she took instead was another disco musical, *Xanadu*. "In which she plays a fucking Greek muse on roller skates!" he screamed. Allan called her, among many other things, "ungrateful."

"He was mad," she recalls. "Allan didn't talk to me for two years."

He did, however, talk to Olivia's agent, screaming at him, "I made her a movie star!"

Just as the Village People movie was conceived under the influence, the development of the script also had much to do with consumption—or lack thereof. "Bronte Woodard and I went to a fat farm in Durham, North Carolina, to lose weight and write the movie *Discoland*," says Bruce Vilanch. Allan planned to join them, but business kept him fat and occupied in Los Angeles.

It was not a typical diet, this Durham regimen. "You ate nothing but rice for a month and lost thirty pounds," says Vilanch. Allan believed in the diet, having done it a number of times with spectacular results—until the weight returned in a month or two. That he didn't accompany Woodard and Vilanch to North Carolina came as something of a pleasant surprise to the two writers, who preferred that their temperamental third wheel stay behind on the West Coast.

The two writers were at slightly different points in their respective careers. Vilanch had just come off writing a Broadway bomb called *Platinum,* in which Alexis Smith played a stage actress who reinvents herself as a recording artist. It was billed as "the musical with a flip-side," and ran thirty-three performances.

Woodard, on the other hand, had written *Grease,* now the top-grossing movie musical of all time, and he'd gotten good reviews for his first (and only) novel, *Meet Me at the Melba,* a southern tale of romance that was based on his parents' courtship. It was a very personal project. "And Bronte's sole mission in life was to get that novel made into a movie," says Vilanch. Allan optioned it and kept announcing everyone from Meryl Streep to Jill Clayburgh to play the female leads. "So here Bronte was writing *Discoland* with hopes that Allan would eventually produce *Melba.*" His intentions were admirable. "But Bronte's property didn't really appeal to Allan's sensibilities," says Vilanch.

While Allan never made it to North Carolina to help write the *Discoland* script, his long-distance phone calls were a constant in Durham. When Olivia Newton-John refused the project, Allan phoned Woodard and Vilanch. "Now it's Cher! Rewrite for Cher!" he ordered.

The next day, their editor from Hilhaven Lodge instructed them, "We're writing for Henry Fonda!" Shirlee Fonda, the actor's wife, had been a recent guest of Allan's, and she promised to show her husband the finished script. Allan thought Henry Fonda would be perfect to play the cameo of a stuffy law-firm executive in the film.

There was also input from the Village People's lead singer, who was the sole hetero of the group. "Victor Willis didn't want people to perceive him as being gay," says Vilanch, "so he insisted we write the role of a girlfriend, to be played by his wife, Phylicia Rashad," aka the future Mrs. Huxtable of *The Cosby Show* fame.

Equally problematic was the continuing debate over how to cast the movie's leading lady. After Woodard and Vilanch wrote the supermodel role for Cher, Allan phoned to tell them, "Cher is out! Now it's Raquel Welch. She will be the supermodel in the movie. Write for Raquel Welch. Think Raquel!"

Screenwriter contracts are complex affairs written on many pieces of paper. Myriad situations are covered in minute detail, more than a few of which are open to interpretation by any number of parties. In this instance, it was the opinion of Vilanch that "step two of the deal had kicked in." He had been put through numerous rewrites as various actresses came and went in the imagination of Allan Carr. According to the contract, each rewrite necessitates more money, and at this point in the leading-lady marathon, Allan had asked his screenwriters to embark on at least their third rewrite, by Vilanch's calculation.

"I need more money," he told Allan.

Allan's response: "Bronte will write it!"

Thirty pounds lighter but not much richer in the pocketbook, Vilanch returned to Los Angeles.

If any piece of the casting puzzle didn't get shuffled, it was a hunk who'd never acted before. Allan invited Bruce Jenner, the Olympics 1976 triathlon champion, to one his Hilhaven parties in the mid-1970s, and listened with sympathy as the former athlete and current Wheaties box cover boy mused about the on-again, off-again negotiations for his starring in the new *Superman* movie, a role that eventually went to Christopher Reeve. After one such bitch session, Allan told his new athlete-friend, "I want to do a movie with you."

"Great," said Jenner.

"I just don't know what it is, but I will find the right vehicle."

"Great," said Jenner.

And then, as with the *Superman* project, the waiting began. There were more parties at Hilhaven, but no movie deal. Then, six months later, Allan phoned to inform Jenner, "I've been thinking about this project. I've finally got the idea. I was with the Village People the other day. There's a story there. You could play their lawyer. To put you together with them is brilliant casting. It's Mutt and Jeff."

Jenner harbored a few reservations when he heard the words "the Village People." As the Wheaties model, he couldn't afford to blow his all-American image. "And at that point in time, people didn't know how to take the Village People," he recalls. The six singers occupied an odd, amorphous place in pop culture. "They were promoted as a disco group." But were they gay? Were they macho men? Were they gay macho men? Only later did Jenner get the picture: "In the casting, boy, you learned quickly, this is a gay group!"

When Cher nixed the idea of making a film called *Discoland,* the next head on the chopping block belonged to Raquel Welch. The ultimate arbiters here, however, were neither Allan Carr nor Raquel Welch but rather the Village People.

David Hodo, the group's construction worker, began his career in show business in a Broadway bomb called *Doctor Jazz,* and had already heard too many horror stories about La Welch. And while she did display the courage to strap on a dildo ten years earlier in *Myra Breckinridge*, the six men insisted, "No Raquel."

The news came to Allan during one of his many sojourns in Cedars-Sinai. Valerie Perrine happened to be visiting him in the hospital after the Village People's edict came down. Five years earlier, the former Vegas showgirl had created much hoopla with her Oscar-nominated portrayal of Lenny Bruce's drugged-out bimbo wife in *Lenny*. In more recent years, her star slipped a bit with below-the-title roles in *The Electric Horseman* and *Superman,* in which she played Lex Luthor's paramour. Allan and Perrine were old friends, and in the midst of their usual gossip treadmill of extramarital affairs, career misfortunes, and plastic surgery mishaps, the blond actress noticed something about Allan that had previously escaped her attention. "Allan kept looking at my legs," she recalls. And there was plenty of leg to check out under Perrine's microminiskirt. Considering her friend's sexual orientation, "I thought that strange." His fixation on the lower part of her anatomy continued until, finally, he announced, "You can play a supermodel!"

Allan's impromptu choice to play the supermodel—sometimes referred to as "a woman," as Janet Maslin described the role in her *New York Times* review of the film—impressed the Village People. The actress's mildly risqué screen persona preceded her and she certainly seemed like a fun, good-old party girl that five, if not six, gay men could relate to.

How much fun the Village People did not know until they performed at Madison Square Garden, a venue of 17,000 seats, which, to Allan's promoter eyes, made it the ideal place to announce his *Discoland* cast. Before entering the Garden, Allan saw a sign for the new Broadway play *The Elephant Man*. He scrunched up his face. "What's *that* about?" he asked Bruce Vilanch.

"It's a play about the ugliest man in the world" came the reply.

Allan let out a whiff of disgust. "Good, I won't turn it into a movie."

He entertained more attractive plans.

The Garden gig came near the end of the Village People's 1979 national tour—one that had already taken them to forty-six cities in a fast, if not numbing, fifty-four days. The Village People looked dead on arrival at Madison Square Garden, but nonetheless anticipated with excitement their first movie, even if it left them only a short two-week break between their tour schedule and the first day of filming. Backstage at the Garden, Allan took the opportunity not only to introduce them to Valerie Perrine and Bruce Jenner but to hand each of the six men his own copy of the long-awaited *Discoland* script. The words "By Allan Carr and Bronte Woodard" were nearly as large as the title itself.

The Village People collectively dropped their scripts when Allan introduced Perrine. "Valerie turned around, bent over, and mooned us," Hodo says. "She had on a g-string." Yes, this would be a fun shoot.

"Valerie scared the shit out of Bruce Jenner," says his then-publicist, Kathy Berlin. "Bruce had never kissed anyone onscreen. He hadn't spent any time around gays. This movie was really out of his element."

The plan that evening was for Allan to introduce his *Discoland* cast during the intermission at the Garden. If Allan was the showman, Perrine was the showgirl, who, once again, did not disappoint. Just before she took the stage to greet the Village People's many adoring fans, "She tweaked her nipples so that they stood up through her dress," says Hodo. The effect may have been lost on many in the crowd that night, but not on those who mattered most. "It was driving our roadies crazy," says Hodo.

Crazy, too, was Allan, who genuinely loved the Village People. He couldn't believe the audience's ovation for each and every number they performed. "Wow!" he exclaimed afterward. "You guys are more popular than Farrah Fawcett!"

More than ready to unwind, the Village People took to their respective hotel suites after the show, ready to hunker down with a good script, in this case, Allan Carr and Bronte Woodard's *Discoland* screenplay. They couldn't wait to see what the genius behind *Grease* had wrought this time. During their many, many evenings on the road, the six men had often dreamed about the kind of movie they wanted to headline. They batted around various story lines, but the concept they liked best was to play vampires—vampires who would perform their disco show in a different town every night, and when they left the next morning, a dozen dead bodies trailed their tour bus. They even had thought about what they'd wear: "Red, white, and blue costumes with lots of stars and stripes," says Hodo.

The costumes were the least of it.

On Saturday, June 9, 1979, with a few more weeks left on their national tour, the Village People opened in Los Angeles at the Greek Theater, an open-air venue plunked down among the chaparral and pine trees in one of the most spectacularly scenic ravines of Griffith Park. If Henri Belolo and Jacques Morali had traveled to Griffith Park rather than Fire Island Pines, it might have been "the bushes" of this wooded glen that inspired them to write an ode to the splendiferous dangers of cruising al fresco.

Just as Allan used the Madison Garden gig to introduce *Discoland* to the Village People's fans, he worked the Greek Theater engagement to advertise it to his closest hundred friends in the Hollywood press corps. Allan was in L.A. The Village People were in L.A. What did it matter that the movie's release date loomed a year away? From a publicity point of view, Allan wanted to celebrate *Discoland*'s "pre-first-anniversary," as he put it, with a series of bashes that would effectively promote the film's new tag line, "Where the Music Never Ends." Those words were the theme of his West Coast kickoff, as duly noted in the *Los Angeles Times,* which obliged with a headline, "Hollywood's Party Champion Defends His Crown," that Allan himself could not have bettered.

The local journalists' biggest query was whether Hollywood's ultimate partygiver had planned four or five fetes that evening or just one long affair, which took them from a 6:30 p.m. cocktail party at the Bistro Garden to the Greek Theater concert to Hilhaven Lodge, where festivities ended at around 1 a.m. for the heterosexual crowd and about 3 a.m. for everybody else. That was three parties right there. And that didn't count the party on wheels (complete with box dinners and the ubiquitous Cristal) that whisked dozens of reporters on two buses (one marked "Y.M.C.A.," the other "In the Navy") between the Bistro, the Greek, and Hilhaven. Entertainment journalists are always in search of a hook, an angle, or a twist to help make their breathless words coalesce into a cogent thought. Allan was there, ready as ever, with his "where the party never ends" line.

For his *Discoland* launch, he played it casual—blue jeans, blue blazer, and white shirt with an AC monogrammed on the breast pocket. His only ostentatious touch was a rather humongous diamond pin on his lapel. "A gift from Ann-Margret," he said whenever asked—or not asked. There would be no theatrical changes of his outfit tonight. It was 6:30 p.m., and he wasn't getting home before midnight. He also sported a beard, which prompted him to proclaim, repeatedly, "I'm in my Francis Coppola period!" The *Godfather* director was very much on everyone's mind as he readied his much-anticipated *Apocalypse Now* for release later that summer.

At the evening's first party, at the Bistro, Allan described his *Discoland* as, alternately, "*Singin' in the Rain* for the disco crowd" and "It's a 1950s musical. It's *My Sister Eileen*. It's New York the way you wish it were. No dog do-do, no garbage, no killings." He also billed *Discoland* as the first in an ongoing musical trilogy, which would soon put Goldie Hawn in *Chicago* and Diana Ross in a Josephine Baker biopic.

Was it any wonder Allan got quoted more than, say, Robert De Niro or Diane Keaton? On the red-tile patio of the Bistro, shaded by a dozen colorful umbrellas, Allan repeated his comments with minor variations. Two tuxedoed violinists serenaded, and a hundred reporters wrote down what he said as they were catered to by no fewer than ten waiters, six press agents, and ten security types, led by Gavin de Becker, who liked to flaunt his business card, which advertised the "International Terrorist Research Center in El Paso, Tex."

Beyond the overabundance of liquor and hors d'oeuvres, Allan plied his reporter friends with other goodies as well. He especially prided himself in the makeover he'd achieved with newcomer Steve Guttenberg, who'd been cast in the Morali/Morell role. While some of the movie's participants would call his attention to the twenty-year-old actor's body "obsessive," Allan made no apologies. "I worked with Steve for two months to prepare him physically and mentally for playing a starring role. He's lost a lot of baby fat, and his face now, it lights up the screen."

Guttenberg was but the first of many young actors whom Allan, as a producer, lusted after. "He had a lot of little crushes," says Kathy Berlin, who did publicity chores on every Allan Carr film. "'I'm going to make you a star, boy!'"

At the Bistro Garden, Allan lavished only a little less hyperbole on his director, Nancy Walker, calling her "the next Alfred Hitchcock," and his choreographer, Arlene Phillips, who he claimed would be "the next Michael Bennett," which left it to Bruce Jenner to give the reporters the only other line worth reprinting.

"Bruce, why are you making this movie?" asked one journalist.

"You can't live on Wheaties alone," said Jenner.

Even before the cameras rolled on *Discoland,* a slight freeze had already chilled the working relationship between male star and producer. Jenner had recently received a script from producer Howard Koch, who was making a new comedy. "You'd be perfect to play the pilot," Koch told him.

"I love the script," said Jenner.

But before he committed, Jenner wanted to inform Allan that this other film would be coming out next summer at about the same time as *Discoland*. It was such a small request. Jenner thought that Allan wouldn't mind.

"Fuck no!" Allan screamed. "I don't want you in another movie! You can't do that!"

Jenner felt he had no choice, "out of loyalty" to Allan, but to refuse the other offer. Disappointed, Koch cast another athlete-turned-actor, Kareem Abdul-Jabbar. Still, Jenner had to wonder as he did press chores for *Discoland* at the Bistro, "Did I make the right choice? Would this other film—*Airplane!*—be a big success?"

As the revelers left the Bistro to go to the Greek Theater, each of them received either a blue lapel dot or a yellow lapel dot. Yellow meant they were relegated to the "Y.M.C.A." bus; blue translated into a seat on the "In the Navy" bus. The latter bus qualified as the preferred mode of transportation since it carried Allan, who, after renditions of "Red River Valley" and "The Irish Washer Woman," gave the assembled reporters even more grist for their newspapers when he brayed at the lone violinist onboard to play something else. "Could we please have some Strauss waltzes?" he insisted, pointing a diamond-encrusted finger at the offending fiddler.

When the two buses unloaded their cargo in front of the Greek Theater, more alcohol and more hors d'oeuvres awaited everyone in yet another hospitality suite. In concert, the Village People were the Village People, singing the same rotation of "Best of Hits," from "San Francisco" to "Fire Island," that they had performed in forty-five other cities. Then it was back on the buses to the night's final party, at Allan's house.

A few partygoers—Robin Williams, Candy Clark, and Sam Bottoms, among others—chose to forgo the live entertainment in favor of a late-night dip in Allan's disco basement. The Village People were thrilled nonetheless that the movie celebs made at least one appearance in their honor that evening.

"Wow! Our very own Hollywood party!" exclaimed David Hodo, who had his hardhat wired to pulse visually to the beat coming from Don Blanton's DJ booth. Allan insisted that all six Village People stay in costume for his party. "Makes for better photos," he believed. And photos galore were taken in the poolside tent, its ceiling festooned with multicolored balloons like a children's birthday party on triple-sugar-overload.

Marvin Hamlisch thought it was all a bit too costumey, especially when the party population threatened to violate fire regulations. "Take off your head-dress!" he told Felipe Rose. "It's in my way."

Rose growled back, "It's my party!"

"There was a Hawaiian theme thing," recalls Steve Guttenberg. "Man, Allan made it like heaven. He knew how to treat people—spectacular food, incredible music, pretty people. There was something for everybody, every sexual orientation, you could get what you wanted at that party." And that included, on the buffet table, a scantily clad boy and girl whose bodies were otherwise covered with edible tidbits.

Even the claustrophobic basement disco impressed Guttenberg. "Yeah, it was small, the disco. But it was cool. It was like getting on a private jet—they're small but cool."

If there was any restriction on indulging yourself sexually or pharmaceutically, it came courtesy of Allan's one hundred friends in the Fourth Estate. "Allan always made sure the press was there," says Guttenberg. "There was a reason for the madness. He was crazy like a fox."

At 2 a.m., Felipe Rose let out a series of war signals as his long feather earrings began to droop in the early morning mist, otherwise known as June gloom. Rose's cry was a call of the wild, as if to announce that there was not a movie star or a heterosexual to be found on the premises, and that included Steve Guttenberg. As if on cue, what happened is what always happened at a certain hour at Allan's parties.

As producer Craig Zadan explained the general scene, "It would be late at night and when the movie stars had left, you would look around the living room and think, 'Where has everyone gone?' And then out there in the hot tub, the guys were having sex."

Sometimes hetero stragglers got caught in the gay melee. "Robin Williams came into the DJ booth to hide," says Don Blanton.

Tired as they were, the Village People booked one more gig before filming began. At the request of the U.S. Navy, they performed their hit song "In the Navy" on the USS *San Diego* in front of an audience that included Bob Hope, Henry Kissinger, and over 2,000 sailors. "They gave us everything we wanted," says Henri Belolo, who, in return, requested that the Navy pick up the cost of filming the music video. "They were going to use it as a recruiting advertisement."

The brief concert went off without a hitch. Bob Hope even joined the Village People onstage to reprise "In the Navy." All that free publicity was for naught, however, as soon as conservative pundits chastised the armed services for consorting with homosexuals. The Village People's military promo never left the cutting room.

It was a minor blip, and filming on *Discoland* began, only a few days late, on August 20, 1979, in New York City. A major bump, however, took form in the person of Victor Willis, who never got around to making his film debut in *Discoland*. He unexpectedly quit the Village People, tired of performing with them. Allan wasn't unhappy to see him go. After Willis nodded off during a reading of his *Discoland* script, Allan wanted him fired, but the singer beat him to it and left the group. Allan did get to indulge his urge to ax somebody, however. When Ray Simpson replaced Willis, Allan saw no reason to indulge Mrs. Willis and unceremoniously dumped Phylicia Rashad from *Discoland*. She was replaced by Sammy Davis Jr.'s wife, Altovise Davis.

fourteen

Can't Stand the Music

The streets of Manhattan were hotter than normal that August, not because of the usual summer-in-the-city temps but because of the sociopolitical climate in Greenwich Village. Director William Friedkin preceded Allan in taking to the Gotham streets to film his crime story *Cruising,* and the *Village Voice*'s gay journalist Arthur Bell used his column, "Bell Tells," to rally the homosexual community against the production. Having secured a purloined copy of the *Cruising* script, Bell proclaimed it wildly homophobic for its portrayal of an undercover cop, played by Al Pacino, who infiltrates the gay underworld of S&M clubs to solve a series of murders. Gay activists, spurred on by Bell, papered Greenwich Village with leaflets protesting the movie, and threatened boycotts of any bars or businesses that cooperated with Friedkin. Busloads of leather-encrusted movie extras were brought to the street scene, only to be splattered with eggs and epithets of "traitors" and "sellouts." The production called in extra cops for protection, and when the police barricades kept the public out of eyeshot of the filming, the protesters quickly adopted a technique that made it impossible for the filmmakers to acquire any usable sound recording: They distributed hundreds of plastic whistles, and from dusk to dawn, a collective high-pitched squeal turned the streets of Barrow, Bleecker, and Washington into an aural hell for Friedkin and company, as well as anyone living there.

Into this cauldron of unrest and provocation dropped Allan Carr's sweet, innocuous, and quasi-gay celluloid marshmallow, *Discoland.* On the first day of filming, which happened to be on Sixth Avenue and Waverly Place (only a few blocks east of Friedkin's camp), the police cautioned Allan, "You'd better be out of here before dark. We've got this *Cruising* movie going on, and it might not be safe for you."

It didn't matter that *Cruising* was primarily a night shoot and sunny *Discoland* filmed most of its exteriors during the day. Even at twelve noon, protesters often confused the two productions. More than once, Allan felt compelled to hoist his chubby frame unto a crane, and through a bullhorn, he politely chastised the activists, "No, we're the good guys. We're the good gay movie. *Cruising* is filming three blocks that way!" And he would point in the direction of the meatpacking district and the Hudson River.

Gotham's denizens rarely got to see many movie people, so it was understandable that some pissed-off homosexuals never understood the difference. On the second day of shooting, one man found his way past the police cordon surrounding the *Discoland* production, and confronted Valerie Perrine. "You should be ashamed of yourself for making a film like *Cruising*!" he screamed. "Shame on you!" He spit a big wet wad of gunk in her face.

"*Cruising*?" Allan screamed back. "This is *Discoland*!"

Stunned, Perrine wiped the man's spittle away with the back of her hand. "A good old New York cop took him away," she recalls.

Although it was only the second day of production, irate homosexuals were already the least of Perrine's problems. Even under the very controlled environment of a Hollywood soundstage, directing one's first movie is a difficult, formidable task. Confronting the chaotic street life of Greenwich Village, Nancy Walker crumbled. Completely. Then her leading lady got slimed.

"This guy spitting at Valerie happens in the middle of a scene," Bruce Jenner recalls. "Nancy Walker was just overwhelmed by it all." The four-foot-eleven director kept telling herself, "I will be OK. I will be OK. I will be OK."

And that was only Day 2.

By Day 4, Perrine barely remembered the spit in her face. The bigger problem, she believed, was Nancy Walker. The actress had already started relying on Bill Butler for direction, and for good reason. In one street scene, the cinematographer set up his camera and an assistant sounded the clack board: "Take one!" Several seconds into the scene, Walker yelled out, "Cut!" and turned to Perrine. "Would you shut up?! Don't you know not to talk during a take?!"

"But the camera's rolling," Perrine replied.

"So shut up!"

"But it's my scene. I'm acting!"

When Walker repeated the tirade the following day, Perrine let it be known. "Nancy," she said, "no matter how hard you scream and yell at me, my tits are real and I'll always be taller than you!"

Allan, who had busied himself directing gay protesters to the meatpacking district where *Cruising* had taken up residence, ordered Perrine and Walker into his stretch limousine parked over on Carmine and Bleecker Streets. At first, it looked as though Allan was going to ply them with kindness. But soon, "The car was rocking," says David Hodo. He and other cast members gathered around to listen as Allan brayed at the guests in his limo, "If you two cunts don't start getting along, I'm going to publish it in every magazine and newspaper in America!"

But it wasn't all rancor that first week of production. Allan immediately gratified his Steve Guttenberg obsession by shooting the title sequence—an exercise in minimalism that focused exclusively on the now-buff actor, poured into T-shirt and cutoffs, skating through the streets of New York for no fewer than four minutes of screen time. For further release, Allan led his cast on nightly pilgrimages uptown to Studio 54, that temple of lust and coke dust. Or, as Perrine described the joint, "They used to say that if you remember going to Studio 54, you didn't have a good time there."

In the two weeks they filmed in New York City, Bruce Jenner conscientiously resisted all invitations to Steve Rubell's pleasure dome. But his wholesome Wheaties image could endure only so much polishing, and after much persuasion, Allan finally convinced his uptight athlete-turned-movie-actor to indulge himself and attend the famed disco on the last night of location filming in Manhattan.

"Hey, the whole cast and crew are going," Allan told his reluctant star, who had to mull the proposal for days. Being seen out with the notorious Village People was one thing, but Jenner found safety in the fact that the film's female contingent—Valerie Perrine, Nancy Walker, and the very pregnant choreographer Arlene Phillips—would also be along for the ride.

For the *Discoland* cast's final night in Manhattan, one grand entrance did not suffice. Allan wanted several entrances, and ordered up a whole fleet of limousines, one for each of his people, Village and otherwise. "Allan made a big deal of getting everyone into Studio 54," says Jenner. He especially played up his close-close relationship with owner Steve Rubell, and let the long line of would-be patrons on the street know, "Make way for the stars of *Discoland!*" as the limo flotilla, one by one, discharged its starry cargo at 254 West 54th Street.

Inside, Bruce Jenner took several deep breaths as socialites, drag queens, beautiful girls in bikinis, and muscled boys in jockstraps danced by him like so many moths on their way to a lightbulb electrocution. The painted wood cutout of the man-in-the-moon dangled overhead, its face winking as a big spoon miraculously filled with white powder. It signaled all revelers to follow suit while a metal Aztec sun god spewed smoke across the 5,400-square-foot dance floor. "This is not your Wheaties crowd!" Jenner told his host, who luxuriated in the expression of shock on his cereal-box cover boy. "This is obviously where you go to look at people," Jenner added, gulping for air.

The one thing Allan liked better than shocking heterosexual men was introducing famous people to even more famous people, and he beelined his way right to the first one he saw at the bar. "Mischa!" cried Allan, giving Mikhail Baryshnikov a big hug. "You must meet my good friend Bruce!" Two years earlier, the Russian émigré danseur had enjoyed a great success in the movies, playing a Russian émigré danseur in *Turning Point*. Hollywood even honored him with an Oscar nomination for his effort at playing himself. Allan wanted to follow up that success with another Baryshnikov headliner, an original MGM musical called *Riviera* to costar Grace Jones.

"Mischa, darling! Bruce is making a movie, *Discoland,* with me!" Allan took both men by the arm and led them to one of the banquettes. Since Jenner had been to the Soviet Union a number of times, he tried to make polite conversation by asking Baryshnikov about his homeland and, in turn, Baryshnikov asked Jenner about winning the triathlon at the Olympics. But Studio 54 was not designed for conversations, and even as intriguing as the Bruce and Mischa tête-à-tête might have been, it soon turned into a trial of disco din over polite words from their respective résumés. Baryshnikov gave up making small talk. "Bruce, do you want to dance?" he asked.

Jenner choked. "Uh, uh, no, but thanks." Having never confronted this situation before, he didn't quite know how to turn down another man's invitation to boogie.

Allan looked on, bemused. "You're turning him down? You're turning down the opportunity to dance with Mikhail Baryshnikov? You're turning down a dance with the greatest dancer in the world!?"

Jenner's smile tightened. "At least it's Baryshnikov asking me to dance."

Ultraprotective of his all-American image, Jenner got squeamish when it came to homosexuality. The other big taboo was drugs, and he could only envision tomorrow's *New York Post,* its cover emblazoned with a photo of a coke spoon up his nose or of him dancing with another man. It didn't take much imagination to envision the morals clause of his Wheaties contract as it burst into tabloid flames.

And so the *Discoland* production completed its two-week shoot in New York with a two-week hiatus. Cast and crew were happy to leave the hectic city streets to move west to the more controlled environs of the grand old MGM studio in Culver City, California. The break was especially appreciated by the film's British choreographer, Arlene Phillips. While everyone else used the time to relax and set up camp in Los Angeles, Phillips went into labor to give birth to her first child, a baby girl, whom she named Alana in honor of her current, beloved movie producer.

Allan had met the young Brit when he was doing publicity chores for *Grease* in London. Phillips had never choreographed a movie or a major stage production before, but her dance group, Hot Gossip, did perform at a prelaunch party for *Grease* at the Embassy Club on Bond Street. Olivia Newton-John came with Allan, and singer Sarah Brightman, who would later marry Andrew Lloyd Webber (and then divorce him, but not before he tried to make her a star with *The Phantom of the Opera*), performed with Hot Gossip. It wasn't your usual dance troupe. For starters, both the men and the women in Hot Gossip wore garters and stockings and bras—"sex shop clothes," as Phillips describes it—that were made out of plastic, rubber, and torn fabric, and Phillips's dance moves sometimes simulated various sex acts. In other words, "This is exactly the kind of choreography I need for *Discoland!*" Allan gushed to Phillips after seeing her dancers perform. "You must come to the *Grease* premiere next week. You must come to America to choreograph *Discoland!*"

As was often the case with Allan, the hire was just that quick and easy.

But there were complications. Shortly after Phillips signed the contract, she learned of her pregnancy. She checked the production schedule and noted that between the shoots in New York and Los Angeles, there was a two-week hiatus beginning September 3. The baby was due September 3.

Phillips knew she had no choice. She phoned her new boss. "Allan, this is the most unforgivable thing: Can I have a week off during the September hiatus?" she asked.

"Why?" he asked.

"I'm going to have a baby then."

"Sure. Fine. Whatever you need."

Fortunately, Alana arrived right on schedule, September 3, at Cedars-Sinai Medical Center in Los Angeles, and when Phillips got back from the delivery room, she found her hospital room filled with literally hundreds of flowers, courtesy of Allan.

"His generosity didn't stop there," says Phillips. When production started on the MGM lot, he ordered up a nanny and a Winnebago large enough to satisfy any star's ego. "Sometimes Allan's exterior could be harsh," says Phillips, "and then there would be these immense acts of generosity that just couldn't be believed."

Allan always chose to show his best side to family people. Like his production manager, Neil Machlis, who confronted his own major crisis that summer. "It was a bad time for me. My two-year-old son had cancer. I was on the set, in the hospital, on the set, in the hospital. Allan was great," says Machlis.

While Phillips and Machlis grew to adore Allan, they sometimes glimpsed another side of the man. This "other" Allan first made his appearance at the MGM studios when Phillips began rehearsals for one of the movie's big production numbers, "Red," which featured several female dancers from her Hot Gossip troupe. "They couldn't give all of the Village People girlfriends," jokes Phillips, "so they just surrounded them with women." One of those girls was chunkier than the others. "Allan couldn't stand her. He hated her," says the choreographer.

During rehearsals one morning, Allan shot up from his director's chair and pointed at the girl. "Put her in the back!" he yelled at Phillips. "Hide her waaaaaay in the back!" It didn't matter that the zaftig dancer stood right beside Phillips and Allan's finger nearly poked her in the nostrils.

In the homosexual community of *Discoland,* Phillips became the production's unofficial female mascot, which made her more privy to the overload of drugs on the set than some of the other straight participants.

"There were a lot of drugs around," says Phillips, who developed such a gay rapport that *Discoland* screenwriter Bronte Woodard invited her to his otherwise all-male parties at his Hollywood Hills home on Mulholland Drive. "I'd be the only woman there. They were just chock full of young boys and drugs. Cocaine right, left, and center. The party started at the swimming pool and ended up in the bedroom."

They were quite the A-list orgies. "Bronte was into Falcon models, Al Parker, among others," says celebrity photographer Greg Gorman, who scored one of his first major assignments with the *Discoland* production. "Bronte lived larger than life." Woodard cultivated his thick Georgia accent and wore white broadband hats. Having written the southern romance *Meet Me at the Melba*, he considered himself another Truman Capote or Tennessee Williams. But late in the *Discoland* production, Woodard's energy began to wane, and he often had to cancel some of the weekend fetes at his house or simply not show up for them. Then he stopped coming to the set altogether. Allan told people, "Bronte's not feeling well."

On at least one occasion, the Bronte free-for-all spirit surfaced on the set of *Discoland*. Instead of re-creating a disco on the MGM soundstage, Allan took over Studio One for one scene, and dressed up the West Hollywood club with several towers of light so that it resembled Studio 54. In the scene, the Jack Morell character gets his big break when he convinces the local DJ to break the Village People's first single. It was a simple scene between Steve Guttenberg and Don Blanton, Allan's real-life DJ, who, two years earlier had actually debuted the Village People's song "San Francisco" at the Odyssey. Blanton wasn't the only bit of typecasting. Allan also larded the background with several of his ex-boyfriends, whose on-set behavior drastically delayed the filming. "It got out of control," says Blanton. "Everyone was having sex with one another. Guys would come by your dressing room and ask, 'Can I give you a blow job?' Allan got angry because it was costing him money because they weren't able to find the people to do the scene."

Allan had no choice but to issue a warning: "Anyone caught having sex will be thrown off the set!"

A modicum of order returned when the production moved back to MGM; unfortunately, the nostalgia of filming where Esther Williams and Judy Garland once cavorted brought little cohesion to the production. "Everyone had ideas for that movie," says Bill Butler, who, in effect, became the de facto helmer on *Discoland*. While he had never directed a film, the cinematographer had worked with some of the best: Milos Forman on *One Flew Over the Cuckoo's Nest*, Steven Spielberg on *Jaws*, Francis Ford Coppola on *Rain People*. "You learn tons from these people," says Butler. And what he learned that came in most handy on *Discoland* was how to direct actors who can't act.

"When you have actors like the Village People who are not actors but performers, they tend to go over the top. They throw their emotions in, and it looks unreal," says Butler.

Nancy Walker, who had trained on Broadway and was, in essence, a theater actor, didn't know how to coax natural line readings from her six nonprofessional performers. Which left it to Butler to take each of them aside to advise, "Say your lines with absolutely no emphasis, just read them flat." According to the cinematographer, "That's how we got through the scenes."

Amidst such ineptitude, Belolo and Morali's enthusiasm for their movie receded along with Walker's control of her actors. In the beginning, Belolo chose to take the philosophical route. "This is Hollywood," he said. "Perhaps it is going to be big." Good, of course, was another story. But even an eccentric Parisian knew there was no way to salvage the "Milkshake" number, a musical extravaganza that shot on Stage 28 at MGM and required no fewer than fifty-seven camera setups.

The scene begins with the taping of a TV commercial in which Perrine's supermodel character serves milk to six children dressed up as the Village People. The camera then segues from the kitchen to an all-white soundstage, where the adult Village People replace the kids. Perrine, now dripping in hand-sewn beads and perched atop a large Plexiglas champagne glass, listens to them sing the joys of having a milk shake with lyrics that could not have been more nutritious: "When you're at work today, and it's time for your coffee break, why don't you treat yourself to a big thick and frosty shake. . . . Just get a glass of milk. It's not very hard to do."

The Village People complained about the wholesome song and their glitzy all-white costumes, and Belolo and Morali were there to back them up. "We had imagined the film would be more street," says Belolo. "Suddenly it became a kind of nightmare, it became burlesque."

Allan could only shrug his shoulders. "The Milk and Dairy Association has paid $2 million to have a milk shake number in the film," explained the master of product placement.

Nancy Walker cared even less about the film's musical sequences than about the dialogue scenes. "She left it to Bill Butler and me to direct most of those numbers," says Phillips. "She wasn't on the set." But since the "Milkshake" number involved Valerie Perrine, the director made an exception. Slumped in a king-size champagne glass, the actress spoke only one line. "One more time!" she told the Village People. But no matter how she delivered those three words, Walker cried, "Again!"

After twenty takes, Perrine fired back, "How many fucking ways are there to say, 'One more time!'?"

Something had to be done about Walker, and Perrine put it to Allan in so many words: "Either she goes or I go." Allan made his choice. After the "Milkshake" number wrapped, any scene featuring Perrine found Walker offset watching *All My Children*.

It didn't matter if *Discoland* was good, bad, or indifferent as a movie. Of greater concern to the powers behind *Discoland* was the January 23 *Variety* headline that declared, "Disco No Longer a Priority Item with Diskeries."

Belolo and Morali heard the death knell even before the editors of *Variety*. "The radio stations were dropping the disco format," says Belolo. "Suddenly, in the middle of filming, everyone was predicting the end of disco, and here we had a $20-million movie about disco."

They couldn't reshoot their movie, which was almost in the can. Instead, they did what they always do in Hollywood when a movie runs into trouble. "We had a creative meeting," says Belolo. *Discoland,* everyone knew, was a lousy title in light of the music industry's turnaround. "We need to find a new name," Allan decreed. Since Can't Stop the Music was the name of Belolo and Morali's American company, Belolo wondered aloud. "Why not *Can't Stop the Music?*"

"That's fabulous!" said Allan. End of discussion. Meeting adjourned.

Allan continued to be a constant presence on the set, and on those days he didn't make a pilgrimage to MGM, he busied himself scouting weight lifters, swimmers, wrestlers, gymnasts, and other athletes to populate the big "Y.M.C.A." number. Allan allocated days, not hours, to searching every gym and athletic field in the Los Angeles area to find just the right 1,000 or so male contestants who could be whittled down to no fewer than 250 specimens of absolute masculine perfection. In essence, the musical number was a parody of a parody, ripped from Howard Hawks's 1953 film, *Gentlemen Prefer Blondes,* starring Jane Russell and Marilyn Monroe as two gold diggers en route to Europe aboard a luxury ocean liner. The classic film features one deliciously improbable scene in which Russell wanders into a gym filled with male athletes who pay absolutely no attention to her as she sings Hoagy Carmichael's "Ain't There Anyone Here for Love?" Allan envisioned something similar for the "Y.M.C.A." production number, only he jettisoned the lead female and radically multiplied the number of men, using split screens to cram as many glutes, pecs, and abs as possible into each frame.

If Butler had become the de facto director of the movie, he essentially went back to his cinematography duties on "Y.M.C.A." Allan Carr sat in charge at the Glendale YMCA, where filming ensued for a luxurious four-day shoot for approximately four minutes of film.

"If we did it once, we did it a hundred times," Phillips says of the choreography. Every dive, every jump, every squat press was never quite good enough. "Do it again!" Allan cried from his director's chair. "Boys, let's see your muscles, let's see your body!"

Belolo used to tease his producer friend, "So tell me, Allan. Exactly how do you have sex? You can't screw because of your gut. Do you take it?"

Allan laughed. He would have strangled another gay man for saying such a thing. But he liked to trade sex talk with the straight guys. Allan bonded with Belolo, but now that Allan surrounded himself with attractive young men for the "Y.M.C.A." number, he and fellow homosexual Jacques Morali grew wary of one another.

"I want that boy," said Allan.

"No, I want that one," said Morali. And so it went guy after guy after guy.

"They had very similar taste in men, and if one wanted one guy, then the other wanted that guy, too," Belolo says.

Except for their vocals, the Village People made only a cameo appearance in the "Y.M.C.A." flesh-a-thon as their hit song blared over multitudes of ripped, pumped, hairless, young male bodies. "Allan essentially made two movies," says Don Blanton. Bill Butler shot the PG-version, while set photographer Roger LeClaire presided over the X-rated one. "There was nudity in the showers and steam room and pool," Blanton says of the latter film, which Allan made for his own private amusement. The assignment won LeClaire a special mention on the end credit roll, which read, "consultant: YMCA."

To cap *Can't Stop the Music,* Allan flew the entire cast and crew to San Francisco to shoot the film's conclusion in the city's largest gay disco, La Galleria. "That was out of sight!" says Butler. "The place was four stories. It was ideal for the finale."

The Village People, along with the principal cast members, were to perform the movie's title song on a Broadway-size stage in front of a few hundred adoring fans. To prepare for the spectacular number, Allan sent advance people to promote the filming throughout the streets of San Francisco. It would take a lot of extras to fill up the gargantuan Galleria, and it wasn't in Allan's nature to pay retail when he could get a discount—or, better yet, charge these nonprofessionals fifteen dollars a pop to be in his movie.

"Allan puts out this letter, inviting people to a fantasy party with the Village People," Jenner recalls. "It read: 'Come in your wildest outfit!'"

And that they did.

On the first day of shooting, Neil Machlis stood with Allan on the fourth tier of the disco and looked down at the multitudes below. The mass of throbbing flesh, pulsing to the same tribal beat, looked very theatrical. La Galleria, in addition to its four levels, featured a roof that retracted to expose a festive spaceship out of *Close Encounters of the Third Kind,* which slowly descended over the dance floor to give off a dazzling light display. Machlis believed the crowded dance palace would make a great final reel for their movie, but he felt compelled to put one question to Allan. Screaming above the din, he asked, "Where are the women?"

The movie's production manager watched as Allan stared at him, then broke out laughing. "He loved to shock me," says Machlis. He wasn't the only family man to be disarmed by the scene at La Galleria. "It was the first time I saw truck-driver types dancing with other truck-driver types. Mostly it was men," observed Warren Cowan, whose firm, Rogers & Cowan, handled publicity chores on the film.

When Allan stopped being convulsed with laughter, he looked back at the dance floor below and realized that his hetero production manager had a point. Within the minute, Allan issued a most urgent edict: "Find females!"

Machlis dispatched every available crew member—grips, gofers, and costumers alike—to round up any woman they could find. Allan didn't care. Young or old, pretty or not. He would forgo the fifteen dollars a head to fill La Galleria with members of the opposite sex.

Despite the crew's efforts, "It was just this whole group of sexy, seething, dancing men," says Arlene Phillips. "There were a few girls down front in the first five rows, but not very many."

Amidst the four-day shoot in San Francisco, Allan petitioned the mayor to give the Village People the keys to the city. Which meant more promotion, more fliers, more newspaper ads.

"But boys, you won't have to sing," Allan told his headliners, who complained repeatedly of being tired, exhausted, burnt out. "Just pick up the goddamn key and then go home to your hotel." Of course, this extra duty was planned *after* a full, hard day of shooting at La Galleria.

The always-docile Village People once again did as they were told and limoed themselves over to city hall to pick up the keys to San Francisco. And Allan, once again, did not disappoint. The square in front of city hall bulged with fans as the songs "Y.M.C.A." and "In the Navy" blared over loudspeakers. Otherwise, it was a fairly ordinary press event: One of the mayor's assistants presented the Village People with a gold plastic key to the city. The boys smiled. Photos were taken, and with a quick wave to the assembled masses, the six pop stars climbed into their respective limousines for a well-deserved night at the Fairmont Hotel.

"But the crowd had it in their head that we were there to sing, to perform a whole show," says David Hodo. "When they saw us get into our limousines, they started to boo and carry on. Boy, were they pissed off!" Fliers were wadded up and pelted the performers as they made their quick escape.

The real dramatic fireworks that night, however, took place not in front of city hall but back at La Galleria. Filming had ended hours before when Belolo returned to the Fairmount for a room-service dinner with his wife, Daniele. At 10 p.m., the phone rang in his hotel suite. It was Morali, who yelled into the receiver, "You've got to come over here. Now!" Belolo asked what was wrong. In the background, he could hear Allan screaming.

"I can't tell you what's the matter," cried Morali. "You just have to come right over here. Allan has gone mad."

Belolo left his wife and jumped into a taxi to return to La Galleria, where Allan had set up his office in the basement. It was there that Belolo found Allan and Morali in full battle mode. For one very tense moment, neither man seemed to be aware that Belolo had made an across-town dash to play mediator at a moment's notice.

"That fucking boy is not going to be in the movie!" Allan screamed at Morali.

"If Dennis isn't in the movie, then I'm leaving as producer!" Morali threatened, "and you can't use any of my music!"

"I'll sue you, you fucker! I'll sue! We've got a contract!"

As Belolo quickly deciphered the situation, Allan refused to put Morali's newest boyfriend, Dennis Parker, in the movie. Morali insisted on the casting, and was ready to use his leverage as owner of the Village People franchise to get his way. Belolo understood the problem. "Allan and Jacques shared a similar taste in men," he says, and in this case, Morali had won out with Dennis Parker. In one of his rare moments of piety, Allan claimed that he didn't want Parker in the movie because the twenty-year-old was "that *porno* actor!" The adjective "porno" had never before been uttered with such abject disgust by Allan Carr. But it was the truth. Dennis Parker possessed an impressive X-rated résumé, cranking out several gay porn movies per year under the nom de cinema Wade Nichols. Playing matchmaker, Belolo eventually succeeded in convincing the two warring parties that "le boyfriend" could be cast—but only as an extra.

The next day on the set, back at La Galleria, Allan thanked Belolo. "You are the Henry Kissinger of this movie!" he said, giving him a big kiss.

As Randy Jones observed, "Parker's wasn't a very big part." In the finished film, "You can see Dennis standing there with Bruce Jenner and Valerie Perrine on a balcony." It was only five seconds of screen time and no lines, but lots of on-the-set peace as Allan's big blowout in San Francisco finally came to an end. His movie now rested in the can, ready for the editor. Standing there on the La Galleria balcony, he looked down as his crew began to dismantle the stage and move their equipment from the building. "I remember him at the end of it," says Steve Guttenberg. "He was higher than God. And tired, just exhausted."

Back in Los Angeles, the film spawned two, not just one, wrap parties. The official one, under Allan's careful supervision, took place at the MGM studios in Culver City, and Allan implored his cast and crew "to savor the moment. Do you realize this is the very sound stage that used to house Esther Williams's pool?"

The following night there was to be a more intimate farewell party at Jacques Morali's rented house in the Hollywood Hills. Still smarting from their catfight at La Galleria, Allan took a dig at Morali when he told the assembled cast and crew, "Don't forget to take these centerpieces for tomorrow night's party."

If Allan thought that Morali didn't have the clout, or cash, to throw a memorable party, he guessed wrong. For his event, the Frenchman got the Ritchie Family to perform, but the highlight of the party came when the Village People presented Allan with a life-size doll of himself. "It looked like Allan," says Felipe Rose, "right down to the glasses, the muumuu, the necklaces, the little sneakers."

Allan recoiled at the sight of it. "What is that?" he groused.

"It's you!" said Rose.

Allan was not pleased.

"It looked like a big Muppet," says Belolo.

"Actually, it looked like a very old Muppet," says Rose.

For the most part, "The party was fun and wild," says Arlene Phillips. At least, while it lasted. "But there was a strange feeling at that party. It was over. It was like somehow disco had soured."

fifteen

Mike Todd Jr.

Allan had been nearly a constant presence on the *Can't Stop the Music* set, given a stop or two at Cedars-Sinai. Now it was time to indulge his real expertise: promotion. Much of it was planned, but some of the press attention even Allan didn't want. When word came down that ABC's *20/20* planned to air an exposé of the Village People, one that would reveal the true sexual orientation of its members and their fan base, the producers were genuinely worried. Allan cautioned Belolo, "You better take care of Jacques."

Belolo put it delicately to his effeminate partner. "Don't act like a woman," he cautioned. To assuage Morali's ego, Belolo advised the ABC producers that they introduce Morali as "the man who created the Village People," and that they call him, simply, "the money man."

"But Jacques couldn't contain himself," says Belolo, and five minutes into the TV interview, his wrists went limp and his hands started flying as he went from sounding like a pseudobasso to a castrato. Otherwise, it was a tame profile by even 1979 standards, and hardly qualified as an exposé.

While ABC revealed that "Homosexuals brought their clothes and lifestyle out of the closet and into the streets of Greenwich Village," the network never identified any of the Village People members as being gay. Morali, despite his flamboyant gestures, said nothing controversial. He kept it simple. "A lightbulb went off inside my brain," he said, referring to the "American icons" of the cop, construction worker, and sailor, which he knew would make a great singing group. His G-rated comments were interspersed with footage of the Village

People recording a new song, "(I Like It) Sleazy," because, as Morali explained, "'Sleazy' is the new in word."

Allan, for his part, barely appeared on *20/20*, and received only enough airtime to say of Morali, "I didn't know him. He didn't know me." Elsewhere in the report, Nancy Walker called the Village People "adorable." That's as controversial as it got, and everyone aboard the *Can't Stop the Music* production let out a collective sigh of relief.

Allan now directed his full attention to the real press campaign, which kicked off with a supersize billboard on Sunset Boulevard. At Allan's prompting, Los Angeles mayor Tom Bradley proclaimed it "Can't Stop the Music Day," and to return the favor, Allan rented the biggest billboard on the Sunset Strip, at the juncture of Havenhurst Drive, just south of the famed Chateau Marmont hotel, where John Belushi would famously overdose two years later.

At least, Allan called it "the biggest billboard on Sunset Strip." He also claimed having "the longest red carpet in the world," which was the one he unrolled for more than a city block, all the way from Schwab's drugstore at Laurel Drive and Sunset Boulevard to the billboard, which had been covered with enough white fabric to drape, well, a very large billboard.

Before the momentous unveiling, the Village People and other cast members got ripped at Schwab's, as did Allan's usual press corps hangers-on, who'd grown fat on his liquor and food ever since he announced the film's production a year ago. This band of imbibers made a motley ensemble as they stumbled together down the long, long red carpet to the big, big billboard. The *Hollywood Reporter*'s Robert Osborne called it "the biggest photo op ever," and to take advantage of that fact, a grandstand filled with fans greeted the *Can't Stop the Music* entourage in front of the Chateau Marmont.

"Are we supposed to perform?" the Village People asked each other, still crowd-shy after their city hall run-in with several angry San Franciscans.

As Allan carefully explained his billboard stratagem, the cast would march down the red carpet, then be hoisted high above the street on a platform, where Valerie Perrine would pull a trigger to set off a huge fireworks display. The white fabric draping the billboard would drop as fans shrieked, applauded, and carried on at the sight of the triple-life-size image of their idols, the Village People.

The publicity stunt went as planned until Perrine pulled the trigger—at which point the vast fireworks display that Allan had promised produced a few red-white-and-blue sparks and a *pphfffft* noise. David Hodo turned to Randy Jones: "Uh oh, not a good omen."

From there, the *Can't Stop the Music* cast retraced their steps on the Sunset Boulevard red carpet for a sit-down dinner at the Director's Guild, but not before Allan physically pulled the Village People from the buffet line and ordered them to wait until the media and industry guests had been served. Such treatment chafed the group's hirsute leather man, Glenn Hughes, who complained to a reporter, "It's constantly shoved down our throats that everything is out of our control. We're pushed around, told what to do, and put into embarrassing situations."

Morali threatened to fire his leather man, but it was too late. The *Can't Stop the Music* train had already left for New York City.

"*That* was my initiation to pharmaceutical drugs," says Tamara Rawitt.

As VP of publicity and marketing at AFD, the company releasing *Can't Stop the Music*, Rawitt held sway over several plans to promote the film on the East Coast. From the beginning, she didn't expect the Allan Carr assignment to be an easy one since "the buzz" around the company, based on early screenings, pegged the movie as *Can't Stand the Music*. Then again, two years ago those in-house pundits at Paramount had dismissed *Grease*. Rawitt shared several phone conversations with Allan prior to his arrival in New York City. Her first face-to-face confrontation, however, didn't come until his first morning in New York. It began with a 3 a.m. phone call. It was Allan. He was screaming, "The stems of the calla lilies in the Indian's room aren't tall enough!" The Indian in question was the Village People's Native American, Felipe Rose, and as Rawitt well knew, he and the rest of the *Can't Stop the Music* cast, along with Allan, were now staying in the tony Plaza Hotel on Central Park South.

Allan's tirade didn't stop with the calla lilies. "There aren't enough champagne truffles in my room!" he continued to scream.

Rawitt threw on some street clothes, and fearing that she might be fired from her AFD gig, cabbed it to the Plaza Hotel to beg forgiveness at 3:30 a.m.

When she arrived, Allan sat draped in a caftan, posing commando-style in a French provincial chair. The stems of the calla lilies and the meager number of truffles were, in his estimation, "egregious errors that could not be repeated." The success of *Can't Stop the Music* depended on it. Rawitt knew then that the next few days would require an hourly intake of Valium.

In some respects, she deeply admired the man. "Allan was astoundingly astute," she says. "He had a sixth sense that was almost psychic, telepathic. He could just read a room right away."

For instance, the board room of Baskin-Robbins in New York City.

Despite its frothy fun product, the ice cream company is a highly corporate place, and for his pitch to use B-R to help promote *Can't Stop the Music,* Allan left his dark blue Ralph Lauren jacket in the closet and chose instead to wear a red, white, and blue bejeweled caftan. Rawitt tried to contain her laughter as she watched Allan, his fingers encased in more diamonds and gold than a Vegas showgirl, introduce himself to a half-dozen uptight, two-piece-suited VPs. Having disarmed, if not stunned, them, Allan proceeded to deliver his spiel to the men from Baskin-Robbins.

"I've got a new flavor for you!" Allan began. "This new flavor will be called Can't Stop the Nuts."

Rawitt called the Baskin-Robbins pitch "one of the great moments in Jimmy Glick showbiz," since Allan presented his new flavor as if it were the greatest invention since rocky road ice cream. Or possibly "since the Holy Grail," says Rawitt. As he had done throughout his career, Allan so assaulted straight men with his blatant, seemingly frivolous brand of homosexuality that they found themselves, in the end, totally receptive to, if not downright beguiled by, his hard-sell pitch. "After the board got over the shock of Allan, they did agree to make Can't Stop the Nuts their sixtieth flavor," says Rawitt. "Considering what the movie was about, that name—Can't Stop the Nuts—was a double, if not triple, entendre."

Allan's wooing of Baskin-Robbins was only the beginning, as he soon lined up Famous Amos, Fleishmann's, Sports-in-Motion, and Roach Inc. to market, respectively, Can't Stop the Cookies, Can't Stop the Spirits, Can't Stop the Fashion, and Can't Stop the Accessories.

Now, suited up with all that tie-in armor, he prepared to do battle with the moviegoing public. To premiere his movie in New York City or Los Angeles would have been the obvious choice. "But being the hometown boy who made good was very important to Allan," says Kathy Berlin, another publicist on the movie. Allan went aquatic in the Windy City. "I remember mermaids in a fountain," says David Hodo. To keep the finned ladies company, Allan put his bartenders in hip boots and yellow slickers to wade through the pool to serve 2,000 guests in the Hyatt Regency's Glass House atrium, which also came equipped with a three-story waterfall and circular staircase that Allan filled with balloons.

"I saw Michael Todd do his *Around the World in 80 Days* party when I was six or seven," Allan announced to his guests, "and I thought, well, we want to do that." From a balcony in the atrium, he called out, "Come on up here to the second level, where there's even more food." And he had other reasons to celebrate. At nearby Lake Forest College, his alma mater, they had just renamed a building the Allan Carr Theater, inspired by his recent $100,000 donation.

As he often did, Allan took out press insurance by casting journalists in his film. With *Can't Stop the Music,* he gave his old friend and *Chicago Tribune* reporter Aaron Gold a cameo in the film. In his column, Gold ignored the movie and instead wrote about the party and its "18,000 pounds of ice that were used for the various ice sculptures and the 27 musicians, including female violinists in evening gowns, [who] played continuously."

The *Hollywood Reporter* columnist Robert Osborne attended the Chicago premiere with his friend actress Barbara Rush, who played Bruce Jenner's mother in the film. The two of them sat directly in front of the diminutive Nancy Walker, and being a gracious man, Osborne turned to the director of the hour to offer, "Don't worry. When the movie starts, I'll scrunch down."

Walker waved away his concern. "You think I'm sitting through this piece of shit again?" she replied, and she exited the room as soon as the movie started.

Just as Walker grew bored by her opus, Allan's inordinate interest in one of the film's headliners waned as well, and shortly after the Chicago screening, he confided to friends, "Steve Guttenberg should have remained in dental school."

Before he left his hometown, Allan phoned his old friend Joanne Cimbalo to offer an invitation to the New York premiere of *Can't Stop the Music.* "I've chartered a plane. Come join us!" Allan insisted. He even ordered up a limousine so Cimbalo and her young daughter, Margaret, could get to the airport in style. In fact, Allan made sure that everyone, from his many stars to the cinematographer, Bill Butler, each had a limousine.

"It was such an Auntie Mame thing," Cimbalo says of her six-mile-high rendezvous with the Village People. It was an exceedingly happy crowd. Even the flight attendants put down their napkins and tea bags to tweak each other's noses with something that looked like powered sugar.

Since his childhood in Highland Park, Allan had dreamed of replicating the showbiz miracle that his idol Mike Todd created at Madison Square Garden to launch *Around the World in 80 Days.* "Allan was affected by Mike Todd's party, and he always wanted to make a film out of Todd's life," says Thom Mount. But that impresario's bit of 1950s derring-do raised a dilemma: Todd had already used up the biggest venue in town. Yankee Stadium might be available. But who wanted to trek up to the Bronx? Allan thought out-of-the-box to top Todd. The Metropolitan Opera house was more prestigious than Madison Square Garden, but at a mere 3,800 seats, it was woefully inadequate in size.

At last, he had it. "We'll hold the party on the plaza of Lincoln Center!" he announced to the people at AFD. As Allan planned it, the premiere screening at the plush Ziegfeld Theater would afford invited guests a very short trip (ten minutes in evening traffic) uptown to the party at Lincoln Center. Allan did borrow at least one aspect of his *Can't Stop the Music* party from Mike Todd, and that was his circus theme. AFD wags gave it a very contemporary spin. "It was Cirque du So Gay," says Rawitt.

Granted, the Canadian circus extravaganza was a good four years away from being founded, in 1984, not that Allan ever took credit for inspiring the multimedia circus franchise. In some respects, his Lincoln Center party easily trumped the *Around the World in 80 Days* event at Madison Square Garden. Unlike Mike Todd's event, Allan's would be an outdoor affair. Also, "The logistics at Lincoln Center were insane," says Rawitt. Circuses pulled in and out of Madison Square Garden on a regular basis back in the 1950s. But no one had ever built trapezes over the pool garden in front of the Vivian Beaumont Theatre at Lincoln Center. "We had to bring in circus equipment and rig everything, and there wasn't time for rehearsal," she says. "Could the acrobats do all their stunts? The safety provisions were just amazing."

In the beginning, the AFD folk didn't believe Allan's threat to stage his party on the Lincoln Center Plaza, because no one thought he could shepherd the necessary paperwork through the arts complex's enormous bureaucracy. But they didn't know Allan.

"He bludgeoned everyone with money," says Rawitt.

"He gave Lincoln Center a major contribution," says Kathy Berlin.

Despite the enormous preparation that the Lincoln Center gala required, Allan never lost sight of the fact that he also had a movie to debut. Where the party would be a magnificent hodgepodge of excitement—trapeze artists, jugglers, clowns, brass bands—the premiere itself was to be an exercise in minimalism, albeit extravagant minimalism.

"It will be white!" he proclaimed, taking a cue from the already infamous "Milkshake" number. He ordered Theoni Aldredge to make all-white outfits for the Village People's movie debut. Whereas the performers had started their career wearing flannel and jeans and leather, Aldredge encased them in white silk and satin and matching beads and glitter. Each star got his own white stretch limousine for the night. White was definitely the look, if not the theme. And it went beyond the mere visuals.

"It's the only movie premiere where they asked, 'Do you want your popcorn powdered?'" Rawitt joked.

And there were other drugs of choice. David Hodo took a Quaalude or two during his limousine ride to the Ziegfeld Theater. He'd given up on the white powder sometime earlier. "We were traveling around the world, eight times in a couple of years." And the cocaine got him up and going. "This is great, this is the answer," he thought. But one day in Norway he poured his stash out the window, and "never touched it again."

Quaaludes were another story. The powerful sedative, if it didn't induce instant narcolepsy, left some adherents feeling floatingly mellow. In Hodo's case, it also made him fall flat on his face as soon as he stepped out of the rented white limousine and onto the rented red carpet. He'd never worn the Theoni Aldredge–designed white metallic construction boots before. "They were cheesy, and the toes caught the rim of the limousine," he recalls. And combined with the debilitating wooziness of the Quaaludes, he landed on his hands and knees. "God never lets me get too grand," he said on the spot, sprawling out like a sun-bleached starfish.

To ensure an appropriately adulatory opening night for their *Can't Stop the Music,* Henri Belolo and Jacques Morali flew over forty friends from Paris. But even that core group of fans didn't help to goose the opening-night response at the Ziegfeld. "It was a very cold reception," says Belolo. "There was polite applause. Not wow!"

Publicist Kathy Berlin feared as much, and worried that no one would go to the party after seeing the movie. "Which is why we spent so much on limousines," she recalls. Allan insisted, "Do what you have to do to get the celebrities there." As a result, all VIPs, from the Metropolitan Museum's Thomas Hoving to Stockard Channing, had a limousine at their service for the entire evening. (The limo bill for all U.S. premieres of *Can't Stop the Music:* $118,000.)

The movie had its supporters. Allan's friend Jack Martin, now with the *New York Post,* said it was the "best film musical since *Singin' in the Rain,*" and Martin's old boss Liz Smith wrote not one but two love letters to *Can't Stop the Music* in her syndicated column.

Elsewhere, "People were relieved," says Kathy Berlin, to be out of the theater and at the party, where the naysayers gathered in a tent to eat and, more
important, dish what they'd just seen onscreen. The all-white motif at the
Ziegfeld spilled over to Lincoln Center, and white plastic hard hats found their
way into everybody's hands so that they could all be part of the lack-of-color
scheme. The hard hats effectively reflected light from the several dozen mir-
rored disco balls that were suspended on wires across the north plaza. Allan
knew how to make a grand entrance, not just for himself but his entire cast,
which entered the Lincoln Center Plaza between two gospel choirs. The *Can't
Stop the Music* cast, together with Allan, then stepped onto scaffolding that
hoisted them up over the crowd as they were serenaded by the choirs and a
high school marching band that began its procession from the opposite corner
of the plaza.

Perhaps the grips and riggers were more cautious securing the circus high
wires and trapezes, because no sooner did Allan and his actors begin their rise
above the multitudes than the scaffolding started to shake and groan as the
crane lifted them skyward. Only Allan exuded absolute serenity in the face of
possible disaster. "He was Mussolini on the balcony," says Ron Bernstein. "He
was the great emperor meeting his people."

In case anyone had time to look elsewhere, there were clowns on stilts, acrobats in silver lamé leotards doing back flips, trapeze artists swinging high in
the air, and—just like at Mike Todd's Madison Square party—elephants. If the
assembled guests were jazzed by the sheer spectacle of it all, the Village People
were not. Smiling, they waved by rote. "At that point, it wasn't a thrill to be
someplace at ten o'clock at night in your gear," says Hodo. "Basically, we weren't
into any of it at all."

For the novices at such Allan Carr–inspired commotion—Bruce Jenner and
Steve Guttenberg among them—it was another story. "It was the biggest party
I'd ever been to in my life!" says Jenner. "I'd never seen anything like it."

"It was totally out of control!" says Guttenberg. "There were 5,000 people,
and Allan was there totally controlling, being bigger than life, and directing people, telling people what to do: laugh, eat, drink. He lived it!"

The Lincoln Center event so psyched Allan that he actually underwent an
out-of-body experience and started to refer to himself only in the third person.
"Doesn't Allan Carr know how to give a great party?" he asked. "New York City
asked for an Allan Carr party and New York City got an Allan Carr party!"

The party was a circus. In addition to the elephants, the tightrope walkers, the trapeze artists, and a couple hundred singers and musicians, Allan made sure that any guest could become part of the show—and he provided the costumes and extravagant makeup. Those makeover stations, however, proved to be a minor waste of money.

"The crowd was a lot of gay guys and a lot of skin and lots of drag," says Rawitt. "It was Studio 54 outside and put front and center." In other words, it was the West Village Halloween parade brought uptown. Photographers had a field day, but not captured in their pictures were the many faces of the Irish cops who'd never been to Studio 54. Incredulous, insane, and unapologetically homophobic—their craggy-faced expressions congealed with a childlike wonder mixed with abject horror. "That party was this last bastion of freedom, of excess and sexual carelessness," says Rawitt. "Allan Carr italicized the end of an era with that party."

Whatever hoopla ensued at Lincoln Center, the press flotsam it produced failed to translate into human bodies buying tickets at the Ziegfeld Theater the next day: The gargantuan movie palace sold virtually no tickets for its first matinee.

Into this BO void dropped the *New York Post*'s film reporter Stephen M. Silverman, who, days earlier, had scheduled an interview with Allan. His newspaper had loved the party, gushing in print, "Not since Cecil B. DeMille parted the Red Sea has Hollywood produced a more spectacular show."

But a party is not a movie. When Silverman arrived at the Plaza the day after the film's premiere at the Ziegfeld, Allan's many assistants scurried about the hotel suite, running back and forth to answer phone calls, locate pieces of lost paper that were the wrong pieces of paper, and otherwise nurse the bruised ego of their producer, who kept braying into various phone receivers, "This movie is so great. Great! Fabulous! It's doing blockbuster business!" In fact, *Can't Stop the Music* had tanked on its very first public screening.

Allan soldiered on regardless. "Do you know that Walter Mondale requested no fewer than fourteen tickets to the Washington, D.C., premiere?" he asked the reporter.

Silverman knew Allan to be a quote machine, a journalist's dream. But that Friday he confronted a very different Allan Carr, one he'd never seen before. This was the distraught Allan Carr. "Allan had been hit with a brick in the head and was still trying to conduct an interview, but his mind was elsewhere," says Silverman. Allan's thoughts, much less his sentences, didn't segue, and his agitated body language belied the calm of a producer who knew he sat on top of a hit movie. *"Can't Stop the Music* was a disaster," says Silverman, "and Allan obviously knew it on Day 1."

As did the world by Day 4: *Can't Stop the Music* racked up a dismal $1.6 million in 423 theaters during its first weekend.

None of which stopped Allan from playing the savvy marketer, and he immediately launched Plan B, which included a month-long tour around the world to promote *Can't Stop the Music.* Bruce Jenner found a certain educational element in the many screenings that greeted him from St. Louis to San Francisco, where Dykes on Bikes escorted Allan into the Golden Gate Theater, and Los Angeles, where Allan attempted to replicate the streets of Greenwich Village on the plaza of the Music Center, and secured the Dorothy Chandler Pavilion, home of the L.A. Philharmonic, to unspool *Can't Stop the Music,* the first movie ever to play the august performance hall. Most audiences were respectfully quiet, but in San Francisco, they guffawed at the movie's strong current of homoerotica. "There's one scene where one of the Village People turns and we see a red handkerchief in his back pocket," says Jenner, referring to a gay symbol for fist fucking. "It got a big laugh in San Francisco. People didn't get that in St. Louis." Otherwise, as he traveled from city to city, Jenner became increasingly squeamish at having to watch himself morph from conservative lawyer to boy toy, complete with short-short cutoffs and bare midriff, in screening after screening. More painful were the radio interviews. After he said goodbye on air, DJs told him, "Our listeners didn't want any more disco."

It was not a great time to release any movie, much less a disco movie. As *Variety* reported on its front page that September, "Summer B.O. Worst in Four Years as Ticket Sales Off More than 10% from 1979."

Costing $20 million, *Can't Stop the Music* brought in only $2 million at the U.S. box office. Overseas sales were even more disappointing, with the exception of three markets: Japan, Australia, and Bali. When decidedly upbeat numbers from those countries rolled in, Allan took solace and referred to *Can't Stop the Music* as "my island picture."

Jacques Morali took no comfort, and began referring to it as "a 1955 Doris Day movie," and not in a good way.

Allan would go on to produce other films and projects, but none with his close friend and scriptwriting partner. On August 6, less than two months after the release of *Can't Stop the Music,* Bronte Woodard died of AIDS. The memorial service in Beverly Hills was distinguished for the prominent number of

porn stars in attendance, many of whom had been unofficial guests of honor at
Woodard's various Saturday afternoon parties over the years. Randal Kleiser
and Allan spoke at the memorial, and it was obvious from what the two men
said, as well as the music played, which Allan Carr/Bronte Woodard movie the
deceased writer preferred. The service included several selections from the
Grease soundtrack but not one song by the Village People.

sixteen

The Queen and I

Can't Stop the Music didn't play out as Allan dreamed, but it did lead him to a former, if not first, love. "Allan had flown to Paris on the Concorde, and I suggested he see *La Cage aux folles*," says Henri Belolo. The film *La Cage aux folles* was yet to be released, but its source material, Jean Poiret's stage comedy of the same name, had been running for five years on the Paris boards, and it was that show that Belolo recommended to Allan when they first embarked on their *Discoland* project. Belolo rightfully assumed that the stage farce, about a drag performer who must impersonate a woman in order to impress the future in-laws of his male partner's son, would delight his flamboyant friend from Hollywood.

"Allan immediately saw it as a musical," says Belolo. It was summer 1978. At the time, Allan had little interest in something called *La Cage aux folles*. In fact, "I dreaded going," Allan said. "I thought it was going to be another boulevard comedy in a language I wouldn't understand." But not wanting to disappoint Belolo, he saw the play. "And of course that night it hit me: I had to have the American rights," he said.

Upon returning to New York, Allan phoned John Breglio, the lawyer he'd worked with on *A Chorus Line* and *Survive!* Breglio immediately put out feelers only to learn that David Merrick was already in touch with Poiret about turning the play into a stage musical. Allan had never produced a Broadway musical, while Merrick had birthed dozens, including the hits *Gypsy*, *Hello, Dolly!*, and *Promises, Promises*. Eager to play Broadway's David to Merrick's Goliath, Allan ultimately settled on the only strategy that always works.

129

"Allan put a lot of money on the table," says Breglio. "He paid $100,000 for a one-year option. No one in his right mind had ever done that before. Most [options] were $50,000 tops then."

Merrick, a shrewd businessman, knew an outrageous price tag when he saw one. He was, after all, David Merrick, the greatest producer of Broadway musicals. Allan Carr was merely someone with a lot of money who had never produced anything on the Great White Way. It was no contest, obviously.

Poiret took the money and Allan won.

So many great Broadway musicals are, at their core, shows about putting on shows—*Annie Get Your Gun, Gypsy, Funny Girl, Cabaret, Chicago. La Cage aux folles* fell into that time-honored vein, even if it would break new ground as the first Broadway musical ever to feature same-sex lovers. Then again, the movie version of *La Cage aux folles*, starring Ugo Tognazzi and Michel Serrault as boyfriends, turned into a surprise hit. "The Broadway musical will be even bigger," Allan believed. Movie gender benders like *Tootsie* and *Victor/Victoria* did well at the box office in 1982, and top-drawer talents like director Mike Nichols, book writer Jay Presson Allen, and choreographer Tommy Tune soon shared Allan's enthusiasm for turning the material into a stage tuner. With such expensive talent at his disposal, it's possible that Allan felt just the slightest urge to economize, or at least mix things up, when he rounded out the creative team with a songwriter who'd never composed a Broadway show.

Maury Yeston, a professor of music at Yale, had written incidental music for Tune's off Broadway production of Caryl Churchill's comedy *Cloud Nine,* and he was also "in talks" to adapt Federico Fellini's autobiographical film *8½* for Broadway, again with Tune. When Tune mentioned the *La Cage aux folles* project to Yeston, he cautioned him that Marvin Hamlisch, Cy Coleman, and Jerry Herman were already circling to be the tuner's composer.

Herman, especially, had his cheerleaders.

Producer Martin Richards (*Sweeney Todd, Chicago*) also wanted to turn *La Cage aux folles* into a stage musical. "I saw the movie one afternoon with a bunch of ladies who carried their shopping bags into the movie theater," he says. "They loved it. I flipped out over it." When he checked on the stage rights, he found they were held by Allan Carr. "He was a genius with press and publicity, so far ahead of his time in so many ways. I suggested Jerry Herman to Allan," Richards says.

Richards and Allan were not strangers. They'd already joined forces to try to bring *Chicago* to the screen, and regarding that movie project, Allan promised "a celebrity in every cell." On *La Cage,* his brain blossomed forth with even more ideas.

An occasional resident of the UN Plaza Hotel, Allan invited Richards to his East Side pied-à-terre to discuss *La Cage aux folles* and possibly have him come aboard as a coproducer. Over the phone, Allan told Richards that "Jerry Herman is perfect!" Richards thought he'd sweeten the meeting by bringing a potential book writer, James Kirkwood, who had done similar duties on *A Chorus Line.* Allan was in a typically festive mood that day, serving champagne, strawberries, and heavy cream. "And he wore a little nightgown down to his rear end," Richards recalls. Allan couldn't contain his excitement at meeting Kirkwood, and he launched into fond recollections of managing Marvin Hamlisch and saving *A Chorus Line* from the ego of Michael Bennett. Finally, he got right to it.

"So, Marty?" he asked. "Can you get Jerry Herman to write a couple of songs to show us how he'd handle this material?"

Richards smiled. Pleasantries were exchanged, and then Richards departed the UN Plaza Hotel, realizing that Allan didn't know the ways of Broadway. Seasoned talent like Jerry Herman wrote *nada* on spec.

Herman always considered *La Cage aux folles* the show he most wanted to write. "It's hard finding source material. I knew in my heart that I knew how to do this material," says the composer of *Mame* and *Hello, Dolly!* "But I just wrote it off as the show that got away."

Unlike Herman, Yeston had no such qualms about putting his talent and reputation on the line. "Look, give me a chance," Yeston told Allan. "Let me write something on spec. I'll write six songs."

Allan never balked at getting something for nothing, so he handed Yeston the musical's book, titled *The Queen and I* by Jay Presson Allen, who'd written the play *The Prime of Miss Jean Brodie* and the *Cabaret* screenplay. "Call me when you've written your six songs," he added.

Yeston promised he'd have them in two weeks, and he set to work. "Mike Nichols, Allan Carr, Jay Presson Allen. It was overwhelming for me. I had nothing to lose," he says.

Yeston liked that Jay Presson Allen had Americanized the material by switching the *La Cage aux folles* locale from Saint-Tropez to New Orleans. Yeston knew that jazz milieu, and the first song he wrote was "The Queen of Basin Street," about the female impersonator Zaza, the show's lead character.

Nichols loved the song, and so did Allan. "*That* will be the title of the show. *The Queen of Basin Street!*" Allan announced. He had his composer. Who cared that few people knew of Maury Yeston? "He's got talent!" Allan said. "Tie him to the sofa!"

Instead, Yeston took a leave of absence without pay from Yale after his agent, the legendary Flora Roberts, won him an advance of $10,000 to write *The Queen of Basin Street* score. "It was a thrilling, heady experience," Yeston recalls. "At that point," he adds ruefully.

Indeed, problems were already brewing in the august law offices of Paul, Weiss, Rifkind, Wharton & Garrison. Breglio, head of the firm's theater department, quickly discovered that negotiating the contracts for creative talent of the caliber of Mike Nichols, Jay Presson Allen, and Tommy Tune was not easy, and as their deals grew richer and richer, Allan only grew poorer and poorer as a producer. Breglio soon found himself in an awkward position. Despite the star power of the show's creative triumvirate, the lawyer "simply couldn't recommend" the package's economics to Allan.

While Roberts repped Yeston, the remainder of Allan's creative team— Nichols, Tune, and Allen—shared just one agent: Sam Cohn. ICM's mighty agent lunched daily at the Russian Tea Room and never returned phone calls or wore a tie—all of which made him the most powerful, as well as elusive, agent on the East Coast.

When Breglio told Allan he couldn't make financial sense of the *Queen of Basin Street* creative package, Allan didn't waste a breath. "OK, I'm flying in to deal with Cohn," he said. Allan got on the next airplane to New York City, but prior to meeting with Cohn, he called a powwow in his new apartment. Now that he was a Broadway producer, Allan decided it was time to move out of the UN Plaza Hotel and into the penthouse at the St. Moritz, once the living space of the most famed and feared columnist in America, the red-baiting Walter Winchell. The St. Moritz penthouse is a historic triplex that, in addition to its view of Central Park from three terraces, offers its residents a sauna and a greenhouse in the sky. Even the most sophisticated New Yorkers were impressed by the space, and many of them didn't notice, at first glance, that Allan had decorated the art deco apartment in a very California style, with lots of matching, oversized pale furniture.

Sitting atop the St. Moritz, Allan welcomed Jay Presson Allen, Maury Yeston, and the composer's agent, Flora Roberts, to his new apartment, which he'd already dubbed Viewhaven in honor of his other "havens" around the world. He avoided the fact that, in this case, he rented and did not own.

Jay Presson Allen came ready for a fight that day. She began by saying that she loved Yeston's music for *Cloud Nine,* the show Tommy Tune had directed at the tiny Theatre de Lys on Christopher Street in the West Village. Niceties out of the way, she then leveled her sights at *The Queen of Basin Street.* "This show has too many directors," she said. "Fire Mike Nichols and replace him with Tommy Tune." Instead of registering dismay or even surprise, Allan's eyes grew big. "Fire Mike Nichols?" he asked.

Yeston blurted out, "Nobody fires Mike Nichols!"

Allan's eyes more than glistened behind his tinted aviator glasses. "Fire Mike Nichols? I'll be a legend!" he whispered in his best Norma Desmond impersonation.

"Don't break this team up," Yeston begged.

Jay Presson Allen ignored the Broadway novice. "It could work," she said.

The next day, wearing a sports coat and tie, Allan walked into the offices of ICM on West 57th Street. He brought Breglio with him. No longer the flamboyant party-giver, Allan presented himself as "the hardened businessman," according to the lawyer. There was no stroking of Cohn's massive ego as Allan took him to the mat.

"Sam, it's too much," he began. "I love them. Mike, Tommy, and Jay. But they are too famous and they are too rich for me. I can't afford it. I'm going elsewhere."

Allan left Cohn speechless. It was over. Finished. Allan had done what he always wanted and turned himself into a legend. What Cohn must have been thinking is what everyone else in the New York theater world would soon be shouting in Shubert Alley: "No one fires Mike Nichols!"

Chaos among the original team ensued. "It was a big uproar. Everybody got mad at one another," said Jay Presson Allen. "Mike and I still don't speak." (That is, until the writer died in 2006.) But somehow she remained sanguine regarding her onetime theater producer. "Any production is a series of disasters," she offered. "If you're going to do that kind of work, it is wonderful to have someone who can deal with it humorously, and Allan Carr could see the humor in almost anything. Allan was honest, and did pretty much what he said he was going to do." Except for firing practically everybody on the original team.

For a moment, rumors circulated that Allan would increase Tune's responsibilities on the project, keeping him on as choreographer *and* making him director. *Cloud Nine* had opened to rave reviews and great box office, and on

Broadway his little musical-that-could, *A Day in Hollywood/A Night in the Ukraine,* also scored.

But Tune could never bring himself to pick up the directorial pieces—or continue as choreographer. As Tune told Yeston, "My friendship with Mike is more important and takes precedence."

Jay Presson Allen recalled the situation, "Tommy was very nervous about it and correctly so." She and Yeston, however, found themselves in different boats since they had essentially completed their respective work on book and score. Allen, a famous writer, could proceed to one of the many other projects that she currently juggled. Yeston, on the other hand, had no other project—or source of income.

Allan remained jubilant regardless of a creative team that now numbered only one: Yeston. With casual fanfare, he insisted that the composer meet him for lunch at the Fairmont Hotel in San Francisco. It didn't matter that Yeston remained on the East Coast, leaving him no choice but to fly west to salvage his career and finances. There on Nob Hill, Allan laid it out for his composer. "You'll write the score and the book, and I've just hired this great new director, Michael Smuin."

Smuin?

"He's got a big hit on Broadway with *Sophisticated Ladies,*" continued Allan, referring to the Duke Ellington revue. Blithely, he changed the subject: "Now, I want you to be my date tonight. I want you to go to Finocchio's. It's a great drag club. It's research!" The switch from Mike Nichols to Michael Smuin left Yeston stricken. He couldn't hide his disappointment. "What's the matter with you?" Allan asked, oblivious of his composer's concerns.

Yeston tried to explain. "I can't help it. I have a nine-year-old son, I'm a professor. I left my job with no pay. And I thought we were doing this show."

Without saying a word, Allan reached into his pocket to pull out a checkbook and began writing. "Use this if you need it," Allan said, handing his cash-strapped composer the check. It was made out to "Maury Yeston" for $150,000.

Yeston didn't know what to say, but he knew enough to be cautious. "Remember, these were the cocaine years," he says of Allan's magnanimous checkbook maneuver. "It was the quintessential Allan Carr gesture. It was the flamboyance of the gesture. In that gesture, he showed both the extraordinary generosity of the man, his desire to be loved, and, at the same time, the narcissism of it." In essence, Allan was telling his impoverished songwriter, "Look at me! I can write a check for $150,000!"

That evening, Allan held court at Finocchio's as he introduced Yeston to the world of drag theater. *"This"*—he waved—"is what our show is all about!" Allan soaked it up. He drank champagne. He signed autographs. He basked in being the most famous person on the premises. This was his milieu, gay San Francisco, and, in Allan's opinion, Yeston merely had to fill in a few missing pieces and *The Queen of Basin Street* would mint money on Broadway. Allan knew it to be true.

When the Finocchio emcee took the stage, he coughed loudly into a handkerchief. "Tonight I have a frog in my throat," he began. "Last night, it was a prince." It was the cue for the entrance of the show girls, all of whom were boys but one.

"That's what I want in our musical," Allan whispered to his bewildered professor-friend. "One girl, the rest are guys. You won't be able to tell. All the chorus girls in our show will be boys—except for one. And she will keep the audience guessing." As far as Allan was concerned, he'd just found the key to unlock the success of his *La Cage aux folles.*

More research meetings with Allan ensued over the following weeks, whether the city was New York, San Francisco, or Honolulu. Then, just as suddenly as they began, the itinerant tête-à-têtes stopped and Yeston couldn't get his producer on the phone.

In the end, Allan needed to break with Yeston, too. The composer had worked closely with Jay Presson Allen, and many of his songs were intrinsically bound to her words in situation and dialogue. To use those songs in a new book written by a different writer risked exposing the project to copyright infringement. What portended an even greater obstacle to Yeston's continued participation was Allan's having purchased the stage rights to only the play *La Cage aux folles.* Unbeknownst to either Yeston or Jay Presson Allen was that Allan had failed to also secure the rights to the movie *La Cage aux folles.*

While the writing duo changed the locale of the story, they "borrowed whole scenes from the movie that never appeared in the play," says Yeston. And in a turn of fate worthy of the Greek gods, those very precious movie rights were now no longer available at any price since they'd been purchased, ironically, by Mike Nichols, who would later fashion the French movie into his own Hollywood movie comedy *The Birdcage,* starring Nathan Lane and Robin Williams as the two lovers, and set in Miami's South Beach. Describing Nichols's one-upmanship, Yeston says, "The best way to achieve revenge is just to wait."

seventeen

Why *Grease* Again?

And there were other reasons that Maury Yeston couldn't get Allan Carr on the phone. Allan's *Grease* agreement with Paramount required that he begin production on the sequel within three years of the original movie. A $5-million check from Paramount depended on Allan's quick segue from *The Queen of Basin Street* to *Grease 2*.

Allan had defied Hollywood wisdom by hiring Nancy Walker to direct *Can't Stop the Music*, and he risked the odds a second time by going with another female director, Patricia Birch, on *Grease 2*. She, at least, had some affinity for the material, having choreographed the first *Grease* movie, as well as the original stage show. But she harbored qualms about undertaking the sequel. "Why *Grease* again? I think I've done it" was her first reaction. It also troubled Birch that neither the original composers, Jim Jacobs and Warren Casey, nor John Travolta and Olivia Newton-John would be doing the sequel.

"I had an idea that John and Olivia would be in the last reel, running a gasoline filling station," says Birch. But even that minor nod to the original was not to be.

Laurence Mark told Allan, "Don't do a sequel without the original stars." But who listens to wise advice with a $5-million check hanging in the balance?

For a moment, Robert Stigwood and Allan toyed with turning *Grease 2* into a vehicle for Bee Gees' brother Andy Gibb. A quick screen test, however, put to rest any thought of Gibb's being an actor.

As that rocker's movie fortunes cratered, a young Scottish actor began to attract attention stateside for his portrayal of a bisexual hustler in an Off-Broadway production of Joe Orton's *Entertaining Mr. Sloane*. His reviews were ecstatic, and such notables as Diane Keaton, Rudolf Nureyev, and Tennessee Williams came to the little Cherry Lane Theatre in Greenwich Village to see the play. A few others came not to see Maxwell Caulfield act but to see him get naked, which he did eight performances a week. One of those voyeurs was Allan Carr.

The night Allan arrived, he brought a date, Valerie Perrine, and afterward, they made the obligatory trip backstage to meet and congratulate the twenty-two-year-old actor. Even though Allan was the producer in search of a new leading man, he was, as usual, a magnanimous host as he led Perrine to Caulfield's dressing room. "Are you going to have him or am I going to try my luck?" Allan asked his friend.

Caulfield's stint in *Entertaining Mr. Sloane* was not the first time Allan had seen the actor in the all together. "I was the It Kid in New York City, and I was being photographed by Bruce Weber and Kenn Duncan and a lot of the hot photographers, specifically known for a somewhat homoerotic style of photography," says Caulfield. "That piqued Allan's interest."

While Allan focused on who would be his leading man, he left it to Patricia Birch to come up with a new femme lead.

Michelle Pfeiffer came in at six-thirty at night for an audition, Birch recalls. "It was a huge dance call. I saw immediately that she had something. She could move." A few months earlier, Pfeiffer had been working at the checkout counter of a Von's supermarket in Orange County. She'd also done a little modeling, when her agent sent her to the *Grease 2* cattle call.

"There were about 1,500 people dancing," Pfeiffer recalls. "They were professional dancers. I almost left halfway through it, but [Birch] was really supportive. I'd hide behind somebody, but I stuck around. When the day was over, I just wanted to die."

Birch saw something beyond Pfeiffer's footwear—"the only way I was able to pick her out was because she was wearing these purple boots," says Birch—and she ordered up a screen test. "She just ate up the camera."

No one ever thought to test her with Maxwell Caulfield. "They were all in love with Maxwell," Birch reveals. "Stigwood and Allan saw him onstage without his clothes."

Stigwood even went so far as to tell Caulfield, "We will be making movies together forever!"

Ready to make his film debut, the young actor took his new status in stride when he described himself to *Life* magazine as "this year's piece of pop meat." He'd beaten not only Andy Gibb but Shaun Cassidy, Rex Smith, Rick Springfield, and, as Caulfield put it, "These guys [who] couldn't act their way out of a paper bag."

Pfeiffer won out over Pat Benatar, Andrea McArdle, Lisa Hartman, and Kristy McNichol. Allan liked to brag that he got Caulfield and Pfeiffer for a mere $100,000 apiece. Cheap, but also not bad for actors whose recent gigs were playing a two-hundred-seat theater in Greenwich Village and a cash register at Von's supermarket. Then again, Allan didn't see it that way, quoting the figure of $1.8 million for pairing those *Blue Lagoon* stars Brooke Shields and Chris Atkins if they reteamed.

It was an arduous audition process not only for Pfeiffer and Caulfield but Judy Garland's daughter Lorna Luft, who would essentially take over for Stockard Channing in the role of bad girl Paulette Rebchuck. Luft recalls, "I did my audition three times for all those suits at Paramount, including that crazy guy who died, Don Simpson, who never took off his sunglasses even though it was night. How many drugs have you taken, Don?" Although Allan said that he had the final say and that the auditioning process was a "mere formality," most actors learned the hard way that "it wasn't enough for Allan to say yes, because of the powers at Paramount," says Luft.

Allan also promised his two new stars, Caulfield and Pfeiffer, that "you are going to be Elvis and Ann-Margret," when instead they ended up, as Caulfield described it, "with my being Olivia Newton-John and Michelle got to be the Danny Zuko character." He wanted to "sing rock and gyrate, except they never let me cut loose like Elvis," for the simple reasons that Caulfield could not sing and gyrate.

Composer Louis St. Louis pinpointed the major casting dilemma. "I couldn't get permission to dub their voices," he said.

St. Louis's bubblegum score didn't require opera singers, but it did need charismatic performers, and the much hoped-for chemistry between Caulfield and Pfeiffer never materialized onscreen because, in part, it never existed offscreen. Caulfield described their relationship alternately as "Michelle and I got along infamously" and "The only thing we had in common was discussing our imminent stardom."

Caulfield, who was married to Juliet Mills, an actress eighteen years his senior, couldn't have been more different from the character he played in *Entertaining Mr. Sloane*. In some ways, Caulfield represented the yin-yang of Allan's attraction to straight men.

"Allan liked that I was a family man," says Caulfield. "He lent my wife and our daughter his beach house in Diamond Head. He threw it over to us for ten days, and there were all these fabulous houseboys running around at our beck and call."

At the same time, Allan found himself sexually attracted to Caulfield. "He didn't come on to you, but you could see it in his eyes," says Caulfield. "They lit up." And in that way, Caulfield's role of a bisexual hustler in *Entertaining Mr. Sloane* was the perfect entrée to Allan's id. He went for Caulfield's onstage character in the Orton play but wound up getting his stay-at-home persona onscreen in *Grease 2*.

A frequent houseguest at Hilhaven Lodge, Patricia Birch saw up close and personal her host's sex drive at work. "He had some pretty rough characters in and out of the house. I worried for him, and I told him so. That rough trade might be the reason he had so much security at Hilhaven," she says, voicing a sentiment that other Allan Carr friends confirm.

Birch soon learned that Allan had problems controlling all his appetites, sexual and otherwise. His teeth wiring, for example, led to his jamming chopped liver through his braces. "It was such a tragic but brilliant portrait of addiction," says his friend Joel Schumacher. "That's what addiction looks like."

Attempting to thwart Allan's lethal intake of food, Birch took it upon herself to lock up the refrigerator that Allan kept at his bedside, and he retaliated by scolding her whenever she came home after hours. "Too late," he would say. If Allan couldn't take care of himself, he liked being "a mother hen" to others, says Birch. Or as Stockard Channing put it, somewhat more darkly, "He had this Mommie Dearest thing."

eighteen

Big B'way Babies

Even though he didn't return Maury Yeston's phone calls, Allan never forgot about the musical *La Cage aux folles* as he readied *Grease 2* for the cameras. Three years after Allen purchased those stage rights, he was back where he started—without a creative team or a director.

But not quite. Shortly before the Sam Cohn showdown, Allan put out feelers to a hungry composer. "Even though there was no deal, Allan knew he had Jerry Herman in his pocket," says John Breglio.

The new *La Cage* team was, in many ways, the artful handiwork of two lovers, Fritz Holt and Barry Brown, who, as the latter put it, "had just come off three huge flops" back-to-back-to-back: *Platinum, The Madwoman of Central Park West,* and *Wally's Café.* "They left us without the money for dinner," says Brown. Allan, more than ready with his checkbook, gave them $10,000 to come aboard as executive producers of *La Cage aux folles.*

To jump-start Holt and Brown, he gave the producing duo a copy of Jay Presson Allen's book. Neither man much liked *The Queen and I;* in fact, they pretty much hated it, and despite their financial straits, the two partners knew not to go forward with the project. No one needs a fourth Broadway flop to his credit.

Allan begged. "I need you, I need you," he said. "How would you do it?"

Jerry Herman's love of the material was now legend in the Broadway community, and a quickly arranged dinner with the *Hello, Dolly!* composer at Ted Hook's Backstage restaurant on West 45th sealed the deal. Holt and Brown had seen Harvey Fierstein's Off-Broadway hit *Torch Song Trilogy,* which presaged

140

by at least a decade the hot topic of gay couples with children. They considered Fierstein a bold but logical choice to write the book about another fictional gay family, and Allan championed the pick. "Because it will increase our credibility in the gay community," he said. Allan saw *Torch Song Trilogy* numerous times, and never forgot to leave his calling card. Whenever he visited the Actors' Playhouse in Greenwich Village, its house manager always commented on the number of Cristal bottles left behind in the aisles.

The wooing of Fierstein didn't require arduous effort. Summoned to Allan's St. Moritz penthouse, the author of *Torch Song Trilogy* wore a big down coat held together by gaffer's tape and staples. Greeting him at the door, Holt and Brown presented the thirty-year-old writer-actor with two dozen red roses, while Allan positioned himself in the middle of the living room, surrounding himself with magnificent views of midtown Manhattan and Central Park. Better yet, Allan held a check for $10,000 and handed it to Fierstein with the greeting, "Go buy a decent coat."

"The idea was to sweep me off my feet," says Fierstein, "and they did." They also made sure that he returned the two dozen red roses before leaving the St. Moritz.

At that meeting, Allan wanted to talk about *La Cage aux folles*, but he made one thing very clear to his new book writer. "We have the rights to the play, not the movie," he said.

"That's OK," replied Fierstein, "since I haven't seen the movie."

Unlike most producers, Allan didn't flinch at his book writer's casual dismissal of the original source material. He liked Fierstein's explanation that he loathed straight actors playing homosexual characters, and how he avoided any and all such efforts in plays and films. (Fierstein would, in time, be forced to make an exception with his first Broadway musical.)

With Fierstein aboard, it was Jerry Herman's turn to pay a visit to Greenwich Village to see *Torch Song Trilogy*. He arrived with his *Hello, Dolly!* star Carol Channing, and the two of them honored the ritual of visiting Fierstein backstage after the performance. The actress wore white. "Like she was going to play tennis," Fierstein recalls. "Even though it wasn't summer."

"Harvey!" she exclaimed in her raspy basso profundo. "Your play reminds me of a gay *Raisin in the Sun*."

Fierstein didn't hold this comment against her date, Jerry Herman.

When it came to picking a director, Brown thought back to his and Holt's 1974 Broadway revival of *Gypsy*, starring Angela Lansbury and directed by

Arthur Laurents. Laurents's book for that bio musical about stripper Gypsy Rose Lee is oft cited as the gold standard.

Holt, however, blanched at the idea of working with Laurents on *La Cage aux folles*. After their success with the *Gypsy* revival, he and Brown tried to find a star actress to appear in Laurents's new play *Scream* but came up empty-handed, and the two parties stopped speaking to each other. When Brown thought of Laurents to direct *La Cage aux folles*—"And who better to help Harvey write the book than the author of *Gypsy*?" said Brown—his partner threw up his hands. "I want nothing to do with him," said Holt, who promptly left for California on a business trip. Undaunted, Brown pursued the mercurial Arthur Laurents to Quogue, Long Island, where the writer-director summered on the ocean.

Laurents expressed both interest and no interest in the project. In characteristic form, he let go with his objections first. "If you want me to write *La Cage aux folles,* the answer is no. That's not what I want."

"Would you consider directing?" Brown asked.

"Do you have writers?" asked Laurents.

Brown mentioned Herman and Fierstein.

"Have you signed them?!" Laurents wanted to know.

"Yes."

"Then yes, I'll do it."

And then, as if the *Scream* dispute had never happened, Laurents launched into a detailed discussion of designers and tech people he wanted to bring aboard the project.

Allan greeted the news with unbridled enthusiasm. "I love it, love it, love it," he exclaimed.

Not everyone was so sure how much Arthur Laurents, Jerry Herman, and Harvey Fierstein would love it, and that included Jerry Herman. "It was a risky situation. Here we were, three people from three totally different worlds. We were so different, but Allan purposefully left us alone, which was good."

The three men were gay and Jewish. Otherwise, they had nothing in common. The chemistry of the theater's greatest contrarian (Laurents), gentlest man (Herman), and edgiest activist (Fierstein) threatened to make very dissonant music. (Fierstein called his two collaborators "the sunshine boy and the grump.") Putting these three together would be Allan's grandest gamble to date.

Over the next three months, Jerry pushed Harvey to be more Broadway and Harvey pushed Jerry to be more political, which left it to Arthur Laurents to play mediator. Allan almost always took Laurents's side, making it three against one. He told Fierstein, "Listen to the old men. We're making a musical here," not a political treatise. Then again, Allan liked that Fierstein gave Herman's show tunes some much needed edge. Of the three, Herman was probably the happiest, or at least, the most grateful, as the three of them set out to create a new show. Working on *La Cage* made him feel like he'd been given a second chance. "I'd been brooding about losing it. It seemed like a miracle that this was happening," says the composer, who hadn't had a big Broadway hit for almost twenty years.

Allan put only one major question to Herman when he signed on. "How do you feel about putting these characters in New Orleans?" he asked, referring to Jay Presson Allen's book for *La Cage aux folles*.

No way, said Herman. "They should be set in Saint-Tropez. It's a flavor that's crucial to the piece."

Herman, Fierstein, and Laurents bonded over their shared opinion of Allen's book. "I got to the first stage direction: 'The décor is old faggot,'" Laurents said of the original *Queen and I* script. "I stopped reading."

In other words, the three men were starting from scratch.

nineteen

Diller's Curse

As the creative team began its work on *La Cage aux folles* in New York City, Allan spent the winter of 1982 in Hollywood watching over his *Grease 2* production, which, at $11.2 million, boasted nearly twice the budget of the original. Paramount was also in production with *Star Trek 2*, and callers to the studio's press department were sometimes greeted with the line, "Paramount Sequels. May I help you?" Everyone thought that *Grease 2*, sequel to the most successful movie musical ever, would demolish *Star Trek 2: The Wrath of Kahn* at the box office. (Instead, the *Star Trek* sequel did nearly $100 million worldwide on its $11-million budget, down from the original's $43-million budget.)

Grease 2 began as the classier of the two fluff projects, even if it was filming not on a Hollywood soundstage but the abandoned Excelsior High School in Norwalk, which clocked in as a twenty-minute drive in good traffic from downtown L.A. That distance was by design, since Paramount's Barry Diller personally banned Allan from the Melrose Avenue lot.

"Barry Diller was not happy with Allan Carr," says Carol Green, the unit publicist on *Grease 2*. Since it was her first gig for Paramount, she didn't know why the two men loathed each other. It only mattered that Diller wanted "the caftan-wearing producer" nowhere near him or his studio. The Paramount honcho also had his eye on an upcoming *Grease 2* profile in the *Los Angeles Times*. "Barry Diller issued an edict that if Allan got a quote in that article, everybody under [Diller] at the studio would be fired," says Green.

144

It fell to Green to deal with the *Los Angeles Times* writer Paul Rosenfield. "It was so absurd, but it was my job to keep that [Allan Carr] quote out of the newspaper, and I managed to do that by appealing to Paul," says Green. "He wanted to remain cooperative with Paramount."

Rosenfield, one of the higher-profile and lower-maintenance journalists (until his death by suicide in 1993), eschewed the Diller/Carr wars in his reporting, and instead focused on movie trivia. Who among the *Times*'s readers knew that the residents of Norwalk, California, hadn't seen this much movie activity since Lana Turner and John Garfield spent an afternoon filming there at the local train depot for *The Postman Always Rings Twice* back in 1945? And since the name Allan Carr couldn't be mentioned in the article, Rosenfield was prevented from reporting on little idiosyncrasies like Allan's demand that his personal assistants check the toilet to issue their opinion on the kidney stones he passed each day. The omission of Allan's name also forced Rosenfield to ignore what was fast becoming a stylistic flourish in all Allan Carr–produced films. Allan insisted that *Grease 2,* like *Grease* and *Can't Stop the Music,* climax with a big party onscreen. For his latest opus, he fashioned a multinight shoot around a big poolside luau, in which several bikers literally crash the high school party by performing Evel Knievel stunts over the open water.

"The weather was really cold and we had to be in the water," Lorna Luft recalls. "To make matters worse, they put ice in our mouth so that our breath wouldn't show."

To keep everyone warm, the caterers served chili at three in the morning. "Not a good choice," says Green. "It was an economic choice rather than a socially conscious choice."

For five days, Allan played pasha as Patricia Birch tried to direct the choreographed mayhem of the party finale. He adored his director and showed it by occasionally letting her know, "Hey, Pat, we wanted Marge Champion but we had to settle for you." Allan let Birch, unlike Nancy Walker, be the director, and for five days he rested poolside, out of shot in his big raccoon coat and "loving every minute of the boys in their short grass skirts and the little flip-flop that covered their penis," says Green. "Allan was so happy to be there, even though it must have been thirty degrees."

The party was fun while it lasted, but in the end, all films must be released. At a preview screening, Birch gave Allan the news. "We're in trouble," she said.

"They're all waiting for John, Olivia, and the others to show up. And we've only got Didi Conn," who makes a brief appearance as Frenchy in the sequel.

The bad omen delivered on its promise at *Grease 2*'s world premiere at Hollywood's Pacific Cinerama Dome. A relic of the futuristic 1960s, the theater looks like a spaceship, but instead of Steven Spielberg aliens, Allan Carr popped out of the limousine that night on Sunset and Vine. Perhaps Barry Diller, who was MIA that evening, did put a curse on *Grease 2*, because no sooner had Allan emerged curbside than he saw his composer of the hour, Louis St. Louis, and gasped out loud. Both men were wearing the same Kenzo sweaters! Allan nearly turned around to go home.

"Would Dolly Parton and Lily Tomlin wear the same outfit to a premiere?" he admonished St. Louis.

Then there was the cut-rate party nearby at the Hollywood Bowling Club on El Centro. Plagued by his kidney stones and other maladies, Allan had left it to Paramount to produce the premiere party. Now, stuck at a bowling alley, he passed on the greasy burgers and hero sandwiches, and wondered why the DJ Phast Phreddie was playing Chubby Checkers's "The Twist" and Marvin Gaye's "I Heard It Through the Grapevine" instead of the *Grease 2* soundtrack.

A reporter asked Allan if he bowled. "Bowl? Sure I bowl," he cracked. "It's the only thing I *could* do in high school." But that night he didn't bowl or eat or even smile very much. "Where's Michelle?" Allan wanted to know.

Still bruised by his fashion faux pas, Louis St. Louis kept his distance from Allan and instead tried to chat up the film's other producer. "There's no way I can thank you for this opportunity," St. Louis told Robert Stigwood.

Stigwood, who had imbibed much that evening, merely smiled. "Oh, yes there is!" he replied.

Allan tried to put a positive spin on his new movie. "If *Grease 2* earns half as much money as our first *Grease* earned, we'll all be very happy," he told well-wishers.

But no one would be happy. Paramount released the sequel against an oddly titled movie by Steven Spielberg, and immediately regretted the contest. "*E.T.* creamed us," says Maxwell Caulfield. Despite the stiff competition, the actor took much blame for the failure of *Grease 2*, and Allan was there ready to give credit whether credit was due or not.

Before and during the shoot, he adored Caulfield, and even lent him his Hawaii home as soon as the film finished production. But just as Allan came to reexamine his lust for Steve Guttenberg after a screening or two of *Can't Stop the Music,* the same fate befell Maxwell Caulfield when *Grease 2* tanked at the box office. Allan told friends that it was Paramount, not he, that wanted Caulfield, and it was Paramount that objected to his first choice. "Tim Hutton came, sang, and danced in my living room. He had done *Guys and Dolls* in college, and that's who I wanted and preferred. But they didn't consider him sexy enough," Allan said postrelease.

And there were other apocryphal tales. "Another prospect came over and, like Timothy Hutton, sang and danced in my living room. He just oozed stardom," Allan revealed. "If I had had my way, it would have been Tom Cruise and Michelle Pfeiffer."

Those stories eventually reached their desired target. Juliet Mills heard them from her friend Joan Collins, who heard them from her friend Valerie Perrine: "Allan is over Maxwell with a vengeance."

twenty

Make It a Croissant

Back in New York City, *La Cage aux folles*'s triumvirate of Jerry Herman, Arthur Laurents, and Harvey Fierstein held to a disciplined regimen, meeting once a week at the songwriter's townhouse on East 61st Street. Years earlier, Herman had converted the brownstone's fourth floor into one large floor-through studio. It was a spectacular room, especially for space-restricted Manhattan. A balcony overlooked a small garden in the back, and skylights bathed the room in an afternoon sun that often blazed against the cool, neutral tones of the walls. Herman called them "stone and mushroom," which he felt emphasized the bright, primary colors of the posters from his tuners *Mack and Mabel*, *Mame*, and *Hello, Dolly!* which decorated the walls.

Each week, Laurents made his critique as Fierstein read a new scene, and Herman, in turn, sang whatever song he'd written for the material that Fierstein had given them the week before. Herman did his own singing and piano playing, seated at a huge Mason & Hamlin grand piano, which had been hoisted up four flights and lifted through the front window of the studio. On especially chilly afternoons, Herman's housekeeper, Damian, lit a fire in the fireplace, and otherwise busied himself serving home-cooked meals as the three men worked on *La Cage aux folles*. "Damian kept us well fed and up to date with the latest gossip from Broadway and Hollywood," says Fierstein.

Laurents and Herman would suggest a bit of stage business or dialogue, but if it was terribly clever, alarm bells went off in Fierstein's head. "Is that from the movie?" he shot back. He continued to pride himself on never having seen

148

the movie *La Cage aux folles,* from which Herman and Laurents had, on occasion, inadvertently pilfered. Fierstein feared violating the movie copyright, not to mention his own prickly sense of originality. When it came to guarding against plagiarism, "I became the arbiter of *that!*" says Fierstein. Laurents admits, "It got ticklish, but we never infringed."

Regarding arguments with his director, Fierstein claims, "I only walked out of Jerry's house twice." It was, all in all, a quick pregnancy. At the end of three months, Allan decided it was time to hear and see something. "I've been patient," he told them.

At that very first reading, Herman played the piano and sang, while Laurents and Fierstein divvied up reading the roles. It was an extraordinarily small audience: Allan attended with his executive producers, Barry Brown and Fritz Holt, and his lawyer, John Breglio. "He wanted to keep a tight control on things until he felt [the show] was ready to be exposed. Which was very smart of him," says Brown.

Sometime during Act II of the reading, Allan began to hyperventilate, and it was genuinely feared by those present that their obese producer was suffering a heart attack. But Allan waved them away. "I'm all right," he whispered dramatically. When they finished the reading, instead of joining in the applause of a dozen hands slapping together, Allan escaped to the nearest sofa to sprawl himself out on the pillows. Then he smiled a beatific smile. "He was in love with the show from the very beginning and never lost any of that enthusiasm," says Herman.

"His excitement was palpable," says Brown.

After extensive jiggering on the book, Laurents deemed the show ready for a series of backers' auditions for potential producers, major investors, and the three big Broadway theater chains: the Shuberts, Jujamcyn, and the Nederlanders. Again, these subsequent readings were casual affairs, held in Herman's top-floor studio, but eventually Gotham gossip doyenne Liz Smith got wind of the soirees and wrote that they were "the in place to be" in New York City, and she went on to give a long tally of theater celebrities who'd been invited.

Despite the positive feedback, *La Cage aux folles,* the musical, remained an extraordinarily fluid venture. "We made it up as we went along at the backers' auditions," says Laurents.

At one such reading, a potential investor asked the director, "Why aren't there any girls in the chorus line?" This money person wanted girls in the Broadway chorus line, since it hadn't occurred to him that *La Cage aux folles* was set in a male drag club in Saint-Tropez.

Laurents thought fast. "Well, two of the Cagelles are girls," he blurted out. "It's up to the audience to decide who are the real girls. They won't know until the curtain call when the real boys tear off their wigs."

The potential investor considered it. "That's great!" Herman loved the idea and so did Allan because, actually, it was his idea, stolen from the drag show at Finocchio's two years earlier.

Fierstein, for his part, hated mixing the sexes in *La Cage aux folles*. "They sold it to me as 'Wouldn't it be fun if we make the audience guess which are men and which are women?' It was a silly cop-out," he says. "They were so scared of the material. I was openly gay. I didn't ever consider making apologies for what we were doing."

"Apologies" is a strong word. Curiously, Fierstein was the only one among the principal creatives who dared mention out loud that *La Cage aux folles* would be the first Broadway musical to feature two male lovers. "Allan never mentioned it. No one," says Brown. "It was always an entertainment."

Herman agrees. "We were looking to do an entertainment that had something to say, which is very different from a message piece." It's what Allan wanted. "And it's why it worked," Herman adds. "It was never a piece of activism, even with Harvey involved."

Laurents, however, worried about the controversial, groundbreaking material. "The subject of two men living together is still dicey," he said many years later. "Americans still do not grasp two men living together; they do not want them buying property next door."

Despite Liz Smith's efforts to tout *La Cage aux folles* as Broadway's next big hit, it remained a tough sell. "The money didn't walk in the door," says Allan's friend Manny Kladitis, a Broadway manager-producer. "I don't know if it was the gay theme, but he didn't have an easy time raising money."

To please skittish investors, who blanched at an all-male chorus line, two women were cast as Cagelles despite Fierstein's vehement protests. (Fierstein jettisoned the concept for the 2004 Broadway revival to make it an all-male chorus line.) Otherwise, the backers' auditions delivered only one major potential blow to the creative team of three.

In the hurly-burly world of Broadway, the show that opens is often the show that can secure a theater, and in the Gotham landscape there are only a dozen venues, at most, that are large enough to house a musical on the scale that Allan envisioned. One organization, the Shuberts, owns half the Broadway real estate.

It's a power that gives them the strength to pull strings—strings long and twisted enough to demand significant changes in a show's makeup, both creatively and financially.

"I'd heard that the Shuberts didn't want me as director," says Laurents. "They told Allan if they got Michael Bennett, they would give him a theater." Bennett, although he'd suffered a disappointment with the box office bomb *Ballroom* during the 1978–1979 season, remained a darling of the Shuberts. His hit musical *A Chorus Line* was only halfway through its fifteen-year run at the organization's cornerstone Shubert Theater on West 44th Street when *La Cage aux folles* began its series of backers' auditions. "Allan hadn't produced on Broadway before," observes Laurents, who felt he had reason to be worried about his rather tenuous position with this nascent musical. "Allan used an awful lot of coke. You never could tell when he was in his right mind. But for some reason he was extremely loyal to me. He said no to the Shuberts."

Allan instead went with the Nederlander Organization, part owners of the venerable Palace Theater, famed for having housed Judy Garland's 1951 Broadway debut engagement, as well as such full-scale musicals as *Sweet Charity* and *Applause*.

The two men, Allan and Laurents, didn't exactly like each other but they shared an understanding. It was one that the old pro, Laurents, brokered with the new kingmaker on the block, Allan. "Your territory is from the back of the house to the orchestra rail, and my territory is from the orchestra rail to the backstage," Laurents told him. And Allan honored Laurents's word. "Once he knew the protocol of the theater, such as, the producer doesn't talk to the actors, he never broke it."

Occasionally, Allan did—very diplomatically—make a directorial suggestion.

"There's the scene in the second act where Georges is trying to make Albin a man," Laurents recalls. The moment requires Albin to pick up a piece of toast and butter it with a nonlimp flick of the wrist, which he has great difficulty mastering. Allan carefully approached his autocratic director. "Instead of toast, make it a croissant," he offered.

Laurents liked the idea. "It was his penis," Laurents says of the croissant. "It was funny."

But not all of Allan's ideas found a receptive audience with the show's creatives, and in time, the three men developed a nickname for their tyro producer. They called him Flo, short for "menstrual flow," since they never knew what mood they might find him in. Even in Allan's company, they could be heard to remark, "Did you hear what Flo said today?" Allan had no idea what they were talking about.

After a few more backers' auditions, Allan flew Fritz Holt and Laurents to his house in Honolulu for a more relaxed powwow. Here was one of Diamond Head's more famous houses, called Rakuen, which means "paradise" in Japanese. The two-story house, which Allan nicknamed Surfhaven and purchased for $5.7 million, had been built with an abundance of silk-paneled doors, or shojis, in nineteenth-century in Japan and reassembled in Hawaii in 1912. The grounds' arching stone bridge, waterfall, and koi pond lived up to the house's original name, "paradise," and even though every plant and architectural piece had been transported across the Pacific Ocean, that strict attention to Asian detail didn't stop Allan from hanging a large crystal chandelier amidst the shojis in the living room. He also added a few throw pillows, which were a gift from his neighbor down the road, Clare Booth Luce—one of them read NO GOOD DEED GOES UNPUNISHED—who had needlepointed them herself. Also strategically placed about the house were photos of Surfhaven guests, people like Robert Redford and Doris Duke and Bruce Jenner at his wedding, which took place on the grounds, and John Travolta, who stayed there so often that Allan put up a copper plaque on one of the bedroom doors. It read THE JOHN TRAVOLTA ROOM.

Shoji screens divided the rooms, and in the morning, some guests from the mainland complained of the bright morning light flooding their bedrooms. Every room opened to the outside, and occasionally Allan would forget to warn a novice guest before he or she descended a few stone steps to the beach and triggered the alarm system. Within seconds, half a dozen security guards would appear and point their guns.

Most people found it to be a very impressive house. Arthur Laurents wasn't one of those people. "It was on a ratty beach of rock and cut glass," he recalls. Even more unappetizing was the sight of Allan in swim trunks. "Not pleasant," says Laurents. "He had his jaws wired shut and he ate like a pig."

Chocolate cake, it seems, topped Allan's list of favorite foods the weekend that Laurents and Holt visited Surfhaven, even though not much of it got through the wires coursing through his teeth, which had recently been snapped shut—again. "Allan took a knife and cut through the cake, spreading the chocolate all over his breasts. Don't ask me why," says Laurents.

He then made a kind offer to his two guests from the *La Cage aux folles* battlefield. "Why don't you take a nap and I'll have this guy come in and blow you?" Allan offered.

Holt and Laurents declined the invitation. The potential blow-jobber was, in Laurents's estimation, "a kid who had done *West Side Story* in high school, and Allan was using me to impress him. He looked like a frightened lamb."

twenty-one

Spring Breakdown

As *La Cage aux folles* came together, Allan attempted to resuscitate his reputation in Hollywood after the ill-fated double blowouts of *Can't Stop the Music* and *Grease 2*. It was not an especially auspicious choice with which to make his comeback, but *Where the Boys Are* spoke to Allan. Just as *Grease* was his hopelessly romanticized rendition of what were tragic times at Highland Park High, *WTBA* symbolized his Lake Forest College days as he wanted to relive them, with the Fort Lauderdale spring break thrown into the mix. No matter that the original *Where the Boys Are* is a fairly standard-issue run-of-the-mill beach-blanket-bingo movie circa 1960. Its ultrawaspish stars, from Jim Hutton and George Hamilton to Yvette Mimieux and Paula Prentiss, loomed as the idealized copies of the Illinois frat boys and sorority girls whom Allan wrote about incessantly in his "Through the Keyhole" gossip column.

Equally important, Allan could make the remake fast, he could make it cheap at $5 million, and he could do what he did best: create a few new stars and party with them in the process.

The new *Where the Boys Are* let Allan reexperience spring break, albeit thirty years later, the upshot being that he got laid this time around. "We shot scenes of spring break, driving up and down the beach looking for beautiful people to be in the movie," says the film's production manager, Neil Machlis. As they cruised down the boulevard off the beach, Allan waved from his rented Cadillac. As always, it was the casting process that really got his juices, creative and otherwise, flowing. "Want to be in a movie?" he cried to every shirtless buff guy on the sidewalk. "Hi, I'm Allan Carr. I'm the producer of *Grease*." It was his Florida update on his recent pickup line, "Cash or career?"

For any college boy or coed who doubted his sincerity, Allan pointed to a couple of cameramen in his entourage, who followed in another car. Allan possessed an eye for talent—or, at least, physical beauty—and to prove it, the footage shot on his Fort Lauderdale tour convinced the film company ITC to green-light the *Where the Boys Are* remake.

For a few days in April 1983, as Arthur Laurents and company toiled away on *La Cage aux folles* in New York and Allan trolled the beaches of Fort Lauderdale, it was for Allan the best of both worlds, combining as he did the Hollywood of *Where the Boys Are* with the Broadway of a new musical. Once he finished with the Florida college boys, Allan took his talent search to Los Angeles, where he found himself completely smitten by a twenty-six-year-old actor named Howard McGillin. In time, McGillin would earn himself a place in *The Guinness Book of Records* for clocking in more performances in the title role in *The Phantom of the Opera* than any other human being. But in 1983, McGillin struggled to support his wife and son, and needed to establish himself in the entertainment business. Along with dozens of other actors who auditioned for the role of the "son," Jean-Michel, in *La Cage aux folles*, McGillin waited his turn to sing the love song "With Anne on My Arm," in which the character Jean-Michel professes his love for his fiancée.

Unlike those other contenders, however, McGillin inspired Allan to call the long, arduous audition process to an abrupt halt. Suddenly, it wasn't the sweet strains of Jerry Herman's ballad that kept Allan's ears buzzing as he followed McGillin out of the Debbie Reynolds Studios and into the asphalt heat of the parking lot on that unduly warm spring day in North Hollywood.

"You're going to be a star!" Allan called out. He then reintroduced himself to McGillin, and launched into a promo of not *La Cage aux folles* but *Where the Boys Are '84*. Since McGillin had never seen the original beach-blanket movie, the on-the-spot offer to appear in the remake impressed him. "You must come up to my house," Allan continued. "It's a great house. Ingrid Bergman used to own it. You're going to be the star of *Where the Boys Are!*"

Despite McGillin's audition for *La Cage aux folles*, that Broadway project quickly evaporated into the white glare of the sun-baked smog over the San Fernando Valley. For an actor in search of any and all credits, those seven words—"You're going to be a movie star!"—summed up, if not his every dream, then at least next month's rent.

Over the next few weeks, as Allan shuttled back and forth between New York City, to take care of *La Cage aux folles* business, and Fort Lauderdale, to scout *Where the Boys Are* locations, he found ample time to entertain McGillin at Hilhaven Lodge and introduce him to potential writers and directors for *Where the Boys Are*. McGillin reread the script many times to help audition other actors whom Allan liked. "I was drawn into this crazy roller-coaster period of about two months," says McGillin. There were incessant phone calls to McGillin's house. When the actor's wife answered, Allan wanted to know, "Is the star there?" Every time Allan called, the conversation would lead to "Get up here. Right away."

It didn't much matter what day of the week or what time of day. Early one Sunday morning, McGillin found himself unceremoniously summoned to Allan's house. "I was leery, and it didn't help that he came to the door wearing a bathrobe. But Allan was very respectful of [heterosexual men]. That's true," says McGillin, who years later came out as a homosexual.

Only once did McGillin consider saying no to his movie mentor's demands, and that minor stab at recalcitrance coincided with his son's second birthday party. McGillin had invited his closest friends to celebrate the big event, held on a Saturday, when the phone rang early that morning. "You must be at the Universal Sheraton today. It's the final audition," announced Allan.

McGillin couldn't help but wonder: Hadn't he already been put through several final auditions?

Two hours later, the currently unemployed but future movie star walked down the hallway of the Universal Sheraton, where dozens of other twenty-ish actors were preparing to audition for *Where the Boys Are '84*. Many of them brought entire wardrobes. In the middle of such planned chaos, McGillin watched as Allan jumped from suitcase to suitcase to check out clothes. "This shirt is fabulous!" he told one boy. "My dog wouldn't be caught dead in those shorts!" he told another.

What McGillin didn't know was that sometime between his first audition for *La Cage aux folles* and his umpteenth reading for *Where the Boys Are*, Allan needed a haircut, which led him to Jerry Esposito's small hair salon, which operated in a cottage on Fountain Avenue in West Hollywood. While having his hair shampooed, cut, and blow-dried, Allan happened to glance up at his haircutter's mirror and spotted the black-and-white headshot of an attractively broody young man who reminded him of Monty Clift before the car accident. He asked Esposito, "Who's that cute guy?"

Always the performer, Alan Solomon dons a Cub Scout cap and shows some leg at his home in Highland Park, Illinois, 1940s.

Ann-Margret and Tina Turner share a laugh over Allan's gift, at the *Tommy* subway party, New York City, 1975.

Elton John, decked out in his Local Lad–inspired regalia from *Tommy*, enjoys a pensive moment in the subway during the premiere party, 1975.

SAL TRAINA / *WWD* © CONDE NAST PUBLICATIONS

Ann-Margret goes all out, and then some, to play Roger Daltrey's mother in *Tommy*, 1975.

PHOTOFEST

The Cycle Sluts delight Allan's more liberal guests, but shock Hugh Hefner, Rex Reed, and a few charter members of Hollywood's old guard, 1975.

ONE INSTITUTE COLLECTION

Roman Polanski receives a standing ovation amidst roving violinists at the Rolodex Party, Malibu, 1977.

PETER C. BORSARI

Allan brings together the worlds of Hollywood actors and Hollywood rockers, in this case Joan Collins and a pink-wigged Elton John.

FREDDIE GERSHON COLLECTION

The ultimate fan, Allan re-creates Sandy's bedroom from *Grease* in Hilhaven Lodge, and dubs it THE OLIVIA NEWTON-JOHN ROOM.

PHOTOFEST

John Travolta and Olivia Newton-John pay the proper respect to their newly svelte producer on the gymnasium set of *Grease*, 1978.

PHOTOFEST

Grease producer Robert Stigwood, in stripes, shares a laugh with the Bee Gees. Barry Gibb, far right, writes the movie's title song, 1978.

PHOTOFEST

During the *Discoland* shoot in New York City, gay protesters confuse the film with *Cruising* starring Al Pacino. Regardless of those problems (and others), Steve Guttenberg, Randy Jones, Valerie Perrine, David Hodo, and Bruce Jenner continue to romp through the streets of Greenwich Village, 1979.

PHOTOFEST

Valerie Perrine, surrounded by the Village People, lands in a big glass of champagne for the "Milk Shake" song in *Can't Stop the Music,* 1980.

How many pecs can one pool hold? Allan goes for the maximum number with the big "Y.M.C.A." muscle fest in *Can't Stop the Music*, 1980.

Can't Stop the Music opens in New York City with an extravagant outdoor circus-themed party at Lincoln Center, 1980.

Siblings unite: Liza Minnelli offers her congratulations to sister Lorna Loft during the *Grease 2* festivities at Studio 54, 1982.

ROBIN PLATZER/TWIN IMAGES

Allan ogles Maxwell Caulfield at the *Grease 2* party in Hollywood, 1982. Later, he has serious second thoughts about his casting choice when the movie tanks at the box office.

PETER C. BORSARI

Allan manages a discreet striptease that upstages his *Grease 2* star Michelle Pfeiffer, who arrives at the New York City premiere with her husband, Peter Horton, 1982.

Allan demands that the *La Cage aux folles* cast album be ready in record time for the opening-night party. At work in the recording studio are (left to right) Jerry Herman, Arthur Laurents, George Hearn, Gene Barry, Thomas Z. Shepard, and Fritz Holt.

Harvey Fierstein and Jerry Herman celebrate with Angela Lansbury at the Broadway opening of the two writers' new musical, *La Cage aux folles*, 1983.

La Cage aux folles star Gene Barry shares the stage, but not the Palace Theater elevator, with one of the Cagelles.

PHOTOFEST

"You're a star": A barber-shop photo leads Allan to his *Where the Boys Are '84* favorite, Russell Todd, 1984.

Just follow the stars: Oscar statues, plus a few million tulips flown over from Holland, adorn the Shrine Auditorium in downtown Los Angeles on March 29, 1989.

PHOTOFEST

Rob Lowe's Prince Charming serenades Eileen Bowman's Snow White to the tune of "Proud Mary" during the Cocoanut Grove opening number of the Academy Awards, 1989.

LOS ANGELES TIMES

Before the bad reviews roll in, Allan looks upbeat in the company of Goldie Hawn, Kurt Russell, Bob Hope, and Corey Feldman in the Club Oscar greenroom, 1989.

Rob Lowe, an instant Oscar disgrace, hides in the background as Patrick Swayze, Bruce Vilanch, and Allan smile for the camera during the Academy Awards telecast, 1989.

Allan inaugurates his basement discotheque at Hilhaven Lodge, its walls (and his caftan) festooned with ersatz Egyptian hieroglyphics, 1978.

PETER C. BORSARI

"An actor," the haircutter replied. "He comes in here. His name is Russell Todd."

"Put me in touch," said Allan. Which led to his pushing aside McGillin for the male lead in *Where the Boys Are.*

Allan's turn of affection may have had less to do with love, lust, or anything in between than pure business. Where McGillin chose not to sign with Allan's new company, Anonymous Management, Russell Todd became a client. The result: McGillin ended up playing second stud, his role reduced to the bookends of humping Lorna Luft over the credits and reuniting with her in the film's last reel.

As Allan prepped *Where the Boys Are,* he continued to work on casting *La Cage aux folles,* where "Everyone from Danny Kaye to Milton Berle to Dick Shawn to Jack Carter to Robert Alda" wanted to star, he told people. Instead, Arthur Laurents cast two actors somewhat less known to the general theater-going audience: George Hearn and Gene Barry.

The two actors had their doubts. Wearing a blue blazer, Barry looked like he'd just walked off Rodeo Drive for his audition and sang "What Kind of Fool Am I?" but not before having long talks with his wife and children about playing a gay man onstage. ("I don't play the homosexual part of Georges," he would later say. "I play the love he feels for Albin.") Hearn also felt he'd put his masculinity on the line, and required a shot of whiskey before he sang "My Heart Belongs to Daddy" in drag. "It was the longest walk I took in my life," he said of taking the stage that day. Regardless of the actor's inner turmoil, Allan bought it.

"Hearn walked in wearing a dress and looking like Arlene Dahl," Allan said of the winning audition, "and he walked out looking like Ann-Margret at Caesars Palace." After hearing Hearn and Barry, Allan opined, "We knew we could go ahead with the show," as if the project was ever in danger of falling apart for lack of thespian interest.

While Fierstein considered George Hearn and Gene Barry gifted performers, he knew dozens of talented gay actors from his Off-Off-Broadway days, and felt strongly that only a fellow homosexual could bring the required pathos to the roles of Georges and Albin.

"I insisted on openly gay leads for the show, and Laurents called me a bigot. He called me a lot of things," says Fierstein.

Laurents didn't think a performer's sexual orientation made much difference. "Harvey, an actor is an actor," he kept saying.

Fierstein challenged him. "You can have the greatest twenty-year-old actress with natural talent and star quality and you can train her brilliantly, but she cannot play a grandmother. There are things life hasn't shown her. Most gay actors have been beaten all their lives on some level, economically, politically, emotionally."

In the show's anthem, "I Am What I Am," in which Albin defiantly registers his pride in being a gay cross-dresser, Fierstein found special fault with casting a heterosexual: "George Hearn gave his body and soul to that role, he worked that thing. He worked his ass off. He cared about that role. But there is a lifetime of shattered pain in 'I Am What I Am.' Those were the battles." (Later, when the show had run on Broadway for over a year, Laurents cast a gay actor in one of the lead roles. According to Fierstein, "I'm probably one of the three people in the world, living or dead, who Arthur apologized to. He called me to say, 'You are so right. What a difference it makes!'")

Allan supported Laurents in these contretemps. "An actor is an actor," he believed. Also, he felt strongly that his director, a Broadway veteran, knew best, adopting Laurents's credo "from the orchestra rail to the backstage" as a kind of iron-curtain divide that protected him from Fierstein's complaints.

Casting wasn't marketing, and it was here, on Allan's turf of how to promote and advertise *La Cage aux folles*, that Laurents and his producer finally butted egos.

While everyone involved with the musical saw it as "an entertainment," the gay subject matter continued to make it a difficult sell, and investors weren't the only ones to resist its charms. Broadway's significant homosexual contingency could keep the show running for, maybe, six weeks. But how did Allan capture that much larger core audience—that is, very mature heterosexual tourists—and get them to fall in love with the first gay couple in Broadway musical history?

"Not an easy task," said the show's marketing director, Jon Wilner. While some participants—namely, Laurents—found Allan to be "tasteless," Wilner called *La Cage*'s producer "one of the smartest people I knew," as well as one of the most unapologetically gay. Or, as Wilner describes him, "Allan was very flamboyant long before *Queer Eye for the Straight Guy*." With *La Cage aux folles*, Allan wanted to push the envelope. In Wilner's expert opinion, there might have been misjudgments, like Allan's desire to mess with the Palace Theater. "Let's paint it pink!" Allan exclaimed.

To which Jerry Herman replied, "Over my dead body!"

Or, as Herman put it more circumspectly years later, "Allan's flamboyance and his wanting to be a P. T. Barnum did cause some conflicts with regard to tasteless advertising." Allan, according to Herman, displayed a dual personality: "He was inherently shy and uncomfortable in certain aspects of how he looked and acted. There was a reticence that he covered by doing the opposite and being flamboyant."

The show's publicist, Shirley Herz, noticed this personality split. "Before we walked into a room, Allan would be absolutely shaking. He'd take my hand. And then we would walk into the room and he was the consummate showman, totally in control," she recalls.

Herz, a Broadway veteran, feared Allan from afar. But once she met him, she found "if you talked back to him, he respected you. If he saw he could bulldoze you, you were dead."

If, in fact, Allan followed Laurents's edict that the producer's world ended at the orchestra rail, then by extension it swept across the orchestra seats and out the front doors to the street. And it was this larger domain that Allan claimed with a vengeance: The overall print and TV campaign belonged to him, and he had no reason to disguise what he wanted to sell with *La Cage aux folles*. Allan was selling drag queens and, by extension, himself as a caftan-wearing man. If *Grease* and *Where the Boys Are* celebrated his youth, *La Cage* embodied everything he wanted to say about his life as an adult. Again, as with *Can't Stop the Music*, he was that accidental gay activist.

To brand the show with one image, marketing director Jon Wilner eschewed the usual Broadway illustrators and instead went with a Saks Fifth Avenue window dresser named Bill Berta, who promptly delivered four sketches. Allan loved them. "They were essentially the *Mame* poster twenty years later. *La Cage* was a sister to *Mame*," says Wilner. In that historic 1966 poster, also designed by Berta, a caricature of Angela Lansbury came whirlwinded in a lavish swirl of a costume, with an oversized trumpet jutting from her left hand. For *La Cage*, Allan liked the portrait of a similar bigger-than-life "female" figure swathed in what could be construed as a gigantic feather boa, and he suggested that "she" be winking at the viewer. "Because if she's winking," Allan explained, "we're in on the joke with her. We're laughing with her. We're in on it." He also suggested that a sailor's tattoo decorate "her" exposed shoulder. (The tattoo remained, but the wink got cut from the final poster.) Herman also loved the she-male image, which came to be known as "Berta," an homage to the poster designer.

But Laurents loathed "Berta."

"There were horrible fights between Arthur and Allan on advertising," says Wilner. "Allan wanted it flamboyant. Arthur wanted it to be mainstream. Arthur wanted it straight," which translated into no images of men dressed up in women's clothes. "Drag turned me off," Laurents had maintained, and "drag in the theatre wasn't to my taste, either."

Allan insisted the show's campaign play up its transvestite roots. "Arthur met his match with Allan Carr and Allan won," says Wilner, who went ahead and featured Berta in a full-page ad in the *New York Times*. The first day it ran, the line to the box office snaked around the corner of the Palace Theater. "The artwork worked, it clicked," says Wilner.

Laurents did not agree. "Look at the ads for *La Cage*. It's a carnival," he complained. And he blamed Allan. "It makes sense he would do that stuff. He had this childish idea of Hollywood glamour. That was his dream. He would love to have lived in a Busby Berkeley movie."

Laurents agreed with Jerry Herman that Allan was "a big kid," but not in a positive way. "Allan was a boy. He was not a man," Laurents offers. Boy or man, Allan fought like a pro, and he got what he wanted in Bill Berta's campy drag-queen image (complete with shoulder tattoo), despite Laurents's objections.

At last, *La Cage* was ready for out-of-town previews in Boston. "Oh, conservative Boston!" moaned Fierstein. He had to wonder why these experienced Broadway hands wanted to open a show about drag queens in notoriously uptight Beantown. It was the city, after all, that coined the phrase "banned in Boston."

twenty-two

Mickey & Judy Time

With *La Cage* ready to pop, Allan flew back to Los Angeles to meet and congratulate his *Where the Boys Are '84* ensemble. In many ways, the four actresses in *Boys* were a precursor of the all-femme chemistry that made hits of *The Golden Girls* and later *Sex and the City*. There was Lisa Hartman's ultrasmart Jennie, Lynn-Holly Johnson's sex-crazed Laurie, Wendy Schaal's conservative Sandra, and Lorna Luft's sardonic Carole. Russell Todd and Howard McGillin would play their boyfriends.

With the actors' deals yet to be finalized, Allan decided to throw a party for them at Hilhaven. He wanted to introduce the various cast members to each other and also to dream out loud among them. The actors had their questions, too. After months of waiting, McGillin wanted to know what he'd be paid for his reduced gig in *Where the Boys Are*.

That answer came as soon as Allan took center stage by the Hilhaven pool to reveal, "This movie is going to be like Mickey and Judy putting on a show in a barn." Although no one was swimming, everyone's heart sank into the pool like a plaster lawn ornament. As McGillin described the general feeling of deflated hopes, "We all realized then that this was going to be a down-low budget. We were going to be working for not very much money."

Eventually, the actors did sign—for not very much money. Most of them did their signature writing in an agent's office or were mailed a copy of the contract. Russell Todd's big moment was cause for somewhat more celebration since Allan insisted that the actor return in person to Hilhaven Lodge. The two men sat at opposite ends of the long oak table in the dining room, and Allan watched intently as the young actor signed the contract. Allan almost had to shout as he stared him down. "So tell me," he began once the papers had been signed. "Are you gay or straight?"

"I'm straight," replied Todd.

"Thank God!" exclaimed Allan, clapping his hands. "We're going to get along great!"

The celebration didn't stop there. Over dinner at Mortons restaurant, Allan presented his fledgling star with a black velvet box. Inside, Todd found a beautiful gold bracelet, which, to please his benefactor, he immediately wrapped around his left wrist. Over his mushroom risotto, Allan enjoyed showing off his newest talent acquisition to everyone who stopped by the centrally located table. Later, when it came time to speed away in Allan's Cadillac, Todd noticed that his left wrist felt a few pounds lighter. He looked down.

"Allan, the bracelet! It's missing!" he gasped.

A quick tour of Mortons did not produce the errant bracelet. "Don't worry about it," Allan said. "It's insured. I'm getting you another one tomorrow."

Todd remembers feeling "two inches tall." But the following day, true to his word, Allan presented him with an identical gold bracelet and an invitation to Century City to see a screening of the new big Oscar contender, Richard Attenborough's biopic *Gandhi,* about the great pacifist leader of India. Both men were excited to see the film that many in the industry were calling a shoo-in for the Academy Award.

If Todd was impressed, the film left Allan downright shaken. The young actor couldn't help but notice that tears covered Allan's face when the lights came up in the theater. "It was a very emotionally moving film. But why are you crying?" Todd asked.

Allan sobbed, "That's not why I'm crying."

"Why then?"

"Because I know I'll never make a movie that good!"

La Cage aux folles rolled into Boston on a June heat wave. But the producers' perspiration had less to do with the temperature than with the subject matter of their show. Transvestites in Beantown? That marriage made everyone nervous. One of the show's producers, Martin Richards, thought, "We're going to Boston with that orthodox Catholic population and open a show about a drag queens there!?"

Regardless of the subject matter, Allan charmed the town. "He set up a piano in the middle of Boston Commons and everyone sang 'The Best of Times' and we got the key to the city," says Richards.

Arthur Laurents was a little more philosophical. "There wasn't a choice with Boston. It was the only place we had," he says of theater availability. The other choice was Washington, D.C. "Not exactly a liberal town either," he observes.

As the musical loaded its sets into Boston's Colonial Theater, Allan basked in the venue's rich history. Built in 1900, the Colonial opened its doors with a touring company of *Ben-Hur* that featured chariots and live horses onstage. "Even I wouldn't go that far!" exclaimed Allan. His show went so well in its first preview at the Colonial that it had to be canceled.

As Laurents and set designer David Mitchell envisioned it, *La Cage aux folles* would open with two turntables that caused the streets and townhouses of Saint-Tropez to revolve before parting to reveal the marquee lights of the club La Cage aux Folles. It was to be a wildly technical opening to what was, at its heart, a rather intimate musical about a family. "Smoke and mirrors, smoke and mirrors," says Laurents.

In its very first performance before a paying audience, *La Cage aux folles* opened with that spin of the turntables, but instead of every element gliding together in a beautifully orchestrated symphony of movement, the various pieces crashed into each other to resemble nothing more than a bunch of painted flats.

The paying audience got more, as well as less, than it expected that first night in Boston. After about two minutes of stage time, the big red curtain at the Colonial Theater fell to the stage. "There was no way we go could on with the show that night," says Barry Brown.

Fortunately, on the following night, after a long tech rehearsal, the stuccoed walls and red-tiled roofs of Saint-Tropez danced together to create an illusion that the audience was peering out a big picture window at the French Riviera.

Allan and his creative team sat in the back of the Colonial. He noticed a typical Bay Area couple in their seventies. He had white hair and wore a blue blazer; she had a purple rinse in her hair. They probably knew the subject matter of *La Cage aux folles,* having seen the movie, but they were nervous and fidgeting in their seats. The movies are so much light play on an inanimate screen. The theater is in-your-face, and here Mr. and Mrs. Middle America were about to witness real live drag queens only a few feet away. The couple's body language read stiff. They weren't comfortable. Then, at the end of the show's first musical number, "We Are What We Are," in which the male dancers in female attire pulled off their wigs, Allan held his breath. So did about 1,500 other people.

Near the end of Act I, Gene Barry began his ballad, which he sings to George Hearn. It's called "Song on the Sand," and it's a love song about memory, about young lovers walking on a beach, about two guys holding hands.

"My heart was in my mouth. I stopped breathing," Jerry Herman recalls, fearing what the old couple in front of him might do. Instead of bolting, the man took his wife's hand and held it, and a few more bars into "Song on the Sand," they put their heads together.

Herman called it "the single most exciting moment" in the whole series of previews in Boston. "The song reminded them of themselves, and they laughed and their whole body language changed—it was loose and comfortable—and they stood up at the end of the show and shouted."

It's also the moment that Allan knew he had a hit. He wasn't the only one. "They had to hold me down!" Harvey Fierstein says of seeing the musical with its first paying audience. "People were leaning against each other, we were beside ourselves. It was a very exciting thing. We'd all come from different places. They hadn't seen it," he says of Laurents, Herman, and Allan. "I'd seen it a lot, but not in a Broadway show. I'd written six shows Off-Off-Broadway, all musicals with gay characters singing love songs. But to see it on a big stage? America is about money. It's a capitalistic country. If you make money, *that* makes you American."

Allan came off the high of *La Cage*'s first out-of-town preview by taking an early-morning flight to Fort Lauderdale to visit *Where the Boys Are,* which had already begun on-location production. Wendy Schaal compared the days and nights of filming to a "slumber party," but when Allan arrived for a visit, the vibe changed to something less high-schoolish. "Oh, Uncle Allan is coming!" someone would announce, giving them about twenty-four hours or less to prepare.

Sometimes Allan surprised everyone and showed up unannounced. After *La Cage*'s success in Boston, he arrived well lubricated at the cast's hotel. They spotted him in the lobby, where he was trying to cash a check at the reception desk. "He was far gone, really drunk," says Howard McGillin. Allan turned to say hello to his actors when, holding a big wad of cash, he dropped to the floor. "Allan passed out, and all this money was floating in slow motion in the air." The young actors looked at each other and gasped, in unison, "Oh my God, this is soooooo Hollywood!"

The next day, completely recovered from his in-flight debauchery, Allan rounded up "my kids," as he called them, and crammed everybody into his rented red Cadillac convertible. On previous outings with Allan, the cast had accepted the key to the city of Fort Lauderdale and, on another trip, they did a photo op with some dolphins at the local water park. What would it be today?

"Today we're doing research. I'm taking you back to school!" Allan announced. He was to receive an honorary degree at the College of Boca Raton at the commencement exercises for the class of 1983, and it was an event he had no intention of missing. As he would tell the assembled students, faculty, and alums of Boca Raton, "I never graduated from college, so this means so much to me!" And he meant it, even though the degree was coming from the College of Boca Raton, which, in Spanish, means "mouth of the rat."

It could be fun making an Allan Carr movie. It could also be life-threatening.

One night, Allan departed the hotel and ran into Wendy Schaal. "Oh, there's one of my girls, one of my stars!" he announced to no one in particular. And scooping the petite brunette into his arms, Allan tried to maneuver a deep dip, as if the two of them were Astaire and Rogers doing the hustle. But his weight and her weight overtook him and he proceeded to crash into a bed of succulents and gray pebbles. The next day the cast presented Schaal with a specially made T-shirt. It read: "Allan Carr fell on top of me and I lived to tell about it."

If Allan treated his young cast like royalty, they were all mere dauphins compared to Russell Todd, who had the advantage of claiming Allan as his manager. Where Howard McGillin had once been given the rush, now it was Todd's turn. Allan couldn't help but look at him and announce, "You're a star. How do you like your new life so far?"

Todd smiled and nodded. "It's pretty good," he said.

There were benefits to being Russell Todd on the set of *Where the Boys Are*. As Allan did with so many straight men, he showed special concern when Todd experienced family problems and needed to take a long weekend to visit his wife, Kim, back in Albany, New York. The actor approached Allan with trepidation. *Where the Boys Are* was not a luxurious shoot; each day the production clocked in a great deal of film time. Allan brushed aside all of Todd's concerns. "You're sick for the next two days. I'll fly you on Pan Am," Allan announced, cashing in on his *La Cage aux folles* connections with the airline. "We'll film your scenes later."

Yes, it was good being Allan's favorite.

twenty-three

Here Come the Cagelles!

The success of that second preview at the Colonial Theater turned out not to be a fluke. The positive audience reaction to the show only grew with the following performances, and by opening night in Boston, *La Cage aux folles* had emerged, as entertainment confections go, as American as apple pie with gruyere cheese on top. "Allan was just overjoyed with the success of the show," says Jerry Herman. "He had been through some rough times. Because of *Can't Stop the Music,* his reputation in Hollywood was a little soiled. He needed for his own self-esteem to do something successful and be the captain of the ship that didn't sink."

It helped, too, that, much to everyone's surprise, Gene Barry came alive in front of an audience. There had been worries in rehearsals that the former TV star would never give a Broadway-worthy performance. The Boston run dispelled those concerns. "Gene turned on in Boston," says Jon Wilner. "Then we knew it would be OK." Up to that point, Arthur Laurents had been a difficult taskmaster. "He didn't trust Gene Barry to have that green light come on. That's the way Arthur works. He'll break you down," Wilner adds.

Both Allan and Barry suffered from that West Coast thing—a Hollywood species out of water in the Broadway pool. "Gene wanted to be the star, have people kiss his ass," says actor John Weiner, who played Barry's son in the show. "But nobody did. He had to be one of us."

Worse, from the very first rehearsals, the TV actor was not respected by George Hearn, who played his stage lover. "Gene felt it, but George never showed it onstage," says Weiner.

If the audience reaction delighted *La Cage*'s team, the critical reviews only heightened their euphoria. That general bonhomie, however, came crashing down like a fire curtain at the opening-night party in Boston. A party wouldn't be an Allan Carr party if it didn't have klieg lights. Did it matter that Beantown wasn't Hollywood? Allan rented a few tinseltown-style lights to burn in front of the Nine Lansdowne dance club, and not being accustomed to such overlit city streets, a reporter from the *Boston Globe* mistook the klieg lights for "rotating World War II searchlights." Borrowing from his *Can't Stop the Music* launch in Los Angeles, Allan took pains to make the trek from venue to party as simple, and as impressive, as possible. Four double-decker buses fetched theatergoers at the Colonial Theater and promptly deposited them at the entrance of the Nine Lansdowne with its yards of red carpet, multiple bright lights, and enough reporters to restaff a small newsroom.

Fierstein arrived, took one look at the mob scene inside the club, and grabbed his mother's arm. "Oh my God! Cir-cus! Cir-cus!" he exclaimed.

Herman let it be known, "I've tried out many shows in Boston, but I've never heard the audience roar like this."

Relieved that he had not been fired by Laurents, Gene Barry exuded such excitement—"It's bigger than anything I've ever been in," he crowed—that he felt compelled to reveal too much of the tuner's plot, forcing Allan to grab the WXKS microphone away from his star and yell, "Don't tell any more! It's thirty-five dollars a ticket!"

John Travolta, Olivia Newton-John, and Rod Stewart were promised to be there but didn't show up, much to the reporters' disappointment. Neither did Senator Teddy Kennedy's ex-wife, Joan, who had recently broken off with Dr. Gerald Aronoff. Allan had provided the former Mrs. Kennedy with ten freebie tickets to the show, which went unused—except for the two that somehow fell into Aronoff's pocket. The good doctor even attended the party, but refused all interviews. "What does he think he's here for?" cracked one wag.

Allan arrived fashionably late for his own party. Waiting for him at the Nine Lansdowne was Arthur Laurents, who turned his producer's entrance into a Bette Davis moment. In his one attempt to economize, Allan had relegated the team of Laurents, Herman, and Fierstein to one table, while reserving a number of other tables for the musical's various producers, investors, and friends. Laurents saw the three name cards on the one small table, and let Allan have it as soon as he walked into the party.

"Out!" he told Allan. "Your kind isn't wanted here!"

When Allan decided to stay put at his own party, it was Laurents who walked out, and he led the cast and creatives to a nearby bar to celebrate sans the money people. Since Allan had no intention of leaving his own party, he cut the cake. And it was such a big cake, too. Allan's fetes typically featured grand displays of baked goods fashioned into novel shapes, and this particular cake sculpture mimicked a chorus girl's (or boy's) leg. Allan posed with it, he hugged it, and the photographers shot him as he obediently stuck his fingers in the icing and licked them clean. Playing off the tuner's showbiz theme of "Break a leg," Allan brought out several gift-wrapped eight-pound chunks of solid chocolate modeled in the form of a leg wrapped in a bright red garter. Each carried the tag "Break it or eat it." Most recipients chose to "leave it" since they'd already abandoned the Nine Lansdowne to hang out with Laurents at a nearby watering hole.

On that breath of contentious air, *La Cage aux folles* rolled into New York City. Some investors were shocked at an interview Fierstein gave to the *Boston Globe,* in which he called for a boycott of the almighty *New York Times* due to "the paper's lousy, slipshod treatment of AIDS."

As some irate money people put it to Allan, "You just don't say those things about the *Times* when you're opening your musical the next month!" Allan, on the contrary, was amused and claimed that another Fierstein profile—this one in *New York* magazine—goosed the show's advance ticket sales, which came to an unprecedented $4 million. It was early August, *La Cage aux folles* looked like a hit, and they hadn't done battle yet with the infamous Gotham critics.

Even an old-timer like Jimmy Nederlander believed that Allan had a foolproof hit on his hands. As part owner of the Palace Theater, he felt the show needed an even bigger venue to fill the ticket-buying demand. "Why not open the second balcony?" he asked, referring to the "nosebleed section" of the theater. It had been closed since 1966 when Gwen Verdon played there in *Sweet Charity.* Allan, despite his weight and bad hip, traipsed up to the second balcony, where no elevator existed, and thought he saw rats. "OK," he said, escaping back to terra firma. "You can open the second balcony. But clean it up first and don't charge anymore than fifteen dollars a seat. That's all it's worth, if that."

On opening night, Allan's favorite review came from the *Daily News*'s Douglas Watt, who remarked of the critics, "This show doesn't really need us. I'd have to say the show will soar with us or without us." It certainly soared without the seal of approval from the *New York Times*'s Frank Rich, known as the

Butcher of Broadway. Although he very much liked Jerry Herman's score and a few of the performances, Rich criticized the show for sometimes being "as shamelessly calculating as a candidate for public office." Fortunately, most of the other reviews were upbeat, if not downright raves, and as Watt opined, the buzz from Boston had essentially inoculated the show against naysayers like Rich, who wouldn't love an old-fashioned Broadway musical if it kissed them. "The show was a huge hit, and because of the kind of hit it was, it didn't matter what the reviews were," says Fierstein.

After their last curtain call, Allan did kiss Fierstein, and said, "We're just like Tommy Tune and Twiggy." Fierstein never asked if he was him or her, because someone took him aside backstage to say, "Now get out of here! The problem lots of people in the theater have is they write a huge hit and then they stand in the back of the house too long. Get out of the theater. Collect your checks and get on with your life."

If only Allan had heard those words. For the next four years he would try to recycle *La Cage aux folles* in as many ways as possible, using it, unsuccessfully, to regain his foothold in Hollywood and London. But those dark days were well into his future. On the night of August 21, he threw yet another Allan Carr party, and Allan never felt more alive than when he was about to enter an extravaganza of his own making. The Village People party at Lincoln Center might have been bigger, the *Tommy* subway party was edgier, the Truman Capote Jail House Party more novel. But this was Broadway. It had to be classy, and to that end, Allan turned on his grand spigot of cash.

Months earlier he told his party planner Elaine Krauss, "You can have whatever money you need, but it just has to be the most spectacular Broadway party ever thrown. It can't be a Sardi's roast-beef-and-peas number," he added, referring to restaurants like Sardi's and Tavern on the Green, which, in his opinion, served no better function than to get the cast fed and the investors drunk before the reviews rolled in. Allan, donning his *Tommy* hat, wanted to give a party in a venue that defied everyone's expectations, and to that effect, he thought back to a famous *Life* magazine photograph of screen legend Gloria Swanson, decked out in an evening gown, her arms stretched up to the heavens, standing amidst the rubble of the famed Roxy Theater after its demolition in 1960.

The Helen Hayes and Morosco Theaters on Broadway were currently being razed to make way for a big Marriott hotel in Times Square. Those adjoining lots, Allan thought, were the ideal spot for his *La Cage aux folles* party. He only needed to convince the Marriott people of the fabulousness of his idea. "They tore down the Morosco and the Helen Hayes, now they get a chance to welcome the biggest play to hit Broadway in years," he said, working the phones.

When insurance concerns felled his party-among-the-ruins concept, Allan let PR concerns trump his imagination. "Pan Am is a sponsor of *La Cage aux folles*. I want the party held in the Pan Am lobby," he ordered.

The airline's headquarters towered over Grand Central Station, and Allan devised a travelogue for the party in which guests were greeted with a phalanx of ticket booths outside the Pan Am building. "We built an airport at which you checked in and picked up your tickets," says Krauss. "And then when you walked into the building, the lobby of the Pan Am, it was as if you had landed in Saint-Tropez."

From there, guests wandered through a Saint-Tropez street, the Pan Am lobby turned into a veritable Potemkin Village of the French Riviera. They could "shop" for everything from cheese and pastries to flowers and beachwear—with *La Cage aux folles*'s logo attached, of course—and pick their way through carts overflowing with snails, crabs, chicken, roast beef, wine, and glacés. Allan also made sure to haul in truckloads of sand to help steady dozens of umbrellas and beach chairs, the entire tableau set off by a huge cyclorama that replicated the Mediterranean sky and sea.

Tickets to the party proved to be more in demand than those to the opening-night performance itself. "They're calling me Mrs. Hitler. The whole world wants tickets," Krauss noted with pride. If Elaine Krauss was Eva, that made her producer-boss Adolf himself, and Allan could not have been happier to handle each ticket request with Prussian-like precision. He called it his "VIP problem," and he loved every minute of the hours he spent in his St. Moritz penthouse as he shuffled names, tickets, bodies, seats, and egos. It was great, for one short month, to be the king of Broadway.

And he wasn't about to disappoint any of the 1,200 invitees. Allan wanted live music. "A band?" asked Krauss. "No, an orchestra," Allan corrected. Twenty-five pieces, to be exact, as many as there were in *La Cage*'s orchestra at the Palace Theater. He liked the idea of a revolving dance floor, which meant that one had to be built in the lobby—and at the center of it all, Allan envisioned a thirty-foot-high replica of *La Cage*'s "lady" Berta, covered in nothing but a few strategically placed ostrich feathers. (The *Village Voice* would refer to it as "Carmen Miranda" in its party coverage.)

And so it went.

On the night of the party, even the French were duly impressed. "We just got back from Saint-Tropez, and this lobby certainly has more class," said Dolores Bosshard, whose husband, Peter, was executive vice president of Credit Suisse.

The original *La Cage* scribe, Jean Poiret, also voiced his approval. "This is more extraordinary, more glamorous than Parisian opening-night parties at Maxim's," said Poiret, who revealed that August 21 was the tenth anniversary of the play's premiere in Paris.

Allan demurred. "Tonight is a tasteful minor extravaganza," he noted.

Allan also splurged on opening-night gifts. Elaine Krauss, for her efforts, received a ring of Burmese sapphires and diamonds from Fred's of Beverly Hills. Costume designer Theoni Aldredge unwrapped a gold pin with the words "La Cage" spelled out in diamonds, again from Fred's.

The evening's most symbolic gift, however, went to Arthur Laurents. Allan gave him an antique Hero Derringer handgun. A Hero has only one shot, and if that fact was lost on the director, Allan made sure to let him know with a handwritten note, which read: "Dear Arthur, I'm so glad I didn't have to use this. . . . Though the thought crossed my mind a few times. And vice versa, I'm sure."

When a *New York Post* reporter, Diana Maychick, asked if there were any gifts for his actors, Allan could only sniff. "Just the promise of five years of employment!" he shot back angrily. What he didn't give George Hearn and Gene Barry were any points in the show's profits or receipts. Each actor received $7,500 a week for the show's first year, a fact that Maychick duly noted in the next day's edition of her newspaper.

The biggest gifts of the night, surprisingly, came from Pan Am. The soon-to-be-defunct airline offered the principal creatives and producers two round-trip tickets apiece to anywhere in the world Pan Am flew, and more than a few *La Cage* participants cashed in with flights to China.

Even the party's goodie bags were unique for Broadway since each one contained *La Cage aux folles*'s cast album. "RCA had to have it pressed and ready and on every table that night," says Jon Wilner. Such a fast turnaround had never been managed before in Broadway history. Whereas most shows record shortly after opening night, Allan insisted that they use the three-day hiatus between Boston and New York to make the album. Record producer Thomas Z. Shepard had no choice but to stage a marathon fifteen-hour session, giving RCA only six days to press the album. "It's what I want," Allan said. End of discussion.

The price tag for the party came to a record-breaking $150,000. In 1983, $50,000 would have been considered excessive.

"It cost $150,000," says Barry Brown, "but we got a million dollars worth of publicity."

Who actually paid for the party remains open to question. Most participants say the funds came from *La Cage*'s budget. But Wilner insists that Allan was too smart to pay out of pocket when he could get somebody else to pick up the tab.

"It was the summertime. Pan Am was trying to sell Kennedy [Airport]-to-Saint-Tropez flights," says Wilner. It was Allan who sold the airline on The Clipper La Cage, because, as he put it, "*La Cage aux folles* is gay and gay people buy first-class tickets."

Although most people from the insular Broadway world found Allan excessive, they could never fault him for thinking small. "Allan was the first person to come up with a national marketing campaign for a Broadway show," says Wilner. "Pan Am paid for that opening-night party." Certainly Allan knew how to treat the Pan Am executives, seating celebs like Marlo Thomas and Mary Tyler Moore next to veteran airline VPs. "Allan knew that the best deals are made on the golf course and at parties, he knew that," Wilner adds.

Allan's various deals, however, won him few friends among the show's participants that evening, And the frosty divide in Boston between him and his creatives resurfaced at the New York fete. "It was a mixed-up party, somehow with the producers and the investors and the director," says Theoni Aldredge. "They didn't get along beautifully. It was very 'This is my side and that's your side.' It wasn't a real company party."

Allan made sure to give Laurents, Fierstein, and Herman each his own table. "But the best tables were reserved for Allan's friends from Hollywood," says cast member John Weiner. "Those of us in the show looked at them, like, 'What are you doing here?'"

Laurents agreed. "The party was lavish. But it was too big and gaudy and just too much. It wasn't a party for the company. It was a party for Allan Carr and his world, whatever that was."

Allan knew the press better than most Broadway types. Reporters only cared to interview Hollywood stars at such events, and fortunately for them, Mary Tyler Moore played along. "I know drag," said the actress, decked out in her own decorative ensemble of paisley print pajamas. "I've been to San Francisco." A Cher look-alike approached Moore, who brushed off the guy with a quick, "I like your peplum skirt better than mine."

For his *La Cage* party, Allan retired his Mike Todd ringleader role and spent most of the evening holed away offstage reading the reviews. As if the intoxication of those notices wasn't heady enough, despite there being a Frank Rich in the ointment, he goosed the situation by getting stoned *and* inebriated, and was definitely smashed by the time he walked into the Pan Am lobby to make a speech. "Don't give me the bill for this party!" he brayed to his guests. "Give it to the Nederheimers," he added, mangling the name Nederlander.

The party came with only one other hitch: Allan's old nemesis at the *Village Voice*, writer Arthur Bell, had somehow secured a ticket despite the best efforts to keep him off the premises. Years earlier, Bell wrote a hatchet job on Ann-Margret, and outraged at the offense, Allan threatened the journalist with a pointed "I'm going to get you!"

"It was very Mafia-style," says the *New York Post* reporter Stephen M. Silverman. Bell feared for his physical safety, until someone at the *Village Voice* suggested, "If you have a column, no one can touch you." Bell liked that idea and lobbied his editors to up his workload and give him a weekly column, which they did, called "Bell Tells." That column soon featured the annual Ann-Margret Awards, a dishonor that the columnist bestowed upon famous people he considered major twits.

At *La Cage*'s party, Allan wanted to protect Ann-Margret from a face-to-face confrontation with their mutual nemesis at the *Village Voice,* and so he placed the actress in a roped-off section. In the end, Ann-Margret, a major investor in *La Cage aux folles,* didn't need the ropes. With flowers in her hair, she arrived at the party with husband Roger Smith and no fewer than four bodyguards. Jerry Herman, for one, came unprotected and soon found himself on the receiving end of one of Bell's more pointed questions—pointed, at least, for 1983. The columnist wanted to know if Herman was ready to "make a pronouncement" in light of the show's out-of-the-closet anthem "I Am What I Am."

According to Bell, the composer "blushed" and proceeded not to answer his question. "*La Cage* isn't [auto]biographical" is how Bell recorded Herman's response in his *Village Voice* column a few days later.

But journalists have a way of telling only their side of the story. What Bell left out of his *La Cage aux folles* report was the full extent of Herman's retort, which included the words "Do you think an author has to write about himself? Do you think I was Molly Picon in *Milk and Honey*?" he said of his first Broadway musical, from 1961. "Or do you think I know anything about how Dolly

Levi felt when she came down those stairs to return to the human race? You have to have an imagination, Arthur!"

Herman agreed wholeheartedly with Allan on the scourge from the *Village Voice*. "Arthur Bell was one of the classic cranky 'queens'—that's not a word I use often—who give homosexuals a bad name. I was never hiding what I was when I went to theater openings."

A member of the militant gay group Act-Up, Bell positioned himself at the forefront of AIDS awareness in the New York press, and as the only openly gay person who wrote a weekly column in a widely circulated Gotham newspaper, he held sway over other homosexuals when it came to what they saw or didn't see on Broadway. Bell gave *La Cage aux folles* a decidedly mixed review: "The show's an old-fashioned formula musical which comes to vivid life during the drag production numbers. The first act has moments of high hilarity. The second act falls flat."

Homosexual men created and produced *La Cage aux folles,* but that didn't mean all of their brethren approved. "We were criticized in the gay press," says Barry Brown. Arthur Laurents said he didn't care what gay people thought of his show. "If we gave them the show they asked for, we would have closed in three weeks," he offered. With a then-record advance of $4 million and first-day sales of nearly a quarter million, *La Cage* had no fear of running only three weeks.

Broadway audiences wanted romance and glamour. Gay activists demanded politics and protest. The latter's response stung some members of the all-gay *La Cage* team, but Laurents took heart that the musical, in addition to being a mere entertainment, did change hearts and minds. A professor at New York University, Laurents taught theater, and after one class, a graduate student gave him the upbeat report: He had come out to his parents after taking them to see a performance of *La Cage aux folles*.

That was the good news. As for the other news, *La Cage aux folles* opened on Broadway just as the epidemic known as AIDS—it had been referred to only two years earlier as GRID (gay-related immune deficiency)—began to enter the public consciousness. On Broadway, a significant number of important creatives had already begun to die, and the disease's presence even made its insidious way into the Palace Theater.

From the first rehearsals, Gene Barry was not popular with many in the company, who considered him "too Hollywood," and to make matters even more precarious, his interviews with the press were patronizing, at best, when it came to the subject of playing a homosexual on stage. His standard lines were "People never think you're a murderer if you're playing a murderer" and "I have nothing against homosexuals, but I have no part of their polemics."

Allan didn't take offense at such remarks, but Fierstein did. "Gene would say horrible things in the press," he recalls. Those comments were endured by gay members of the cast and crew, but not tolerated was Barry's backstage behavior, especially when the chorus boys noticed that he actively shunned them. As they explained it to Fierstein, "Gene Barry won't ride in the elevator with us because he's afraid of catching AIDS."

It was the truth. John Weiner, who played Barry's son in the show, listened repeatedly as the star expressed his fear of being infected with the AIDS virus. One night, in the wings of the Palace Theater, shortly before their entrance, Weiner put it to Barry in blunt terms: "Gene, you really have nothing to worry about. You're not going to catch AIDS unless you're bending over and take it up the ass."

"OK. OK," said Barry.

As the show's publicist, Shirley Herz felt that Barry's concern went beyond the disease. "He kept asking me if people would think he was a homosexual because he was in *La Cage aux folles*," says Herz. The publicist kept telling him, "Not if you aren't."

Allan fiercely obeyed Laurents's edict that he never speak to the cast about any problem. Which left it to Fierstein to confront Barry, albeit in a roundabout way: "I went to Gene's wife, Betty, and told her, 'This has to stop.'"

And it did. Betty talked to her husband and Barry started riding the elevator with the Cagelles, whether he liked them or not.

In some respects, the Gene Barry problem should have been handled by Allan, not Fierstein. Allan, however, was not a favorite among the chorus boys, more than a few of whom found him arrogant. Allan showed respect to the principal actors but often mistreated the chorus members, whom he considered on the level of assistants, secretaries, gofers. At one party for the show, John Weiner stood at the bar with a Cagelle. "And after Allan congratulated me on my performance, he completely ignored this other actor, who was quite upset by the slight," says Weiner.

Even a misanthrope like Arthur Laurents noted Allan's dark side. "He could say cutting things and behave badly," he recalls. "But Allan didn't mean to be a killer. Rather, he was filled with self-loathing, because of his weight, I think."

Gene Barry's "problem" with *La Cage aux folles* was not entirely without basis. The show had a definite "vibe," as cast member Mark Waldrop recalls.

"We all knew Allan had a wild party reputation," he says. "There was a great atmosphere around the show: It was a gay show and there were these gay men in charge of it. There was a sort of an early 1980s charge of sexuality surrounding the show, with the older men choosing up among the younger men. That was the impression."

Whether that bonhomie among cast, creatives, and producers qualified as a bad thing or not depended on how one looked at it. As Jon Wilner describes the scene backstage at *La Cage,* "It was incestuous. Everyone was sleeping with the Cagelles. Everyone had a Cagelle. It was a great time."

twenty-four

Choreographed Chaos

When the party ended in the Pan Am lobby, Allan moved it to the beaches of Fort Lauderdale, where his update of *Where the Boys Are* continued to film. "There were always plenty of Hollywood-style good-looking guys who were being interviewed and then stuck in the background of the film," says Howard McGillin.

The film's party quotient hit its greatest density when, in one scene, a flotilla of motor boats, yachts, sailboats, Jet Skiers, and two parachutists literally crash (one boat leaves the water to beach itself in the front lawn) a private gathering hosted by a rich kid, a character evocatively named Camden Roxbury (Daniel McDonald), and his mother (Louise Sorel). The movie never reveals how these spring-break students, who couldn't afford decent hotel rooms, lucked into owning, renting, or even hijacking such expensive watercraft. Not that Allan didn't consider the expense.

It sent him into a phone-calling frenzy when one manufacturer wouldn't provide the Jet Skis free of charge. "Are they crazy? They'll see Kawasaki all over the movie!" he cried. When the sportsware company wouldn't buy his pitch, Allan sought to apply pressure and ordered an assistant to start making phone calls. "Bo Derek's father used to be a Kawasaki executive," he began, "but let's start with Bruce Jenner. I think he did a Kawasaki ad in Hawaii."

When Bo and Bruce's connections proved worthless, Allan took subtle revenge. "Make sure you tape out the name," he said of the Kawasaki logo. "I ain't giving away free publicity to people who aren't nice."

In what came to be known as the Jet Skis scene, Russell Todd plays the fire-brand leader, who, in addition to leading the rowdy rebels à la George Washington across the canals of Boca Raton, rescues Lisa Hartman from a no-good rich boy and a fate worse than warm Dom Perignon. Filmed at the end of summer, the scene was "chaos," says Todd, "and I was wearing this really heavy, itchy sweater. It was hotter than hell, at least 110 degrees."

McGillin had never experienced anything like it before—or since. "There were cranes everywhere," he recalls. "There was even an airplane involved in the shooting." For the most part, Hy Averback, the sixty-two-year-old director, took a backseat, having found himself a piece of shade under a big magnolia tree.

With the opening of *La Cage* out of the way, not to mention Arthur Laurents, Allan relished being at the helm of a big production that he got to direct. From the balcony of a rented Boca Raton mansion, Allan led the charge as he yelled through a bullhorn, "OK, start your engines. Let's rip! Action!"

By walkie-talkie, he cautioned Russell Todd. "Don't fall off the boat!" he cried. "I don't want to lose you."

The thought did enter Todd's mind: Dozens of motorboats crisscrossed the canal, making the water choppier than the open seas, and while there were no boating accidents, "One parachutist did miss his mark, and ended up in the bushes instead of on the ground," says Todd. "It was a mass assault coming in at all directions and angles."

Amidst the not so carefully organized chaos, Allan positioned himself high on a balcony or crane. Whatever his perch, he could be heard yelling, "Boys, take your shirts off!"

The film was replete with fantastically proportioned young men and women in Speedos and bikinis. "*That* made sense," says McGillin. "But what no one could figure out were some of the other extras." Many of them looked vaguely familiar, and, in fact, bore uncanny resemblances to Michael Jackson, Elizabeth Taylor, and Marilyn Monroe. "Allan liked celebrities at his parties," McGillin surmises. "There was this need he had to surround himself with celebrities. Even if he couldn't have the real thing, he'd get the look-alikes. And up there on the balcony was Allan, perhaps a little chemically borne, yelling, 'More boys around the pool!'"

Farther back under the magnolia tree sat Averback, fanning himself with the script. "I just remember thinking, I feel so sorry for him," says McGillin. On calmer days, the director enjoyed kicking back with the young actors and recalling his early days in television when he acted in *Dragnet* and *I Love Lucy* and, later, directed episodes of *The Beverly Hillbillies*. It puzzled some cast members why a man his age had been hired to direct a teen beach comedy. But then no director could have competed with a hands-on producer like Allan, who knew exactly what he wanted, especially for the big party that capped the Boca Raton scene.

He had handpicked the mansion, owned by an Australian industrialist who now grew oranges in Florida, and in Allan's opinion, it was a "wet dream of a house." The house inspired him to think big and he wanted that personal vision recorded so that it would end up in the film. "I want a couple screwing under the stairway," Allan told a note-taking assistant. "I want some girl with big tits lying on the staircase, drunk, saying, 'Does anyone wanna take me upstairs?' I want four tits looking out those bay windows behind the wet bar and two tits over by the fireplace and two more on the couch. I want a girl with big tits being pushed around on a serving cart like she was an hors d'oeuvre. I want another girl coming around with franks on a skewer, saying, 'You want my dogs?' In other words, in this scene more is not enough."

Allan took a breath, then turned to the esteemed owner of the house. "And now I want to go swimming," he said. "It's a fabulous pool."

When *Where the Boys Are* wrapped, Allan busied himself with dreams that *La Cage aux folles* would win the Grammy for best cast album against such formidable competition as Andrew Lloyd Webber's *Cats*. Allan gave much thought to which song should be performed on the telecast, and instead of choosing one of the more innocuous numbers, Allan insisted that actor Walter Charles (subbing for George Hearn, who didn't want to fly to Los Angeles during the show's run) deliver the Act I curtain dropper, the gay anthem "I Am What I Am." It's a defiant, almost militant, song, and standing on the stage of the Shrine Auditorium, Charles delivered it in full drag, tearing off his female wig at the song's angry conclusion.

Fierstein liked Allan's determination to show some political defiance on network TV. "But out of context the song makes no sense for an audience that doesn't know the show," he says. "The audience was going 'Why that? Wha's that?'"

When it came time to announce the winner, Allan braced himself, ready to take the stage. "And the Grammy goes to . . . *Cats!*"

Cats. La Cage aux folles. The two titles don't sound alike, but to Allan's ears on that particular night, after too much Cristal and cocaine, *Cats* came out sounding exactly like the title of his show. Excited, overjoyed, his adrenalin pumping, Allan rose in his seat to accept the Grammy. What he didn't immediately realize was that friends were begging him to sit down.

Suddenly, as if crossing a busy street on a green light only to see red midway, Allan crumpled back into his seat and began sweating through Andrew Lloyd Webber's acceptance speech. He waited for a commercial break so he could hightail it back home to Hilhaven Lodge.

There was more ignominy to come. Rather than rescue his reputation in Hollywood, *Where the Boys Are '84* sank it completely, preceded as it was by *Can't Stop the Music* in 1980 and *Grease 2* in 1982. At least, *Boys* disappeared before anyone noticed it had opened. Only the party at Studio 54, with its re-creation of Fort Lauderdale and three tons of real sand, lingered in anyone's memory. "The parties were always great," says publicist Kathy Berlin. "Only the movies stank."

But Allan still had *La Cage*.

While the Grammy meant nothing to Broadway's box office, the Tony was the cake as well as the frosting, and *La Cage*'s nomination for best musical of the 1983–1984 season, plus seven other Tony nominations, was balm on Allan's filmmaking wounds. Fortunately, *Cats* was not in awards contention, having won the season before. Ever since *La Cage* opened in August, no real competition reared its unwanted head over the course of the Broadway season, what with such lackluster tuners as *Baby*, *The Tap Dance Kid*, and *The Rink* presenting the only threat. That is, until Stephen Sondheim and James Lapine's *Sunday in the Park with George* held its premiere in the last days of the season, coming in just before the cutoff deadline for Tony nominations, on May 2, 1984. Critics hailed the Sondheim show as a masterpiece, and opening so late in the season, "They have the momentum," Allan rightfully feared. He held the *New York Times* responsible. "It's relentless. It's like they're giving it their political endorsement," he said. Every time he picked up the newspaper, there was another article proclaiming it a total triumph. "This went on for months."

Still, *Sunday in the Park*, an intimate and cerebral show, would have difficulty on tour in the sticks, Allan felt, whereas his show had wowed them in Boston. "They'll love it in San Francisco, Los Angeles, Miami, and New Orleans," he claimed. As he knew, many of the Tony voters were out-of-town presenters who needed the imprimatur of the Tony to sell shows on their home turf. Why waste the award on Sondheim's tuner, a show that only the cognoscenti could love and appreciate?

Allan ordered up tons of expensive ads to tout *La Cage*'s Tony potential. But in his head, if not his heart, he didn't really believe his dream would come true. "We all felt that *Sunday in the Park* would win," says Shirley Herz.

The year before, Fierstein won two Tonys, for starring in and writing *Torch Song Trilogy,* which transferred to Broadway after its run downtown. At those 1983 Tonys, the lead producer of Fierstein's play, John Glines, shocked many in the audience with his simple, heartfelt thank-you speech: "I want to thank my producing partner and lover, Lawrence Lane, who never said it can't be done." Such an affront to mainstream sensibilities was a first for the Tonys, as well as network TV. Award winners at the Tonys, the Oscars, and the Emmys had been thanking their opposite-sex spouses and lovers for decades. But no homosexual had ever dared mention his or her same-sex partner in the high-profile glare of a nationwide telecast. At the ball following the Tony sweep of *Torch Song Trilogy,* many stalwart members of the straight Broadway community, which had always prided itself on being liberal, found themselves defensive, if not under attack, by the sizable gay minority among them. "You could hear people across America flicking off their TV sets," said one producer, who feared that the heartland would be offended by Glines's audacious thank-you to his boyfriend.

Alexander Cohen, who produced the Tony telecasts, also worried about the TV audience. In 1984, the year of *La Cage aux folles, The Tap Dance Kid, The Rink,* and *Sunday in the Park with George*—shows that involved many homosexual writers, directors, and producers—Cohen was not about to endure a repeat of Glines's public gay gesture from the year before.

When he put on his tux for the Tonys, Harvey Fierstein entertained no plans to rock the heterosexual boat at the Gershwin Theater. He'd already won his Tonys, for *Torch Song Trilogy.* "And besides, I was actually hoping not to win that night," he says. "I loved *Sunday in the Park with George.* James Lapine had done a magnificent job with the book."

At least that's the way he felt *before* Cohen took the stage off camera to lecture the Gershwin Theater's live audience, giving them the dos and don'ts of on-camera etiquette. In closing he added, "And let's not have a repeat of last year's embarrassment with *Torch Song Trilogy* when it comes to giving acceptance speeches."

Fierstein saw red. He turned to his lover, Scott, and growled, "I want to win."

And win he did, along with Jerry Herman, George Hearn, Arthur Laurents, and Theoni Aldredge. Fierstein relished breaking Cohen's rule by, first, kissing the presenter, who happened to be fellow homosexual Larry Kert, and, second, telling the TV audience, "And I'd like to thank my lover, Scott, who typed the whole thing."

Hearn accepted his Tony for lead actor in a musical, and displayed a minor case of hetero skittishness when he said of his drag turn, "What a man won't do! . . ."

Allan gave Jerry Herman a standing ovation of one at the Gershwin when his *La Cage* score was awarded. With Tony in hand, Herman felt compelled to take a swipe at Sondheim's more sophisticated score. "There's a rumor going around for a couple of years that the simple hummable show tune was no longer welcome on Broadway. Well, it's alive and well at the Palace," he said.

The evening, however, belonged to Dustin Hoffman, who emerged as a surprise presenter. The actor had not been nominated for his performance as Willy Loman in *Death of a Salesman*. Many theatergoers considered it an oversight, if not a snub, and Hoffman milked the moment by wearing his *Salesman* hat onstage to give out the award for best play.

At evening's end, Michael Bennett announced the winner for best musical. Since the show had won the other big honors, it was no surprise when he announced, "*La Cage aux folles*," and Allan bolted to the stage, his legs carrying him faster than even he thought possible. He used his long-awaited moment of glory to indulge in an uncharacteristic bit of humility. "I'm just the conduit," he said, then stroked his new theater cohorts while dismissing his old movie ones. "This is the only awards show where people who aren't nominated show up. Hollywood, take a lesson from Broadway," he said, pointedly referencing the unexpected appearance of Dustin Hoffman.

Offstage, the Tony apparatchiks picked up Allan's award shortly after he walked into the wings of the Gershwin Theater. They told him it needed to be engraved. "I'm not leaving New York until I get mine back!" he promised. Following the telecast, Allan held court at the ball. He was Broadway's premiere producer, and for an hour or two, it didn't bother him that his creative team— Laurents, Herman, and Fierstein—had thanked each other in their acceptance speeches but not him. "He was happy, and it was fun to watch that kind of happiness," says Fierstein. Allan's Tony moment effectively erased every personal insult and career mishap of his forty-seven years—that is, until he woke up the next day.

Allan's friends—and some who weren't friends—joked that Allan Carr produced *La Cage aux folles* on Broadway so that he could eventually bring it to

Hollywood to show that he still had the stuff of a real producer. With Tony in hand, he concentrated on his grand return to the West Coast as the proud presenter of *La Cage aux folles*. The musical should have played there in a medium-size theater, like the Shubert in Century City. But the Shubert Theater (1,700 seats), in 1984, continued to house *A Chorus Line,* which the mighty theater organization had produced on Broadway. The Ahmanson Theater (2,000 seats) was a bit large, but it housed only limited runs due to its status as a nonprofit theater. Allan didn't want a limited run for *La Cage*. Not in Los Angeles, anyway. He wanted the real thing, a first-class sit-down production that wouldn't run for weeks or months but years. Since the Nederlander Organization, one of the show's producers, owned the Pantages Theater on Hollywood Boulevard, that venue emerged as the logical, if not the perfect, fit. At a gargantuan 2,700 seats, the mighty Pantages, a former home of the Oscars, is twice the size of the average Broadway theater.

It made economic sense to put out a national company of *La Cage aux folles*; there was its big Tony win and the show continued to sell out on Broadway. But once again, despite its New York success, the musical's gay content proved a hard sell. Broadway wasn't like the rest of America. To ease into the California market, Allan decided to open in homophilic San Francisco for a few weeks and then bring the show down to Los Angeles for an open-ended run.

"Allan wanted to show his pals in Hollywood what he could do," says Barry Brown. The San Francisco engagement scored. "We played fourteen weeks there and sold out, and could have stayed another six months."

Los Angeles, however, rotated in another orbit in the theater universe. The positive reviews there exceeded the New York notices, and instead of his Pan Am lobby extravaganza, Allan brought a hometown touch to the L.A. opening by taking over one of Hollywood's favorite eateries, the legendary Chasen's restaurant. He even renamed the place Chez Jacqueline, after the restaurant in *La Cage aux folles*, and made it a veritable children's playground with sand drifts of plastic confetti on the floor and colorful balloons within balloons suspended from the oak rafters. If Allan didn't get his wish to paint the Palace Theater pink, he indulged that fantasy by hanging huge swaths of pink fabric throughout Chasen's, which turned the restaurant into a very festive-looking Chinese laundry.

At the opening-night party in Los Angeles, Allan kept repeating his formula on how to entertain as if it were his new mantra: "What does it take to make a great party? It takes Alan Bates, Phyllis Diller, Christopher Atkins, Sidney

Poitier and Audrey and Jayne Meadows and Peter Falk in the same room still talking to each other. This is old Hollywood and new Hollywood. We made Chasen's a cross between 21 and Joe Allen's." He then nearly slipped on all the plastic confetti under his shoes. "I've gotta sweep this stuff up! Somebody thought it was cocaine on the floor," he grumbled with good cheer.

For a while, the publicity and positive reviews worked. The Pantages sold out, but only for a few weeks. Twenty-seven hundred seats is equal to filling two Broadway-size theaters on a nightly basis, and within a couple of months, the place was half empty on most week nights. "You needed binoculars even if you were sitting in the first row. It was like playing on a football field" is how Arthur Laurents described it.

La Cage aux folles ran one year in Los Angeles, not exactly the record longevity of *A Chorus Line*, but four times as long as most Broadway shows played in this notoriously nontheater town. The loss: $2 million. "Los Angeles should have been a stop on the national tour," says Barry Brown.

Allan did not tempt fate with a London production; instead, he licensed *La Cage* to some British producers. Laurents busied himself with that overseas project, while Allan and Jerry Herman concentrated instead on finding future Albins and Georges for their New York production, which continued to do, in *Variety* slanguage, "boffo biz." On Broadway, Allan wanted to replace the ailing Gene Barry, who had suffered a heart attack, with Regis Philbin. Laurents balked. He found daytime TV personalities "not classy enough" for his musical, and went with 1940s heartthrob Van Johnson instead.

Johnson, in time, grew increasingly tone-deaf in the role—"He would have sung it forever, if they let him," says cast member John Weiner—and eventually the former movie star also required a replacement. Two years earlier, Robert Stack had auditioned for Allan and Arthur Laurents at Hilhaven Lodge, where, Jerry Herman recalls, "There was a Lucite grand piano in the living room. It had absolutely no business being there." Laurents thought the actor needed singing lessons, to which Allan replied, "But Bob's aunt was an opera singer!" Laurents also expressed concern that Stack, best known for his portrayal of Elliot Ness on TV's *The Untouchables,* had never appeared on Broadway and his stage experience "was limited to five weeks of summer stock twenty years ago," according to the director.

Allan did not heed Laurents's advice. When *La Cage aux folles* needed a Georges replacement after Van Johnson's departure, Allan went ahead and signed Stack. Advertisements were printed to announce the new cast member, and with Laurents still putting the London cast through its paces, it fell to Fritz Holt and an assistant director, Jim Pendecost, to rehearse Stack for the New York production. Then Laurents returned to New York City on a Sunday night. It had been a bumpy opening night in London.

"Everyone was in a bad mood because of the bad reviews," says Jon Wilner. "You don't tell the English how to do drag in the Palladium." Indeed, weeks earlier, Harvey Fierstein had complained about putting *La Cage* in the 2,400-seat theater in the West End. "I stood in the back of the house and looked down at that stage so far away, it was like I was seeing it from Passaic." The thought hit him, "They had forgotten what the show is about. It is a show about a couple in love. It's about human emotions. The ego of these people." And there were other problems. Despite the appearance of George Hearn, "It wasn't well cast in the West End," says Shirley Herz.

Into this maelstrom of nasty news from London dropped Robert Stack, who was to have his first run-through with a jet-lagged Arthur Laurents on the very day, Monday, that the autocratic director got his first look at the full-page ad in the *New York Times* heralding the appearance of TV's Elliot Ness in *La Cage aux folles*. If Allan could get his way when it came to taking out advertisements, Laurents was about to show the Broadway community that he controlled everything from the "orchestra rail to the back wall of the theater."

That Monday morning, Stack performed the role of Georges onstage with the full cast. Georges's opening monologue, in which he invites everyone to club La Cage aux Folles, didn't go well. According to Laurents, the meeting that led to Stack's leaving the show took place between the two men. "After the rehearsal, I met with Bob onstage alone. They had all gone. They fled," Laurents says, referring to the cast, management, and producers.

Producer Barry Brown and actor John Weiner recall being present that day, and they tell a slightly more theatrical story.

Sitting in the auditorium of the Palace Theater, surrounded by a few cast members and assistants, Laurents was not a happy director, according to Brown and Weiner. "I'm going to be rid of him after this rehearsal," he said of Stack.

Someone whispered back, "Oh, he's just nervous."

"It's not going to get better," Laurents cracked.

Among other problems, Stack found it difficult to negotiate the furniture onstage. Worse, his role required that he function as the evening's emcee, and he simply lacked the requisite charm and bonhomie that Van Johnson and Gene Barry exuded. Laurents made minor adjustments in Stack's performance, but it soon became clear that Stack had progressed from clumsy to downright scared. Then Stack launched into "Song on the Sand," the love song he sings to Albin.

No sooner had he finished than Laurents called a halt to the rehearsal, and made his way to the stage. It's never a good sign when the director leaves his orchestra seat to confront an actor face-to-face onstage. Again, Laurents made minor suggestions to Stack. At first, they were delivered sotto voce, but soon his voice began to escalate, and in front of the full company, who had gradually made their collective way to within earshot, he told Stack, "You can't sing. You can't act. What can you do?"

Marvin Krauss, the show's general manager, materialized from the wings. "Everybody in the lobby!" he announced as if speaking to a room of eavesdropping schoolchildren. But the company of actors didn't leave fast enough, and as they shuffled out, they were able to catch Stack's defense. "Jerry Herman and Allan Carr heard me sing and thought I sang very nicely," he said.

"Well, I resent Jerry Herman and Allan Carr saying that," Laurents replied.

"You think I'm doing this show?" Stack sputtered.

It's exactly what Arthur Laurents wanted to hear. He didn't have to fire Robert Stack. Robert Stack fired himself.

Laurents wrote in his book *Mainly on Directing* that he delivered his rejection of Stack in private and that the actor took it "without a trace of resentment," that "we shook hands, he quit that day, and I never saw him again."

Regardless of who was present (or eavesdropping) during the infamous showdown between Laurents and Stack, there's no doubt that the director's next encounter with his producer, via a letter, was not so amicable. In a missive posted from Quogue, New York, Laurents chastised Allan in withering detail: "You, the Veteran Producer (according to your theatre program bio which, however, lists absolutely no previous experience worth mentioning), waited until I was in London and then insisted on signing Stack without anyone hearing him read, let alone sing, in a theatre. Now you were in high gear and really on a power trip." Laurents went on to accuse Allan of costing the production $100,000 as a result of the Stack hiring/firing: "Did you pay? No, the show did, the investors did. Will they ever know? How creative is your bookkeeping? As creative as your ducking responsibility? Because who, in this whole painful and unnecessary episode, who got off scot-free? You did."

There it was, finally, out in the open. The two men hated each other, and that animosity only escalated *La Cage*'s ongoing marketing wars. Laurents had always loathed the print ads that stressed the show's transvestite subject matter. "After three years, we were sick of Arthur complaining," says Wilner, who, along with Allan, decided to release what was called their "straight campaign," one that featured the young lovers, Jean-Michel and Anne. No sooner did the new advertisements appear in newspapers than the gay activist group ACT UP voiced its objection in the "Page Six" gossip column of the *New York Post*.

Allan consulted no one. He read the *Post*'s ACT UP item and ordered, "Get rid of the new ads! We didn't do this show to hurt the gay community. Pull everything. Go back to the original."

Early in the show's run, Rock Hudson and his longtime friend and occasional lover Tom Clarke paid a visit to *La Cage aux folles*. They even made the obligatory visit backstage to say hello to the show's stars and pose for photographs. If AIDS would eventually claim many of Broadway's finest in the 1980s, including one of the show's executive producers, Fritz Holt, it took its most famous victim, Rock Hudson, on October 2, 1985. His death came on a Wednesday, and by the end of that day's matinee, CBS had already dispatched its camera crew to the sidewalk in front of the Palace Theater to ask theatergoers what they thought of not only the movie star's death from AIDS but Broadway's only gay musical, *La Cage aux folles*.

"*La Cage aux folles* had nothing to do with AIDS, but in people's mind it was about gay people and the equation was made," Allan lamented. After the CBS report aired, box office at *La Cage aux folles* took an immediate tumble, never to return to its former superhit status. The impact was even greater elsewhere. "The AIDS epidemic was partially responsible for the show's failure in London," says Barry Brown. And on the West Coast, it didn't help *La Cage*'s box office when the Screen Actors Guild responded in the press to reports that homosexual actors were being discriminated against because of AIDS.

The media stoked the AIDS frenzy, which quickly turned into a gay backlash, especially in the once-friendly terrain of the downtown nightlife. In *New York* magazine, Bianca Jagger was quoted as saying that she appreciated the heterosexual atmosphere at Steve Rubell's new club, the Palladium. And Rubell himself remarked, "Gay, it's an empty life," despite the fact that he was already taking the drug AZT to control his HIV, which, four years later, would take his life.

By summer 1987, *La Cage*'s company was ready to traipse a few blocks north from the Palace to the smaller Mark Hellinger Theater. AIDS wasn't the only thing that forced the planned move: Air rights had been sold over the

Palace Theater, to make way for a new DoubleTree Hotel. The move looked
like a sure thing. Actor Lee Roy Reams from *42nd Street* had been rehearsed,
the Hellinger sported a new *La Cage* marquee, and while the show's box office
continued to dwindle in the wake of the AIDS crisis, the marketing director,
Jon Wilner, welcomed the move away from the discount tickets booth, known
as TKTS, that sat directly in front of the Palace Theater in Duffy Square. *La
Cage* had heretofore never been able to take advantage of the booth, because
"If you sold half price, you could never get full price," says Wilner. In residence
at the Hellinger, the musical would finally be able to go the discount route.

Wilner never got to test his theory. Shortly before the planned transfer to
the Hellinger, Marvin Krauss called a meeting in lawyer John Breglio's office.
It was not a good sign. "You never have a meeting at a lawyer's office," says
Wilner, "because it means you will be canceled." Allan didn't attend. Suffering
from his kidney stones, he remained in California.

Breglio got right to the point. "There is no [current] economic justification
for *La Cage*," he said. The show's advance ticket sales were in freefall, and according to the lawyer, the show's box-office decline was due to forces outside
anyone's control. "It was sad and depressing," Breglio later observed. "Because
of the AIDS crisis, [the subject matter of *La Cage*] was no longer something
you could easily fool with."

Broadway itself was reeling. In addition to Fritz Holt, the theater community
had lost Michael Bennett, *Company* star Larry Kert, and many others to AIDS.
"No one closes a hit show. *La Cage* had run four and a half years. It had run its
course," says Brown.

Arthur Laurents took the opportunity to blame Allan for the early closing,
and he offered a bizarre explanation: "We were set to move to the Mark
Hellinger. The Moonies, however, wanted the Hellinger for their tabernacle.
They offered Allan Carr a lot of money. . . . He took it, and that was the end of
La Cage aux folles, the musical."

The followers of Sun Myung Moon, of course, had nothing to do with the
show's shuttering. The Mark Hellinger Theater eventually became the home
of the evangelical Times Square Church, but not before another musical, the
Peter Allen flop, *Legs Diamond*, opened and quickly closed there.

If Allan was too indisposed to make it to Breglio's office to deliver the bad
news, he didn't miss the opportunity to attend a good party two weeks later.
After their final performance on November 15, 1987, the cast members of *La*

Cage said good-bye to each other at a small restaurant on the corner of Amsterdam and West 79th Street.

"We were surprised that Allan came to the party," says cast member Mark Waldrop. "Everyone was mad at him."

Wilner disregarded the cast's negative attitude. Many of the actors were young, and didn't know that *La Cage* had been a rather atypical Broadway experience. Producers often replace casts on a yearly basis, but Allan proved much more generous and loyal to his actors. As the marketing director points out, "The cast kept getting raises on a regular basis. There were few defections. They didn't go to other shows."

John Weiner, who never left the Broadway *La Cage* during its entire four-year run, agrees: "We had parties all the time, they treated us like gold." He recalls one of the older cast members telling him, "This is a real special kind of thing."

Regardless of Allan's largesse for the preceding four years, the sudden posting of the closing notice made for hurt feelings. If Allan sensed that *Macbeth* atmosphere, he didn't advertise his outsider status. At the closing party, he even smiled when three of the Cagelles sang the tune "Brother, Can You Spare a Dime?" but changed the lyrics to reflect the occasion. As *La Cage*'s trio put it to the newly unemployed among them, "Hey, don't you remember? I was a star in my fabulous prime. I once did a show for Allan Carr. Brother, can you spare a dime?"

twenty-five

Goya, Goya, Gone

Before he shuttered *La Cage aux folles*, Allan made a visit to the Metropolitan Opera as the guest of Sybil Harrington. A Texas oil heiress worth close to a billion dollars, give or take a few barrels, the silver-haired Mrs. Harrington was such a dutiful patron of the opera house that the management named its 3,800-seat theater in her honor while she could still enjoy it. Before the Texas heiress did ascend to that great Valhalla in the sky, Harrington liked to show her friends the newly placed bronze plaque on the orchestra level. It read "The Sybil Harrington Auditorium." One flight of marble stairs up, on the parterre level, she often took up residence in the general manager's primo left-corner box. On this particular evening, her guests were Placido Domingo and Allan. During the first intermission, the opera novice among them made the faux pas of asking the great Spanish tenor a naive question.

"Placido," Allan began, "who does the sound system in this house? It sounds so natural. I don't see the microphones."

Domingo laughed. "This is opera," he informed Harrington's opera-challenged friend. "We don't use microphones here."

"Amazing!" said Allan.

During the second intermission, it was Domingo's turn to ask the ingenuous question. "I want to do a Broadway show," he said. "Is it possible to create a new show for me?"

"Of course" came the quick answer. "But it's easier said than done," said Allan, thinking back to the seven years it took to create *La Cage aux folles*.

"I just did a pop song with John Denver," Domingo added. "One day I will have to make the graceful and gracious move away from opera. I can't do *South Pacific,* that's Ezio Pinza's role."

"Like Pinza, you need an original role," Allan agreed.

As the house lights dimmed for the third act of *Madama Butterfly,* Allan added, "We will discuss this after the opera." He had already begun writing the new intro paragraph of his *New York Times* obituary: "Allan Carr, the impresario who brought Placido Domingo to Broadway . . . " Allan thought of nothing else for the next thirty minutes of unrequited love, child abandonment, humiliation, and suicide. Cio-Cio-San's tragedy came and went. Allan didn't notice. Instead of listening to Puccini's music as it pumped through the Met's nonexistent sound system, he compiled a list of questions for his eager Broadway debutant. After the performance, over drinks and a late-night dinner at the Ginger Man restaurant, he set out to get Domingo's answer to each and every one of them.

Over their endive salads, Allan put forth the greatest unknown. "What famous Spanish figure would you like to portray onstage?" he asked Domingo.

The tenor didn't have to think long. "What about a bullfighter like Manolete?"

Allan looked at Domingo, who was svelte for an opera singer but not svelte for a Broadway star. He carefully composed his response as Domingo proceeded to tell him all about Manuel Rodríguez Sánchez, aka Manolete, a great bullfighter who expired in the bullring in 1947 after being gored by a fierce Miura bull. Manolete's only solace, as Domingo told it, was that the Miura also died in battle.

"A great story!" said Allan, his hands clapping as Domingo finished his bullfighting profile. "A great story, perfect for the opera. But Broadway? Placido, funny, but you don't look like a bullfighter. A voice you have, but the body of a bullfighter? You will have to wear a bullfighter's costume on Broadway, and the sequins will not cover all the pasta and paella you've consumed."

Allan knew the only way to criticize a person's weight is to level the attack with tongue planted firmly in his own jowly cheek. Domingo digested Allan's critique of his physique along with his pasta that evening, and said he'd think about it. "I will give you a list of other famous Spanish people," Domingo added. "In the meantime, you must come hear me perform at Madison Square Garden. I sing zarzuela. It's like a Broadway musical." Domingo devoted several engagements a year to performing in the Spanish folk idiom, which, like American musical theater, weaves together songs and spoken dialogue. His family in Madrid, where Domingo was born, ran a zarzuela company, which they later moved to Mexico City.

Allan made his pilgrimage to hear the great Domingo sing at Madison Square Garden, and backstage the tenor kept his promise. He presented his list of famous Spanish personages, any one of whom he wanted to portray on stage.

Allan looked over the list. "Goya?" he asked. "What do you know about Goya?"

Domingo knew everything about the Aragonese Spanish painter, including his full name, Francisco José de Goya y Lucientes, and the fact that he went mad due to the lead powder he mixed into his paints to give his portraits their trademark luminescence.

Allan loved the idea, and he didn't fall out of love with it when Domingo later informed him that the American composer Gian Carlo Menotti had already written an opera titled *Goya,* commissioned by the tenor and performed on public television the year before. It didn't matter. Opera and Broadway were two different audiences, as Allan kept repeating. All that mattered was that he would follow his *La Cage aux folles* success with an even greater triumph by bringing Placido Domingo to Broadway. He wallowed in that thought as he contemplated who should write this opus. "This Goya musical will be my *Gandhi,*" he told people.

The phone call surprised Maury Yeston. He hadn't heard from Allan since 1981 when he went off to make *Grease 2* and left the composer-lyricist with a batch of songs for an unproduced musical called *The Queen of Basin Street.* Since then, Yeston had written a Tony-winning musical, *Nine,* based on Federico Fellini's movie *8 ½.* That major accomplishment aside, it was as if the last half dozen years were but a weekend. Then again, Yeston couldn't be too angry at Allan: For his efforts on *The Queen of Basin Street,* the composer received 0.25 percent of the weekly box-office take from *La Cage aux folles.*

Allan started the phone conversation with Yeston on an upbeat note, retelling his opera faux pas in which he asked Domingo "Who does the sound system?" at the Met Opera. Then, as often was the case when Allan wanted to make things happen, he presented his business plan without delay: Domingo wanted to perform in an original musical on Broadway, and would Yeston like to write a show for him based on the life of Goya. "I mentioned your name to Domingo and he loves your score for *Nine,*" Allan added.

The phone call "came out of the blue," says Yeston, and despite their *Queen of Basin Street* misfire, the composer couldn't refuse such an offer. "Anyone would jump at the chance to write for Domingo," says Yeston. He did a little research on Goya, and soon discovered why Domingo found the painter to be an ideal subject for the musical theater: Goya was the last of the Old Masters and the first of the moderns. He indulged in several great love affairs, passionately espoused pacifism, went deaf like Beethoven, and effected no fewer than three revolutions in art. Yeston knew precisely how to deliver this great portrait to the Broadway stage. As he pitched it to Allan, "What if this show reflected those style changes of traditional musical theater and gradually more and more got to be acid rock at the end?"

"Perfect," said Allan. "I love it."

Although Allan knew about the Menotti *Goya*, he didn't mention it to Yeston. "I just naturally assumed that Placido envisioned a musical theater role as tailored to him as the King of Siam was to Yul Brynner or Tevye was to Zero Mostel. And I thought that was a very smart idea," says the composer.

Yeston set to work, and a few months later, he was ready to play some of the score for Domingo, Freddie Gershon, and Allan. The four men met backstage at the Metropolitan Opera, where Domingo had just finished a performance of Verdi's *Otello*. Everyone wanted Domingo's feedback on Yeston's score, but Allan and Gershon also needed to lock in dates for *Goya*'s Broadway production. Opera singers commit to the Met, La Scala, and Covent Garden years in advance, so Allan and Gershon braced themselves. They both realized that this project could take awhile.

Having just performed Otello, his most arduous role, Domingo felt ebullient that night as he wiped away the Moor's makeup and listened to Yeston play a few *Goya* songs on the dressing-room piano. "Allan Carr delivered good to me," he kept saying. He was especially enthusiastic about a love ballad that Yeston had written for him, "'Till I Loved You."

"I love this so much! This is so pleasing to me," Domingo continued.

But as for the dates he could perform on Broadway . . .

In the opera world, Domingo is well known as a numbers man, someone who can recite from memory how many times he has performed every opera in his massive repertoire. Domingo also displays total recall of every date he is scheduled to sing in the future. He didn't have to look at notes when he informed Allan and Gershon of his upcoming schedule. Regarding *Goya*, he was fully prepared to set aside three months next year in the spring and a couple of weeks later in the summer and a few more weeks at the end of 1989. For a busy opera superstar, four or five months equals a small eternity to devote to one project.

Allan may have produced only one Broadway show, but he knew that no musical production could recoup its capitalization in fewer than six months. When Domingo told them of his schedule, "We all just went pale," Yeston recalls.

Within an instant, Allan segued from glad-hander to seasoned businessman to undertaker. There was no way he could adjust the project's basic time requirements. "We need a minimum guarantee of six months. Six months at least," he told Domingo. "Unless you have another great tenor who can substitute for you until you're able to return. I need a commitment of six consecutive months. Otherwise, I cannot do it. I cannot do it." Now he knew how the Met impresario Rudolf Bing felt when he fired Maria Callas.

The world's greatest tenor could only say no to his Broadway debut.

Gershon walked up West 65th Street with a suddenly "bloodless" Allan Carr and Maury Yeston. "Domingo couldn't understand why we were disappointed," says Gershon.

The opera singer's affection for Yeston's score, however, was genuine, and he didn't let go of the project. He firmly believed that "'Till I Loved You" would be his signature song, and to show his commitment, the singer convinced CBS Records, where he had cut many opera albums, to make a CD of Yeston's musical, which was to be called *Goya: A Life in Song*.

"You want to have *My Fair Lady* in your regime?" Domingo told Walter Yetnikoff, head of CBS Records. "Wait until you hear this score."

Again, Yeston was called upon to return to the piano, this time to audition his score for the powers at Black Rock on Sixth Avenue in New York City. Again, it was a success. Yetnikoff agreed wholeheartedly with Domingo. "If we as a company cannot get behind something with this kind of integrity, why are we in this business?" said Yetnikoff, who wanted to match the tenor's star power with pop icons like Barbra Streisand and Richie Havens. This was to be a class project, and Yetnikoff demanded no less a producer than Mike Berniker, heir to CBS's Goddard Lieberson, the man who "invented" the original cast album. Since Yetnikoff felt that Domingo's talent required something better than a Broadway pickup band, tracks were laid down instead with the London Philharmonic, as well as the New York Philharmonic, and Domingo recorded a couple of the ballads, including his favorite, "'Till I Loved You." It was this version of his musical that Yeston would refer to as the "classical" *Goya*.

Finally, it was time for the powers at Black Rock to listen to what Berniker had produced before approaching the big pop guns of Streisand and Havens to perform alongside Domingo on the record. What Yetnikoff heard impressed him but not in a good way. "This sounds like musical theater," he said. The comment astounded Allan and Yeston, because "Isn't that what we were doing?" asked the composer.

"No," said Yetnikoff. "I want this ballad 'Till I Loved You' to be a hit song. I'd like to get a whole other audience. Everybody should know *Goya*. I'd like to get Phil Ramone to produce this album."

What Allan didn't know is that Yetnikoff, while considered a genius music executive despite his tone-deafness, had recently suffered yet another nervous breakdown brought on, in part, by his addiction to cocaine and alcohol. Bruce Springsteen called him "the craziest music exec north of E Street," and the Boss said so with no hyperbole intended.

But who was to argue with the man at the top of CBS Records, then home to not only Springsteen but Michael Jackson, the Rolling Stones, Bob Dylan, Billy Joel, and James Taylor?

Allan did what any man in his position would do. He said, "I love the idea!"

And so, crazy or not, Yetnikoff replaced Berniker with Ramone on *Goya*. Ramone was definitely not musical theater. He had produced every Burt Bacharach song and many by Billy Joel, which meant that the budget on the *Goya* LP ballooned from the $250,000 that Berniker had envisioned to the $1 million that Ramone needed to bring on pop stars Gloria Estefan, Dionne Warwick, Richie Havens, and Seiko Matsuda.

Yeston found it all very thrilling. "But it wasn't musical theater," he says. "And it wasn't rock." This was the version that Yeston would refer to as the "pop" *Goya*.

Whether it ultimately could be categorized as pop, rock, opera, or Broadway, "It was a great project that failed," says Gershon, who, together with Allan, took producer credits on the project. The classical audience considered the CD a bit déclassé, a step down for the great Domingo. And the pop audience thought, "What the hell are these pop stars singing with this guy who bellows? And they didn't understand his accent," says Gershon.

Allan hoped that the concept album might spur a full-scale Broadway production. "Maybe we would cast it with a singer other than Domingo," Yeston surmised. But there was no money interest.

Not ready to let go of the project, Allan plotted how to revive *Goya*. His answer came in autumn 1988 when the Music Center Opera Company approached him about staging a benefit at the Hollywood Bowl. Domingo had sung with the fledgling company and sat on its board of directors. The idea struck Allan, "What if we present a concert version of *Goya* with Domingo, Gloria Estefan, and a few others who appear on the album? Who knows? We might even be able to get Barbra Streisand!"

If the Metropolitan Opera is grand at 3,800 seats, the Hollywood Bowl is the true behemoth of performing spaces with its 18,000 outdoor seats. There weren't 18,000 people in all of Los Angeles who had even heard of Goya, much less *Goya*. To bring in the masses, Allan relegated his new musical to the benefit's second half, and kicked off with a much more conventional and crowd-pleasing first act.

"The first half of the show was great moments from Broadway," Gershon recalls. Elaine Stritch reprised her "Ladies Who Lunch" from *Company*, Patti LuPone sang "Don't Cry for Me, Argentina" from *Evita*, Tommy Tune performed "It's Not Where You Start" from *Seesaw*, and Carol Channing did "Diamonds Are a Girl's Best Friend" from *Gentlemen Prefer Blondes*. But Allan's coup de théâtre was getting a seventy-five-year-old Mary Martin to cap the benefit's first half with renditions of "Cockeyed Optimist" from *South Pacific* and "My Heart Belongs to Daddy," which, as she explained to the adoring Bowl audience, was the song she used to audition for Cole Porter in 1938. Best of all, the night marked Martin's fiftieth anniversary in show business. Few impresarios other than Allan Carr could pull off such a grand star-packed event.

Act I of the opera benefit appeared to be finished, and the audience had yet to see Domingo, when suddenly his inimitable tenor voice could be heard singing "Some Enchanted Evening," the great Ezio Pinza song from *South Pacific*. He then walked onstage to take Mary Martin in his arms and the two proceeded to make the great American aria into a duet. It was a one-night-only feat, since Martin's original *South Pacific* contract stipulated that she not be required to sing onstage with the great Pinza. Allan convinced her otherwise for the great Domingo.

"It cost $500 to sit in the boxes, and it was wonderful," Gershon recalls. The crowd went into ovation overdrive and couldn't wait to hear Domingo sing more beloved music from the great Broadway repertoire.

Instead, Allan devoted the entire second act to *Goya*, billed that evening as a "work in progress." After a long intermission, Domingo took the stage with Gloria Estefan. Despite his never having performed any *Goya* song in public, the evening registered as a disappointment for the opera tenor. He had looked forward to making "'Till You Loved Me" his signature song and a crossover hit— that is, until, Barbra Streisand recorded her own version of it earlier that year, performing it with her current boyfriend, Don Johnson. The single, which quickly went platinum, was produced by . . . Phil Ramone.

The *Hollywood Reporter* review of the gala summed up the schizoid nature of the event. "No discredit to *Goya,* the second half was, understandably, anticlimactic to the time-capsule-worthy first half."

Some of *Goya*'s participants were a little less forgiving. "There was a large Latino audience there that night to hear Domingo and Gloria Estefan," says Gershon. "And I don't think anyone knew what was going on."

Yeston agrees: "It didn't land. It wasn't a show."

In typical showbiz style, when people mentioned the opera benefit to Allan, they congratulated him on the stupendous first half and diplomatically ignored the second half. He had gambled on giving *Goya* the world's biggest backers' audition, and he failed. There was the solace, however, of having raised over $600,000 for the opera, and as Allan himself summed it up, "Who else raises $600,000 for opera in L.A.?"

Goya might have made it to Broadway, with or without Domingo, had it been handled properly. But at every turn, instead of being nurtured quietly in readings and workshops, the project developed an early, fatal case of Brobdingnagitis—first as a million-dollar concept album produced by Phil Ramone, and second as a Hollywood Bowl concert produced by Allan Carr.

Yeston believes that Allan had two goals in life, goals that were always at odds with each other. "He had a deep love of the material and the wonderful world of entertainment. He also had a personal goal to create a legend for himself, and if that second goal resulted in some bad or wild behavior, that was all to the good." He saw himself in the constellation with the great flamboyant producers and impresarios like David Merrick and Mike Todd. "That was terribly important to this overweight, spoiled Jewish kid who wanted to make good on both coasts. It is a classic American tragedy, because everything Allan wanted to do he undermined by being too flamboyant."

If *Goya* defined Allan Carr's fate, his next project was the one to seal it.

twenty-six

What He Prayed For

Ready to give his joints a rest after climbing the Hollywood Bowl, Allan tried to prepare himself emotionally, as well as physically, for yet another trip to Cedars-Sinai, this time to replace his delinquent hip with a hunk of plastic. The operation had been scheduled for October 17 when, three days earlier, Allan received a phone call from the president of the Academy of Motion Pictures Arts and Sciences. Richard Kahn wanted to meet in person, and since Allan remained immobile in Beverly Hills, the Academy honcho agreed to come to his house on the hill. Kahn didn't say much over the phone, but Allan suspected that he wanted him to work his magic on the Governor's Ball that followed the Oscar telecast. Perhaps the "Broadway at the Bowl" gala sparked Kahn's memory. Eleven years earlier, Allan had produced the post-Oscars ball, and it won him universal raves. Then again, in his short phone conversation, the Academy president never mentioned the Bowl event, and for good reason. "I didn't go," reports Kahn, who had other, more important things to talk over with Allan on that October morning.

Allan prided himself in being shockproof, but poolside at Hilhaven, Kahn offered him his ultimate dream: to produce the 1989 Oscars telecast. Short and much more than sweet, the meeting left Allan elated, and if he was momentarily speechless, he recovered himself enough a few hours later to tell the *Los Angeles Times,* "Dick came over to see me for fifteen minutes, and asked me." Allan didn't play coy with Kahn. He didn't have to think about it. He accepted the assignment on the spot with blunt delight. Like any other awards-show devotee, Allan had been mouthing his acceptance speech to himself every Oscar night since he listened to the 1940s radiocasts in his pj's back in Highland Park. Now the night, if not the statue itself, would be his to control and, in essence, own. Allan grabbed the opportunity because he wanted it. He wanted to prove that he could still produce—if not a movie, then Hollywood's biggest night. And more than he wanted it, he needed it.

At such defining moments in life, a man of Allan Carr's unbridled enthusiasm never stops to recall the truism about the ill fortune that comes to those who get what they pray for. If he ever did stop to think, Allan would have said that such reservations were for losers. Here was a task he'd prepared for his entire life, even before he bestowed his beloved Poopsie Awards on undeserving no-talents at Lake Forest College. Not for a moment did Allan want Kahn to believe him when he said, "I can't believe you picked me for the show. I never thought anyone would ask me to do it." What he really thought was that someone should have asked him years ago, because Allan had talked about wanting to produce the Oscars ever since he took over the Academy's Governor's Ball in 1978.

"My wife still talks about it being the greatest of the Governor's Balls," Kahn told Allan. And it was the truth. The black-and-white décor that year transformed the tent in front of the Dorothy Chandler Pavilion into an elegant Rainbow Room–style nightclub, complete with a revolving dance floor. The stunningly attired venue induced a number of celebrities to spend more than a few obligatory minutes there, as had been the custom for years. Allan even upped the gourmet level that year by having individual one-ounce containers of Petrossian caviar and chilled Stokskayvia vodka at each place setting. More important, he took the edge off the Oscar competition and delivered the coup of publicly congratulating each and every Oscar nominee, not just the winners. "It was a very generous touch," says Kahn.

Regardless of his past association with the Academy, Allan Carr was a different, if not downright out-of-the-box, choice to produce the Oscars telecast. In previous years, Kahn played it safe, making his picks from the old establishment pool of Hollywood—men like *West Side Story* director Robert Wise and *Singin' in the Rain* director Stanley Donen and producer Samuel Goldwyn Jr., whose father practically invented the film industry. Allan was younger than any of those men, he was openly gay, and more significant, he wasn't a buttoned-down guy like Goldwyn, Wise, or Donen.

"I picked Allan because he was a great showman," Kahn says.

Unspoken was the fact that Allan didn't have another gig at that moment in his career. Sherry Lansing explains why it's so tough to pick an Oscar producer: "It's sort of a thankless job, producing the Oscars. You don't get paid and it takes up a lot of time," says the former Paramount CEO.

With *Goya* a no-go and Allan's hip under repair, the project seemed predestined. Or as Allan told Kahn, "This will be a nice thing to do in my recovery period, when I can't climb the stairs that lead from my house."

Allan and Kahn spoke for only fifteen minutes at their first meeting, but Allan knew precisely what to do with the 1989 Oscars. "I want to bring glamour back to the awards," he told the Academy president. "Women watch the Oscar show to see what the women are wearing." For Allan, it was an occasion for style to trump substance, as if the latter were ever in danger of rising phoenix-like at an awards show.

It's doubtful if Goldwyn, Wise, or Donen thought of fashion as their first point of business, but then none of them was a five-foot-six 300-pound homosexual whose closet contained over 100 designer caftans and enough women's jewelry to sink Cleopatra's barge. Kahn wouldn't have picked Allan Carr if he didn't want to shake things up, and that included the ratings of the telecast, which had fallen over the years to an all-time low in 1988. Allan was, first and foremost, a showman, and like any great showman, he did what they all do when embarking on a major enterprise. He hired a personal publicist.

Linda Dozoretz had already worked with Allan on an ill-fated Lana Turner movie, based on the book *Detour*, by Turner's daughter, Cheryl Crane, who had stabbed and killed the actress's paramour Johnny Stompanato a few decades earlier. Even for a seasoned Hollywood flack like Dozoretz, Allan was an unusual client-producer. He didn't ask her to drum up publicity. He told her *how* to drum up publicity.

"Allan would kick around these ideas about the Oscars and get excited like a little kid," Dozoretz recalls. "Sometimes I was a sounding board." Allan talked; the soft-spoken publicist listened. When she talked, he didn't always listen: "Every one of his ideas, he thought it was the best thing ever." Rather than disagree with him, Dozoretz simply let Allan's weaker ideas die on the vine of his attention deficit.

Allan sought to goose the Oscar telecast's ratings, and to that end he pushed what many considered his greatest Oscar innovation. "He wanted to stage an Oscar fashion show, which had never been done before," says Kahn.

Allan's second "hire" was the man they called "the father of Rodeo Drive." Fred Hayman first met Allan shortly after he opened his store, Giorgio Beverly Hills, in 1961. "Rodeo Drive was primitive then," says Hayman. "Allan used to come in to try on women's caftans." By 1988, when Allan approached the boutique owner to work on the Oscars, Hayman was so famous that he dropped the Giorgio moniker to make his store eponymous.

Prior to Allan's involvement, the Academy Awards telecast kicked off with sixty seconds of red-carpet gawking, followed by a parade of actresses in gowns that ran the gamut from Armani to Beene to Mackie to sheer chutzpah. The following week, *People* and a few tabloids published the sartorial hits and misses, and that was the extent of Oscar fashion.

"But it doesn't have to be," Allan insisted. "This should be the world's greatest fashion show." Hayman, in Allan's opinion, was the perfect fashion nexus because Hayman didn't design clothes. He instead represented lots of designers and sold their dresses, and besides, "Fred Hayman's is the best place to buy evening wear!" exclaimed Allan, never afraid of the definitive overstatement. "I want you to be the Oscar's first fashion consultant," he told Hayman.

In truth, people like costume designer Edith Head had served as de facto fashion consultants on the telecast over the years, but their obligations had less to do with style than censorship, and they often held court backstage, ready with pieces of lace and fabric to cover a too-exposed décolletage for the TV cameras. Allan didn't want to wait until the big night to correct any fashion faux pas. He wanted Hayman to show actresses how to dress for the Oscars *before* the big night. "The fashions have gotten boring," Allan said. "The concept of Hollywood is far from boring. It's an illusion."

Allan promised to extend the red-carpet section of the broadcast. "Let's give it five, ten minutes!" he announced. Even more radical, he conceived a fashion show to be staged pre-Oscars, as part of a press conference that would unveil a "new and improved, more exciting and glamorous" Oscars to the world. "And show the women of Hollywood how to dress," proclaimed the man who often dressed like a woman.

Having given Hayman his fashion dictate, Allan took up his third point of business and phoned an old friend in San Francisco. He'd been a big fan of *Beach Blanket Babylon* ever since director Steve Silver conceived the Frisco revue back in 1974. Silver wrote that original show with *Tales of the City* scribe Armistead Maupin, and while it had radically morphed over the years, *Beach Blanket* continued to be the acropolis of camp in a city that practically invented the gay aesthetic. With its outrageous costumes, split-timing derring-do, and wicked send-ups of every entertainment figure from Elvis Presley to Snow White, Silver's show stood as the antithesis of the ossified, endless Academy Awards telecast. Allan knew it in his gut: This genius helmer on the Barbary Coast would be his ticket to reinventing the Oscars in a way it hadn't been overhauled since Bette Davis moved the awards across Hollywood Boulevard from the Roosevelt Hotel to Grauman's Chinese Theater in 1945, put it on the radio for the first time ever, and invited 200 servicemen to sit onstage. Allan dreamed as big as Bette.

Allan particularly adored Silver's rococo overlay of ornate costumes and huge headdresses. Those hats, in fact, were so big that one creation carried the entire cityscape of San Francisco, complete with fog machine and a running trolley car. The revue changed from year to year, and Allan had seen practically every incarnation, but his absolute favorite was one titled "*Beach Blanket Babylon* Goes to the Stars," in which Silver re-created the Cocoanut Grove nightclub, replete with dancing tables. "That's what Allan saw and remembered—the dancing tables," says Silver's widow, Jo Schuman Silver. "And he loved the big hats. The *Beach Blanket Babylon* trademark is the big hats. The concept was all Steve's."

Allan and Silver were an even draw when it came to worshipping at the altar of Oscar. Like Allan, Silver could parody entertainers because he adored entertainers. *Beach Blanket Babylon* might have started as a cult show, but it had since spawned a sister act in Las Vegas, and there were plans to take it to New York City. Silver wanted his *BBB* to go mainstream, and it doesn't get any more public than directing the opening act of the Oscars. The director got so excited about the Academy Awards assignment that he rejected all other invitations—including offers to take his revue to the White House for the Christmas holidays and to perform at one of George H. W. Bush's 1989 inauguration balls. It seemed, at least for a while, that all of San Francisco blessed Silver's Oscar fixation. The local press, which usually disdained everything SoCal, couldn't have been more supportive and happy to see its local boy make good. As the director told the *Contra Costa Times,* "Life in my book is nothing more than crossing things off your list. The more you cross off, the clearer your path in life becomes. On [March] 19th, I'm crossing a big, big line." Silver so anticipated his March 29 date with Oscar that he mistakenly moved it up ten days.

While Silver worked to replicate the camp glamour of his *Beach Blanket* costumes for the Oscar telecast, Allan hired production designer Ray Klausen to re-create what would be the Cocoanut Grove, Grauman's Chinese Theater, and a box of popcorn big enough to accommodate a superstar's entrance on the

Oscar stage. Klausen had always wanted to design for the stage but got "side-tracked into TV work," he says, when ABC hired him to do a show called *Hooray for Hollywood*. For Allan, Klausen represented the perfect mix of Broadway dreams and Hollywood illusion, and he knew he'd made the right choice when, during their first meeting, the set designer mentioned what he hated most about the Academy Awards.

"I don't like it when the presenters say, 'And the winner is.' It makes everyone else look like a loser," the designer groused.

Allan didn't miss a beat. "That's a really good idea," he said. "We'll change it to . . . 'And the Oscar goes to . . . '"

Allan was out to burn other Oscar bridges to the past as well, including the sacrosanct best-song category. He personally detested all the eligible songs from 1988 films. "If I'm lucky, might I be able to get away with having only two or three nominated songs?" he wondered. None of them, in his opinion, were TV-worthy. He petitioned the Academy's songwriters division to nominate only those songs that received a certain number of votes. It was a long shot, but the songwriters, surprisingly, agreed, and as a result, Allan succeeded in having only three tunes nominated.

It was then that Allan broke out in what he called "an Oscar rash."

In its December issue, *Los Angeles* magazine took a first potshot at the new Oscar producer. The rag published a two-inch item that opined, "Carr . . . has some of the Academy's conservatives edgy about what the flamboyant producer may come up with." Allan knew what "flamboyant" meant. It meant "fag." He didn't mind their pointing out the "black-tie dinner dance in honor of Truman Capote at the Lincoln Heights jail" in the article or that he "even hired the man who streaked the 1974 Oscars to do the same for another get-together." But flamboyant? Allan could only be happy that *Los Angeles* magazine failed to mention his hiring Steve Silver from "San Francisco," that other gay code word. Linda Dozoretz recalls, "There were some whispers: It's going to be too gay, whatever words were used. Allan, though, just shrugged that off."

Or maybe he baited it.

Ebullient over his Oscar gig, Allan defied any and all naysayers. "What did they know?" he said of *Los Angeles* magazine. He was on a roll. Good or bad, the speculation fueled him, and when he was inspired, he thought up his best ideas—or so he claimed.

One night, it came to him in the middle of an Academy Award dream. "The Oscars was not about the winners. It was all about the presenters," he believed. "The presenters would be compadres, costars, couples, and companions!" He

phoned Dozoretz the very next morning. She liked the idea. If she hadn't like
it, he would have gone with it anyway.

It was such a lovely disease, this "Oscar rash," and to give it a good scratching,
Allan retreated to Fiji for Christmas. "Whenever he went on vacation, he took
three or four twinkies with him," says Kathy Berlin. "Most of the time, he didn't
even know the guys' names." He also took with him every combination of star
pairings that could be crammed into the presenters' rubric of "compadres,
costars, couples, and companions." He also packed a couple of suitcases full of
old-movie videotapes, as well as arcane information on gift baskets and green
rooms and limousines that ranged from rules like "Don't argue with your driver"
to "How can we keep the bottles of Coca-Cola chilled?" He would leave nothing
to chance with this Oscar production, whether it be the correct pronunciation
of the foreign film titles or how many buckets of ice to dump into the Shrine
Auditorium's urinals.

Roasting himself on the beaches of Fiji, Allan put together his dream list of
star pairings: Warren Beatty and Jack Nicholson. Robert Mitchum and Deborah
Kerr. Janet Leigh and Tony Curtis. Paul Newman and Joanne Woodward. Mia
Farrow and Robert Redford. Roseanne Barr and Meryl Streep. Roger and Jessica Rabbit. New movie couples, classic movie couples. He could dream. And
with a big enough carrot, he could lure anyone to the show. He wondered aloud,
"What about a tribute to Sophia Loren and her producer husband, Carlo Ponti?"

On Fiji, everything was possible.

Back in Hollywood, reality fouled his fantasy when word arrived in early January that Joanne Woodward refused to fly from her Connecticut home.
Roseanne Barr considered herself "too TV" for the Oscars. Beatty, Farrow, and
Kerr were being difficult. And cartoon Jessica Rabbit was deemed too expensive. "The real stars are cheap compared to the animated ones!" Allan ruefully
learned. He could take only small comfort in pulling some strings at *Variety*
and the *Hollywood Reporter*, both of which agreed to publish a new, rotating
feature called "Oscar Watch." In effect, it was a day-to-day drumroll to announce all those stars who were confirmed to present, and over the following
weeks, Allan took pleasure in releasing the names of such real-life couples as
Demi Moore and Bruce Willis, Goldie Hawn and Kurt Russell, Geena Davis
and Jeff Goldblum, Melanie Griffith and Don Johnson, and legends like Kim
Novak and Jimmy Stewart, Lucille Ball and Bob Hope.

Allan came up with a new mantra: "The night is 10 percent for the town and
90 percent for the world!" He especially liked his young star couples, but he

needed a coup—a genuine Hollywood legend who hadn't shown up at the Oscars for decades, which in Hollywood was as close to eternity as anyone ever got.

"What about Doris Day?" Allan asked Dozoretz.

Dozoretz had long toiled as publicist for Hollywood's longest-living onscreen virgin, and knew better than anyone how difficult a catch Doris would be.

"She won't do it," Dozoretz replied.

Allan smiled, and asked his publicist why Doris Day wouldn't do the Oscars when she was scheduled to appear on the Golden Globes later that month.

"Doris was kind of tricked into coming to the Golden Globes," Dozoretz surmises. The Hollywood Foreign Press Association, which gives out the Golden Globes, lured the retired actress back to Hollywood with its Cecil B. DeMille lifetime achievement award. It helped, too, that her son, Terry Melcher, had been nominated by the HFPA for writing the song "Kokomo" for the Tom Cruise movie *Cocktail.*

If Dozoretz had been wrong about her client never again basking in the Hollywood limelight, she made up for it by getting Allan seated at Doris Day's table at the HFPA's 1989 awards ceremony. It was there, in the Beverly Hilton Hotel ballroom, that Allan made his pitch. "I'm doing the most glamorous Academy Awards show ever," he told the reluctant star during commercial breaks. "So many of your costars will be there." Doris listened patiently, politely. She found Allan extremely funny and wondered where he got all his energy and enthusiasm. She didn't say yes. She didn't say no.

"But as the night went on at the Golden Globes, she got uncomfortable," Dozoretz recalls. When it came time for the presentation of the Cecil B. DeMille Award, Clint Eastwood took the stage. His was a gracious speech, but as the encomium passed the sixty-second mark, Doris Day's all-teeth smile began to harden under her equally famous freckles. "It was the length of the clips from her old movies, and the TV camera was on her constantly. She is not one to look back," says her publicist.

Later that evening, the retired actress told Dozoretz, "I can't do this again." Allan never believed those words, and since he didn't actually hear Doris Day speak them, he interpreted her silence as yes or, at least, maybe. Dozoretz warned Allan, but it didn't matter what she said. His fantasy had jelled into reality, and the name Doris Day soon made the list of presenters in *Variety*'s "Oscar Watch."

twenty-seven

Proud Mary

Shortly after the Academy announced its many nominations in mid-February, Allan decided to give his Oscar rash to all those old establishment "conservatives" in Hollywood who had complained about such a "flamboyant" man producing the Academy Awards. To tweak their squeamishness even further, he hired as the telecast's one and only writer the Chicago-born Bruce Vilanch, who'd been openly gay from the moment he first set foot in the Hollywood Hills over a decade ago. Since Vilanch had never written any material for the Oscars, much less the entire telecast, it was appropriate that Allan's protégé be introduced to the big brass at the ABC network by having them all visit Hilhaven Lodge for a meet and greet.

Before the suits arrived, Allan put out several bottles of Cristal on ice. "But they're coming here to talk business," Vilanch pointed out to his producer-boss. "I don't think anyone will be wanting to drink champagne in the middle of the day."

Allan brushed aside the comment. "It doesn't matter," he said. "Just make sure the label shows. I want those bastards to know I have class."

He also placed a glossy photograph of Ingrid Bergman in the foyer, and slipped it into a silver frame, but not before he inscribed it to himself:

> To Allan,
> I'm glad to see the Swedes are still paying for this house.
> Love, Ingrid

For the high-level confab with ABC, Allan wore a caftan. Vilanch wore T-shirt and jeans. ABC vice president John Hamlin played it only slightly more formal in a dress shirt and slacks. Everybody sat down on pillows in the poolside white tent to talk about the Oscars, leaving the Cristal to sweat in buckets of ice, as Vilanch predicted.

"One pair of presenters will follow another," Allan began. "It is the passing of the baton that keeps the show moving," he said, elaborating briefly on his four C's: the "compadres, costars, couples, and companions," of which he continued to be very proud.

The ABC VPs asked about the telecast's host.

"There won't be a host. We don't need a host," Allan said, who segued to another controversial subject: the three nominated songs. It was his opinion, which he delivered as fact, that the songwriters' division of the Academy had rightfully chosen only three songs, and none of them deserved to be performed. "They're awful," said Allan. "I can't get performers for these three turds. So let's not do them."

Carly Simon's "Let the River Run" from *Working Girl* was the best of the lot. "But Carly has legendary stage fright and won't perform," Allan informed them. Then there was Lamont Dozier and Phil Collins's "Two Hearts" from a movie no one had seen, *Buster*. "Collins had been nominated four years ago for his song 'Take a Look at Me Now' from *Against All Odds*, and it got turned into a ballet for Ann Reinking and he's pissed off, so he won't perform. And, of course, Bob Telson's 'Calling You' from *Bagdad Café* is no song at all."

These nominated songs, Allan told the men of ABC, would be announced but not performed. "There's no reason we have to endure sitting through any B-list singer trying to put over those songs. And besides, it gives us more time for the opening number," he concluded.

Having dismissed the three Oscar-nominated songs, Allan jumped off the pillows to act out the telecast's much-anticipated opening number. It was as if Judy Garland had been reborn to perform that bare-bones production number called "Somewhere There's a Someone" in Vicky Lester's living room in *A Star Is Born*. Judy didn't need costumes and locations to take her fans around the world, and neither did Allan when it came to duplicating what the stage would look like at the Shrine in six weeks. With his gestures and expressions, he recreated the huge headdresses, the palm trees, and the dancing tables of the Cocoanut Grove.

"I'd never seen anyone so excited about his dream coming true," says Hamlin. "And I've worked on over forty Oscar shows. It was truly amazing to see such enthusiasm."

In passing, Allan mentioned the San Francisco revue *Beach Blanket Bingo* with its send-up of Snow White, which he wanted to replicate.

Hamlin wondered out loud, "Will that go over the heads of our TV audience?" Allan said not to worry. "We'll make it work!"

While no one mentioned anything about copyright infringement regarding the Disney character, there was much talk about keeping the show "young." The demographics for the Oscars had grown increasingly older over the years, a problem that Allan hoped to solve. "We've got a 'Young Hollywood' number planned for the second half of the show. It will be young, young, young, and these stars of tomorrow will all be singing and dancing. Hollywood has never seen anything like it since Mickey and Judy put on a show in the barn!" he said.

So much for the ABC brass.

At a meeting later that February, when Allan shared the Snow White concept with his creative team, set designer Ray Klausen worried about how they'd pull it off. He didn't mention his concerns to Allan, but he wondered nonetheless: "Everyone at the Oscars is in tuxedoes and evening gowns. They're expecting an elegant evening. And this wasn't an elegant number." It was the designer's opinion that if you're going to parody something, like having Snow White serenaded by Prince Charming, "You need to tip off the audience that you're having good fun."

Klausen hated to puncture the fantasy, since Allan was so clearly in love with Steve Silver's campy San Francisco concept of the beloved Disney princess and prince. Fortunately for Klausen, Marvin Hamlisch beat him to it.

Allan's former composer-client would conduct the Oscar orchestra and be musical director for the event. "You know, Allan, I'm having problems with this opening number," Hamlisch said at the creative-team meeting. "We need to let the audience know that this is a spoof. Otherwise, I'm not sure how they'll react."

Hamlisch said it would be a simple thing to accomplish. Klausen also thought the whole concept missed "just one beat."

Allan smoldered, then nearly attacked Hamlisch. "It's brilliant! It's perfect! It will be different!" he said as he quickly segued to the next topic of business: who would play Snow White. After seeing Allan's reaction to Hamlisch, Klausen wisely chose to remain mute. "There wasn't any point," he says. "Allan was going to do what Allan was going to do."

The production number had its supporters. "It was grandiose," says the telecast's director, Jeff Margolis. "Allan thought big, like a film person. He wanted to push the boundaries of television." Margolis's recent work on the Emmy and the American Music Awards telecasts had impressed Allan, who hired the director for what would be the first of many Oscar assignments. The sheer extravagance of having Snow White segue into a big Cocoanut Grove number followed by a Broadway-like dance routine at Grauman's Chinese Theater thrilled Margolis, who loved the challenge. "It's possibly the biggest thing that had ever been attempted in the history of TV. Plus, we were going to be doing it live!" he says.

David O. Selznick took nearly a year to test hundreds of actresses for the coveted role of Scarlett O'Hara in *Gone with the Wind*. Allan didn't have that much time to find his Snow White and Prince Charming. Surprisingly, the latter half of that duo turned out to be the easy part. Allan asked Rob Lowe and Rob Lowe said yes. Four years earlier, the handsome actor found himself a charter member of the so-called Brat Pack due to his appearance in the film *St. Elmo's Fire*. In the following years, along with his costars Emilio Estevez, Demi Moore, Judd Nelson, and Ally Sheedy, he had suffered from the media fallout of being labeled a movie-star brat. Perhaps Lowe felt he needed the imprimatur of the Oscars, and if he couldn't give an Oscar-worthy performance, then an Oscar-night performance would have to suffice. Besides, "[Allan Carr] had produced one of my favorite movies, *Grease*," Lowe explained years later. "I figured he knows about musicals. And you have to understand. I'm from the Midwest, and Midwestern values tell you, if someone asks you nicely, to say yes, especially if it is the Academy of Motion Picture Arts and Sciences."

Sometime that winter, Lorna Luft also received a breathless phone call from Hilhaven Lodge. "Come over to the house. I've got an exciting project I want you to be a part of," Allan told her. She, of course, wanted to know more, but Allan enjoyed the suspense. "I have to tell you face-to-face."

The phone call intrigued Luft. She had landed her two film gigs, *Grease 2* and *Where the Boys Are '84*, thanks to her producer friend, and she hoped there would be a third. "Bring your husband," Allan added. "We can make a fun day of it!"

When Luft and her husband, Jesse Hooker, arrived at Hilhaven, Allan appeared ready to give birth to an epic endeavor. He introduced her to a pianist,

already seated at the Lucite grand, then showed Luft a number of easels, each
of which held a sketch of a colorful stage set. It sure looked like a movie. "As
you probably know, I'm producing the Oscar telecast," Allan began. "It's a
dream come true for me. And I'd like you to be a part of it."

Although not quite the movie offer she wanted, the Oscars is not a shabby
second option with its worldwide audience of over 1 billion people. Lorna Luft
had never appeared on the Oscars. She listened attentively.

"I want you to play Snow White in the opening number for the Oscars this
year," Allan continued. "It is going to be an extravagant, big number. Like something you would only see on Broadway but much, much grander. And you'll be
singing Tina Turner's song 'Proud Mary,' but with new lyrics and it will be a
duet. You will be singing with Prince Charming."

Allan paused to check her reaction.

Luft paused, too, to take a breath. "And who will be playing Prince Charming?" she wanted to know.

"Rob Lowe. You wouldn't believe it, but he has a great voice."

Luft glanced at her husband, who was seated behind Allan and looking a
little nonplussed.

"Now here's the best part," Allan said. "You will be wearing a wig and dressed
up like Snow White, and no one will know it's you!"

Luft shot her husband another look. "Can I hear the song I will be singing?"

Allan motioned to the pianist, who in turn broke into song: "Keep those cameras rollin', rollin' rollin'. Used to work a lot for Walt Disney starring in cartoons
every night and day. Late nights keep on burnin' . . . keep the cameras rollin'."
Yes, she thought, it sure sounded like Tina Turner's anthem "Proud Mary."

Even though Luft hadn't sung a note, she cleared her throat. "What is Snow
White doing at the Oscars?" she asked.

Allan tossed the question aside with a flip of his fingers. Instead, he talked
about Steve Silver's revue in San Francisco. Had she seen it? he wanted to know.

No, she hadn't.

"Well, you should. We can fly you up there," he offered. Regarding Snow
White, "She can't find her way into the theater," Allan explained. "So we'll have
Army Archerd from *Variety* show her the way. And then Merv Griffin will be
singing at the Cocoanut Grove and onstage we'll have some of the great stars
who used to go to the Cocoanut Grove—Alice Faye, Lana Turner—and then
Merv will introduce you to your blind date, Rob Lowe. He's Prince Charming.
And then you sing the 'Proud Mary' song together, which leads into this fabulous

number with the ushers of Grauman's Chinese doing a chorus-line kick right out of *A Chorus Line*—Marvin Hamlisch is conducting the orchestra—and then the Chinese Theater turns into a big box of popcorn and Bette Midler pops out of it all!" Allan jumped off the sofa. "Let me show you the sketches. The sets are fabulous too."

Luft tried to match Allan's level of excitement—never an easy feat. Granted, Ray Klausen's sketches looked impressive, but she had serious doubts about the number Allan wanted her to perform. "There's a lot to think about here," she said.

It wasn't what Allan wanted to hear. "People have never seen an Oscar show like this. It will be the most exciting, the biggest, the most glamorous ever," he promised.

Luft repeated herself. "There's a lot to think about."

When she didn't phone the next day, Allan took it upon himself to call her. His voice was major key, hers minor. "I'm sorry, Allan, I can't do that," she said.

"Why not?" he demanded.

"I just can't. I'm so sorry."

"Why wouldn't you want to do the Oscars? No one will know it's you. We'll put you in a wig, lots of makeup."

"Why would I want to do that?"

The conversation digressed from there until he let her have it. "I made you!" he screamed, referring to *Grease 2* and *Where the Boys Are '84*. Many four-letter words colored what Luft considered one of the worst telephone calls of her life. "I finally hung up the phone sobbing," she says.

If Lorna Luft wasn't going to cooperate, Allan put out the word to Lucie Arnaz, Ellen Greene, and others. Steve Silver thought it better to go with an unknown and suggested a girl who played Snow White in his Las Vegas production of *Beach Blanket Babylon*. If one of the celebs didn't want to do it, Eileen Bowman would. The challenge excited Allan. "We'll make her a star!" he promised.

While Allan fretted over his Snow White, the first-ever Oscar fashion show began to take shape in Fred Hayman's imagination. He agreed with Allan that the actresses didn't dress well enough for the telecast. But it was a problem: How do you tell the most fussed-over, catered-to beautiful women in the world that their taste in fashion sucks?

Mr. Rodeo Drive put out the call, and while many designers were phoned, not many answered. "The designers weren't eager to loan," Hayman recalls. "This was before all the top designers fought to get an actress to wear their fashions at the Oscars. There's been a whole evolution, and it began with Allan Carr." That first year, most of the clothes came from Karl Lagerfeld, Giorgio Sant'Angelo, and Halston, whom Hayman had championed early in their careers. "We had to promise to return the clothes," says Hayman. "A few of the actresses bought the clothes. This was before the designers *gave* the actresses the clothes."

Allan envisioned a full-scale fashion show, but like so many first steps, the 1989 event was something less than grand. It took place in the restaurant at the tony L'Ermitage Hotel in Beverly Hills, and at 9:30 a.m. movie-musical legend Cyd Charisse found herself leaning against the bar, sipping coffee, with a tray of desserts ready at her elbow if she wanted to indulge. Wanting to look svelte, she ignored the sweets.

Allan stressed to Charisse his concept of using this press event to goose up the fashion quotient of the Oscars, and he'd seduced her into attending his dog-and-pony show by promising her an appearance, together with husband Tony Martin, in the show's opening number at the Cocoanut Grove. It was important to Allan that Charisse look great that morning, and he personally approved her outfit that day: a pale pastel silk dress with a gold necklace and medallion, which, in his estimate, weighed a ton and cost something more. "Angie isn't here yet?" asked Charisse.

No sooner had that complaint taken wing than Angie Dickinson materialized, bringing a somewhat more business-like tone to the affair in her subdued white blazer. "Joe Namath would approve," Allan said, patting Dickinson's padded shoulders. He kissed her hello, and then the two actresses, likewise, greeted each other.

Where the Hollywood press corps had been accustomed to getting their meager Oscar news via printed releases, Allan initiated the more showy route of a series of press conferences, complete with Cyd, Angie, and a free breakfast buffet. On March 8 at 10 a.m., he welcomed the reporters, all three dozen of them, from a small makeshift stage. He didn't mess around when it came to making promises about the 61st Academy Awards. "It's a Hollywood industry party and Broadway show! Everything's bigger than life. It'll be very much like a Broadway musical. It will be the most glamorous, fun, funniest, and shortest Academy Awards in years," he bragged.

To show just how big Allan dreamed, Ray Klausen unveiled his sketches and talked up the "thirty-foot-high curtain" he'd designed for the Shrine Auditorium stage. "Enough to cover one whole side of the Empire State Building. I've designed it with more than 50,000 beads and sequins, to be hand applied."

"There will be 11 sets and 106 stagehands," Allan added. "A red carpet will cover the street in front of the Shrine Auditorium. The second largest banner ever made will hang outside the auditorium." Allan even gave names to Klausen's sets, names like "Stars and Diamonds," "Tiffany Jewels with Crystal Beads and Chiffon Swags," "Beaded Victorian Flowers," and "The Grand Drape."

Off in the wings, one of the models for Hayman's fashion show wisecracked, "It sounds like planning an invasion."

"There will be sparkling drapes," said Klausen.

"But we have to have beautiful people in front of them," said Allan, cutting him off. It was time for the fashion show. Allan could tell the reporters were already starting to crash from their pastry-coffee rush, and he quickly introduced Fred Hayman, who, in turn, brought out three models who wore a white form-fitting gown by Bill Travilla, a shimmering silver and bugle bead number by Oscar de la Renta, and a Bob Mackie ensemble that appeared to have been constructed with whatever drapes Klausen had left over from the Empire State Building.

Most members of the press didn't know a Givenchy from a Valentino, but if they were impressed or simply waiting to get back to the donut tray, Hayman promised that designs by Calvin Klein, Karl Lagerfeld, Donna Karan, Giorgio Armani, and others would be seen on the telecast.

Most journalists bolted L'Ermitage's press conference to make an early deadline. Others dove for the remaining croissants and wondered if they could possibly turn this breakfast buffet into lunch. Some reporters groused that Allan's ego had exploded, but his publicist saw the logic behind the ambition. "He wanted to do something every day, every week to hype the awards. He wanted the biggest ratings ever," says Linda Dozoretz.

If Allan couldn't micromanage every detail of the event, such as who actually received the Oscars, he would personally pick who handed them out and man the phones himself, afraid to leave any of the big presenters to a flunky booker. Occasionally, he left Hilhaven to spend the day at ABC's rented second-floor offices on La Cienega and Santa Monica Boulevards in West Hollywood. A few white sterile rooms formed a horseshoe of offices around an assistants' area. Allan called it Oscar Ground Zero, even if he made few visits there. It was the kind of mundane workaday office that made him happy he never held a nine-to-five job in his life. Leo's Flowers did business under Oscar Ground Zero. Allan would gaze up from the florist's shop at the one flight of stairs and complain, "Couldn't ABC afford a place with an elevator?" In addition to his hip replacement, he had recently torn his knee cartilage and needed a cane to walk. As he fought his way up the stairs, Oscar's worker bees could hear him coming, his cane stabbing at each difficult step.

When Allan first visited the rented ABC offices, he laughed out loud at Bruce Vilanch's office door. It read MISS GRABLE'S DRESSING ROOM. Vilanch worked the phones to try and explain his material to a recalcitrant star's publicist. "So she's not gonna shoot you; blame me," he said. "And point out to her that he may have the most lines but she has the big joke." As Vilanch explained to Allan, "A lot of people are afraid to give their clients the material," the "material" being his patter for the various presenters.

Allan had his own problems with celebrity wrangling. He loved to bask in the presence of the legends—but only *if* they cooperated. When their ego got in his way, he had to wonder what else they had to do "except change their Depends" on a Wednesday night. Case in point: Loretta Young. She adamantly refused to be paired with anyone. "I stand on my own two feet," she told Allan during their fierce negotiations. Better yet, she liked the idea of repeating her 1982 performance at the Oscars when she capped the show by warning against "smutty" pictures, and presented the best-picture award to *Chariots of Fire*.

"But dear, you would be presenting an award with Nureyev!" Allan replied.

If Loretta could play hardball, so could Allan, who declined her services altogether. "And I was offering her Rudolf Nureyev!" he fumed.

The logistics had gotten awfully convoluted. For some reason, Lana Turner wasn't responding to his calls, even after Allan enlisted her daughter, Cheryl Crane. He wanted Lana for the big opening Cocoanut Grove spectacular, to appear alongside Dale Evans and Roy Rogers and Alice Faye. "Lana doesn't want to take part in the program. I don't know what her problem is, but I'm working on it," he informed Vilanch. (Perhaps Allan had forgotten that, ten years earlier, when he booked talent for the Oscars, he told the *Los Angeles Times*, "Lana Turner will not take my calls. I think that should be printed. How dare she?")

Movie couples were even tougher. Whom did he call first: Demi or Bruce? Ryan or Farrah? Melanie or Don? Geena or Jeff? "Can't these people use the same publicist?" Allan wanted to know.

Allan had talked to Goldie Hawn and Kurt Russell about a possible on-air joke regarding their wedding announcement, even though they had no plans to get married. The couple was mulling the gag. There was also the good news that Brigitte Bardot wanted to be on the show. But the bad news: "She wants to talk about animal rights?!" screamed Allan. He assured her long-distance that there would be no furs on the show. "But also no speeches. We are not planning on Sacheen Littlefeather—or a speech on animal rights."

Word had already gotten back to Allan that Gregory Peck was pissed that no one asked him to present an Oscar. Allan rolled his eyes. The American Film Institute tribute to Peck had aired recently—and even worse than being over-exposed, Peck pulled in no ratings for the NBC telecast. In any other year, Allan would have done pliés to get Elizabeth Taylor to present. Unfortunately, a week before the Oscars, ABC was scheduled to air its tribute to the star. So no Liz. Paul Newman loomed as a possibility, but Allan wanted him to appear with Joanne Woodward, and since she wasn't flying to Los Angeles, Allan didn't re-extend an invite to her willing husband. Also not flying was a very pregnant Susan Sarandon, who looked forward to popping her first kid any minute.

Genuine excuses or poor reasons, Allan accepted every rejection as if the star had pummeled him with his or her Guccis. He went from loving the potential presenter to hating anyone who said no. Like Sophia Loren, who announced that she couldn't show up for her own tribute. "Whaaaaat?" Allan brayed at the news. "I offered her the moon—Oscar tickets for her kids—anything." Rightly or wrongly, Allan blamed it on her acting coach, Anna Strasberg, and her publicist, Bobby Zarem. "So instead, she accepts a benefit in Florida for the University of Miami, three nights later?! And she could have done both." Allan retaliated by canceling the Pontis' tribute.

Or when John Travolta wouldn't say yes or no to introducing a montage of musical clips. "He appeared in *Grease,* for Chrissakes!" said Allan, as if he owned the actor. The offer then went out to Patrick Swayze, hot off *Dirty Dancing,* which had outgrossed Travolta's last movie, *Perfect,* in which he played a *Rolling Stone* reporter investigating health clubs. "The ungrateful!" Allan called any star who wouldn't cooperate. He took no delight in the second-choice Swayze pick, but kept it civil, professional. "I want Patrick Swayze's people to see the tape of the movie musical montage," he said. "I want to see how he feels about it."

In the middle of the booking madness, Allan took a call from an A-list publicist, who was pushing a B-list client. "I like her," Allan told the flack. "We were at the fat farm in England together three years ago—she's terrific. But I've got biggies on the waiting list. . . . Love you, too." Then he hung up without thinking to say good-bye.

Someone in the office delivered a pseudobombshell. "Don Ameche can't do the show. He is in New York to be in *Our Town.*"

Allan didn't even bother to look up from his bagel. "I knew that three days ago. What world are you people living in? They better wake up."

There're no demands like show-business demands. Allan tried to indulge them all. His patience, which was nonexistent for friends and family, knew no limits for a star. If Doris Day required a dog sitter to make the trip to Los Angeles, "Then get her a fucking dog sitter!" he ordered no one in particular. She also wanted to be driven, not flown, down from Carmel. Her neighbor Kim Novak wanted to be flown, not driven, from her home on Big Sur. Both women insisted on hotel suites, wardrobe, hair and makeup, and a certain size of dressing room. And of course neither of them would sit in the audience with the Oscar nominees and other stars during the telecast. Alice Faye wanted to be limoed from Rancho Mirage. She'd do her own hair, but insisted she sit onstage next to Dorothy Lamour, who didn't really care one way or the other about much of anything. The real troupers of the affair, Dale Evans and Roy Rogers, would get themselves to the Oscars on time and even bring their own horsy wardrobe. But they didn't much care for the accommodations at L'Ermitage and preferred to stay at the Tolucan. "Whatever they want!" Allan harrumphed.

He wanted the entire Oscar experience to be a party for his stars, and to that end he created a green room, or hospitality suite, at the Shrine. "He did everything to make them feel like stars," says Richard Kahn, "and he wanted to create that kind of a private protective enclave for them to relax in." Other producers might have provided them a bare-bones room to sit and watch the telecast in before their appearance. "Allan was the first to put a label on it," Kahn says of the fancy green room. Allan called it Club Oscar, and he even made a sign to hang on the wall. Club Oscar would be a party room not only on the big night but during the four days of rehearsal leading up to the show. Dom Perignon, Moët & Chandon, and cuisine by Fernaud Page would be served to the star participants, "who never get to see each other," Allan said. Sometimes it seemed as if he had truly thought of everything. He even had the green room sponsored by Waverly fabrics, "so that the Academy wouldn't have to pay the costs of decorating it," says Dozoretz.

Club Oscar emerged as an oasis of overstated relaxation in the midst of the general decay and grime of the Shrine. "You never would have known that you were backstage in a theater," says Jeff Margolis. "It was like you were in some highfalutin' club in West Hollywood or New York City."

The closer it came to Oscar Day, the more Allan's dream solidified as a triumph in his brain. "His ego was becoming the size of the Academy Awards.

Everybody was calling Allan," says Dozoretz. "And everyone was bowing. He liked that in real life. He had all this power. I couldn't believe who was calling him for favors and asking him. Allan knew for a few days that he would never have again that power. Allan, who was not always the most polite man, burned bridges. He was the king of the world."

Even one of Allan's most admired Hollywood major players, überagent Swifty Lazar, offered his respects. Swifty's annual Academy Awards party had, over the years, eclipsed the telecast in star power, draining the talent pool of A-list celebs, who preferred to watch the TV proceedings in the comfort of Spago restaurant rather than embarrass themselves at the Oscars and remind everyone that they hadn't been nominated.

Allan saw it as the passing of the torch when Swifty graciously accepted his invitation to make a brief appearance in the Cocoanut Grove opening number. Allan gushed, "He's a legend. Swifty is as much a legend as the Cocoanut Grove." And Swifty returned the favor. In no less a forum than the *Sunday Los Angeles Times,* the agent predicted that the 1989 Oscar telecast would be "the best party we've had. There's a greater feeling of fun than I've ever had before. There are so many new people who are going to be here after the telecast, new blood. Allan Carr is such a great showman, and he's having about 40 people present the awards, up from about 20."

Allan dramatically upped the telecast's celeb population. "We won't show the movie clips all in one big clump at the end of the telecast!" he ordered his Oscar bookers. "Instead, we'll have each nominated film and its clip introduced by a big star and intersperse them throughout the evening. It gives us five more star participants!"

Allan referred to the seven days before March 29 as "White Knuckle Week," and if he fretted unduly over the presenters and the movie clips, he bet the show's success on his two big production numbers, each of which was clocking in at a whopping twelve minutes. ABC was also feeling the pressure, and insisted in the final days that Allan hire Hildy Parks, who'd written several Tony Awards telecasts, to join Vilanch as cowriter.

Rehearsals began on a Thursday only six days before the actual broadcast. With Marvin Hamlisch at the piano, Allan stood on the bleachers in Rehearsal Hall No. 1 at the ABC Studios on Vine in Hollywood. Together with lyricist Fred Ebb, Hamlisch had written the "(I Want to Be) an Oscar Winner" for the fourteen young actors and actresses who were now watching their leotarded reflections in a giant mirror set on rollers. Only one of the scheduled performers, fifteen-year-old Savion Glover, remained behind on the East Coast, having to appear on Broadway in the new musical *Black and Blue* before he flew to Los Angeles on Monday for the final run-throughs. The other showbiz newcomers were ready to go, and that included such to-be-or-not-to-be stars as Blair Underwood, Patrick Dempsey, Christian Slater, and Ricki Lake, as well as those here-by-the-grace-of-their-famous-parent kids like Patrick Cassidy, Carrie (Burnett) Hamilton, Patrick O'Neal, and Tyrone Power Jr. Allan didn't mess around when it came to making predictions about their future success. He called them, simply, the "Break-Out Super Stars of Tomorrow."

Despite his new plastic hip, Allan jumped up and down on the bleachers or, at the very least, he bounced a little, his body like jelly in aspic. It thrilled him that he'd rounded up the children of the famous in this one room, while in Rehearsal Hall No. 2 he held court with the real legends, everyone from Vincent Price and Alice Faye to Buddy Rogers and the Nicholas Brothers. Allan had sold Rob Lowe on playing Prince Charming in the opening Cocoanut Grove number as an homage to old Hollywood "and those who came before us." But in rehearsals the twenty-five-year-old actor grew leery of the concept as soon as it became clear that "a lot of the legendary old Hollywood folk could not walk unassisted," Lowe observed firsthand.

Their overall immobility didn't disturb Allan, who quickly ordered Vincent Price and others to simply sit at the tables and wave. Or if need be, he got a chorus boy to help walk them across the stage.

Allan had one eye on the past and one finger on the current pulse. He also had to watch his rear. "That Young Hollywood number was the direct result of ABC's edict that he 'young-up' the show," says Bruce Vilanch.

Allan wanted to sex-up the Oscars as well, and he hired *Dirty Dancing* choreographer Kenny Ortega to put his Young Hollywood troupe through its paces. Christian Slater agreed to do the production number on one condition: "If I could swing in on a rope," he said. Ricki Lake claimed some expertise. "I had a year of ballet when I was five," she said, "but I don't think that really counts." Tracy Nelson, granddaughter of TV's Ozzie and Harriet, had actually studied ballet and did a mean pirouette, but other than her and Savion Glover, there wasn't a lot of innate talent or training for what these novice performers would be required to do in front of the vast television audience—for twelve long minutes.

Could Tyrone Power's son sing? Could he dance? If Allan didn't ask these questions, it's because he had fallen in love with the charm of the future—and his role as star maker. "Allan was like a little kid jumping up and down," Linda Dozoretz says of the rehearsals. "The excitement of his meeting Tyrone Power's son!"

Allan gave Kenny Ortega only four rehearsal days to perform his miracle. While other producers might want to cloak such protégés in a secure blanket of secrecy, Allan chose to invite select members of the press to the rehearsals. "People put down Young Hollywood as a group of actors who are pretty but not very talented," he told reporters. "There are a lot of talented, caring young actors out there. On Oscar night, we're going to acknowledge them. I think it's going to be a showstopper."

Power Jr. put his finger on the challenge faced by these showbiz newbies. "All of the production numbers on Oscar night are usually so serious," he told Allan's phalanx of reporters. "This is just a bunch of young actors, none of whom are really singers, dancers, or fencers, goofing around and having fun. Hopefully everyone else will too."

The next day, the *Los Angeles Herald-Examiner* gossip Kevin Koffler wrote up the rehearsal. He titled his column, "Hooray for Nepotism!"

While choreographer Kenny Ortega worked with the kids, Hamlisch played nursemaid to a nervous Eileen Bowman, who only a year before had been singing in the chorus of Youth for Christ. "Snow White is a bigger celebrity than anyone else in that audience," Hamlisch assured her.

Bowman wasn't so sure. Earlier in the day, she'd fought back nausea just thinking about Wednesday night. If she feared that she might "look at one person and forget my lines," Allan harbored no such doubts as he threw out ideas. "It will be gold if we have Snow White greet and shake the hands of the celebs in the audience," he said.

Steve Silver hated having actors interact with the audience. "It won't work," he told Allan. "It never works."

Vilanch also cautioned, "The Shrine will be lit up. There's no place to hide. I don't think you can take a woman dressed up as Snow White and put her in the audience with Tom Hanks and Sigourney Weaver and Geena Davis and expect them to react to her. They'll freeze and not play along."

"You're wrong," said Allan. "It's going to be gold!"

Silver tried to explain: What made *Beach Blanket Babylon* a success was its speed. "Things are always edited down," he said. But he saw the reverse happening with the Oscar telecast's opening number, which only grew in size as more and more celebs were added. "Everyone wants input," Silver said. And the more the input, the more that got put in. Instead of lasting eight minutes, the number soon clocked fifteen. Rather than cut, Allan added yet another legendary actor to the Cocoanut Grove parade. Silver worried about the extra minutes that the Snow White meet and greet would add. He timed it. "Sixteen minutes!" he exclaimed. "Nothing should be sixteen minutes!"

Allan took his director aside. "Look, you've got your show in San Francisco. *This* is my next job!"

The rehearsals continued. While Eileen Bowman practiced shaking the imaginary hands of movie stars, another crooner substituted momentarily for Merv Griffin, who would not only sing "I've Got a Lovely Bunch of Coconuts" but introduce the evening's Prince Charming: "And your blind date for the Oscars, Snow White, is none other than Rob Lowe!" At which Bowman and Lowe would break into "Proud Mary," singing the new lyrics, "Keep those cameras rolling, rolling, rolling." It worried Allan that Merv Griffin couldn't rehearse on the Shrine stage. Then again, Griffin had already sung "I've Got a Lovely Bunch of Coconuts" a thousand times when he used to deliver it with a cockney accent for $150 a week at the real Cocoanut Grove in the 1940s.

Allan watched "the dinosaurs," as they came to be called, walk across the rehearsal hall. Or, at least, they tried to walk. Fortunately, Cyd Charisse's legs still looked great and she could dance, as could Fayard and Harold Nicholas, who hadn't stopped tap-dancing since they appeared with Eubie Blake and his orchestra nearly sixty years ago.

Ray Klausen's Cocoanut Grove set also moved well, segueing seamlessly into his rendering of Grauman's Chinese as a chorus line of high-stepping ushers led up to the big box of popcorn from which Lily Tomlin would descend a long flight of stairs. It was supposed to be Bette Midler, but she departed the telecast soon after her name was not announced as one of the best-actress nominees, for her over-the-top performance as a pop singer in *Beaches.* It fell to Tomlin to cap the production. The comedian did it as a favor to her friend Bruce Vilanch. But in rehearsals she was having second and third thoughts, so Vilanch wrote her an opening line, "How do you follow this?" It was a tacit acknowledgment of all the questionable extravagance that would precede her. Vilanch also thought it might be funny for Tomlin to lose her shoe on the set—"Like what else could go wrong?" he surmised—at which she would say, "So on with the shoe. I mean, show," as a chorus-boy-usher slithered down the stairs to pick up her errant slipper.

If it bothered Allan that his handpicked head writer and star were secretly hedging their bets, it didn't matter. He hadn't been seeing straight ever since he came down with a less than healthy appreciation of the talents of his Prince Charming. "He thought Rob Lowe could sing," says Linda Dozoretz. "He had great belief in Rob Lowe and where his stardom would go. And Rob Lowe thought he could sing. There was nothing tongue-in-cheek, it was serious. Allan believed Rob Lowe was Prince Charming and Lowe believed that, too. Everyone thought he was cute."

Prince Charming's date with Snow White at the Oscars worked its charm even on people not named Allan Carr—none of whom thought to ask, "Do you hear what he sounds like?" And if not beguiled by Allan's romantic fantasy, at the very least, the concept came as no surprise to anyone at ABC or the Oscars, including Richard Kahn. Some producers talk to the president on a weekly basis. "Others on a daily basis, which was my relationship with Allan," says Kahn. Regarding Snow White, "Allan wanted to return glamour to the Oscars and somehow marry that to the eclectic excitement of Steve Silver's show up in San Francisco with Snow White," adds the former Academy president.

Whatever the qualms—and there were few among Allan's coterie of Oscar workers—most doubts evaporated as soon as the lavish costumes arrived. "Everyone was laughing," Dozoretz recalls. They were so spectacular and outrageous, these giant headdresses and the tables that danced. "The excitement was that the show would just be bigger and better than anything."

Coupled with Ray Klausen's equally kaleidoscopic sets, the costumes jazzed the performers, and the jump from ABC's sterile rehearsal halls to the stage of the Shrine Auditorium propelled Allan's fantasy to life. Except for Kevin Koffler's "nepotism" comment in the *Herald-Examiner,* the press reports of the rehearsals were uniformly upbeat. It helped, too, to see Army Archerd in person. The *Variety* columnist, who had presided over the Oscars' red carpet for almost three decades, made a brief appearance at the rehearsals. His mere presence gave a showbiz imprimatur to the project, and Allan expected him to write a flattering notice of the rehearsals in his *Variety* column. According to the telecast script, Archerd would greet Snow White in front of the Shrine, where she asks him how to get to the Oscars. "Just follow the stars" was the reply.

"The rehearsal was fun," said Archerd. "We all thought it would be terrific, an amusing way to introduce the Oscars and not the usual send-off into one of the secondary awards. Allan wanted to do something different." And Archerd wasn't the only one who approved. "They all loved the idea of Snow White," Freddie Gershon says of the powers at the Academy and ABC.

As moods go, ecstasy is not one of the more enduring. Some of the Oscar youngsters, accustomed to performing in the close confines of the ABC rehearsal hall, froze on the gargantuan 65-by-185-foot stage as they looked out over the Shrine's 6,500 seats. The old-timers harbored other problems. Alice Faye complained that she'd been reduced to "a dress extra" along with her friend Dorothy Lamour. And worse, the Nicholas Brothers needed to be cut completely from the Cocoanut Grove number. The decision devastated Allan.

"People hadn't seen the Nicholas Brothers for a long time," says Dozoretz. "Allan was so excited about bringing those guys back." It worried him too that people would criticize him for excising the only two African Americans in the entire production number.

No sooner had Allan eliminated the Nicholas Brothers than the bad karma came knocking. Swifty Lazar sent word that he wouldn't be able to appear, as promised. "Too busy," he said. Then Doris Day phoned to say that she had tripped over a sprinkler at her home in Carmel. A swollen ankle prevented her from making the trip down the California coast.

Allan endured these hits, buoyed by the in-house praise surrounding his Cocoanut Grove opening number. Occasionally he tempered his excitement by acknowledging the ephemeral nature of the event. "Two nights after Oscar is the *Vanity Fair* party in honor of the Man Ray exhibit. The next night is something else. So if you are lucky, it's only for one wonderful moment," Allan said. But what a moment! He couldn't help but dream.

The rehearsals behind him, Carr walked out of the Shrine to inspect the hanging of the Oscar banners over the building's Moorish arches. Tulips don't have much odor, but six million tulips flown over from the Netherlands do, and their sweet aroma was so pungent that people kept having this urge to slip into wooden shoes. At least the Shrine wouldn't stink like a toilet, even if the management didn't live up to its promise that the place would be something less than filthy. "What is that muff in my face?" Allan asked. The feathered boom mike belonged to a cameraman from *Entertainment Tonight*. "I thought you were here to clean the Shrine," he cracked.

Located on Jefferson Boulevard near Figueroa Street, the sixty-three-year-old Shrine Auditorium occupies that busy street corner with its towering 100-foot walls and elaborate Arabesque filigree. The façade of the Shrine had faded, if not actually started to crumble, and to hide its faded glory, Allan ordered up a few gold statues of Oscar that loomed up twenty-four feet to help highlight, along with all those banners, the theater's multiple entrances. Allan was ready for the day he'd been planning all his life.

Swifty Lazar. Doris Day. The Nicholas Brothers. Suddenly, they were minor irritants that disappeared into the city's smog as it drifted eastward over Pasadena. Unbeknownst to Allan, however, was this pesky lawyer who'd been calling the offices of the Academy every day for the past week. The lawyer wanted the Academy to know that he and others at the Walt Disney Studios had heard rumors that there was an "unauthorized and unflattering reference to Disney material" planned for the telecast. These phone calls had been going on for a week, but it was only on Wednesday, March 29, the afternoon of the ceremony, that an Academy spokesperson finally deigned to return the call, assuring the Disney lawyer that there was no foul play regarding a beloved animated icon. No one bothered to mention any of these things to Allan.

twenty-eight

Snow Blight

That Wednesday, otherwise known as Oscar Day, the arrivals of the stars started early—and Allan made sure that every minute of their procession into the annals of Hollywood royalty would be recorded for posterity, even if not every momentous second could be included in the ABC telecast. "Before Allan, the red carpet had been just a frill, a minute of montage," says Bruce Vilanch. "There wasn't the frenzy of now. Allan made that happen."

The traffic was so clog-free around the Shrine that Glenn Close, who had been forced to hoof the final block the year before, joked about the improved car flow. "We had to circle the Shrine three times so we wouldn't be the first to arrive," she told the TV cameras. The dubious distinction of being first went to Sylvester Stallone, who at 4 p.m. jumped the official arrival time by thirty minutes. At 4:30 p.m., Army Archerd announced, "Good evening, movie fans!" Publicists whispered the names of their clients in Archerd's ear so that the seventy-seven-year-old reporter could accurately welcome newlyweds Kevin Kline and Phoebe Cates, along with John Cleese, Billy Crystal, and Olivia Newton-John, whose nubile husband, Matt Lattanzi, would be performing in the Young Hollywood number. Meryl Streep, having perfected her role as the Hollywood interloper despite eight nominations and two wins, told onlookers, "I'm still not used to all this." While speculation swirled that Rob Lowe might show up with his new girlfriend, Fawn Hall, fresh from her Oliver North shredding episode, Allan's new Prince Charming disappointed by making a tedious choice: He brought his mom, Barbara. If Fawn didn't show, another Washington, D.C., scandal girl, Donna Rice, who'd brought down presidential hopeful Gary Hart on a boat called *Monkey Business,* walked the red carpet. Behind police barricades on Jefferson Boulevard, four men in Mae West wigs and gold lamé gowns, known as the Sisters of Perpetual Indignity, came "to show our support for Allan Carr," they said, because this was the first "gay Oscars." These Frisco refugees failed to notice when Allan himself entered the arena wearing a black sequin dinner jacket by Luis Estevez. The transvestites' view had been blocked by placards that petitioned MAKE MORE G-RATED MOVIES.

Married or not, couples on the red carpet included Demi Moore and Bruce Willis, Tom Cruise and Mimi Rogers, Geena Davis and Jeff Goldblum, Farrah Fawcett and Ryan O'Neal, Don Johnson and Melanie Griffith. Those accompanying less famous women were "comedy star nominee" Tom Hanks, "maestro" Marvin Hamlisch, and the "cuddly" Dudley Moore.

"The doors will be closing in ten minutes!" announced Army Archerd. "Please enter the theater!"

Bob Hope walked a little faster. Dustin Hoffman, Michael Douglas, Willem Dafoe, and Lucille Ball gave a final wave. Cybill Shepherd flexed her biceps for the paparazzi, and then she, too, disappeared inside. The red carpet was relatively empty for a good five minutes before Cher, showing lots of leg in a black lace mini by Bob Mackie, materialized off the asphalt with boyfriend Rob Camiletti and daughter Chastity Bono. With her dangling black earrings and black-beaded headdress and black mass of curls, Cher didn't disappoint the bleacher crowd, who gave the star their longest, most undivided wave of applause of the evening. Weeks earlier, Allan had publicly promised to lock the Shrine doors at 5:45 p.m. sharp, and yet one half hour late, Cher and company gained entrance without incident.

Allan's longtime dream entered its final reality phase when, inside the auditorium, a disembodied voice used the loudspeaker to announce again and again, "The star of all time will be here soon."

Publicist Warren Cowan wondered, Who could it be? Katharine Hepburn? Greta Garbo? "It was Snow White," he recalled.

Right on schedule, the ABC cameras caught Eileen Bowman in her princess-in-exile getup outside the Shrine. "How do you get to the Oscars?" she asked Army Archerd.

"That's easy, Snow. Just follow the Hollywood stars!" Archerd replied on cue.

Bowman traipsed down the center aisle of the Shrine to shake the hands of Michael Douglas, Kevin Kline, Tom Hanks, Dustin Hoffman, Ryan O'Neal,

Glenn Close, and a blushing Michelle Pfeiffer, who giggled ominously. None of them looked happy to be holding hands with a warm, life-size Disney cartoon. As the curtains parted, TV talk-show host Merv Griffin launched into "I've Got a Lovely Bunch of Coconuts," and the audience caught its first glimpse of Ray Klausen's re-creation of the Cocoanut Grove, where Cyd Charisse, Roy Rogers, Dale Evans, Buddy Rogers, Dorothy Lamour, Alice Faye, Vincent Price, and Coral Browne made their respective bows. Merv Griffin stopped crooning long enough to introduce Rob Lowe to Snow White, "Meet your blind date, Prince Charming." It was their cue to break into "Late nights keep on burnin' . . . keep the cameras rollin', rollin', rollin'." Then came the dancing tables, Grauman's Chinese Theater, a chorus line of ushers, and, finally, Lily Tomlin, who walked out of the giant box of popcorn, dropped her shoe on the stairway, and read the lines that Bruce Vilanch had written for her: "I told them if they could just come up with an entrance. One and half billion people just watched it. And they're trying to make sense of it. So sit back and welcome to the shoe. Show."

That's how it looked to the audience watching the 1989 Academy Awards on TV. For nearly everybody else, it played differently.

Walking down the Shrine's center aisle, Eileen Bowman shook the hands of many Oscar-nominated actors. "She was so embarrassed, she could not even give me her hand," Bowman says of Michelle Pfeiffer, nominated for her featured performance as an ex-virgin in *Les Liaisons Dangereuses*. "Then Michelle started to laugh and giggle and that made me feel better. If she was nervous, then why should I be?" For the first time in many years at the Oscar telecast, there was a curtain—the one that Ray Klausen claimed could cover half the Empire State Building—and when it parted, Bowman believed everything would be fine. "I saw all my friends onstage—all the dancers—I felt really great," she says.

In the parking lot behind the Shrine stage, director Jeff Margolis sat in the large "remote truck" that functioned as the ABC control room for the telecast. He'd attended the rehearsals for the Snow White opener, and found its logistics daunting. If this were a movie, he would have worked five to ten weeks to plan every camera shot and angle. The Oscars, on the other hand, is live TV and there'd been less than a week to rehearse. Where most shows use half a dozen cameras, he ordered up fourteen for the opening number. Margolis clocked it: During the number's twelve minutes, instead of fifty cues, there would be at least a hundred for everything from the sets and lighting to the music and actors. In rehearsals, he'd found the Snow White number to be "entertaining." On

Oscar night, he wasn't there to be amused. "It was intense calling dozens of cues within the course of twelve minutes," he says. "It required 100 percent concentration. Something like this had never been attempted before on TV."

Below the Shrine stage in the men's room, Academy president Richard Kahn could hear Rob Lowe and Eileen Bowman launch into "Proud Mary." He couldn't see what was going on, but he knew the staging and felt no need to worry. "Let Snow White take care of herself," he thought. He had to pee now, because in ten minutes he'd be up onstage himself to represent the Academy of Motion Picture Arts and Sciences and thank everyone for being there, either in the Shrine Auditorium or at home watching on TV. Forgetting for a moment about Snow White, Kahn saw that the Shrine lived up to its reputation as a pigsty, as Allan continually warned him. The Shrine may have refurbished its first-floor restrooms, but the men's room in the basement was flooded, one of the toilets or urinals having overflowed. There in the fetid water, Kahn saw a penny on the tiled floor. He would have picked up the coin, but not wanting to contaminate himself with god-only-knows what in the water, he kicked the penny to a dry spot and then reached down to put it in his pocket. "For good luck," he told himself.

Kahn walked upstairs and into the wings—"I was standing downstage right. I could see only the first row of the audience from back there. But the reaction seemed terrific"—and he waited his turn to walk into the spotlight.

Ten miles to the north in Studio City, Lorna Luft sank into the couch at a friend's house to watch the Oscars along with those oft-mentioned other billion and a half TV viewers. It was a rather large gathering of thirty people, many of them friends, and as the telecast began and Luft watched Candice Bergen and Jodie Foster and Sean Connery cross the red carpet to enter the Shrine Auditorium, it occurred to her, "Gee, it might have been fun to do the number. Maybe I made a terrible mistake. Maybe I should have done it." Someone offered her a bowl of popcorn. She nervously downed a handful and watched as Eileen Bowman, dressed as the beloved Disney princess, tried to shake people's hands. Suddenly, Luft didn't feel so left out. "There was such a look on Michelle Pfeiffer's face of 'If you don't get away from me now I'll kill you.' It was shock and dismay," Luft says.

Merv Griffin introduced Snow White to her "blind date," and when they sang the revised "Proud Mary," Rob Lowe found himself fixating on one person in the audience, Barry Levinson, whom most observers picked as a shoo-in to win the Oscar for directing *Rain Man*. Bumping and grinding away, a microphone to his mouth, Lowe should have been gazing lovingly at his Snow White, but instead he caught yet another glimpse of Levinson, who turned to his date to say something. He may have been yards away, but Lowe found that he could actually read his lips:

"What . . . the . . . fuck?"

Lowe continued singing Tina Turner's recrafted anthem, but his mind was elsewhere. "Please God," he thought. "Let me get out of here alive!"

Like all things good or bad, Bowman and Lowe's duet came to an end. The opening number lumbered on, however, for minutes more as Prince Charming and Snow White disappeared only to be replaced by Grauman's Chinese Theater and those high-kicking ushers. Lorna Luft exhaled, and in the comfort of her friend's Studio City home, she heard someone telling her, "If you would have done that song, we would be taking you to Cedars-Sinai right now, because you would have tried to jump off the top of the Shrine."

Seated in the Club Oscar green room, Bruce Vilanch watched the show on one of several TV sets. "They looked at Snow White like she was a plague," he says of Hanks, Pfeiffer, Close. The auditorium looked as overlit as any TV set—hardly the mood for embracing something as outré as Snow White singing a duet with Rob Lowe followed by, as Vilanch put it, "the wax works of Roy Rogers, Dale Evans, Dorothy Lamour, and Alice Faye, who had to be led around by a bunch of chorus boys so they wouldn't topple over." It was obvious that almost no one in the Shrine audience understood why Merv Griffin was there or that he had actually sung "I've Got a Lovely Bunch of Coconuts" at the real Cocoanut Grove umpteen hundred years ago. "It made no sense," says Vilanch. Even his attempt to salvage Lily Tomlin from the wreckage with his line "I told them if they could just come up with an entrance" met with stunned silence.

Down in the Shrine's orchestra pit, baton in hand, Marvin Hamlisch felt a cold wave of rejection push at the backside of his tuxedo. The sweat gathered there as he smiled for the TV cameras. Despite the enthusiastic applause that capped the opening number, "You knew you'd hit a wall," he says. "There was no question. This thing that Allan was so wild about, this Las Vegas/San Francisco thing, didn't translate either to the stage or to TV. It didn't. It just wasn't classy enough. And the rest of the evening was putting a Band-Aid on something that was hemorrhaging. It was obviously a disaster."

Sitting in Row L center, Jo Schuman Silver heard the applause and turned to her husband, Steve. No matter that she'd never been to the Oscars before, the audience seemed to love it, in her opinion. "I'm so proud of you! It's a big hit," she told him.

Steve Silver let out a long sigh, then closed his eyes. "It's a piece of shit!" he whispered back.

Allan stood backstage, watching the show on monitors when, after a commercial break, a very slicked-back Tom Selleck walked into the lights to announce, "We're going to try something different." The 1989 Oscars, he said, would be conducted with "no hosts. People will arrive as couples, companions, friends, costars, compadres."

Allan blanched. Friends? Where did "friends" come from? It ruined the wonderful alliteration of his four C's!

Standing in front of the cameras, Selleck revealed that past Oscar hosts like Chevy Chase, Bob Hope, and Johnny Carson "would have you in stitches by now." As if to prove his point, no one in the Shrine auditorium laughed at Selleck's remark.

In a flop sweat, Rob Lowe wandered into the green room, the Club Oscar sign lit up overhead. In the corner he saw an old woman in a bad red wig sitting alone. She motioned for him to take the seat beside her. It was Lucille Ball. "You're baaaaaad!" she said, indulging in a bit of street jargon. "I had no idea you were such a good singer. Be a love and get me some aspirin." Lowe obeyed, got her the painkiller, and the two of them spent the next hour holding hands as he attempted to figured out what tonnage of bricks had just been dumped on his career.

Despite Selleck's "friends" glitch, Allan was soon feeling no anxiety. To his finely attuned ears, the opening number delivered an ovation, and even if the TV cameras diminished the spectacle of Ray Klausen's clever re-creations of the Cocoanut Grove and the Chinese Theater, it played well to the live audience. "Fabulous!" he kept telling himself and anyone else who'd listen. He got goose bumps when he heard the big applause that capped the number, and a minute later there were tears in his eyes as he walked into Club Oscar arm in arm with Linda Dozoretz. His "star participants" were there waiting to go on—Goldie Hawn, Kurt Russell, Sean Connery, Roger Moore, and Michael Caine—and they actually rose to their feet to give him a standing ovation. Everything was going so well that when a major coup evaporated—Goldie and Kurt told him that they decided not to joke about their nonexistent nuptials—he didn't snap or get mad or blurt out some four-letter expletive.

Allan took solace in the fact that his couples were delivering their lines as rehearsed. First up, Melanie Griffith and Don Johnson came out in matching poodle dog dos to give out the supporting actress award. "It's appropriate because I've supported one or two actresses," Johnson said.

"And a few have supported you," said Griffith.

Like any stage mother, Allan repeated the scripted lines along with his performers.

Sean Connery, Roger Moore, and Michael Caine clowned it up to give out the supporting actor award. "My name is Bond," said Connery. And pointing to Moore, Caine said, "*He's* Bond."

Allan loved the Bond bit and he laughed despite his having memorized it. He especially liked the patter that Bruce Willis and Demi Moore had planned. It was their idea to show bad home footage of their baby, Rumer, which segued into their presenting the cinematography award, which Bruce announced as "and the winner is," to which Demi corrected, "And the Oscar goes to . . . "

Allan appreciated her correction. And he laughed out loud when Robin Williams showed up in big mouse ears and white gloves to joke, "Hello, I'm Michael Eisner. Tonight's Disney movie stars Sylvester Stallone as Bambo."

But the highlight for Allan was watching Walter Matthau introduce Lucille Ball and Bob Hope. The two legends were there to announce the Break-Out Super Stars of Tomorrow number, and when the Shrine audience rose to its feet at the sound of the song "Thanks for the Memory" and Lucy turned to Bob Hope to say, "Look, they're standing!" it was as if they were saluting him, Allan Carr. Tearing up all over again, Allan turned to his publicist to say, "Let's check out the pressroom."

Every time Allan walked into his Club Oscar green room, he scored a standing ovation. Even the crew backstage couldn't stop congratulating him. "So Allan wandered into the pressroom to bask in their applause, too," says Linda Dozoretz.

Allan didn't have to look far to find a friend among the journalists. Seated in the front row was the *USA Today* columnist Jeannie Williams, who had often written enthusiastically about his many projects. He could count on Williams to give things a positive spin. Allan waved. "Hi, Jeannie."

Even though Williams obeyed the Oscar's formal dress code, she looked more than a little rumpled, her blond hair tossed as if by its own wind machine. "Allan!" she exclaimed. "Don't you think the Snow White opening was a bit . . . over the top?"

Dozoretz could feel Allan's fingers burrow into her right arm. "Are you kidding?" he asked Williams. "Did you hear the ovations out there? It was magical."

A veteran gossip, Williams may have been supportive of Allan in the past, but she wasn't letting go of a good story on Oscar night. "But Allan," she continued, "why Snow White? What's the connection between her and, well, the whole Cocoanut Grove theme of the show?"

"It's called theatrical!" Allan was no longer smiling.

"So, Allan, tell us," Williams taunted. "Would you do it all again?"

"Ask me tomorrow," he replied a little too fast.

As soon as the Break-Out Super Stars of Tomorrow number ended, an army of publicists led Ricki Lake, Blair Underwood, Christian Slater, and other youngsters into the pressroom. "Get me out of here!" Allan whispered to Dozoretz. Allan was so shaken by his Jeannie Williams run-in that he actually had trouble walking. "It was piling on him. It hadn't occurred to him that the show had been anything but a huge success until that moment in the pressroom," says Dozoretz. When Allan let go of his publicist, she checked her arm. A dark purple bruise was already growing there. "Protect me," he begged.

In another of his Oscar innovations that year, Allan separated the various categories of the press—print, TV, radio, and a new one called "the Internet"—into separate rooms. He fully intended to jump from one pressroom to the next to bask in the reporters' adulation. But that long journey came to an abrupt end after his impromptu chat with the *USA Today* columnist. "That's as far as we got," says Dozoretz, who escorted her client back to the safe, friendlier terrain of Club Oscar.

As the telecast continued, there were fewer and fewer celebs hanging out in the green room, and Allan watched the final minutes of the show in relative quiet without being hassled or, for that matter, congratulated. The Jeannie Williams encounter, however, left him so stunned that he didn't even comment when Cher, giving out the best picture award, made the ultimate faux pas and said, "And the winner is . . . *Rain Man*."

By now he'd sweated through his black sequined dinner jacket, and there was nothing left to do but face the jury at the Governor's Ball. He could only hope that what he'd witnessed in the pressroom was not replicated among his peers in the Shrine's adjoining Expo Hall.

Ray Klausen watched the final moments of the telecast from the back of the Shrine Auditorium, and couldn't really deconstruct the audience reaction. Lots of applause doesn't always mean lots of excitement, especially on Broadway opening nights or at Hollywood galas, as he well knew. As soon as Cher announced *Rain Man,* he dashed out of the theater to make his way backstage. He wanted to thank his crew for a job well done. The sets for an awards show need to be assembled quickly, and they aren't always the most reliable or well-built structures. "You're just grateful that you didn't have a bad accident and that you got through it unscathed," he surmises. In that regard, the 1989 Oscar production qualified as a success. No one got killed. (Only later, when he saw the show on videotape, did he realize what had happened: "The look on the audience's face was priceless. Oh, my God!" And Klausen didn't mean that in a good way.)

For Klausen, the evening had only hit its halfway mark, since he was also in charge of decorating the cavernous Expo Hall. Playing off the old Hollywood theme of the Cocoanut Grove number, he doused the place in red, white, and gold. "It's kind of like decorating a Bavarian hangar," he says. "But it's become wonderfully glamorous and handsome." If he said so himself.

Along with the 6 million tulips outside, the Flower Council of Holland supplied a few acres of red and white tulips to complement the estimated 5,000 yards of red and white chiffon that draped the Expo Hall walls. As the twenty-piece orchestra played, three giant Oscars slowly revolved in unison with the dance floor, inducing vague nausea in anyone who had already gorged on the poached salmon, arugula salad, free-range chicken breast grilled over alder wood, and the contents of the crisp potato baskets, of which there were an estimated 2,000.

Kevin Kline, who won as supporting actor for his role in *A Fish Called Wanda,* joked about getting a hernia. "This weighs a ton!" he said of his gold statuette, which no pundit had predicted he'd win. "I thought they'd assign someone to carry it for me." To that end, Jodie Foster, the best-actress award-winner for essaying a rape victim in *The Accused,* got her nephew Christian Dunn, age twelve, to carry her Oscar as she pretended to be physically enamored of her walker date for the evening, Julian Sands. But winners aside, the real story that March 29 evening was the Oscar production itself. Away from the Shrine glare, people were only beginning to compare notes on what Allan Carr had wrought.

Richard Kahn and his wife, Gloria, accepted the many kudos with polished restraint. They couldn't tell if the congrats were sincere or forced. Kahn had traveled long enough in the Hollywood world to know that it's difficult to tell the difference. "You try to filter out the pro forma congratulations that come at the end of any show," he philosophizes.

Out of Kahn's earshot, Jeff Berg, who headed up the newly created Creative Artists Agency (CAA), ran into Thom Mount, the former president of Universal Pictures, who was riding high on the hit *Bull Durham*. Standing together at the bar, they both felt the need for a strong drink. "We just looked at each other," says Mount. "What on earth was that?!" He told Berg that the Snow White number had caused him to undergo a "Martian out-of-body experience," and in his opinion, the Shrine audience had been "incredulous and stunned." The Break-Out Super Stars of Tomorrow number didn't get a much better review. "It was painful," says Mount.

The immediate feedback was not all negative, and Peter Guber, *Rain Man*'s executive producer, noted a distinct generational divide in the criticism. "There were two reactions," says Guber. "The view that we've punctured the sacrosanct Oscar awards ceremony was held by the conservative folks. The young people were 'Hoorah, what a breath of fresh air. We're headed for oblivion if we have our eyes in the rearview mirror.' Inadvertently Allan set the tone for folks to take another way to do this staid event."

Mrs. Steve Silver chose to feel the younger, kinder vibe that evening. At the Governor's Ball, well-wishers like Gene Hackman, Amy Irving, Don Johnson, and Melanie Griffith offered their congratulations to her husband. Many of them had seen *Beach Blanket Babylon* either in San Francisco or Las Vegas, and were fans. "Everyone made such a fuss about Steve, how brilliant and wonderful the show was," she recalls. Even some bigwigs from Disney expressed their wholehearted approval, and according to Mrs. Silver, more than one Disney executive asked her husband, "Have you ever thought of doing movies?"

For a moment, the orchestra stopped playing and, from the dais, Richard Kahn thanked Jeff Margolis and Allan, who, in turn, thanked everyone and then escaped to a roped-off area of the Expo Hall. "He wanted to have his own private party at the ball," says Kahn. It was there that Allan holed up with his Young Hollywood kids, who included Patrick Dempsey, twenty-three, who was stepdad to Corey Parker, twenty-three, whose mom, Rocky, forty-eight, was Dempsey's wife. Some of Allan's star participants also showed up, and Allan hugged Goldie Hawn and Kurt Russell as if for support.

"Overall, the reaction was subdued," says Dozoretz. "And Allan definitely picked up on that."

Under other circumstances, Dozoretz might have accepted Allan's invitation to go to Swifty Lazar's party at Spago, but she claimed to be tired, and declined. Exhausted or not, Dozoretz wanted to rush home to check out that new invention, the Internet, to read early reviews. Indeed, the wire services had already posted their pan reviews of the event. Some of the smaller news outlets were also delivering decidedly downbeat verdicts. Her face to the computer, "I saw what was happening," she says. Tomorrow morning, Dozoretz knew, would be her most difficult challenge when Allan called for a rundown of all the reviews.

Jeff Margolis also made an early exit. "To go home and collapse," he told friends.

On the limo ride from the Shrine to Spago, Allan poured champagne for Bruce Vilanch, and told him with no joy, "I burned a lotta bridges with this one."

Vilanch thought that Allan realized how poorly the show had been received. "But in fact he didn't know, not yet," says the writer. "Instead, he was referring to all the people whom he had rejected as presenters."

Swifty Lazar's Oscar party wasn't anything like the Governor's Ball or even the future *Vanity Fair* fetes, where celebrities made an appearance to have their photos taken and then ran out to have their photos taken again elsewhere. "At Swifty Lazar's you sat down to dinner with Audrey Hepburn and Elizabeth Taylor," says George Christy, who wrote the *Hollywood Reporter*'s party column during the superagent's heyday. Swifty greeted everyone at the door like a master general, and it wasn't only movie stars who came. Publishing giants like Random House's Bennett Cerf and Simon & Schuster's Michael Korda and Putnam's Phyllis Gran made the grand trek out west to attend, and there would also be royalty, like Princess Grace's kids, to chow down on Wolfgang Puck's pizza, chef Serge Falesitch's red snapper, and pastry chef Mary Bergin's macadamia nut tarts. "There was heat at those parties, major, sizzling heat; it was like your fingers got burned," says Christy.

At Spago that night, Swifty was there not only to party but to hold nervous, unhappy hands. Like those of Tom Cruise.

"They quoted my mother!" the *Rain Man* star complained to Swifty. "They had the nerve to make up a quote from my mother. They never spoke to my mother!" Cruise was still huffy over reports from England that had him dying of breast cancer. "I had the flu," he told Swifty. "The worst flu I've ever had in my life. My wife had it, too," he said of Mimi Rogers. "They put me in the hospital in Paris because they thought I had malaria. I don't have cancer. It's total bullshit."

Others at Swifty's party had less reason to be testy with the press, and they included Art Buchwald, Jackie Collins, Jack Nicholson, Michael Douglas, Cybill Shepherd, Merv Griffin, and Sean Connery and Michael Caine, both of whom brought their respective wives. Amy Irving came with Richard Dreyfuss and his wife, Jeramie, since Steven Spielberg remained home in Los Angeles on Oscar night, causing everyone to speculate that not all was well with Mr. and Mrs. Spielberg. Alana Stewart, divorced from Rod Stewart, arrived with first former husband, George Hamilton. Shirley MacLaine, pissed over Bob Hope's crack about her reincarnation habits on the telecast, complained, "I think the jokes about me are getting stale. They need updating, maybe some new writers."

Allan arrived at the party with Bruce Vilanch, who had most definitely not written Bob Hope's barb regarding Shirley MacLaine, and to prove it, the writer and the actress spent much of the night together schmoozing. Allan looked for Swifty Lazar, but the host had already gone home.

Robin Williams praised Allan: "I hear he's doing the Nobel Prize next. Lots of singing and dancing."

The *Nightline* TV show corralled Michael Caine for an interview, but after being miked for ten minutes without being asked one question, he finally un-wired himself. "What is this?" the actor asked to no one in particular. "Am I working?" At which he rejoined the party by offering a toast to Allan.

"The reception was very warm, actually," says Vilanch. "People told Allan how much they had loved it." Too often, however, they asked Allan, "Will you produce it again?" He would have preferred to hear, "It was the greatest show I've ever seen."

Allan could only smile and reply, "Ask me tomorrow." Or he said without en-thusiasm, "The scenery didn't fall down. I'm ecstatic."

Tired of repeating himself, Allan left Spago after a brief visit, to make his way home alone to Hilhaven. The greatest day of his life had just ended, and for some reason he wasn't feeling so great.

twenty-nine

Death by Oscar

A few hours later, Steve and Jo Silver rose early in their room at the Beverly Hills Hotel. They were eager to read the reviews, and with a raft of newspapers under their arms, they retired to one of the poolside cabanas. They sat down with their coffee and croissants, and began to read. No surprise, their hometown paper, the *San Francisco Examiner*, gave him a rave: "After a decade-plus of dull, dull, dull telecasts, a shot of good old San Francisco camp restored Oscar to his rightful place as king of TV awards shows."

Variety, on the other hand, suffered from a slight case of press schizophrenia. Army Archerd, who appeared in the Snow White number, called the telecast "a hit." But the newspaper's TV reviewer, Tony Scott, whose notice ran on the same page as Archerd's, had witnessed a different telecast: "The 61st Annual Academy Awards extravaganza—seen in 91 countries including, for the first time, the Soviet Union—turned out to be a TV nyet." Scott went on to trash a "feeble-voiced Rob Lowe" and a "squeaky-voiced Snow White," but saved his real condemnation for the Break-Out Super Stars number with its "youngsters few have heard of, cavorting around a giant Oscar as if it were the Golden Calf."

Since the *Daily Variety* review saved its nastier comments for the telecast's *other* production number, Steve Silver thought he could live with those words. Then came the *New York Times*. "The 61st Academy Awards ceremony began by creating the impression that there would never be a 62nd," wrote Janet Maslin. "The evening's opening number, which deserves a permanent place in the annals of Oscar embarrassments, was indeed as bad as that. Barely five min-

236

utes into the show, Merv Griffin was on hand to sing 'I've Got a Lovely Bunch of Coconuts,' and that was only the beginning. Snow White, played as a simpering ninny, performed a duet of 'Proud Mary' with Rob Lowe, who would be well-advised to confine all future musical activities to the shower."

Silver read no further. Barely did he have time to recover from that assault in print than Gael Love, the editor of *Andy Warhol's Interview,* stuck her head in the cabana. "You're Steve Silver?" she asked. "You directed the Oscars last night, right?"

Silver nodded. "Well, the opening number . . . "

"The one with Snow White and Rob Lowe, yeah." Never one for the delicate touch, Love got right to it. "So what did you think of it? Were you happy with how it turned out?"

Silver took a breath. He even managed to grin. "It's the best thing that ever happened to me!" he exclaimed. He thought a moment, still holding the *New York Times* in his hand. "Janet Maslin says it is the worst production number in the history of the Oscars. I guess you can't top that. The publicity for *Beach Blanket Babylon* ought to be wonderful."

Silver went on to tell Love that the opening number wasn't what he originally envisioned. Then again, his job wasn't on the line. Unlike other people involved with the Oscars, he didn't have to wait for his next gig. "Steve has a hit show in San Francisco," Jo Silver informed the *Interview* editor.

A few blocks east toward the hills, Allan Carr was one of those people waiting for his next job. He had expected to get a phone call from Richard Kahn, begging him to produce the 1990 Oscars. Instead, Allan sat in his white tent by the pool, the copies of the *Los Angeles Times* and the *New York Times* already tattered and blowing in the wind at his feet. Since the phone didn't stir, he picked it up to dial his publicist.

When Dozoretz answered, he didn't introduce himself. "No one has called," said Allan. She commiserated by mentioning the TV ratings, which looked very good. "It's still early," Dozoretz added. There was plenty of time for phone calls and flowers and telegrams to arrive. But it was clear. "Allan didn't know what hit him," she says.

A more circumspect man, Bruce Vilanch decided not to make phone calls or show his face in the wake of the reviews. "I was in bed all the next day cheering up several members of the Young Hollywood number," he recalls.

Resting the morning after in his Beverly Hills home, Kahn tossed off the bad reviews, just as he did in previous years. "Producers usually shrug them off," he says. The Janet Maslin review was a little more bloodletting than usual, he thought, but since when did a *New York Times* reviewer ever like the Oscars? Kahn chose to believe the well-wishers at the Governor's Ball. The critics who watched it at home on TV weren't always the best judge. "When you're watching it in the auditorium, it's a different show. You can have a fabulous time in the theater, and then people say it was so boring on TV."

Pundits made a national sport of attacking the Oscars, saying that each year is the worst, the most boring. Allan, in Kahn's opinion, achieved the impossible: The TV ratings for the 1989 edition weren't just good, they were spectacular, and had reversed the show's five-year numbers slide. "There was a feeling we owned the town," Kahn recalls. The telecast made it into no fewer than 26.9 million homes in the United States, and with a 29.8 rating; the Oscar telecast hadn't done that well since 1984, when it did 30.5.

Kahn took pleasure in analyzing the telecast ratings. Then the phone rang. It was Frank Wells, president of Disney. "Frank, how are you?" Kahn asked, expecting him to say something nice about last night's show.

Wells said, "Dick, we got a problem."

"Oh."

"Yes, we're very unhappy, we at Disney."

"Yes?"

"About the show."

"Oh?"

"Disney is upset over the appearance of Snow White."

It was the first sign that there might be trouble ahead, because no sooner had Kahn put down the phone with Wells than he received a messenger-delivered missive. It was a letter of complaint about the telecast from a former Academy president,—and Oscar-winning actor—named Gregory Peck. "I didn't know why he was so upset," says Kahn. He phoned Peck to find out.

"The show reminds me of those Photoplay Awards!" said the actor, referring to a now-defunct fanzine that published puff pieces on the Hollywood stars and, each year, congratulated itself with a meaningless awards show. Apparently, Peck never liked the Photoplay Awards, and found them tacky, not sophisticated, beneath dignity.

"That was a very difficult day for me as president of the Academy," says Kahn.

Allan, disappointed by the lack of day-after accolades, decided to go hunting for them. Rather than cancel his lunch plans, he kept his appointment at Mortons restaurant that Thursday afternoon, as did Robert Osborne, who happened to be dining there that day. The *Hollywood Reporter* columnist had been very supportive of the *Beach Blanket Babylon* revue in San Francisco, but Osborne's enthusiasm did not extend to Steve Silver's work on the Oscar production.

"I knew Steve Silver. Allan loved that show in San Francisco," Osborne says. "But what Allan did with it—it didn't have any of the humor or the terrificness of Silver's show." He was surprised to see Allan at Mortons the day after the Oscars. "It was foolish. Allan must have known that these powerful Hollywood figures would be there. Maybe it was his way of showing defiance."

More likely, despite the paucity of phoned-in congratulations, Allan continued not to process how much the Hollywood establishment despised his Oscar telecast. At Mortons, many fellow diners turned away from the Oscar producer's table and actually extended their lunch hour, waiting for Allan to leave first. "When they got up, finally, they took the most indirect route to get by Allan. You could tell that he became aware of that," says Osborne.

People read the dreadful reviews and spent that morning gossiping about how bad the telecast had been. The buzz spiraled from bad to godawful, and soon wound its way down to fiasco. "Then it became this megadisaster," says Osborne, "so that by the time Allan got to Mortons, the Oscars were considered enough of a disaster that no one wanted to talk to Allan Carr. I hadn't previously seen that so dramatically displayed by so many people in Hollywood as that day at Mortons—like they'd catch something, like it was a disease."

That evening, Steve and Jo Silver made what they felt was a difficult but obligatory trip to Allan's house. Days earlier, Silver had ordered a crystal-star sculpture from Tiffany's, and engraved it with the words, "You are the Star!" But when he and his wife knocked on the front door of Hilhaven Lodge, an assistant answered to tell them, "Allan is not home." The young man instinctively reached for the gift-wrapped package.

Silver resisted, saying, "No, I just want to set it down. I know where I'd like Allan to find his present." He sensed that Allan was home that evening, and after a few minutes of investigation, Silver found him in the basement, a drink in hand in the Bella Darvi Bar. Allan was alone, drunk, depressed.

The three of them hugged. "I just want to give you this gift," said Silver. "It has been a very special experience for me." Hearing those few words, Allan began to sob.

There were more phone calls from Disney executives to Richard Kahn. He, in turn, consulted the Academy lawyers. But when Frank Wells demanded a public apology, Kahn felt he stood on solid enough ground to refuse that order.

If Kahn had capitulated, "We would have considered the matter ended," said Wells.

The matter didn't end there. Before the end of Thursday's business day, the Walt Disney Company slapped the Academy with a federal lawsuit charging that the Oscar telecast of March 29, 1989, had abused and irreparably damaged the studio's fifty-two-year-old Snow White character. It asked for unspecified damages for "copyright infringement, unfair competition, and dilution of business reputation."

Together with Kahn, ABC's John Hamlin found himself broadsided by Disney, having assumed there would be no problem. As he told the *Wall Street Journal*, "I had always surmised Disney would be very pleased. Disney loves promotion of Disney characters."

Many other members of the press were also working the phones, asking Disney about the Snow White brouhaha. "It wasn't the songs so much, it was her singing," a company spokesman told them. Several Disney employees had remarked, "Snow White sounded like a Martian."

More inquiring minds wanted to know why the studio hadn't also objected to Robin Williams, who donned big mouse ears and made unflattering remarks about Michael Eisner on the Oscar telecast. The spokesman replied that the Williams's ears were not an exact replica of Mr. Mickey Mouse's.

While the comedian got a pass, *Beach Blanket Babylon* in San Francisco did not. The Disney lawyers checked on whether any copyright impropriety had been committed up north, and soon learned that the show axed its Snow White character four years earlier.

Stung by news of the lawsuit, Allan went into spin overdrive, and called every friend he knew in the press. He told *Variety*'s Army Archerd that Ronald Reagan had phoned him personally to congratulate him on the show, and that the president was especially impressed by the opening Cocoanut Grove number. "I used to go there," said Reagan. Or so Allan said he said.

Phoning the *Hollywood Reporter*'s Martin Grove, Allan pointed out that "it was the highest-rated Oscar show in five years. The interesting thing is that the ratings went up as the evening went along as opposed to dropping off, which shows people loved the show." The ratings in England and Australia were the best ever for the Oscars. "This will be great for business!" he exclaimed, referring to the telecast's impact on international ticket sales. In England, *Rain Man* was only in its third week, *Dangerous Liaisons* had just opened there. And did Grove know that there was a line that Bruce Vilanch had written for Anne

Archer when she introduced *Dangerous Liaisons* as one of the five nominated pictures? "She called it *'The Fatal Attraction* of another era,'" Allan pointed out. "That line is being used by the video company that's releasing *Liaisons* as their [ad] tagline!" It didn't seem possible, Allan told Grove, but he had received so many congratulatory flowers, telegrams, and bottles of champagne at Hilhaven that "I've had to put a secretary on just to answer the mail. You know when that happens you've touched the town."

Hollywood was, in fact, so affected that the *Los Angeles Times*'s top film reviewer-reporter, Charles Champlin, wanted to meet with Allan to talk about the show—in person on Friday. Allan looked forward to the interview to clear his reputation. Champlin owed him: Shortly before *La Cage aux folles* opened in Boston, he'd set up a big student confab for the journalist at Harvard. Allan knew he could count on Champlin to help get out his version of events.

Allan decided to go casual for the *Los Angeles Times* interview, and donning yet another caftan, he flicked off his slippers and mixed himself a vodka and grapefruit juice. He was barefoot and nonchalantly sipping the drink when Champlin came to the door. "Chuck!" he exclaimed, as if the reporter were paying an impromptu visit. Allan made sure that flowers filled the living room, and he remarked, "It resembles a flower shop or a gangster's funeral." It was a line that Champlin later noted in his newspaper report.

"There were more flowers," Allan pointed out, "but I've already had most of them shipped to a children's hospital." Allan read aloud a handwritten note from a dear friend: "You delivered. Jennifer Jones." There was another letter from the American Film Institute's Jean Firstenberg: "You put the show back in show business." And it meant so much to Allan that his friend at CAA Michael Ovitz took the time to write, "You brought show business back to the movie business." Ovitz had reason to celebrate regardless of the telecast: The agency's big film, *Rain Man,* had won the top Oscar. "And Candy Bergen called to say how angry she was about the reviews," Allan told Champlin. "Janet Leigh had also called to say how much she disagreed with the reviews."

Allan stopped himself. It was bad form to dwell on the negative when a reporter had his tape recorder going. "And I suppose you've heard," he said. "Ronald Reagan called to say he how much he liked the Cocoanut Grove number."

Champlin smiled and nodded. He'd read that in Army Archerd's *Variety* column. Allan grimaced. He should have known better. That bit of news was a minor coup for Archerd, and reporters, who lived from item to item, hated it when they'd been scooped. Allan's mind raced. If only he could give Champlin some news on the level of the Reagan story. He'd hoped by now that he could announce that, yes, the Academy wanted him back to produce next year's telecast. But while he'd spoken to Richard Kahn about the Disney lawsuit and Gregory Peck's complaints, the Academy president never mentioned anything about the 1990 telecast. Then again, Kahn was retiring from the Academy at the end of July. Lame ducks don't have any power, Allan kept telling himself.

In the end, the only thing Allan could offer Champlin in the way of a firstrate story was his very veiled assumption that there was something homophobic about certain people's condemnation of the telecast. He repeated what Ronald Reagan and Jennifer Jones and Janet Leigh said about his Oscars. But he firmly believed, "If it came from Lincoln Center and not San Francisco . . . ," San Francisco, by way of Steve Silver, being the buzzword for "gay," the reaction would have been uniformly positive.

While Allan looked for scapegoats, he was not alone in believing that the "gay thing" contributed to the brouhaha. "I always thought it was *that*," says Dozoretz.

"I felt there was a surge of homophobia," says producer Craig Zadan. "But Allan played into that. He never attempted to tone it down. He embraced all of that extravagance. Everything was flamboyant and he liked to shock people."

"The fact of Allan's being gay helped fuel in people's minds the anger and the recrimination," says ABC's John Hamlin.

"So what if Allan was gay?" says Fred Hayman. "I have never seen anything so outrageous as the way Hollywood reacted against that show. It was vicious and uncalled for, and they destroyed Allan."

After Allan Carr and Steve Silver, Bruce Vilanch comprised the third big gay component of the 1989 Oscar telecast. He put another wrinkle on the disaster. "Allan had said it was going to be the biggest and best for so long," says Vilanch. "Everyone who'd produced the show before, or knew someone who had done it before, took umbrage."

Then there was the telecast itself. "People didn't hate it because Allan was gay," says David Geffen. "It was a terrible show."

Allan's upbeat words defending himself appeared in the *Los Angeles Times, Variety,* and the *Hollywood Reporter,* but were, in the end, a mere bandage over a deepening, infected wound.

One week after the Oscars, Richard Kahn relented, on the advice of counsel, and issued a statement. It read, "The Academy sincerely apologizes to Disney for the unauthorized use of Disney's copyrighted Snow White character and for unintentionally creating the impression that Disney had participated in or sanctioned the opening production number on the Academy Awards telecast."

As part of the agreement, Disney dropped its federal suit on the condition that the Academy never "reuse the segment" with Snow White or "use Disney's Snow White character in the future without Disney's permission."

Allan could deal with the Disney lawsuit, especially now that it had so conveniently disappeared. But April 7 brought new trouble. If Peter Guber surmised that the younger generation applauded Allan's Oscarcast as a "breath of fresh air," they were clearly not the ones in control of the Academy. No sooner did Kahn clear up the House of Mouse mess than another problem materialized in the form of a letter signed by seventeen of the most prominent (read: "older generation") figures in the Hollywood film community. It began:

> The 61st Academy Awards show was an embarrassment to both the Academy and the entire motion picture industry. It is neither fitting nor acceptable that the best work in motion pictures be acknowledged in such a demeaning fashion. We urge the president and governors of the Academy to ensure that future award presentations reflect the same standard of excellence as that set by the films and filmmakers they honor.

The letter was signed by Julie Andrews, David Brown, Stanley Donen, Blake Edwards, John Foreman, William Friedkin, Larry Gelbart, Sidney Lumet, Joseph L. Mankiewicz, Paul Newman, Alan J. Pakula, Gregory Peck, Martin Ritt, Mark Rydell, Peter Stone, Billy Wilder, and Fred Zinnemann.

Kahn publicly responded to the comments of the Hollywood 17, as they were soon dubbed, with an upbeat remark: "We're delighted to receive them, although I certainly don't agree with them." Kahn went on to give Allan his support, but in effect, he did acknowledge that his chosen producer was a novice when it came to putting on the Oscars. "Allan's next show, whenever that might be, will be a lot better than the first one," Kahn wrote.

Kahn failed to state outright whether Allan would be invited back—the president was retiring from the Academy on July 31—but the news couldn't have been clearer: Allan Carr would not be producing the Oscars next year or ever again.

Kahn launched his own little private investigation into the Hollywood 17, and in his opinion, "the ringleader, the guy who put that letter out, was Blake

Edwards," says Kahn. "He got a lot of those people to sign it." Weeks later, Kahn ran into a producer who attached his name to the letter, and he asked him, "Were you really that unhappy about the show?"

"No" came the reply, "but Blake asked me to sign it."

That fact was not expressed publicly nor was it ever made known to Allan Carr, who took the brunt of the abuse. "People who were friends of Allan showed up on that letter," says Kahn, "and those comments really hurt him. I really think that Allan's declining health in the years following that show are in part attributable to the hurt he felt from some of those people he regarded as friends."

Allan considered them friends because they came to his parties, but many people partied at Hilhaven not because they were his friends but because Allan Carr had become "such a visible Hollywood celebrity," says Gary Pudney. There were also people who came to his parties, overindulged themselves, and then had reason to fear Allan. "They were afraid of his outrageousness. Then, like a pack of hyenas, no one came to his parties after the Oscars. The great thing he wanted in his life was that job, and he got the job and then would spend the rest of his life trying to recover from it. He fell ill," says the ABC executive.

Over the following days, the Oscar loathing spread, and it wasn't only those people who'd drunk Allan's Cristal and eaten his crab legs and snorted cocaine in his basement disco. On April 9, the *Los Angeles Times* devoted its entire letters section to Oscar hate mail and titled it "For Some, the Oscar Show Was One Big Carr Crash." It was official: Ten out of ten letter writers in the *Times* despised the show. Then, almost one month to the day after the 61st annual Academy Awards, Lucille Ball passed away on April 26. The prevailing joke in Hollywood was that the Oscar telecast had killed her.

By the end of April, while most people in Hollywood had already forgotten that *Rain Man* won the top Oscar, the public indignities continued unabated for Allan. On April 28, Kahn announced that the Academy would form an Oscar telecast committee to "figure out why and what we should do in the future. . . . Certain factors this year did involve a lot of comment pro and con." Gilbert Cates, former president of the Directors Guild of America, was named as committee chairman, and would head up the Awards Presentation Review Committee. A most generous individual, Cates took no potshots at Allan in the press, and publicly presented himself as a thoroughly bemused figurehead. "As soon as my name was mentioned as chairman, people started calling saying they loved the show or hated it. It really is a lightning rod of opinion," he told *Variety*.

Meanwhile, Allan continued to defend himself, weakly. "Jennifer Jones loved it! Janet Leigh loved it. Candice Bergen loved it," he said. But no defense could mask his devastation.

Friends in the industry tried being upbeat. Gary Pudney told him, "It will go down in history as one of the highest-rated Oscar telecasts, Allan. And that's all those fuckers care about. Who cares that Blake Edwards wrote a letter to the Academy?"

Allan cared.

It didn't help, as Bruce Vilanch pointed out, that many of those who signed Blake Edwards's letter were on those very bridges that Allan had burned. "He didn't know what was in store for him," says Vilanch. "All those people he'd said no to at the behest of ABC would turn on him. Certainly no one was expecting the Snow White insanity. That number had been cleared by lawyers at the Academy and at ABC and Disney, which were not yet affiliated."

Allan rued the day that he failed to invite as presenters such industry stalwarts as Gregory Peck and Paul Newman. He could only thank God that Elizabeth Taylor, whom he had also rejected as a presenter, didn't sign the petition. By 1989, she was the patron saint of gay people for having championed AIDS care and research as a cause.

It seemed the most improbable thing, but Allan gave up talking to the press for the first time in his life, and became uncharacteristically "unavailable for comment." *Variety* reported that he was traveling in Mexico. "He was such an easy target," says Marvin Hamlisch. "He was bigger than life. He felt wherever he would walk, they were whispering, 'He's the guy who screwed it up.'"

Despite Allan's disappearance to Mexico, the snowball effect of the Oscar disaster only grew. In the beginning, it was bad enough that Rob Lowe couldn't sing. In the beginning, like Allan, Lowe defended himself. "The Academy asked me to take that role. So I was a good soldier and did it. You can't be your own manager and agent and soothsayer—you have to take risks. And on that one I got shot in the foot," said Lowe. And then, like Allan, Lowe just shut up.

And for good reason. In early May of that year, the actor got hit with a personal injury lawsuit regarding allegations filed by a teenage girl's mother. The investigation involved criminal sexual activity with a minor during Lowe's attendance at the Democratic National Convention in Atlanta the previous summer. A videotape had surfaced showing Lowe and another man as they took turns having sexual intercourse with a young woman. Just when the Oscar fiasco began to wind its way out of the newspapers, it resurfaced as part of the Rob

Lowe sex scandal, as if, in his now-infinite bad taste, Allan Carr had managed, with 20-20 foresight, to capitalize on the infamous videotape to help promote his Oscars telecast. That was nonsense, but legends don't always fuel themselves on the facts.

Allan tried to reinvent the Oscars through camp comedy, and thought he could entertain the Hollywood royalty just as he had Gregory Peck and Billy Wilder and Gene Kelly years ago at Hilhaven with the Cycle Sluts. "But the Oscars is the one night Hollywood has no sense of humor," says Lorna Luft. "Their careers are on the line that night. It's not funny, and nobody in the audience that night is having fun. Ask anybody who has hosted the Oscars."

Allan never admitted *ever* that the Snow White number was anything but stupendous. "In Allan's world it was a fabulous number that had Alice Faye and Dorothy Lamour and Buddy Rogers and Roy Rogers and Dale Evans and Merv Griffin at the Cocoanut Grove," says Bruce Vilanch. "It was that old Hollywood glamour. But they were old chess pieces, and they didn't do what had made them famous years ago. And people didn't know who they were."

To his credit, Cates refused to discuss the recommendations of the august Awards Presentation Review Committee, which met that summer. But in time, he did speak to the matter. "Allan did a good job," Cates surmised nearly twenty years later, "but he made one tragic mistake: He put a questionable number at the beginning of the show and he let it run for twelve minutes."

Allan tried to edit it in rehearsals. "Some stuff did get cut," says Vilanch. "But we were in so deep with Snow White that you couldn't cut enough."

In Hollywood, there's an old truism that's popular among film directors: Never show a studio executive more than three takes. Too much material inspires them to get critical. The same could be said of the Oscar audience. "If the number had been only three minutes," says Cates, "Allan would be alive today."

"Allan thought like a film person," says Jeff Margolis. "He didn't understand TV, where twelve minutes is an eternity."

Vilanch and Margolis survived to write and direct, respectively, many more Oscar telecasts. But the 1989 show remains their most memorable, if for all the wrong reasons. "No one involved ever thought it would have the effect it had," says Vilanch.

Despite the criticism heaped on the telecast, Cates kept a number of Allan's innovations in the more than fourteen Oscar telecasts that he produced in the following years. Those Allan Carr touches included the fashion show, the ex-

tended coverage of the red carpet, the separate presentations of the five nominated best pictures, and the line "The Oscar goes to . . . "

That Allan was banned from ever producing the show again seemed like an
extreme reaction, but one with which Cates could identify. "It sounds like our
town," he says. "Banned? What did he do? Fuck the queen?"

Cates didn't witness the 1989 Oscar show firsthand—he saw it on tape—nor
did he ever see Allan Carr again. His last memory of Allan Carr in the flesh
came a few years before the 1989 Oscars. "There was this trapeze act in the
Shrine Auditorium," Cates recalls, "and Allan was seated in the audience. There
was this absolute childlike look of wonder in his eyes as he watched those people
on the trapeze. He loved everything about show business."

Some time after the Oscar telecast, "when the dust had settled," Lorna Luft
mailed Allan a note. "Don't worry," she wrote. "Everything will be fine." But
she never heard back from him. Luft kept his Snow White invitation a secret,
but people found out regardless. Years later, no less a Hollywood personage
than Dreamworks' Jeffrey Katzenberg told her, "Thank God you didn't do Snow
White."

She had to wonder, "How did he know?"

Allan missed all these secondhand humiliations by retreating to his beloved
Hilhaven Lodge. When he did leave the house, he made sure also to leave the
country. When Mexico proved not far enough away, he planned one of his trips
to Fiji.

On a day in December 1989, his assistant Jeff Paul drove Allan to the airport,
where both men ran into James T. Ballard, an attorney, whom Paul knew from
the West Hollywood Swim Club. In his early thirties, Paul was a stunningly built
nonprofessional athlete who spent his days swimming, riding a bike through the
streets of the gay enclave, and not working—except for the occasional gig that
Allan threw him, whether that be as his chauffeur or gofer. "Guys on the swim
team used to ask Jeff Paul why he did these odd jobs for Allan Carr," Ballard
recalls. Paul's response never changed. "Allan will take care of me," he said.

At LAX, Allan was clearly distracted when Paul introduced Ballard to his
patron-boyfriend. Allan wore a discrete beige caftan and carried a small suitcase.
"Allan had a look of panicked depression," Ballard recalls. Before they boarded
the plane to Tahiti, which would carry Allan on to Fiji, Allan briefly commiserated with Ballard, saying, "Oh, it's such a long flight. I'd hate to be flying coach."

Ballard let the comment pass, but took great satisfaction when, a few minutes
later, he took his seat in front of Allan in the airplane's first-class section.

"Oh, you're flying first-class!" Allan exclaimed.

Even before the flight took off, Allan began to rummage through his small suitcase. "I'd never seen so many pills, outside of a doctor's office, in one bag," says Ballard. "Allan Carr took two or three of everything." Then washed them down with cheap complimentary champagne.

Allan eventually dozed off but not before he finished a fifteen-minute conversation with himself. "Those bastards in Hollywood," he mumbled. "Those ungrateful SOBs! I gave them everything. I did everything for them. And then those assholes treat me like this. Those bastards!"

EPILOGUE

No Second Acts

During his *La Cage aux folles* heyday, Allan remarked that he tried doing nothing for four weeks at his Surfhaven house in Hawaii. "My mind turned into mai tais," he said. "The Gemini personality is all or nothing." Now, post-Oscars 1989, Allan experienced *nothing*.

Two years after that debacle, Allan remained sequestered in Hilhaven Lodge. As for so many Americans, the 1991 recession savaged his stock portfolio, and while he was still financially secure, Allan could no longer blithely tear off a check for a few hundred thousand dollars, as he did in 1984 to help bring the Royal Shakespeare Company's productions of *Cyrano de Bergerac* and *Much Ado About Nothing* to Broadway. Parties no longer held any appeal for him, because he feared, quite correctly, that the A-list celebs and powerbrokers would no longer make the trip to his basement disco to dance and get stoned. And most important, Allan's health, always precarious, completely deserted him in the wake of the Academy Awards fiasco. He rarely knew good health, but in the past, Allan bravely coped with the bad hip, the morbid obesity, the dialysis, the kidney stones, and the various bypass infections that prompted frequent visits to Cedars-Sinai hospital. He endured because he willed himself to work, and his work, in turn, became an anodyne for whatever afflicted him physically. Now, he found himself a prisoner not only of his body but his beloved Hilhaven Lodge, with its long flight of stairs to the garage level. He put in an elevator, but even that mechanical conveyance didn't carry him out of the house often enough. He avoided old haunts like Le Dome and Mortons, where former business

249

associates might fail to greet him or, worse, point and whisper, "There he goes. The one who screwed it up."

In spring 1991, his good friend Angie Dickinson phoned him with an invitation. The actress would be speaking at the American Film Institute's gala honoring Kirk Douglas, and she asked Allan to be her date for the evening.

He hesitated. "I don't know."

She wouldn't give up. "C'mon, go with me."

It took more phone calls and "great urging" on Dickinson's part before Allan relented, making the AFI event at the Beverly Hills Hilton his delicate, if not grand, return to Hollywood. Angie Dickinson supported him physically, as well as emotionally, and except for those few minutes that she had to speak onstage, the actress remained at his side to help make conversation whenever a former Hollywood comrade asked, "So Allan, what are you doing now?"

He didn't say much that evening, but appeared to enjoy himself. "It helped him to say hello to many big people who wouldn't say hello to him before," says Dickinson.

Gradually, as the U.S. economy rebounded from the early 1990s recession, Allan's stock portfolio recouped its losses and began to grow again. Where he had previously spent his days in bed watching game shows and soap operas, he now turned his attention to CNBC to fixate on the stock market. "It was amazing to watch Allan," says his business manager Asa Manor. "Making money can be an antidote to depression."

It helped, too, that some studio chiefs remained in touch with him, albeit behind the scenes. While they badmouthed his Oscar telecast and turned their back on him in public, a few continued to phone Hilhaven for his advice. Allan's *Deer Hunter* cohort Thom Mount was one of the few who actually made personal visits, and it amazed the producer how often his reclusive friend's phone rang. It would be a movie-studio macher asking Allan how to handle the X, Y, or Z problem of marketing a movie. Allan would say, "No, move the film three months" or "Yes, audiences will go for it if you change the tag line." He never refused a request regardless of infractions suffered. Mount found the situation both hilarious and sad. No one would give Allan a job, "but he was the secret marketing machine of Hollywood," says the producer. "He was a better publicist than any publicist he met and a better marketing person than any marketing person."

Allan never admitted that his Oscar telecast was anything less than wonderful. And why should he? In 1995, David Letterman hosted the show and put a spinning dog, among other low-rent touches, on the stage. Bruce Vilanch wanted to send Allan a note—"And to think you got in trouble for Snow White. How times have changed"—but never did.

The name Allan Carr still meant something. Asa Manor phoned Allan one day to ask if he had seen the latest issue of *Buzz*. It contained an unwelcome reminder of his current legacy. In an article on Hollywood excess, the magazine mentioned Allan Carr as the man who "produced *Can't Stop the Music*, which he did."

Then there was George Plimpton's book *Truman Capote*, published in 1997. Allan sat in bed reading it, checking the index to see if his famous Jail House Party for the *In Cold Blood* author was mentioned. It surprised him that his name didn't appear. Then he came to page 414, which included a long quote from his close friend Dominick Dunne. It read:

> [Capote and I] were at a party in Hollywood given by this guy who was up-and-coming, trying to make a name for himself, and it was given in the Los Angeles County Jail. It was attended by what they used to call out there in those days a kind of "B" group party list, wannabes and has-beens. It wasn't the kind of party that Truman was used to at all . . . lots of coke being taken, and he was at his table in one cell, my table was in another, and we kind of looked across and saw each other; he understood that I understood that this wasn't how it used to be; his eyes were very, very sad.

Allan put the book down and broke into tears. He was still crying when he phoned Dunne. Their conversation didn't go well despite his friend's contrition. Later, Dunne wrote to Allan, and recalled the financial and emotional support Allan had shown him in the early 1970s, when Dunne's own career was in a "downward spiral" in the movie business.

"I hope you will forgive me," Dunne wrote. "You were one of the people who didn't drop me and I'll never forget that. I remember the trip we took to Puerta Vallarta, and the trip you took me on to Saint-Tropez, when we went out on Harold and Grace Robbins yacht, and then the Plaza Athenée in Paris. I remember the nights and nights of parties and good times at your house, with you at the center, directing, wanting to make everybody happy. I remember the laughs you and I have had together, fall-on-the-floor kind of laughing, because we both have the same take on so much of what happens. . . . with hopes of forgiveness, Dominick."

The blows hurt, but with his stock portfolio now strong again—Allan often told his financial analyst, "Get rid of this turkey, it has gone up only twenty percent!"—he gradually looked to get back into producing for the theater, if not the movies. He hired a private trainer, Rob Bonet, who, like more than a few assistants before him, became a boyfriend of sorts. An underwater treadmill now graced the pool so that Allan could exercise without putting undue strain on his hips. He occasionally went out to eat, and yet, despite Angie Dickinson's best efforts, Allan assiduously avoided events like the AFI gala and instead frequented West Hollywood restaurants, like Marik's and the Abbey, where he could still impress attractive young men and not worry about the unattractive powerful men in Hollywood. Bonet sometimes enlisted the help of his friend Blaise Noto, a publicist at Paramount, to help get Allan into a car and keep him entertained.

The theater world of New York City posed a more difficult trip, especially after Allan lost his beloved Viewhaven atop the St. Moritz. It happened unfortuitously one day when the owner of the Central Park South building, a lady named Leona Helmsley, asked who was living in the penthouse. When she learned that Billy Joel sublet it from the current renter, Allan Carr, the infamous Queen of Mean became so outraged that she terminated the lease.

On one New York trip, Allan went to the theater to see the Ken Ludwig comedy *Moon over Buffalo,* starring Carol Burnett, and immediately pronounced it a perfect West End vehicle for his friend Joan Collins. He contacted Ludwig to obtain the rights, and what ensued was a long transcontinental telephone relationship in which the two men didn't meet but became "good friends," says the playwright. Soon, as happened with so many of Allan's family-man friends, he sent lavish gifts to Ludwig's wife and two young children. No Christmas or birthday went unobserved without a present from Hilhaven Lodge.

Excited about producing *Moon over Buffalo* in London, Allan considered calling in some Hollywood favors for all the free marketing advice he'd given over the years. He also had a new movie property, *Personal Shopper,* that he wanted to pitch to Paramount, and to sweeten the deal, there was the fast-approaching twentieth anniversary of *Grease.* He went to the top at the studio, CEO Sherry Lansing. It hurt that her husband, *The Exorcist* director William Friedkin, was one of the seventeen who signed the infamous "ban Allan Carr from the Oscars" petition spearheaded by Blake Edwards. Swallowing that indignity, he informed Lansing that *Grease* remained the highest-grossing movie musical of all time. (It remained in that exalted position for thirty years, when, in 2008, *Mamma Mia!* replaced it with total ticket sales of over $600 million, compared to *Grease*'s nearly $400 million. Domestically, *Grease* continued to beat *Mamma Mia!* $188 million to $144 million in figures that are not inflation-adjusted.) "It would be wonderful to rerelease *Grease*," he told her.

Allan persisted, but "movie rereleases are difficult," says Lansing. A few years earlier, Paramount's *Godfather* rerelease, after two decades, failed to generate much business. Allan dismissed the comparison, and barraged her with all the *Grease* figures, especially the $188 million that *Grease* had grossed domestically. "And he made that rerelease happen," says Lansing. "It took him almost a year, but he made it happen."

This time around, the Paramount brass were enthusiastic about *Grease*. For the rerelease, they booked the Chinese Theater, where the film had its world premiere, and John Travolta and Olivia Newton-John not only attended but brought their families. Before the screening that night, Allan walked the red carpet. It was difficult, but he walked without a cane. "It was like a whole new person emerged," says Blaise Noto. "The flashbulbs went off, and it brought him back to his past days of glory. He just changed, his whole face and body."

A reporter from *People* magazine tried to dampen Allan's enthusiasm with questions about his recent, inactive past, but Allan refused to be anything but upbeat. "To have a huge Broadway hit and to make this big musical, that's enough," he replied. "I've made my statement, thank you."

In Allan's long phone conversations about taking *Moon over Buffalo* to London, Ken Ludwig did what all playwrights do when chatting up a producer: He mentioned his new project, a musical version of *The Adventures of Tom Sawyer.* Allan responded with his favorite three words: "I love it!" And he quickly snapped up the rights. "He saw it as his next Broadway project," says Ludwig.

But Allan had no intention of taking the musical to Broadway—not right away.

Allan gave Ludwig's agent, Peter Franklin at William Morris, the following bit of theater wisdom on how he wanted to handle the new tuner. "The critical establishment in New York City will never like a show about Tom Sawyer," he said. Instead, his concept was to tour the musical and then "play New York like it is just one stop on the road. You have to make a show look like a hit, because *Tom Sawyer* is something that will be produced in church basements forever," Allan believed.

Franklin was impressed. "Allan Carr knew exactly what to do with that show," says the agent.

The theater was different from film. In Hollywood, a producer is only as good as his last movie. Broadway is more forgiving, and besides, Allan's last show there, *La Cage aux folles,* had been a superhit, and the denizens of Shubert Alley remembered it with genuine fondness. Allan felt good negotiating with Broadway powers; they treated him better than film people did, and he felt secure putting up the money for no fewer than two major workshops, at a cost of a quarter million dollars, for his *Tom Sawyer* musical.

After many months of phone conversations, he and Ludwig finally met face-to-face at the first of those workshops, held at the 890 Broadway rehearsal hall. Allan rolled around in a wheelchair, and there were needles sticking out of his ears. They made him look like a Martian, but Allan was used to being stared at for all the wrong reasons. He said the acupuncture helped control the pain and dizziness from a combination of illnesses, the worst of which was his failing kidneys. His skin, on some days, gave him the appearance of a ripe pumpkin.

For that first *Tom Sawyer* workshop staging, Allan invited 150 guests to observe Ludwig's and composer Don Schlitz's new show. For a brief moment, Allan left his wheelchair to stand up and address the audience of friends, potential investors, producers, and theater owners. "Oh, I'm so happy you are all here," he began. "I forgot when we worked on *A Chorus Line* what a messy and ratty place this is. I'm sorry about that. Enjoy the show."

Sometime between the first and second workshop of *The Adventures of Tom Sawyer,* Allan took time to have one of his kidneys replaced. It was Christmas 1998, and he'd been told by doctors not to leave Beverly Hills. He was on a waiting list, and the kidney might become available over the holidays. It arrived Christmas Eve.

For a couple of months after that surgery, Allan felt great, reborn, ready to do business and throw a party. Friends advised him against such an expenditure of energy, but he dismissed those reservations. While he still worried if Hollywood had forgiven him for the 1989 Oscar fiasco, he took out social insurance by throwing the party not only for himself and his new kidney, which he nicknamed Poopsie, but his friend Mo Rothman, a longtime executive at Universal and Columbia Pictures. Rothman had just turned eighty and suffered from Parkinson's disease.

The party was a success—if success at a party can be measured by the number of invitees who actually show up. Allan made fun of his most recent bout with the surgeon's knife by having Mo's birthday cake include a dedication to the kidney named Poopsie. Even though his orange complexion alarmed some guests, Allan told everyone that he'd never felt better. Then, while they all par-tied away in Club Oscar and drank at the Bella Darvi Bar, he retired to his bed-room. It was from this safe haven that he phoned Cedars-Sinai, which made a discreet ambulance call to 1220 Benedict Canyon Drive. An hour later, Allan was back in the hospital while Donna Summer blared away in the basement of Hilhaven Lodge.

Allan felt well enough to attend the second *Tom Sawyer* workshop in New York, but he looked weaker and, this time, he didn't leave his wheelchair to make a precurtain announcement. On that trip, his *Can't Stop the Music* dis-covery Steve Guttenberg ran into him outside the Pierre Hotel, where Allan was staying. "He was totally different: sweet, considerate," says the actor.

Then, suddenly, Allan was back in Beverly Hills, a recluse again, hidden away as assistants and housekeepers tried, but didn't always succeed, to keep friends away—old friends like Angie Dickinson and Freddie Gershon and Ann-Margret, who came to sing a song and dance a dance for an audience of one. He let a few of those friends know the truth. He had liver cancer. As Allan told it, the immune suppressants he was given to keep his body from rejecting the new kidney had left his body defenseless to the rapid spread of cancer.

He didn't want to talk about his terminal illness, even with close friends, and he invariably changed the subject. "I want to have a party," he announced. This final party, he told them, would be like no other, because it contained an element of surprise. As Allan envisioned it, the party would involve a tour of Hilhaven Lodge in which guests got to put their name on whatever possession it was they wanted. Later, after his death, the item would be messengered to its new owner.

Allan took great pleasure in planning what was to be his final party, but he didn't live long enough to play host. It didn't matter. People took things regard-less when he died on June 29, 1999. "It was like day of the locusts," Freddie Gershon says of those who descended on Hilhaven to loot the place. There were as many fingers pointing at the suspected culprits as Allan had assistants, house-keepers, business associates, and friends. "It's still a mystery who got the money after his death," says Gary Pudney.

Sherry Lansing took it upon herself to give a memorial on the Paramount lot. Over 400 people showed up. Angie Dickinson told amusing stories. Ann-Margret read poetry. And John Travolta, who also attended, made sure that the lobby and auditorium were filled with flowers. The event was so newsworthy that Liz Smith wrote it up in her syndicated gossip column, in which she called Allan "Hollywood's flashiest producer and partygiver."

Two weeks later, Ann-Margret flew to Hawaii to spread Allan's ashes in the ocean in front of Surfhaven. Allan's friend Richard Hach, retired from *TV Guide,* was now living in Hawaii, where he received a big envelope from 1220 Benedict Canyon Drive. Allan wanted Hach to write his biography, and to facilitate that dream, he sent him a large packet of handwritten notes. As always, Allan's penmanship presented a problem. "I couldn't read a word of it," says Hach, who received the pages four days after his friend's death.

Back in Allan's hometown of Highland Park, Joanne Cimbalo mourned the loss of her oldest friend in the world. His successes in the movies and theater left her dazzled, but in spite of those accomplishments, she felt he'd never known real contentment or happiness. "Allan always felt apart. His weight made him, in his eyes, different," Cimbalo explains. "You have a picture of yourself that you carry with you, and that may not have anything to do with reality, but it's your reality. He carried that picture with him his whole life. I would describe Allan as tortured. It's a strong word, but he was so impacted by what he saw as rejection. And it was an incredibly powerful rejection."

At his worst moments, Allan might have agreed with his childhood friend. But on other days, including some that were very dark, he liked the life he lived. Or at least, he liked it better than if he had been born straight, gotten married, had kids, and lived out his days in Highland Park. "I'd be living on Moraine Road with my kids and my wife's money," he fantasized. "It'd be a combination of B'nai B'rith and the Junior League, and no one would even raffle me off."

One day, Cimbalo and her daughter, Margaret, were on a commercial airplane flying from Chicago to Los Angeles. An attendant approached them to ask, "Excuse me, but didn't I meet you many years ago?" Cimbalo didn't recognize the middle-aged woman standing in front of her in the aisle, and she had to apologize. The flight attendant smiled. "You and your daughter were on a chartered flight for the movie *Can't Stop the Music,*" she said. "The Village People were there and Valerie Perrine and Bruce Jenner. It was the kind of Allan Carr party I'd only read about, and I have to tell you, that was the most fun I've ever had."

THE END

ACKNOWLEDGMENTS

This book began with a phone call to my friend Shirley Herz, who handled pub-licity for Allan Carr's original Broadway production of *La Cage aux folles*. "Is Allan Carr a book?" I asked. Herz responded, "I don't really know. But you should call Freddie Gershon, who worked with Allan for years."

Gershon and I spoke for about half an hour, and at the end of that conver-sation, he said, "So yes, I think Allan Carr is a book." That was August 2005 and I finished *Party Animals* four years later.

Over those years, Gershon and Herz have been generous sources who not only gave insightful interviews but put me in touch with other Allan Carr asso-ciates and friends. Henri Belolo, Ronni Chase, and Bruce Vilanch were also es-sential contacts whom I relied on repeatedly. Brett Ratner took time from his busy filmmaking schedule to give me a personal tour of Hilhaven Lodge and share various Allan Carr memorabilia. Michael Riedel provided important the-ater insights. And the alumni office at Lake Forest College graciously put me in touch with Margaret Neely Wilhelm, who, in turn, invited me to the fiftieth reunion of the class of 1958, which led to so many interviews with Allan Carr's classmates. In total, over 200 other people were interviewed, either on or off the record, and each of those conversations proved invaluable. I am deeply in-debted to all of you.

James T. Ballard, Peter Bloch, Anna Stewart, and Nanette Varian are friends who gave me great line-editing tips.

My *Variety* associates Sam Thielman and Chris Jones were kind enough to perform interview and research duties, respectively.

I'd also like to express gratitude to the dedicated librarians at the Los Angeles Public Library, Margaret Herrick Library at the Academy of Motion Pictures

Arts and Sciences, New York Public Library for the Performing Arts at Lincoln Center, and One Institute.

I am deeply indebted to Da Capo Press's production editor Collin Tracy, copyeditor Margaret Ritchie, and publicist Lissa Warren.

Most important, I thank the five major contributors to this book: my Da Capo Press editor, Jonathan Crowe; my agent, Eric Myers at the Joseph Spieler Agency; my photo-research guru, Howard Mandelbaum of Photofest; and my dear friends Denise Smaldino and Don Weise.

BIBLIOGRAPHY

"4.6 mil Dom. Rentals for Par From 'Survive!,'" *Variety,* Oct. 8 1976.

Alexander, Ron, "Opening Party for 'La Cage,'" *New York Times,* Aug. 23, 1983.

"Allan Carr," *Life,* p. 42, Apr. 1979.

Andrews, Nigel, *Travolta: The Life.* London: Bloomsbury, 1998.

Ann-Margret, with Todd Gold, *Ann-Margret: My Story.* New York: Putnam, 1994; Berkley Books, 1995.

Archerd, Army, "Just for Variety," *Daily Variety,* p. 2, July 10, 1975.

Ardmore, Jane, "Back to High School with 'Grease 2,'" *San Antonio Light,* p. 4W, June 6, 1982.

———, "Sunday Woman," *San Antonio Light,* June 6, 1982.

Arons, Rana, "A Genius at Promotion," *Us,* June 21, 1980.

Bacon, James, "Hollywood, a Town Going to the Dogs," *Los Angeles Herald-Examiner,* p. C12, Apr. 28, 1976.

Bart, Peter, "Angst for the Memories," *Variety,* p. 5, Nov. 18–24, 2002.

"The Bash," *Newsweek,* Mar. 24, 1975.

Beck, Marilyn, "Carr's Crusade," *Daily News,* p. 3, June 26, 1980.

Bell, Arthur, "Bell Tells," *Village Voice,* p. 34, Aug. 30, 1983.

Blowen, Michael, "Flamboyant Producer Allan Carr," *Boston Globe,* p. A1, Nov. 4, 1984.

Broeske, Pat H., "Allan Carr, Entrepreneur," *Drama-Logue,* p. 18, Sept. 6–12.

Burns, Howard, "ABC's Oscar Telecast," *Hollywood Reporter,* Mar. 31, 1989.

Byrge, Duane, "Broadway at the Bowl," *Hollywood Reporter,* p. 6, Sept. 1, 1988.

———, "Weather's Just Fine Outside the Shrine," *Hollywood Reporter,* p. 30, Mar. 30, 1989.

"Can't Stop the Party, Either," *New York Post,* p. 9, June 20, 1980.

Carey, Lynn, "'Beach' Producer Opens Oscar," *Contra Costa Times,* Mar. 18, 1989.

"Carr Hears Only the Ovations," *Hollywood Reporter,* p. 6, Mar. 30, 1989.

"Carr's ABC's of Beach Chic," *Los Angeles Times,* p. 3, Aug. 19, 1977.

Cartnal, Alan, "Allan Carr: Clocked by Alan Cartnal," *Interview*, p. 9, June 1974.

———, "The Dream Merchant," *New West*, p. 34, Aug. 14, 1978.

"Cass Elliot's Death Laid to Heart Attack," *Los Angeles Times*, p. B2, Aug. 6, 1974.

Caulfield, Deborah, "Can't Stop the Hype," *Los Angeles Times*, p. T29, June 22, 1980.

Champlin, Charles, *Los Angeles Times*, Apr. 2, 1989.

Chin, Paula, and Kristina Johnson. "Marathon Man," *People*, p. 112, Aug. 22, 1994.

Christy, George, "The Great Life," *Hollywood Reporter*, undated clipping.

Clarke, Gerald, *Capote: A Biography*. New York: Simon & Schuster, 1988.

Clarkson, Wensley, *John Travolta: Back in Character*. New York: Overlook Press, 1997.

Cobb, Nathan, "Acceptance, Accolades at First-Night Party," *Boston Globe*, June 20, 1983.

Collins, Glenn, "Rob Lowe Braves Farce," *New York Times*, p. C11, Jan. 20, 1997.

Collins, Nancy, "The Uphill Racer, Allan Carr," *Women's Wear Daily*, p. 17, Aug. 23, 1976.

Conn, Didi, *Frenchy's "Grease" Scrapbook*. New York: Hyperion, 1998.

Culhane, John, "For Oscar's Producer, the Key Is C," *New York Times*, p. 11, Mar. 26, 1989.

"Cycle Sluts," *Los Angeles Times*, July 10, 1975.

Davis, Ivor, "From Mayer to Cohn," *Los Angeles* magazine, p. 280, undated clipping.

"Disney Drops Snow White Suit," *Daily Variety*, p. 1, Apr. 7, 1989.

"Disney: Suit over Snow White," *Daily Variety*, p. 1, Apr. 12, 1989.

Dunne, Dominick, *The Way We Lived Then*. New York: Crown, 1999.

"Faces & Places," *Us*, p. 18, May 15, 1989.

"A Father's Day Gala Premiere," *Los Angeles Times*, p. AA8, June 8, 1980.

Fink, Mitchell, "Spago Schmooze News," *Los Angeles Herald-Examiner*, p. 2, Mar. 31, 1989.

Galbraith, Jane, "Acad Caught Lookin' Goofy," *Daily Variety*, p. 1, Mar. 31, 1989.

Galligan, David, "New Projects for Allan Carr," *Drama-Logue*, p. 28, Sept. 25-Oct. 1, 1986.

"The Gatsby of Benedict Canyon," *Time*, p. 52, Aug. 30, 1976.

Gold, Aaron, "Tower Ticker," *Chicago Tribune*, June 20, 1980.

Goodwin, Betty, "'Grease' Parties in an Alley,'" *Los Angeles Herald-Examiner*, p. B3, June 5, 1982.

Grant, Hank, "Rambling Reporter," *Hollywood Reporter*, Mar. 14, 1978.

———, "Rambling Reporter," *Hollywood Reporter*, Feb. 15, 1980.

Grant, Lee, "Two Pictures on the Same Subject," *Los Angeles Times*, July 10, 1976.

Grease DVD, special features.

Grobel, Lawrence, *Conversations with Capote*. New York: New American Library, 1985.

Grove, Martin, "Hollywood Report," *Hollywood Reporter*, Apr. 6, 1989.

Haber, Joyce, "Two Parties Hollywood Never Gives," *Los Angeles Times*, p. E16, Apr. 11, 1974.

Haden-Guest, Anthony, *The Last Party: Studio 54, Disco, and the Culture of the Night*. New York: William Morrow, 1997.

Hamlisch, Marvin, and Gerald Gardner, *The Way I Was*. New York: Scribner, 1992.

"Hanging Out with the L.A. Rockers," *Time*, Apr. 25, 1977.

"Insider," *Los Angeles* magazine, Dec. 1988.

"Is This a Competition Prize?" *The [London] Times*, p. 16, Mar. 31, 1989.

Jacobs, Jody, "Capote and His Pen Pals," *Los Angeles Times*, p. G1, Dec. 16, 1975

———, "Carr Gives a Friendship Party," *Los Angeles Times*, May 5, 1980.

———, *Los Angeles Times,* July 16, 1980.

———, *Los Angeles Times*, p. IV5, Aug. 23, 1981.

———, "Show Goes On for the No-Show," *Los Angeles Times*, p. E3, July 13, 1975.

Jewel, Dan, "Showman," *People*, p. 111, July 19, 1999.

Kelly, Kevin, "Harvey Fierstein Dragged into Sudden Stardom," *Boston Globe*, July 3, 1983.

Kenner, Mary, "Can't Stop Carr," *Los Angeles Times*, p. G12, June 20, 1980.

Kilday, Gregg, "Allan Carr—Greasing the Wheels," *Los Angeles Times,* p. 46, June 18, 1978.

———, "Bash Follows 'Tommy' Premiere," *Los Angeles Times*, p. 14, Mar. 21, 1975.

———, "Celluloid Village People," *Los Angeles Herald-Examiner,* p. E1, Sept. 30, 1979.

Kleiman, Rena, "Carr to Produce 'Boys,'" *Hollywood Reporter,* p. 1, May 5, 1983.

Koffler, Kevin, "Carr Puts Oscar Spotlight on the New Hollywood," *Los Angeles Herald-Examiner,* Mar. 22, 1989.

Kroll, Jack, *Newsweek,* July 11, 1977.

"'La Cage aux Folles' Cleaned Up," *People*, p. 125, June 18, 1984.

"'La Cage aux Folles' Coming to Broadway," *New York* magazine, p. 33, Aug. 22, 1983.

Lane, Lydia, "Weight Loss Shapes Personality," *Los Angeles Times*, p. 12, Dec. 9, 1977.

Laurents, Arthur, *Mainly on Directing*. New York: Knopf, 2009.

Leamer, Laurence, *As Time Goes By: The Life of Ingrid Bergman*. New York: Harper & Row, 1998.

Leaming, Barbara, *Polanski: The Filmmaker as Voyeur*. New York: Simon & Schuster, 1981.

Letofsky, Irv, "Glamour? Glory?" *Los Angeles Times*, Mar. 26, 1989.

Levine, Richard, "The Selling of a Used Car," *Esquire,* p. 186, Nov. 1983.

Light, Alan, "Backstage at the Oscars," *Movie Collector's World,* p. 2, June 23, 1989.

Love, Gael, "Allan Carr," *Interview,* Oct. 1984.

Mann, Roderick, "Barry Knows Why the 'Cage' Bird Sings," *Los Angeles Times,* p. 7, Oct. 11, 1984.

Maslin, Janet, "The Oscars as Home Entertainment," *New York Times,* Mar. 31, 1989.

Maychick, Diana, "More Glory than Gelt," *New York Post,* Aug. 23, 1983.

McBride, Joseph, "Panel to Probe Oscarcast Flaws," *Daily Variety,* p. 1, Apr. 28, 1989.

McCabe, Bob, *John Travolta: Quote Unquote*. New York: Paragon, 1996.

McDaniel, Wanda, "Sometimes I Feel like Staying Home to Watch 'Dynasty,'" *Los Angeles Herald-Examiner,* July 9, 1984.

———, "When You're Out with Allan Carr the Parties Never End," *Los Angeles Herald-Examiner*, p B5, June 12, 1979.

McEvoy, Marian, "Subway Siren," *Women's Wear Daily,* Mar. 21, 1975.

McLaughlin, Jeff, *Boston Globe,* June 19, 1983.

Mewborn, Brant, "Circus on Celluloid," *After Dark,* p. 23, July 1980.

Millman, Joyce, "S.F. Puts Some Zip in Show," *San Francisco Examiner,* Mar. 31, 1989.

Morrissey, Paul, "Big Hit in Hollywood: Pat Ast," *Interview,* p. 41, Oct. 1978.

Murphy, A. D., "'Jaws 2,' 'Grease' Set New B.O. Records," *Daily Variety,* p. 1, June 21, 1971.

"No Cooling of Disco Fever as Operators Eye $5 Billion Year," *Hollywood Reporter,* p. 1, July 17, 1978.

Opel, Robert, "Cycle Sluts," *Drummer,* p. 8, Oct. 1976.

Orth, Maureen, "The Baby Moguls," *New West,* June 19, 1978.

Parker, John, *Polanski*. London: Victor Gollancz, 1993.

"Peacocks Flock to 'La Cage' Opening," *New York Post,* Aug. 23, 1983.

Peck, Abe, "From the Navy to the YMCA: The Village People," *Rolling Stone,* Apr. 19, 1979.

Penn, Jean Cox, "It's Greenwich Time at Pavilion," *Los Angeles Times,* June 17, 1980.

Peter, Elizabeth, "Bump in the Night," *Newsweek,* Mar. 24, 1975.

Plimpton, George, *Truman Capote*. New York: Talese/Doubleday, 1997.

Polanski, Roman, *Roman by Polanski*. New York: Morrow, 1984.

Pond, Steve, *The Big Show: High Times and Dirty Dealings Backstage at the Academy Awards*. New York: Faber & Faber, 2005.

Puig, Claudia, "Dressing Up the Academy Awards Show," *Los Angeles Times,* undated clipping.

"Rating the Oscar Parties," *TV Guide*, p. 45, Apr. 15, 1989.

Reilly, Sue, "Producer Allan Carr Waxes Fat and Fortyish on the Gross of 'Grease,'" *People*, p. 49, Aug. 6, 1979.

Rich, Frank, "Hitting Rock Bottom—Maybe," *New York Post*, Aug. 14, 1976.

Rosenfield, Paul, "A Great Big Broadway Show," *Los Angeles Times*, Aug. 28, 1983.

———, "The Oscar Show and the Exercise of Power," *Los Angeles Times*, Mar. 26, 1989.

Russo, Vito, "A Visit with Allan Carr, Hollywood's Can't Stop Mogul," *The Advocate*, p. 36, June 12, 1984.

Schreger, Charles, "Hollywood's Party Champion Defends His Crown," *Los Angeles Times*, p. E10, June 11, 1979.

Scott, Tony, "Oscar Awards Singin' in the 'Rain,'" *Daily Variety*, p. 1, Mar. 31, 1989.

Silverman, Stephen M., *Public Spectacles*. New York: Dutton, 1981.

Smith, Liz, "Can't Stop Shouting About 'Can't Stop,'" *Daily News*, p. 8, July 2, 1980.

———, "The Duchess & the Lord," *New York Daily News*, Aug. 30, 1976.

———, "Paramount Sendoff," *Newsday*, p. A13, Aug. 1, 1999.

———, "Truman Capote in Hot Water," *New York Magazine*, pp. 47–51, Feb. 9, 1976.

"Snow White," *Los Angeles Times*, Apr. 5, 1989.

Solomon, Alan, "Poopsie Picks," *The Stentor*, p. 4, May 18, 1956.

"So Much for Star Wars," *People*, Sept. 5, 1977.

Spoto, Donald, *Notorious: The Life of Ingrid Bergman*. New York: HarperCollins, 1997.

Stein, Jeannine, "Click," *Los Angeles Herald-Examiner*, Sept. 18, 1984.

———, "Oscar: An Overnight Sensation," *Los Angeles Times*, Mar. 31, 1989.

———, "Where the Stars Come Out to Shine After Oscars Show," *Los Angeles Times*, p. 2, Mar. 29, 1989.

"Survive! Tale of Cannibalism," *Los Angeles Times*, July 29, 1976.

Tamaya, Steve, "Closed School Reborn as Studio," *Los Angeles Times*, p. LB1, Jan. 10, 1982.

Taylor, Clarke, "The People's Movie Moves the Village," *Los Angeles Times*, p. L29, Sept. 9, 1979.

———, "Village People Try a New Look," *Los Angeles Times*, p. B3, July 19, 1981.

Terry, Clifford, "Allan Carr, Counselor to the Stars," *Chicago Tribune*, p. 35, Oct. 13, 1974.

Thomas, Bob, "Merv Griffin Dies at Age 82," AP, Aug. 12, 2007.

Thompson, Douglas, *Fever! The Biography of John Travolta*. London: Boxtree, 1997.

———, *Pfeiffer: Beyond the Age of Innocence*. London: Smith Gryphon, 1993.

Todd, Michael, Jr., and Susan McCarthy Todd, *A Valuable Property: The Life Story of Michael Todd*. New York: Arbor House, 1983.

Turner, Richard, "Nobody Ever Said Snow White Had Much of a Sense of Humor," *Wall Street Journal,* p. A8, Apr. 3, 1989.

Weiner, Bob, "Big Man on Broadway," *Sunday News Magazine,* p. 7, Aug. 21, 1983.

"West Coast Maxwell," *Playbill,* Nov. 1983.

Yetnikoff, Walter, with David Ritz, *Howling at the Moon.* New York: Broadway Books, 2004.

NOTES

In the notes, Author Interviews are designated "AI."

Introduction

Facts, quotes, and observations regarding Hilhaven Lodge circa 1999 were obtained from an Author Interview (AI) with Brett Ratner, who also gave the author a tour of the house, on August 18, 2007.

Ingrid Bergman anecdotes: Laurence Leamer, *As Time Goes By: The Life of Ingrid Bergman*, pp. 107, 162–163, and Donald Spoto, *Notorious: The Life of Ingrid Bergman*, pp. 170–171.

viii   "place like Woodland": Paula Chin and Kristina Johnson, "Marathon Man," *People*, p. 112.

xi   "Walk around the": Vito Russo, "A Visit with Allan Carr," *The Advocate*, p. 36.

Chapter 1

1   "streaked"/"private party": Clifford Terry, "Allan Carr, Counselor to the Stars," *Chicago Tribune*, p. 35.

1   "invitation isn't fabulous": AI, Kathy Berlin, Apr. 18, 2009.

2   "in the fabled": Original invitation, Brett Ratner collection.

2   $200,000: AI, Daniel Gottlieb, July 1, 2009.

2   "James Caan": AI, Richard Hach, Aug. 16. 2007.

3   "pig city": Alan Cartnal, "Allan Carr: Clocked by Alan Cartnal," *Interview*, p. 9.

3   "Jewish gymnasium": Nancy Collins, "The Uphill Racer, Allan Carr," *Women's Wear Daily*, p. 17.

3   Kim Novak's brief: Bob Weiner, "Big Man on Broadway," *Sunday News Magazine,* p. 7, Aug. 21, 1983.

3   "walk sideways": AI, Warren Cowan, May 17, 2007.

3   "I stepped off": AI, Bruce Vilanch, Aug. 13, 2007.

3   "so life-threatening": AI, Ann-Margret, Apr. 17, 2008.

4   "I was shocked": Terry, "Allan Carr," p. 35.

4   "He was just": "The Gatsby of Benedict Canyon," *Time,* p. 52, Aug. 30, 1976.

4   "Body by Dr.": AI, Joel Schumacher, Apr. 6, 2009.

4   "the old trick": Collins, "Uphill Racer," p. 17.

4   "Joe Namath's knees": Terry, "Allan Carr," p. 35.

4   "my elephant skin": AI, Freddie Gershon, Apr. 2, 2007.

5   "jaw wired shut": AI, Ann-Margret, Apr. 17, 2008.

5   its title, *Jaws*: *New York Post,* p. 6, Nov. 17, 1978.

5   "confidante to Ann-Margret": AI, Marvin Hamlisch, July 26, 2007.

5   "She's not a": AI, Freddie Gershon, Apr. 2, 2007.

5   "Ann-Margret owes": AI, Roger Smith, Apr. 17, 2008.

5   "did every step": AI, Dyan Cannon, Aug. 10, 2007.

5   "fired Dyan Cannon": Terry, "Allan Carr," p. 35.

6   "She always seemed": "Cass Elliot's Death Laid to Heart Attack," *Los Angeles Times,* p. B2.

6   "Cass Elliot and": AI, Bruce Vilanch, Aug. 13, 2007.

6   a party person: AI, John Kander, Sept. 1, 2005.

6   "bring glamour back": "So Much for Star Wars," *People,* Sept. 5, 1977.

7   "Allan is as rich"/Hackett: Jacobs, Jody, "Carr Gives a Friendship Party," *Los Angeles Times,* May 5, 1980.

7   "only in 3-D": AI, Joanne Cimbalo, Dec. 18, 2007.

7   "Because they're all": Paul Morrissey, "Big Hit in Hollywood: Pat Ast," *Interview,* p. 41, Oct. 1978.

7   "Hello, It's Allan": AI, Mitzi Brill, May 9, 2007.

8   "invited his Rolodex": AI, David Picker, Aug. 6, 2007.

8   "cross-pollinated lists": AI, Richard Hach, Aug. 16, 2007.

8   "instant Elsa Maxwell": "Gatsby of Benedict Canyon," p. 52.

8   "Bianca Jagger showed": AI, Richard Hach, Aug. 16, 2007.

8   "Stigwood disco period": AI, Alice Cooper, Oct. 1, 2007.

9   "the bridge between": AI, Peter Guber, Jan. 10, 2008.

9   "Allan's parties unique": AI, Ron Bernstein, Apr. 8, 2009.

9   "like Noah's ark": AI, Joel Schumacher, Apr. 6, 2009.

9   "loud, vulgar extravaganzas": AI, Rex Reed, Apr. 16, 2009.

9   "Allan Carr's house"/"A list": "Hanging Out with the L.A. Rockers," *Time,* Apr. 25, 1977.

9   "career doctor": "Gatsby of Benedict Canyon," p. 52.

10   "Rock people are": "Hanging Out."

10   "whole rash of": AI, Alice Cooper, Oct. 1, 2007.

11   "You can't go": AI, Freddie Gershon, Apr. 2, 2007.

11   "whether they would": AI, Gary Pudney, Feb. 27, 2007.

11   "daughter Edie Goetz": AI, Zvi Howard Rosenman, July 10, 2007.

11   "these beach kids": AI, Craig Zadan, Nov. 27, 2007.

11   "the twinkies": AI, Kathy Berlin, Apr. 18, 2009.

11   "So many gay": AI, Brett Ratner, Aug. 18, 2007.

11   "If you ever": AI, anonymous source.

11   "really out there": AI, Gregg Kilday, Feb. 13, 2009.

11   "epicene": "Gatsby of Benedict Canyon," p. 52.

11   "making it up": AI, Richard Hach, Aug. 16, 2007.

12   "product-placement parties": AI, Laurence Mark, Aug. 21, 2006.

12   "It was marketing": AI, Richard Hach, Aug. 16, 2007.

12   "comical version of": AI, Zvi Howard Rosenman, July 10, 2007.

12   "a sweet guy": AI, Bruce Vilanch, Aug. 13, 2007.

12   "thick Russian accent": AI, Richard Hach, Aug. 16, 2007.

12   *tout* L.A.: Terry, "Allan Carr."

12   "feel like Secretariat": Joyce Haber, "Two Parties Hollywood Never Gives," *Los Angeles Times*, p. E16, Apr 11, 1974.

13   satin Cossack pants: Ibid.

13   "their clothes off" "No! No!": Terry, "Allan Carr," p. 43.

13   "muscle-bound young": Haber, "Two Parties." p. E16.

13   "Nureyev was sexually": AI, Dominick Dunne, Sept. 19, 2006.

13   "a midnight party": AI, David Steinberg, Aug. 22, 2007.

14   "Nureyev's getting"/"But that wasn't"/"young, hairless boys": AI, Zvi Howard Rosenman, July 10, 2007.

14   his "Marvin"/Nureyev: *People,* pp. 44–49, Aug. 6, 1979.

15   "Easter bush": Terry, "Allan Carr," p. 35.

15   "'being hung'": AI, Alice Cooper, Oct. 1, 2007.

15   "the good Allan": AI, David Geffen, Apr. 21, 2009.

15   "way he lived": AI, Gary Pudney, Feb. 27, 2007.

15   "big Hollywood life": AI, Joan Rivers, Sept. 25, 2007.

Chapter 2

16   "fiesta-colored Civic": AI, Bruce Vilanch, Aug. 13, 2007.

17   "Columbia doesn't"/"The What?"/"Making *Tommy*": AI, Freddie Gershon, Apr. 2, 2007.

17   "I'd only heard": Ann-Margret with Todd Gold, *Ann-Margret*, p. 201.

18   "can she sing?": Ibid.

18   "Allan showed Columbia": AI, Peter Guber, Jan. 10, 2008.

18   "such TV coverage": AI, Warren Cowan, May 17, 2007.

18   "too obvious:" AI, Kathy Berlin, Apr. 18, 2009.

19   "Allan's *Tommy* party": AI, Warren Cowan, May 17, 2007.

19   "subway concept": AI, Kathy Berlin, Apr. 18, 2009.

19    $150,000/$5,000: AI, Bobby Zarem, Aug. 7, 2008.

19   "When Allan hired": Ibid.

19   "*Entertainment Tonight*": AI, Freddie Gershon, Apr. 2, 2007.

19   "white and glass": AI, Bobby Zarem, Aug. 7, 2008.

20   renegade publicist/"Stigwood was already": Ibid.

20   "greatest goof": AI, Freddie Gershon, Apr. 2, 2007.

21   "sphincter arrest": AI, Peter Guber, Jan. 10, 2008.

21   "terrific to terrible": Marian McEvoy, "Subway Siren," *Women's Wear Daily*.

21   50 pounds/"I've never been": "The Bash," *Newsweek*.

21   "costume ball": AI, Kathy Berlin, Apr. 18, 2009.

21   "Who concerts"/"A little bit": "The Bash."

22   silver-plated hypodermics: McEvoy, "Subway Siren."

22   "see Ann-Margret": "The Bash."

22   "I love this"/the centerpieces: McEvoy, "Subway Siren."

22   "It's not easy": Gregg Kilday, "Bash Follows 'Tommy' Premiere," *Los Angeles Times*, p. 14.

23   "cross-sexual cavortings": Elizabeth Peter, "Bump in the Night," *Newsweek*.

23   "totally apolitical": AI, Roger Smith, Apr. 17, 2008.

23   "Allan never": AI, Joan Rivers, Sept. 25, 2007.

23   "If Allan": AI, Gregg Kilday, Feb. 13, 2009.

24   "1970s hedonistic era": AI, Lila Burkeman, July 19, 2007.

24   "Stigwood didn't talk": AI, Kathy Berlin, Apr. 18, 2009.

24   "Allan was synchronistic": AI, Peter Guber, Jan. 10, 2008.

Chapter 3

26   "Michael wanted"/"I was sure"/ "Michael, you": AI, Marvin Hamlisch, July 26, 2007.

27   "They were having": AI, John Breglio, Nov. 15, 2007.

27   "Marvin is really": AI, David Kennedy, July 17, 2007.

27   "People forget that": AI, Marvin Hamlisch, July 26, 2007.

Chapter 4

28   David Geffen, Cher: Jody Jacobs, "Show Goes on for the No-Show," *Los Angeles Times*, p. E3.

29   "We don't pretend": Robert Opel, "Cycle Sluts," *Drummer,* p. 8, Oct. 1976.

29   "Montezuma's Revenge": "Cycle Sluts," *Los Angeles Times.*

29   leopard print bathrobe: Jacobs, "Show Goes On," p. E3.

29   "a bunch of hustlers"/"front lawn": "Cycle Sluts."

29   "chemically altered": AI, Bruce Vilanch, Aug. 13, 2007.

30   "servants change": Jacobs, "Show Goes On," p. E3.

30   "guys in leather chaps": AI, Lorna Luft, July 26, 2007.

30   "future of show": Jacobs, "Show Goes On," p. E3.

30   "his childhood": AI, Lorna Luft, July 26, 2007.

30   "nameless Hollywood": Army Archerd, "Just for Variety," *Daily Variety,* p. 2.

30   "something you know": AI, Dyan Cannon, Aug. 10, 2007.

31   "survival story": AI, Joel Schumacher, Apr. 6, 2009.

31   "Before Allan": AI, David Geffen, Apr. 21, 2009.

31   "virgin until"/"This guy": AI, Gary Pudney, Feb. 27, 2007.

Chapter 5

32   "quite a shock": AI, Dominick Dunne, Sept. 19, 2006.

33   "our getaway car": Jody Jacobs, "Capote and His Pen Pals," *Los Angeles Times,* p. G1.

33   "no ashtrays"/"red tape": Ibid.

34   "bathrooms were fit:" AI, Dominick Dunne, Sept. 19, 2006.

34   "anyone peeking": "West Coast Maxwell," *Playbill.*

35   "party' parties": Jody Jacobs, "Capote," p. G1.

35   "I always"/"I bet": Ibid.

35   "old friend": AI, Richard Hach, Aug. 16, 2007.

35   "La Cote Basque 1965": Liz Smith, "Truman Capote in Hot Water," *New York Magazine,* pp. 47–51.

35   "Carole Matthau and": Archerd, "Just for Variety," p. 3.

36   "Why, if": Ibid, p. 49.

36   "the no place": Gerald Clarke, *Conversations with Capote,* p. 152.

36   "onion soup": AI, George Christy, Mar. 6, 2007.

36   "rice and beans": Jody Jacobs, "Capote," p. G1.

36   "such sadness": AI, Dominick Dunne, Sept. 19, 2006.

36   "fun if Truman": AI, Joseph Wambaugh, Mar. 5, 2009.

36   "kinds of friends": AI, David Steinberg, Aug. 22, 2007.

37   "those occasions": AI, Don Bachardy, Mar. 6, 2009.

37   "The joke": AI, Bruce Vilanch, Aug. 13, 2007.

37   "spectacular"/"inventive": Lawrence Grobel, *Conversations with Capote,* p. 152.

Chapter 6

38   a dinner invitation: Liz Smith, "The Duchess & the Lord," *Daily News,* Aug. 30, 1976.

38   visit Mexico City: AI, Maury Yeston, May 5, 2008, and Gregg Kilday, "Allan Carr—Greasing the Wheels," *Los Angeles Times,* p. 46.

39   "Freddie, you're"/"It will work"/"If we can": AI, Freddie Gershon, Apr. 2, 2007.

40   "first thing I"/"Just give me": AI, John Breglio, Nov. 15, 2007.

41   "Let me fiddle": AI, Freddie Gershon, Apr. 2, 2007.

41   "brilliant job"/*Won Ton Ton*: AI, David Picker, Aug. 6, 2007.

41   "hired thirty dogs"/Marisa Berenson: AI, Laurence Mark, Aug. 21, 2006.

41   Merv Griffin/"want your chair": James Bacon, "Hollywood, a Town Going to the Dogs," *Los Angeles Herald-Examiner,* p. C12.

42   More problematic/erection: Richard Levine, "The Selling of a Used Car," *Esquire,* p. 186, Nov. 1983.

42   "amazing event": AI, David Picker, Aug. 6, 2007.

42   cornflakes: "Survive! Tale of Cannibalism," *Los Angeles Times.*

42   ninety minutes: Lee Grant, "Two Pictures on the Same Subject," *Los Angeles Times.*

42   "It's terrible"/"Whoa!"/Sam Arkoff: AI, Freddie Gershon, Apr. 2, 2007.

43   Sam Arkoff/"This movie can": Ibid.

43   "Paramount had nothing": AI, David Picker, Aug. 6, 2007.

43   "Let's go for"/60-40: AI, Freddie Gershon, Apr. 2, 2007.

44   "strange deals"/"400 prints": Wanda McDaniel, "Sometimes I Feel like Staying Home to Watch 'Dynasty'," *Los Angeles Herald-Examiner.*

44    $1 million: "So Much for Star Wars," *People,* Sept. 5, 1977.

44   "Elizabeth Taylor": Gael Love, "Allan Carr," *Interview,* Oct. 1984.

44   "snuff film": Frank Rich, "Hitting Rock Bottom—Maybe," *New York Post.*

44   "delicatessen movie": Rana Arons, "A Genius at Promotion," *Us.*

44   "The only thing": "4.6 mil Dom. Rentals for Par From 'Survive!'," *Variety,* Oct. 8 1976.

44   "Hey, I didn't": Michael Blowen, "Flamboyant Producer Allan Carr," *Boston Globe,* p. A1.

45   "terribly happy"/"no other project": Lee Grant, "Two Pictures."

46   "After $10 million": Bob Weiner, "Big Man on Broadway," *Sunday News Magazine,* p. 7, Aug. 21, 1983.

46   "Vaseline": *New York Times,* p. C6, July 2, 1976.

Chapter 7

47   "If ever": AI, Marvin Hamlisch, July 26, 2007.

48   "I have to": Didi Conn, *Frenchy's "Grease" Scrapbook,* p. 1.

48   "all wrong"/Lunching at: AI, Kenneth Waissman, Jan. 10, 2008.

48   "I *really* am"/"installment plan": Ibid.

48   "the bastard child": Conn, *Frenchy's,* p. 2.

49    $100,000/"Who are you?"/Eisner/Diller: AI, Kenneth Waissman, Jan. 10, 2008.

50   "legitimate theater": Conn, *Frenchy's,* p. 2.

50   "It can't lose": AI, anonymous source.

50   "'Hey, let's have fun'"/"Broadway thing": AI, Bill Butler, Oct. 14, 2007.

51   "gone glitzier here": AI, Patricia Birch, May 4, 2006.

52   JAMANI: AI, Bruce Vilanch, Aug. 13, 2007.

Chapter 8

53   "high school memories": Didi Conn, *Frenchy's "Grease" Scrapbook,* p. 2.

53   "Money was not": AI, Joanne Cimbalo, Dec. 18, 2007.

53   "whole nitty-gritty": Nigel Andrews, *Travolta: The Life,* p. 102.

54   "Allan's house": AI, Robert Le Clercq, Nov. 1, 2008.

54   "Don't worry"/*Ziegfeld's Follies*: David Galligan, "New Projects for Allan Carr," *Drama-Logue,* p. 28.

55   "That's when": Michael Blowen, "Flamboyant Producer Allan Carr," *Boston Globe,* p. A1.

55   "an embarrassment": AI, Freddie Gershon, Apr. 2, 2007.

55   "very hot": original letter, Freddie Gershon collection.

55   "At home I": Lydia Lane, "Weight Loss Shapes Personality," *Los Angeles Times,* p. 12.

56   "Lake Forest is": AI, anonymous source.

56   "The other fraternities": AI, David Umbach, Oct. 30, 2008.

56   "Our national chapter": AI, James Kenney, Oct. 29, 2008.

56   "Roman Catholic"/nun: AI, Ann-Margret, Apr. 17, 2008.

56   "or bar mitzvah": AI, Joanne Cimbalo, Dec. 18, 2007.

56   "Alan loved": AI, Margaret Neely Wilhelm, Dec. 1, 2007.

57   "Isn't he interesting?": AI, Joanne Cimbalo, Dec. 18, 2007.

57   "Gay or straight": AI, David Umbach, Oct. 30, 2008.

57   "The other boys": AI, Joanne Cimbalo, Dec. 18, 2007.

57   "theater nuts"/"I was green": AI, David Umbach, Oct. 30, 2008.

57   "Mae West at"/Carol Channing: Ibid.

58 "Alan, could"/"Margaret, you're": AI, Margaret Neely Wilhelm, Dec. 1, 2007.

59 "Like many kids": Conn, *Frenchy's,* p. 3.

59 "He advertised": AI, Franz Schulze, Oct. 27, 2008.

59 "Alan wasn't": AI, David Umbach, Oct. 30, 2008.

59 "Alan knew Bob"/"This shouldn't be": AI, Margie Tegtmeyer Cohen, Nov. 3, 2008.

59 "Alan didn't feel": AI, Joanne Cimbalo, Dec. 18, 2007.

60 "We reopened"/"We'll become": AI, Jack Tourville, Mar. 9, 2008.

60 "divorcing"/"thinking of billing": Wanda McDaniel, "Sometimes I Feel like Staying Home to Watch 'Dynasty,'" *Los Angeles Herald-Examiner.*

61 "I don't want"/"Good question": Gael Love, "Allan Carr," *Interview,* Oct. 1984.

61 Cassidy also cooperated: AI, Jack Tourville, Mar. 9, 2008.

61 "It was too"/Tallulah Bankhead/*A Raisin in the Sun*: Ibid.

62 "I was starting": AI, Hugh Hefner, Dec. 2, 2006.

62 Playboy clubs: Nancy Collins, "The Uphill Racer, Allan Carr," *Women's Wear Daily,* p. 17.

Chapter 9

63 "high school kids": AI, Patricia Birch, May 4, 2006.

63 "The 1950s": Wensley Clarkson, *John Travolta: Back in Character,* p. 135.

63 "I based": Didi Conn, *Frenchy's "Grease" Scrapbook,* p. 2.

64 "That kid's": AI, John Travolta, Sept. 15, 2007.

64 "blue black hair": Ibid.

64 "Carrie Fisher": AI, Joel Thurm, July 5, 2007.

64 "One day, Allan": AI, Olivia Newton-John, Oct. 5, 2007.

65 "No one else": AI, Joel Thurm, July 5, 2007.

65 "Allan was adamant": AI, Randal Kleiser, Aug. 3, 2007.

65 "goody-goody two-shoes": AI, Freddie Gershon, Apr. 2, 2007.

65 "screen test"/"I worry": AI, Olivia Newton-John, Oct. 5, 2007.

66 "didn't pop": AI, Joel Thurm, July 5, 2007.

66 "screenplay effectively": AI, Randal Kleiser, Aug. 3, 2007.

66 "That was Allan's!": *Grease* DVD, special features.

67 "I'm making"/"When do"/$5,000: AI, Harry Reems, Sept. 10, 2007.

67 "You're in it"/Eisner sat chin/"Wow! The entire": AI, Lucie Arnaz, Sept. 25, 2007.

68 "We'll know"/*Bye Bye Birdie*: Ibid.

68 "play Rizzo"/"twenty-four hours": AI, Stockard Channing, Mar. 6, 2009.

68   "I had picked"/"my daughter": Conn, *Frenchy's,* p. 2.

68   "ridiculous. My mother": AI, Lucie Arnaz, Sept. 25, 2007.

68   Cedars-Sinai/"Ford knew": AI, Joel Thurm, July 5, 2007.

69   "everybody getting smashed": AI, Stockard Channing, Mar. 6, 2009.

69   Kenneth Waissman introduced: AI, Kenneth Waissman, Jan. 10, 2008.

69   "Good news for": Clarkson, *John Travolta,* p. 137.

69   Kate Edwards: Hank Grant, "Rambling Reporter," *Hollywood Reporter.*

69   Marilu Henner, Priscilla: Douglas Thompson, *Fever! The Biography of John Travolta,* p. 110.

69   "But I was"/"That's Hollywood"/"Don't worry": Sam Thielman interview of Jim Jacobs, Aug. 9, 2007.

70   "Oh yeah, that's": AI, Randal Kleiser, Aug. 3, 2007.

70   John Farrar: AI, Olivia Newton-John, Oct. 5, 2007.

70   "girls' names songs"/"There's the guy"/Scott Simon: AI, Louis St. Louis, Oct. 30, 2007.

70   "most-favored-nations": AI, Joel Thurm, July 5, 2007.

71   Rudolf Nureyev, George: Ibid., AI, Randal Kleiser, Aug. 3, 2007.

71   "stomach staples": AI, Joel Thurm, July 5, 2007.

71   "poodle skirts": Alan Cartnal, "The Dream Merchant," *New West,* p. 34.

71   "very Ava Gardner": AI, Stockard Channing, Mar. 6, 2009.

71   When John Travolta: Cartnal, "Dream Merchant," p. 34, .

71   "They'll go back"/"I've got thirty": AI, Randal Kleiser, Aug. 3, 2007.

72   "'Win a Spot'": AI, Laurence Mark, Aug. 21, 2006.

72   Pepsi-Cola/"Who did this?"/"it's blurry": AI, Randal Kleiser, Aug. 3, 2007.

Chapter 10

73   "Producing *Grease*": Didi Conn, *Frenchy's "Grease" Scrapbook,* p. 5.

73   "cool greasers": AI, Didi Conn, Aug. 9, 2007.

73   that photo/Bermuda shorts: Conn, *Frenchy's,* p. 4.

73   "He just beamed": AI, Stockard Channing, Mar. 6, 2009.

74   "last names A–L": George Christy, "The Great Life," *Hollywood Reporter.*

74   "that *Survive!* bought": Army Archerd, "Just for Variety," *Daily Variety,* p. 3.

74   "Everyone in Hollywood": AI, Zvi Howard Rosenman, July 10, 2007.

74   "It felt like": "Carr's ABC's of Beach Chic," *Los Angeles Times,* p. 3.

74   red carpet/klieg lights: AI, Neil Machlis, Apr. 13, 2007.

74   "them molted": Ivor Davis, "From Mayer to Cohn," *Los Angeles* magazine, p. 280.

74 "expensive"/$35: AI, Ronni Chasen, Aug. 20, 2007.

74 Valentino fabric: Christy, "Great Life."

74 "Get rid of": "Carr's ABC's," p. 3.

74 Dani and David: Ibid.

74 Britt Ekland, having: AI, Alana Stewart, July 14, 2008.

75 "George and Alana": Christy, "Great Life."

75 Keith Carradine came: "So Much for Star Wars," *People.*

75 "It's all wrong": AI, Stockard Channing, Mar. 6, 2009.

75 La Vetta, followed: Sue Reilly, "Producer Allan Carr Waxes Fat and Fortyish on the Gross of 'Grease,'" *People,* p. 49.

75 "I am confident": Lydia Lane, "Weight Loss Shapes Personality," *Los Angeles Times,* p. 12.

75 chef, Tom Rolla: "Carr's ABC's," p. 3.

75 Partygoers John Travolta: Ibid.; and "So Much for Star Wars."

76 Allan motioned for: Ibid.

76 "The DA's case": Roman Polanski, *Roman by Polanski,* p. 401.

76 Polanski a "freak": Barbara Leaming, *Polanski: The Filmmaker as Voyeur,* p. 170.

76 $2,500 bail: Ibid., p. 171.

77 "Only in Hollywood": AI, Alana Stewart, July 14, 2008.

77 "rhymes with star"/"Cash or career": AI, Gary Pudney, Feb. 27, 2007.

Chapter 11

78 "He saw me": AI, Randal Kleiser, Aug. 3, 2007.

78 "Your salary": AI, Bill Butler, Oct. 14, 2007.

78 Stigwood/"The beat": AI, Randal Kleiser, Aug. 3, 2007.

79 "So why don't": Ibid.

79 full 1 percent: Stigwood Group, Ltd., letter, dated Jan. 1, 1978.

79 "Robert was quiet": AI, Laurence Mark, Aug. 21, 2006.

79 "Stigwood nutty": AI, Kevin McCormick, Aug. 7, 2007.

79 "I really like": AI, Stockard Channing, Mar. 6, 2009.

80 "total panic"/"premiere party": AI, Randal Kleiser, Aug. 3, 2007.

80 "Paramount hated": AI, Freddie Gershon, Apr. 2, 2007.

80 126 markets: George Christy, "The Great Life," *Hollywood Reporter,* p. 8.

80 "We sweated": Ibid.

80 Elaine's restaurant/"mink caftan": Ibid.

81 "1950 Chevy": Anthony Haden-Guest, *The Last Party: Studio 54, Disco, and the Culture of the Night,* pp. 54–55.

81 "the authors": AI, Kenneth Waissman, Jan. 10, 2008.

82   valet, John/"Mary Tyler Moore": Allan Carr home video/Brett Ratner collection.

82   "I Feel Love"/"mummified"/*"Holocaust"*: Ibid.

83   "Listen, I am": Vito Russo, "A Visit with Allan Carr," *The Advocate*, p. 35.

83   "The unprecedented": A. D. Murphy, "'Jaws 2,' 'Grease' Set New B.O. Records," *Daily Variety*, p. 1.

83   "I really wracked"/*"Grease"* grosses": AI, Ron Bernstein, Apr. 8, 2009.

84   "Something happens": Bob Weiner, "Big Man on Broadway," *Sunday News Magazine*, p. 7.

84   "Look, she's"/"civil tongue": AI, Freddie Gershon, Apr. 2, 2007.

85   Nile Party: Christy, "Great Life."

85   movie *Cleopatra: Los Angeles* magazine, p. 256.

85   "private parties"/"4 a.m.": AI, Don Blanton, Mar. 27, 2009.

85   Merv Griffin, Roy/The Odyssey: Ibid.

86   "Barry is very": AI, Zvi Howard Rosenman, July 10, 2007.

86   "Barry can't believe": AI, Freddie Gershon, Apr. 2, 2007.

Chapter 12

87   Studio chiefs Lew/"worst preview": AI, Thom Mount, Oct. 2, 2007.

87   postmortem/"We realized"/"I've come": AI, Barry Spikings, Aug. 9, 2007.

88   "That's fine"/"important movie"/"going to market": Ibid.

88   Wasserman viewed cable/"Z Channel": AI, Thom Mount, Oct. 2, 2007.

89   "right audience"/Little Carnegie: Ibid.

89   "I saved *The*": "Allan Carr," *Life*, p. 42.

89   "I want you": David Galligan, "New Projects for Allan Carr," *Drama-Logue*, p. 28.

89   black Bentley/"Allan doesn't": AI, Barry Spikings, Aug. 9, 2007.

89   make Allan head: AI, Thom Mount, Oct. 2, 2007.

90   "new film *Ishtar*"/"spelled backwards": AI, Freddie Gershon, Apr. 2, 2007.

90   "Allan always dreamed": AI, Thom Mount, Oct. 2, 2007.

90   "The Baby Moguls": Maureen Orth, "The Baby Moguls," *New West*.

90   "I'm a baby": AI, George Christy, Mar. 6, 2007.

91   "I hit California": Nancy Collins, "The Uphill Racer, Allan Carr," *Women's Wear Daily*, p. 17.

91   "Allan obviously had"/"did you sleep"/"a long list": AI, Thom Mount, Oct. 2, 2007.

91   "Do you mind": AI, James Randall, April 1, 2008.

Chapter 13

92   "heavily soused": AI, Bruce Vilanch, Aug. 13, 2007.

92   "two fried eggs": Jack Kroll, *Newsweek.*

92   "1000 percent no": AI, Peter Guber, Jan. 10, 2008.

93   "who did *Grease*": AI, Henri Belolo, Aug. 24, 2007.

93   "represent the Village"/"Instantly, I see": AI, Richard Hach, Aug. 16, 2007.

93   "No Cooling": "No Cooling of Disco Fever as Operators Eye $5 Billion Year," *Hollywood Reporter,* p. 1.

93   "Village People movie": AI, Bruce Vilanch, Aug. 13, 2007.

94   "very openly gay"/"macho American men": AI, Henri Belolo, Aug. 24, 2007.

94   hired Victor/100,000 copies: Ibid.

94   "Morali was openly"/"fantastic movie": AI, Henri Belolo, Aug. 24, 2007.

94   "The girls want": Clarke Taylor, "The People's Movie Moves the Village," *Los Angeles Times,* p. L29.

95   "many discussions": AI, Bill Butler, Oct. 14, 2007.

95   warn journalists not: Abe Peck, "From the Navy to the YMCA: The Village People," *Rolling Stone.*

95   "Morali became"/"That's how Hollywood": AI, Henri Belolo, Aug. 24, 2007.

95   "combination of Olivia": AI, Bruce Vilanch, Aug. 13, 2007.

95   "Maybe if Allan": AI, Olivia Newton-John, Oct. 5, 2007.

95   "I made her": AI, Bruce Jenner, Nov. 29, 2007.

96   "fat farm": AI, Bruce Vilanch, Aug. 13, 2007.

96   Streep to Jill: Hank Grant, "Rambling Reporter," *Hollywood Reporter.*

96   "Bronte's sole mission"/"Cher"/"Henry Fonda": AI, Bruce Vilanch, Aug. 13, 2007.

96   "Victor Willis"/"Raquel Welch": Ibid.

97   "Mutt and Jeff": AI, Bruce Jenner, Nov. 29, 2007.

98   "No Raquel": AI, David Hodo, Mar. 29, 2007.

98   "Allan kept looking"/"play a supermodel": AI, Valerie Perrine, Dec. 5, 2007.

98   "What's *that*"/"ugliest man": AI, Bruce Vilanch, Aug. 13, 2007.

99   "mooned us": AI, David Hodo, Mar. 29, 2007.

99   "Valerie scared": AI, Kathy Berlin, Apr. 18, 2009.

99   "She tweaked"/"Farrah Fawcett": AI, David Hodo, Mar. 29, 2007.

99   play vampires/"Red, white": Ibid.

100   "Hollywood's Party": Charles Schreger, "Hollywood's Party Champion Defends His Crown," *Los Angeles Times,* p. E10.

100   "Ann-Margret"/"Francis Coppola"/Allan described his/"International Terrorist": Ibid.
101   "Steve for two": Gregg Kilday, "Celluloid Village People," *Los Angeles Herald-Examiner,* p. E1.
101   "little crushes": AI, Kathy Berlin, Apr. 18, 2009.
101   "next Alfred Hitchcock"/"Wheaties alone": Schreger, "Hollywood's Party," p. E10.
102   "You'd be perfect": AI, Bruce Jenner, Nov. 29, 2007.
102   "Strauss waltzes"/"Wow! Our": Wanda McDaniel, "When You're Out with Allan Carr the Parties Never End," *Los Angeles Herald-Examiner,* p. B5, June 12, 1979.
103   "headdress"/"It's my party": AI, Felipe Rose, Apr. 14, 2009.
103   "Hawaiian theme": AI, Steve Guttenberg, July 20, 2007.
103   At 2 a.m.: McDaniel, "When You're Out," p. B5.
103   "late at night": AI, Craig Zadan, Nov. 27, 2007.
103   "Robin Williams came": AI, Don Blanton, Mar. 27, 2009.
103   "They gave us": AI, Henri Belolo, Aug. 24, 2007.
104   Willis nodded off: AI, David Hodo, Mar. 29, 2007.

Chapter 14
105   gay activists: author's personal observations.
106   "You'd better be": AI, Bill Butler, Oct. 14, 2007.
106   "good guys": AI, David Hodo, Mar. 29, 2007.
106   "should be ashamed": AI, Valerie Perrine, July 20, 2007.
106   "This guy spitting"/"OK": AI, Bruce Jenner, Nov. 29, 2007.
106   "Shut up"/"camera's rolling"/"Nancy," she said: AI, Valerie Perrine, July 20, 2007.
107   "Car was rocking": AI, David Hodo, Mar. 29, 2007.
107   "They used to": AI, Valerie Perrine, July 20, 2007.
107   "cast and crew"/"Make way": AI, Bruce Jenner, Nov. 29, 2007.
108   "Wheaties crowd"/"good friend Bruce": Ibid.
108   *Riviera*/Grace Jones: Alan Cartnal, "The Dream Merchant," *New West,* p. 34.
108   "Mischa, darling"/"Bruce, do": AI, Bruce Jenner, Nov. 29, 2007.
108   "Baryshnikov"/big taboo: Ibid.
109   Embassy Club/Hot Gossip: AI, Arlene Phillips, Sept. 26, 2007.
109   "sex shop"/"This is exactly"/"baby then": Ibid.
110   "My two-year-old": AI, Neil Machlis, Apr. 13, 2007.
110   "Red"/"Put her in"/"lot of drugs": AI, Arlene Phillips, Sept. 26, 2007.
110   "Falcon models": AI, Greg Gorman, Apr. 26, 2007.

111   "Bronte's not feeling": AI, Arlene Phillips, Sept. 26, 2007.

111   "out of control"/"Anyone caught": AI, Don Blanton, Mar. 27, 2009.

111   "Everyone had"/"You learn tons": AI, Bill Butler, Oct. 14, 2007.

112   "This is Hollywood": AI, Henri Belolo, Aug. 24, 2007.

112   Stage 28 at MGM: Gregg Kilday, "Celluloid Village People," *Los Angeles Herald-Examiner*, p. E1.

112   "more street"/"Milk and Dairy": AI, Henri Belolo, Aug. 24, 2007.

112   "She left it": AI, Arlene Phillips, Sept. 26, 2007.

112   "How many fucking"/"Either she goes": AI, Valerie Perrine, July 20, 2007.

113   "The radio stations"/"creative meeting": AI, Henri Belolo, Aug. 24, 2007.

114   "hundred times": AI, Arlene Phillips, Sept. 26, 2007.

114   "I want": AI, Henri Belolo, Aug. 24, 2007.

114   "two movies"/Roger LeClaire: AI, Don Blanton, Mar. 27, 2009.

114   La Galleria/"four stories": AI, Bill Butler, Oct. 14, 2007.

114    $15 a pop: AI, Neil Machlis, Apr. 13, 2007.

114   "Allan puts out": AI, Bruce Jenner, Nov. 29, 2007.

115   "Where are": AI, Neil Machlis, Apr. 13, 2007.

115   "truck-driver types": AI, Warren Cowan, May 17, 2007.

115   "Find females!": AI, Neil Machlis, Apr. 13, 2007.

115   "sexy, seething": AI, Arlene Phillips, Sept. 26, 2007.

115   "But boys"/"But the crowd": AI, David Hodo, Mar. 29, 2007.

116   "You've got to"/"If Dennis"/"Henry Kissinger": AI, Henri Belolo, Aug. 24, 2007.

117   "Parker's wasn't": AI, Randy Jones, Nov. 8, 2007.

117   "higher than God": AI, Steve Guttenberg, July 20, 2007.

117   "savor the moment"/"Don't forget": AI, Felipe Rose, Apr. 14, 2009.

117   "big Muppet": AI, Henri Belolo, Aug. 24, 2007.

117   "The party was": AI, Arlene Phillips, Sept. 26, 2007.

Chapter 15

118   "You better"/"Don't act": AI, Henri Belolo, Aug. 24, 2007.

119   "biggest billboard"/ripped at Schwab's: AI, David Hodo, Mar. 29, 2007.

119   "biggest photo op": AI, Robert Osborne, Aug. 27, 2007.

119   "supposed to perform?"/"Uh oh": AI, David Hodo, Mar. 29, 2007.

120   buffet line/"It's constantly shoved": Brant Mewborn, "Circus on Celluloid," *After Dark,* p. 23.

120   "pharmaceutical drugs"/"calla lilies"/"champagne truffles": AI, Tamara Rawitt, Nov. 30, 2007.

121   Baskin-Robbins/"new flavor": Ibid.

121   Famous Amos, Fleishmann's: Deborah Caulfield, "Can't Stop the Hype," *Los Angeles Times*, p. T29.
121   "hometown boy": AI, Kathy Berlin, Apr. 18, 2009.
121   "I remember mermaids": AI, David Hodo, Mar. 29, 2007.
121   "I saw Michael Todd": Mary Kenner, "Can't Stop Carr," *Los Angeles Times*, p. G12.
122   "18,000 pounds": Aaron Gold, "Tower Ticker," *Chicago Tribune.*
122   "Don't worry"/"You think": AI, Robert Osborne, Aug. 27, 2007.
122   "Steve Guttenberg should": AI, Kathy Berlin, Apr. 18, 2009.
122   "I've chartered"/"Auntie Mame": AI, Joanne Cimbalo, Dec. 18, 2007.
122   "Mike Todd's party": AI, Thom Mount, Oct. 2, 2007.
123   "party on the plaza"/"Cirque du So": AI, Tamara Rawitt, Nov. 30, 2007.
123   "acrobats"/"bludgeoned": Ibid.
123   "major contribution": AI, Kathy Berlin, Apr. 18, 2009.
123   "will be white": AI, David Hodo, Mar. 29, 2007.
123   Theoni Aldredge: AI, Theoni Aldredge, Aug. 11, 2007.
124   "popcorn powdered": AI, Tamara Rawitt, Nov. 30, 2007.
124   "We were traveling"/Quaaludes/"God never": AI, David Hodo, Mar. 29, 2007.
124   "cold reception": AI, Henri Belolo, Aug. 24, 2007.
124   "limousines": AI, Kathy Berlin, Apr. 18, 2009.
124   $118,000: Liz Smith, "Can't Stop Shouting About 'Can't Stop,'" *Daily News*, p. 8.
125   "People were relieved": AI, Kathy Berlin, Apr. 18, 2009.
125   gospel choirs/a high school marching band: Ibid.; AI, Tamara Rawitt, Nov. 30, 2007.
125   "Mussolini": AI, Ron Bernstein, Apr. 8, 2009.
125   "wasn't a thrill": AI, David Hodo, Mar. 29, 2007.
125   "biggest party": AI, Bruce Jenner, Nov. 29, 2007.
125   "out of control": AI, Steve Guttenberg, July 20, 2007.
125   "Doesn't Allan Carr": author personal observation.
126   "Studio 54 outside": AI, Tamara Rawitt, Nov. 30, 2007.
126   "Cecil B. DeMille": "Can't Stop the Party, Either," *New York Post*, p. 9.
126   virtually no tickets/"blockbuster business": AI, Stephen M. Silverman, Aug. 3, 2007.
127   $1.6 million: Marilyn Beck, "Carr's Crusade," *Daily News*, p. 3.
127   Dykes on Bikes: AI, David Hodo, Mar. 29, 2007.
127   Greenwich Village: "A Father's Day Gala Premiere," *Los Angeles Times*, p. AA8.

127 Dorothy Chandler Pavilion: Jean Cox Penn, "It's Greenwich Time at Pavilion," *Los Angeles Times*.

127 red handkerchief: AI, Bruce Jenner, Nov. 29, 2007.

127 "Doris Day movie": Clarke Taylor, "Village People Try a New Look," *Los Angeles Times*, p. B3.

128 porn stars/*Grease* soundtrack: AI, Bruce Vilanch, Aug. 13, 2007.

Chapter 16

129 "Allan had flown": AI, Henri Belolo, Aug. 24, 2007.

129 "I dreaded going": Paul Rosenfield, "A Great Big Broadway Show," *Los Angeles Times*.

129 David Merrick/"$100,000": AI, John Breglio, Nov. 15, 2007.

130 "bunch of ladies": AI, Martin Richards, Jan. 16, 2006.

131 "in every cell": AI, Joel Schumacher, Apr. 6, 2009.

131 "little nightgown"/"get Jerry Herman": AI, Martin Richards, Jan. 16, 2006.

131 "It's hard finding": AI, Jerry Herman, Aug. 31, 2005.

131 "Look, give me"/"Call me": AI, Maury Yeston, May 5, 2008.

131 *"That* will be"/$10,000: Ibid.

132 "couldn't recommend"/"I'm flying in": AI, John Breglio, Nov. 15, 2007.

132 called a powwow: AI, Maury Yeston, May 5, 2008.

132 St. Moritz penthouse/Viewhaven: Jody Jacobs, *Los Angeles Times,* p. IV5.

133 "too many directors"/"Nobody fires"/"a legend": AI, Maury Yeston, May 5, 2008.

133 "hardened businessman"/"Sam, it's": AI, John Breglio, Nov. 15, 2007.

133 "big uproar": AI, Jay Presson Allen, Apr. 13, 2006.

134 "My friendship": AI, Maury Yeston, May 5, 2008.

134 "Tommy was very": AI, Jay Presson Allen, Apr. 13, 2006.

134 "Michael Smuin"/$150,000/"Tonight I have": AI, Maury Yeston, May 5, 2008.

135 "That's what I"/rights to the movie/"borrowed whole scenes": Ibid.

Chapter 17

136 Allan's *Grease* agreement. AI, Maury Yeston, May 5, 2008.

136 "Why *Grease*"/"filling station": AI, Patricia Birch, May 4, 2006.

136 "original stars": AI, Laurence Mark, Aug. 21, 2006.

136 Andy Gibb: Jane Ardmore, "Sunday Woman," *San Antonio Light*.

137 "try my luck"/"It Kid": AI, Maxwell Caulfield, Apr. 25, 2006.

137 "huge dance call": AI, Patricia Birch, May 4, 2006.

137 "1,500 people": Paramount Pictures interview/*Grease,* Michelle Pfeiffer.

137 "purple boots"/"just ate up": Douglas Thompson, *Pfeiffer: Beyond the Age of Innocence,* p. 42.

137 "Stigwood and Allan": AI, Patricia Birch, May 4, 2006.

138 "making movies together": AI, Maxwell Caulfield, Apr. 25, 2006.

138 "this year's piece": George Christy, "The Great Life," *Hollywood Reporter.*

138 "these guys": Ardmore, "Sunday Woman."

138 Pat Benatar, Andrea/$100,000: Thompson, *Pfeiffer* p. 43.

138 "all these suits": AI, Lorna Luft, July 26, 2007.

138 "Elvis and Ann-Margret": AI, Maxwell Caulfield, Apr. 25, 2006.

138 "couldn't get permission": AI, Louis St. Louis, Oct. 30, 2007.

138 "Michelle and I": AI, Maxwell Caulfield, Apr. 25, 2006.

139 "pretty rough characters": AI, Patricia Birch, May 4, 2006.

139 other Carr friends: AI, Manny Kladitis, Aug. 21, 2007.

139 "portrait of addiction": AI, Joel Schumacher, Apr. 6, 2009.

139 "Too late"/"mother hen": AI, Patricia Birch, May 4, 2006.

139 "Mommie Dearest": AI, Stockard Channing, Mar. 6, 2009.

Chapter 18

140 "was no deal": AI, John Breglio, Nov. 15, 2007.

140 "three huge flops": AI, Barry Brown, Sept. 8, 2005.

140 "I need you"/"gay community": Ibid.

141 Cristal bottles: AI, Harvey Fierstein, Jan. 16, 2007.

141 "decent coat"/"not the movie"/"gay *Raisin*": Ibid.

142 "I want nothing"/"answer is no"/*Scream*: AI, Barry Brown, Sept. 8, 2005.

142 "sunshine boy and": "'La Cage aux Folles' Coming to Broadway," *New York* magazine, p. 33.

143 "old men": AI, Barry Brown, Sept. 8, 2005.

143 "brooding about"/"New Orleans"/"Saint-Tropez": AI, Jerry Herman, Aug. 31, 2005.

143 "old faggot": AI, Arthur Laurents, Nov. 1, 2005.

Chapter 19

144 $11.2 million: Steve Tamaya, "Closed School Reborn as Studio," *Los Angeles Times,* p. LB1.

144 "Paramount Sequels": AI, Carol Green, Mar. 13, 2007.

144 "Barry Diller was"/"so absurd"/check the toilet: Ibid.

145 "The weather": AI, Lorna Luft, July 26, 2007.

145   "loving every minute": AI, Carol Green, Mar. 13, 2007.

145   "Marge Champion": Ivor Davis, "From Mayer to Cohn," *Los Angeles Times,* p. 280.

145   "We're in trouble": AI, Patricia Birch, May 4, 2006.

146   Kenzo sweaters/"Dolly Parton": Christy, "Great Life."

146   "Bowl?": Betty Goodwin, "'Grease' Parties in an Alley,'" *Los Angeles Herald-Examiner,* p. B3.

146   "There's no way"/"Oh, yes": AI, Louis St. Louis, Oct. 30, 2007.

146   "If *Grease 2*": Christy, "Great Life."

146   "*E.T.* creamed"/his Hawaii home: AI, Maxwell Caulfield, Apr. 25, 2006.

147   "Tim Hutton"/"Tom Cruise": David Galligan, "New Projects for Allan Carr," *Drama-Logue,* p. 28.

147   "Allan is over": AI, Valerie Perrine, July 20, 2007.

Chapter 20

148   songwriter's townhouse: AI, Jerry Herman, Aug. 31, 2005.

148   "Damian kept us"/"from the movie"/ "Jerry's house twice": AI, Harvey Fierstein, Jan. 16, 2007.

149   "tight control"/"I'm all right": AI, Barry Brown, Sept. 8, 2005.

149   "in love with": AI, Jerry Herman, Aug. 31, 2005.

149   "excitement was palpable": AI, Barry Brown, Sept. 8, 2005.

149   "the in place": AI, Shirley Herz, Sept. 25, 2005.

149   "backers' auditions"/"the Cagelles": AI, Arthur Laurents, Nov. 1, 2005.

150   "They sold it": AI, Harvey Fierstein, Jan. 16, 2007.

150   "do an entertainment": AI, Jerry Herman, Aug. 31, 2005.

150   "two men living": AI, Arthur Laurents, Nov. 1, 2005.

150   "The money didn't": AI, Manny Kladitis, Aug. 21, 2007.

151   "the Shuberts didn't"/"Your territory"/"act where George": AI, Arthur Laurents, Nov. 1, 2005.

152   "Flo said today": AI, anonymous source.

152   called Rakuen: Promotional material, "Rakuen, Honolulu, Hawaii," undated.

152   NO GOOD DEED: Jody Jacobs, *Los Angeles Times.*

152   "ratty beach"/"Why don't you"/"a kid who": AI, Arthur Laurents, Nov. 1, 2005.

Chapter 21

154    $5 million: Rena Kleiman, "Carr to Produce 'Boys,'" *Hollywood Reporter,* p. 1.

154   "We shot scenes": AI, Neil Machlis, Apr. 13, 2007.

155 ITC: Kleiman, "Carr to Produce," p. 1.

155 "You're going to"/"roller-coaster": AI, Howard McGillin, Aug. 2, 2007.

156 Universal Sheraton/"This shirt is": Ibid.

156 Jerry Esposito's: AI, Russell Todd, Aug. 2, 2007.

157 "Kaye to Milton": Paul Rosenfield, "A Great Big Broadway Show," *Los Angeles Times.*

157 "I don't play"/"the longest walk": " 'La Cage aux Folles,' Coming to Broadway," *New York* magazine, p. 36.

157 "Arlene Dahl"/"Ann-Margret": Rosenfield, "Great Big Broadway."

158 "Not an easy": AI, Jon Wilner, July 25, 2006.

158 "paint it pink"/"dead body": AI, anonymous source.

159 "Allan's flamboyance": AI, Jerry Herman, Aug. 31, 2005.

159 "Before we walked": AI, Shirley Herz, Sept. 25, 2005.

159 *Mame* poster"/"she's winking"/"horrible fights": AI, Jon Wilner, July 25, 2006.

160 "Drag turned me": Arthur Laurents, *Mainly on Directing*, p. 115.

160 "drag in the": Ibid., p. 116.

160 "It's a carnival"/"not a man": AI, Arthur Laurents, Nov. 1, 2005.

160 "conservative Boston": AI, Harvey Fierstein, Jan. 16, 2007.

Chapter 22

161 "Mickey and Judy": AI, Howard McGillin, Aug. 2, 2007.

162 "So tell me"/"Allan, the bracelet"/"why I'm crying": AI, Russell Todd, Aug. 2, 2007.

162 "going to Boston": AI, Martin Richards, Jan. 16, 2006.

163 "choice with Boston": AI, Arthur Laurents, Nov. 1, 2005.

163 *Ben-Hur*/"go that far": Paul Rosenfield, "A Great Big Broadway Show," *Los Angeles Times*, Aug. 28, 1983.

163 "Smoke and mirrors": AI, Arthur Laurents, Nov. 1, 2005.

163 "no way we": AI, Barry Brown, Sept. 8, 2005.

164 "My heart was": AI, Jerry Herman, Aug. 31, 2005.

164 "They had to hold": AI, Harvey Fierstein, Jan. 16, 2007.

164 "slumber party"/"Uncle Allan": AI, Wendy Schaal, Sept. 4, 2007.

164 "really drunk": AI, Howard McGillin, Aug. 2, 2007.

165 Boca Raton/"Allan Carr fell": AI, Wendy Schaal, Sept. 4, 2007.

165 "It's pretty good"/family problems/"You're sick": AI, Russell Todd, Aug. 2, 2007.

Chapter 23

166 "Allan was just": AI, Jerry Herman, Aug. 31, 2005.

166   "Gene turned on": AI, Jon Wilner, July 25, 2006.

166   "Gene wanted to be the": AI, John Weiner, Aug. 18, 2007.

167   "War II searchlights"/Lansdowne/"Cir-cus"/Aronoff: Nathan Cobb, "Acceptance, Accolades at First-Night Party," *Boston Globe*.

167   "Your kind isn't": AI, Barry Brown, Sept. 8, 2005; Manny Kladitis, Aug. 21, 2007.

168   "Break it": Jeff McLaughlin, *Boston Globe*.

168   "slipshod treatment": Kevin Kelly, "Harvey Fierstein Dragged into Sudden Stardom," *Boston Globe*.

168   "about the *Times*": AI, anonymous source.

168   *New York* magazine: AI, Shirley Herz, Sept. 25, 2005.

168   "second balcony": AI, Jon Wilner, July 25, 2006.

168   "This show doesn't": Paul Rosenfield, "Great Big Broadway Show."

169   "Tune and Twiggy": "Peacocks Flock to 'La Cage' Opening," *New York Post*.

169   "huge hit": AI, Harvey Fierstein, Jan. 16, 2007.

169   "whatever money": AI, Elaine Krauss, Aug. 23, 2007.

169   big Marriott/"fabulous idea": Richard Levine, "The Selling of a Used Car," *Esquire*, p. 187.

170   "We built": AI, Elaine Krauss, Aug. 23, 2007.

170   "Mrs. Hitler"/"V.I.P. problem": Rosenfield, "Great Big Broadway."

170   "Carmen Miranda": Arthur Bell, "Bell Tells," *Village Voice*, p. 34.

171   Bosshard/Poiret/"minor extravaganza": Ron Alexander, "Opening Party for 'La Cage,'" *New York Times*.

171   opening-night gifts: AI, Elaine Krauss, Aug. 23, 2007; Theoni Aldredge, Aug. 11, 2007.

171   Derringer/"Dear Arthur": Rosenfield, "Great Big Broadway."

171   "years of employment": Diana Maychick, "More Glory than Gelt," *New York Post*.

171   flights to China/$150,000: AI, Barry Brown, Sept. 8, 2005.

172   "Saint-Tropez flights": AI, Jon Wilner, July 25, 2006.

172   "mixed-up party": AI, Theoni Aldredge, Aug. 11, 2007.

172   "best tables": AI, John Weiner, Aug. 18, 2007.

172   "party was lavish": AI, Arthur Laurents, Nov. 1, 2005.

173   "Nederheimers": AI, anonymous source.

173   "Mafia-style": AI, Stephen M. Silverman, Aug. 3, 2007.

173   "Do you think": AI, Jerry Herman, Aug. 31, 2005.

174   "We were criticized": AI, Barry Brown, Sept. 8, 2005.

174   "three weeks"/New York University: AI, Arthur Laurents, Nov. 1, 2005.

175   "People never think": Roderick Mann, "Barry Knows Why the 'Cage' Bird Sings," *Los Angeles Times*, p. 7.

175   "Gene would say": AI, Harvey Fierstein, Jan. 16, 2007.

175   "Gene, you really": AI, John Weiner, Aug. 18, 2007.

175   "He kept asking": AI, Shirley Herz, Sept. 25, 2005.

175   "Gene's wife, Betty": AI, Harvey Fierstein, Jan. 16, 2007.

175   "after Allan congratulated": AI, John Weiner, Aug. 18, 2007.

175   "He could say": AI, Arthur Laurents, Nov. 1, 2005.

176   "wild party reputation": AI, Mark Waldrop, Nov, 8, 2007.

176   "It was incestuous": AI, Jon Wilner, July 25, 2006.

Chapter 24

177   "good-looking guys": AI, Howard McGillin, Aug. 2, 2007.

177   "Are they crazy"/Kawasaki: Richard M. Levine, "The Selling of a Used Car," *Esquire,* p. 188.

178   "itchy sweater"/"Don't fall": AI, Russell Todd, Aug. 2, 2007.

178   "Boys, take"/"More boys": AI, Howard McGillin, Aug. 2, 2007.

179   Australian industrialist/"couple screwing under": Levine, "Selling of a," *Esquire,* pp. 188–189.

179   "out of context"/Allan rose: AI, Harvey Fierstein, Jan. 16, 2007.

180   "The parties were": AI, Kathy Berlin, Apr. 18, 2009.

180   "It's relentless": Wanda McDaniel, "Sometimes I Feel like Staying Home to Watch 'Dynasty,'" *Los Angeles Herald-Examiner.*

180   "momentum"/"They'll love"/expensive ads/"We all felt": AI, Shirley Herz, Sept. 25, 2005.

181   "You could hear": author's personal observation.

181   "I loved *Sunday*"/"last year's embarrassment": AI, Harvey Fierstein, Jan. 16, 2007.

182   "I'm not leaving": "'La Cage aux Folles' Cleaned Up," *People,* p. 125.

183   "pals in Hollywood": AI, Barry Brown, Sept. 8, 2005.

183   Chez Jacqueline/"I've gotta sweep": Jeannine Stein, "Click," *Los Angeles Herald-Examiner.*

184   "You needed binoculars": AI, Arthur Laurents, Nov. 1, 2005.

184   "Los Angeles should"/Regis Philbin/"not classy": AI, Barry Brown, Sept. 8, 2005.

184   "He would have": AI, John Weiner, Aug. 18, 2007.

184   "Lucite grand": AI, Jerry Herman, Aug. 31, 2005.

184   "Bob's aunt"/"limited to five": Arthur Laurents letter, dated June 21, 1986.

185   "bad mood": AI, Jon Wilner, July 25, 2006.

185   "from Passaic": AI, Harvey Fierstein, Jan. 16, 2007.

185   "wasn't well cast"/*New York Times*: AI, Shirley Herz, Sept. 25, 2005.

185   "after this rehearsal"/"You can't dance"/"doing this show": AI, Barry
       Brown, Sept. 8, 2005; John Weiner, Aug. 18, 2007.

186   "without a trace": Arthur Laurents, *Mainly on Directing*, p. 38.

186   "Veteran Producer": Arthur Laurents letter, dated June 21, 1986.

187   "After three years"/"Get rid of": AI, Jon Wilner, July 25, 2006.

187   Rock Hudson: AI, Shirley Herz, Sept. 25, 2005.

187   "do with AIDS": Vito Russo, "A Visit with Allan Carr, Hollywood's Can't
       Stop Mogul," *The Advocate,* p. 36.

187   "AIDS epidemic": AI, Barry Brown, Sept. 8, 2005.

187   Mark Hellinger/Reams: AI, Barry Brown, Sept. 8, 2005; Shirley Herz,
       Sept. 25, 2005.

188   "If you sold": AI, Jon Wilner, July 25, 2006.

188   "[current] economic justification": AI, John Breglio, Nov. 15, 2007.

188   "No one closes": AI, Barry Brown, Sept. 8, 2005.

188   "We were set": Arthur Laurents, *Mainly on Directing*, p. 142.

189   "We were surprised": AI, Mark Waldrop, Nov, 8, 2007.

189   "kept getting raises": AI, Jon Wilner, July 25, 2006.

189   "we had parties": AI, John Weiner, Aug. 18, 2007.

189   "Brother, Can You": AI, Mark Waldrop, Nov, 8, 2007.

Chapter 25

190   "sound system"/"don't use microphones": AI, Maury Yeston, May 5, 2008.

191   "John Denver"/"*South Pacific*": AI, Freddie Gershon, Apr. 2, 2007.

191   "Manolete"/"bullfighter's costume"/"my *Gandhi*": Ibid.

192   0.25 percent: Paul Rosenfield, "A Great Big Broadway Show," *Los An-
       geles Times.*

192   "loves your score"/"out of the blue"/"King of Siam": AI, Maury Yeston,
       May 5, 2008.

193   "Allan Carr delivered"/"went pale": Ibid.

194   "Domingo couldn't understand": AI, Freddie Gershon, Apr. 2, 2007.

194   *My Fair Lady*/Yetnikoff/Berniker/"Ramone to produce": AI, Maury
       Yeston, May 5, 2008.

195   addiction to cocaine: Walter Yetnikoff, with David Ritz, *Howling at the
       Moon*, p. 241.

195   "craziest music exec": Ibid., book jacket.

196   "What if we": AI, Maury Yeston, May 5, 2008.

196   "The first half": AI, Freddie Gershon, Apr. 2, 2007.

196   Elaine Stritch reprised: Duane Byrge, "Broadway at the Bowl," *Hollywood Reporter,* p. 6.
196   "$500"/"Latino audience": AI, Freddie Gershon, Apr. 2, 2007.
197   "It didn't land"/"deep love": AI, Maury Yeston, May 5, 2008.

Chapter 26

198   delinquent hip/October 17: John Culhane, "For Oscar's Producer, the Key Is C," *New York Times,* p. 11.
198   "I didn't go": AI, Richard Kahn, Aug. 24, 2007.
198   "Dick came over": Paul Rosenfield, "The Oscar Show and the Exercise of Power," *Los Angeles Times.*
199   Poopsie Awards: Alan Solomon, "Poopsie Picks," *The Stentor,* p. 4.
199   "My wife still": AI, Richard Kahn, Aug. 24, 2007.
199   Wise/Donen/Goldwyn: Ibid.
200   "thankless job": AI, Sherry Lansing, Aug. 30, 2007.
200   "recovery period"/"Women watch": AI, Richard Kahn, Aug. 24, 2007.
200   *Detour*/"Allan would kick": AI, Linda Dozoretz, Nov. 2, 2007.
201   "women's caftans": AI, Fred Hayman, Aug. 17, 2007.
201   "Fred Hayman's"/"gotten boring": Claudia Puig, "Dressing Up the Academy Awards Show," *Los Angeles Times.*
201   *Beach Blanket*/"dancing tables": AI, Jo Schuman Silver, July 17, 2007.
202   Bush's 1989 inauguration/"big line": Lynn Carey, " 'Beach' Producer Opens Oscar," *Contra Costa Times.*
203   "sidetracked into"/"when the presenters": AI, Ray Klausen, Dec. 10, 2007.
203   "If I'm lucky": AI, Bruce Vilanch, Aug. 13, 2007.
203   "Oscar rash": Rosenfield, "Oscar Show."
203   "Academy's conservatives edgy": "Insider," *Los Angeles* magazine.
203   "were some whispers": AI, Linda Dozoretz, Nov. 2, 2007.
203   "compadres, costars": Culhane, "For Oscar's," p. 19.
204   "four twinkies": AI, Kathy Berlin, Apr. 18, 2009.
204   "Coca-Cola chilled": Rosenfield, "Oscar Show."
204   "too TV"/Jessica Rabbit: Culhane, "For Oscar's," p. 19.
204   "is 10% for": Rosenfield, "Oscar Show."
205   Doris Day: AI, Linda Dozoretz, Nov. 2, 2007.

Chapter 27

206   "drink champagne"/glossy photograph/"three turds": AI, Bruce Vilanch, Aug. 13, 2007.
208   "his dream": AI, John Hamlin, May 18, 2009.

208   "young": AI, Bruce Vilanch, Aug. 13, 2007.

208   "elegant evening"/"I'm having problems"/"It's brilliant": AI, Ray Klausen, Dec. 10, 2007.

209   "It was grandiose": AI, Jeff Margolis, Mar. 12, 2009.

209   "favorite movies, *Grease*": *Jimmy Kimmel Live!* Feb. 23, 2009.

209   "Bring your husband"/"Snow White"/"I made you": AI, Lorna Luft, July 26, 2007.

211   "The designers weren't"/Lagerfeld, Giorgio: AI, Fred Hayman, Aug. 17, 2007.

212   L'Ermitage/"Angie isn't"/"Tiffany Jewels": Rosenfield, "Oscar Show."

212   "Everything's bigger": Puig, "Dressing Up."

213   "hype the awards": AI, Linda Dozoretz, Nov. 2, 2007.

213   Oscar Ground Zero/MISS GRABLE'S/"clients the material": Irv Letofsky, "Glamour? Glory?", *Los Angeles Times.*

214   "with Nureyev"/"Lana doesn't": Rosenfield, "Oscar Show."

214   on-air joke: AI, Linda Dozoretz, Nov. 2, 2007.

215   overexposed, Peck: AI, Bruce Vilanch, Aug. 13, 2007.

215   So no Liz: "Is This a Competition Prize?" *The Times,* p. 16.

215   "her the moon"/"Swayze's people"/"Tom's producer"/Ameche: Rosenfield, "Oscar Show."

216   Both women insisted/Alice Faye: Peter Bart, "Angst for the Memories," *Variety,* p. 5.

216   "He did everything": AI, Richard Kahn, Aug. 24, 2007.

216   Club Oscar: Army Archerd, "Just for Variety," *Daily Variety,* p. 2.

216   "highfalutin' club": Steve Pond, *The Big Show,* p. 5.

216   "His ego was": AI, Linda Dozoretz, Nov. 2, 2007.

217   "He's a legend": Rosenfield, "Oscar Show."

217   "the best party"/"movie clips": Ibid.

217   ABC Studios: Culhane, "For Oscar's," p. 19.

218   "old Hollywood folk": *Jimmy Kimmel Live!* Feb. 23, 2009.

218   "Young Hollywood number": AI, Bruce Vilanch, Aug. 13, 2007.

218   "could swing in"/"year of ballet": Kevin Koffler, "Carr Puts Oscar Spotlight on the New Hollywood," *Los Angeles Herald-Examiner.*

219   "People put down"/"numbers on Oscars": Ibid.

219   "bigger celebrity than"/"forget my lines": "Snow White," *Los Angeles Times.*

219   "going to be gold": AI, Bruce Vilanch, Aug. 13, 2007.

220   substituted momentarily: Alan Light, "Backstage at the Oscars," *Movie Collector's World,* p. 2.

220   "It won't work"/"Sixteen minutes!"/"Look, you've got": AI, Jo Schuman Silver, July 17, 2007.

220   $150 a week: Bob Thomas, "Merv Griffin Dies at Age 82," AP.
220   "the dinosaurs"/Bette Midler/"Like what else": AI, Bruce Vilanch, Aug. 13, 2007.
221   "He thought Rob": AI, Linda Dozoretz, Nov. 2, 2007.
221   "daily basis": AI, Richard Kahn, Aug. 24, 2007.
221   "rehearsal was fun": AI, Army Archerd, Oct. 1, 2007.
222   "They all loved": AI, Freddie Gershon, Apr. 2, 2007.
222   "dress extra": Archerd, "Just for Variety," p. 2.
222   Doris Day: Ibid., Mar. 30, 1989, p. 2.
222   "that muff": Rosenfield, "Oscar Show."
223   pesky lawyer/Disney: Richard Turner, "Nobody Ever Said Snow White Had Much of a Sense of Humor," *Wall Street Journal*, p. A8.

Chapter 28

224   "the red carpet": AI, Bruce Vilanch, Aug. 13, 2007.
224   "circle the Shrine": "Faces & Places," *Us*, p. 18.
224   Streep/Fawn Hall: Duane Byrge, "Weather's Just Fine Outside the Shrine," *Hollywood Reporter*, p. 30.
225   "support for Allan"/Cybill Shepherd/Cher: Ibid.
225   Warren Cowan: AI, Warren Cowan, May 17, 2007.
226   ordered up fourteen/"percent concentration": AI, Jeff Margolis, Mar. 12, 2009.
227   Kahn/"Let Snow White": AI, Richard Kahn, Aug. 24, 2007.
227   Luft/"Pfeiffer's face": AI, Lorna Luft, July 26, 2007.
227   Lowe/Levinson/"Please God": *Jimmy Kimmel Live!* Feb. 23, 2009.
228   "Cedars-Sinai right": AI, Lorna Luft, July 26, 2007.
228   "plague"/"wax works": AI, Bruce Vilanch, Aug. 13, 2007.
228   Hamlisch/"hit a wall": AI, Marvin Hamlisch, July 26, 2007.
229   "proud of"/"piece of": AI, Jo Schuman Silver, July 17, 2007.
229   Lucille Ball/"aspirin": *Jimmy Kimmel Live!* Feb. 23, 2009.
229   Goldie and Kurt/"Let's check out"/Jeannie Williams: AI, Linda Dozoretz, Nov. 2, 2007.
230   "Snow White opening": "Carr Hears Only the Ovations," *Hollywood Reporter*, p. 6.
231   "Get me out": AI, Linda Dozoretz, Nov. 2, 2007.
232   "You're just grateful": AI, Ray Klausen, Dec. 10, 2007.
232   "Bavarian hangar"/crisp potato baskets: Jeannine Stein, "Where the Stars Come Out to Shine After Oscars Show," *Los Angeles Times*, p. 2.
232   "weighs a ton"/Julian Sands: Jeannine Stein, "Oscar: An Overnight Sensation," *Los Angeles Times*.
233   "pro forma congratulations": AI, Ray Klausen, Dec. 10, 2007.

233 Berg/"What on earth": AI, Thom Mount, Oct. 2, 2007.

233 "two reactions": AI, Peter Guber, Jan. 10, 2008.

233 "such a fuss"/Disney: AI, Jo Schuman Silver, July 17, 2007.

233 Kahn thanked Jeff: AI, Jeff Margolis, Mar. 12, 2009.

233 "own private party": AI, Richard Kahn, Aug. 24, 2007.

233 "Overall, the reaction": AI, Linda Dozoretz, Nov. 2, 2007.

234 "To go home": AI, Jeff Margolis, Mar. 12, 2009.

234 "At Swifty Lazar's": AI, George Christy, Mar. 6, 2007.

234 chef Serge Falesitch's: Mitchell Fink, "Spago Schmooze News," *Los Angeles Herald-Examiner*, p. 2.

234 "quoted my mother": Ibid.

235 "the jokes about": Ibid.

235 "Nobel Prize": "Faces & Places," p. 18.

235 "People told Allan": AI, Bruce Vilanch, Aug. 13, 2007.

235 Michael Caine: "Rating the Oscar Parties," *TV Guide*, p. 45.

235 "Ask me tomorrow": Archerd, "Just for Variety," p. 2.

Chapter 29

236 "dull telecasts": Joyce Millman, "S.F. Puts Some Zip in Show," *San Francisco Examiner.*

236 "TV nyet": Tony Scott, "Oscar Awards Singin' in the 'Rain,'" *Daily Variety*, p. 1.

236 "The 61st": Janet Maslin, "The Oscars as Home Entertainment," *New York Times.*

237 Love/"Janet Maslin": AI, Jo Schuman Silver, July 17, 2007.

237 "No one has": AI, Linda Dozoretz, Nov. 2, 2007.

237 "I was in bed": AI, Bruce Vilanch, Aug. 13, 2007.

237 "Producers usually shrug": AI, Richard Kahn, Aug. 24, 2007.

238 26.9 million: Howard Burns, "ABC's Oscar Telecast," *Hollywood Reporter.*

238 Wells/"Dick, we got"/"Photoplay Awards": AI, Richard Kahn, Aug. 24, 2007.

239 Mortons/"megadisaster": AI, Robert Osborne, Aug. 27, 2007.

239 sculpture from Tiffany's/"very special experience": AI, Jo Schuman Silver, July 17, 2007.

240 "copyright infringement": Jane Galbraith, "Acad Caught Lookin' Goofy," *Daily Variety*, p. 1.

240 "Disney loves promotion": Richard Turner, "Nobody Ever Said Snow White Had Much of a Sense of Humor," *Wall Street Journal*, p. A8.

240 "like a Martian": Galbraith, "Acad Caught," p. 32.

240 Reagan: Army Archerd, "Just for Variety," *Daily Variety,* p. 2.

240 "highest-rated Oscar": Martin Grove, "Hollywood Report," *Hollywood Reporter.*

241 journalist at Harvard: Michael Blowen, "Flamboyant Producer Allan Carr," *Boston Globe,* p. A1.

241 "flower shop"/"Lincoln Center": Charles Champlin, *Los Angeles Times.*

242 "I always thought": AI, Linda Dozoretz, Nov. 2, 2007.

242 "homophobia": AI, Craig Zadan, Nov. 27, 2007.

242 "Allan's being gay": AI, John Hamlin, May 18, 2009.

242 "took umbrage": AI, Bruce Vilanch, Aug. 13, 2007.

242 "People didn't hate": AI, David Geffen, Apr. 21, 2009.

242 "Academy sincerely apologizes": "Disney Drops Snow White Suit," *Daily Variety,* p. 1.

243 "an embarrassment"/"We're delighted": Joseph McBride, "Panel to Probe Oscarcast Flaws," *Daily Variety,* p. 1.

243 "The ringleader": AI, Richard Kahn, Aug. 24, 2007.

244 "visible Hollywood celebrity": AI, Gary Pudney, Feb. 27, 2007.

244 Kahn/Cates/Awards Presentation Review: McBride, "Panel to Probe," p. 30.

245 "down in history": AI, Gary Pudney, Feb. 27, 2007.

245 "Snow White insanity": AI, Bruce Vilanch, Aug. 13, 2007.

245 "unavailable for comment": "Disney: Suit over Snow White," *Daily Variety,* p. 1.

245 "such an easy": AI, Marvin Hamlisch, July 26, 2007.

245 "The Academy": Glenn Collins, "Rob Lowe Braves Farce," *New York Times,* p. C11.

246 "sense of humor": AI, Lorna Luft, July 26, 2007.

246 "In Allan's world": AI, Bruce Vilanch, Aug. 13, 2007.

246 "one tragic mistake": AI, Gilbert Cates, July 26, 2007.

246 Too much material: AI, Gilbert Cates, July 26, 2007.

246 "film person": AI, Jeff Margolis, Mar. 12, 2009.

247 "like our town"/Shrine Auditorium: AI, Gilbert Cates, July 26, 2007.

247 "Don't worry": AI, Lorna Luft, July 26, 2007.

247 Fiji/Jeff Paul/"Those bastards": AI, James T. Ballard, Aug. 1, 2007.

Epilogue

249 "mai tais": Wanda McDaniel, "Sometimes I Feel like Staying Home to Watch 'Dynasty,'" *Los Angeles Herald-Examiner.*

249 Royal Shakespeare: Pat H. Broeske, "Allan Carr, Entrepreneur," *Drama-Logue,* p. 18.

250   "There he goes": AI, Marvin Hamlisch, July 26, 2007.

250   Dickinson/"I don't know": AI, Angie Dickinson, July 21, 2007.

250   CNBC/"amazing to watch": AI, Asa Manor, Nov. 2, 2007.

250   "No, move the"/"secret marketing machine": AI, Thom Mount, Oct. 2, 2007.

251   "trouble for Snow": Steve Pond, *The Big Show*, p. 26.

251   "I hope you": letter, Feb. 5, 1998, Freddie Gershon collection.

252   "Get rid of": AI, Asa Manor, Nov. 2, 2007.

252   West Hollywood restaurants: AI, Blaise Noto, Mar. 7, 2007.

252   Billy Joel sublet: AI, Manny Kladitis, Aug. 21, 2007.

252   Ludwig comedy/"good friends": AI, Ken Ludwig, Aug. 14, 2007.

252   Lansing/"wonderful to rerelease"/"movie rereleases": AI, Sherry Lansing, Aug. 30, 2007.

253   "whole new person": AI, Blaise Noto, Mar. 7, 2007.

253   "made my statement": Dan Jewel, "Showman," *People,* p. 111.

253   "next Broadway project": AI, Ken Ludwig, Aug. 14, 2007.

253   "The critical establishment": AI, Peter Franklin, Aug. 16, 2007.

254   quarter million dollars: AI, Ken Ludwig, Aug. 14, 2007.

254   acupuncture/"I'm so happy": AI, Peter Franklin, Aug. 16, 2007.

254   kidney might become: AI, Freddie Gershon, Apr. 2, 2007.

254   birthday cake/ambulance call: AI, Lyn Rothman, Aug. 7, 2007.

255   "totally different": AI, Steve Guttenberg, July 20, 2007.

255   friends away/liver cancer/"I want to"/day of the locust: AI, Freddie Gershon, Apr. 2, 2007.

255   "still a mystery": AI, Gary Pudney, Feb. 27, 2007.

255   give a memorial/"Hollywood's flashiest": Liz Smith, "Paramount Send-off," *Newsday,* p. A13.

256   Ann-Margret flew: AI, Ann-Margret, Apr. 17, 2008.

256   biography/"I couldn't read": AI, Richard Hach, Aug. 16, 2007.

256   "Allan always felt": AI, Joanne Cimbalo, Dec. 18, 2007.

256   "Moraine Road": Clifford Terry, "Allan Carr, Counselor to the Stars," *Chicago Tribune,* p. 48.

256   "Excuse me, but": AI, Joanne Cimbalo, Dec. 18, 2007.

INDEX